the German Shepherd

Today

the

German Shepherd

Today

New and Revised Edition

**winifred gibson strickland
and james a. moses**

HOWELL
BOOK
HOUSE

Howell Book House

A Simon & Schuster Macmillan Company
1633 Broadway
New York, NY 10019

Macmillan Publishing books may be purchased for business or sales promo-
tional use. For information, please write: Special Markets Department,
Macmillan Publishing USA, 1633 Broadway, New York, NY 10019.

Library of Congress Cataloging-in-Publication Data:

Strickland, Winifred Gibson.
    The German shepherd today / Winifred Gibson Strickland and James
A. Moses.
        p.   cm.
    Includes index.
    ISBN 0-87605-154-9
    1. German shepherd dogs.   I. Moses, James Anthony.   II. Title.
SF429.G37S77   1997
636.737'6—dc21   97-38168
                                                            CIP

Design by George McKeon

Manufactured in the United States of America

10 9 8 7 6 5 4 3 2 1

Contents

Winifred G. Strickland with Wynthea's Jack of Hearts, UDX; Falco v. d. Schanzlache, UD; Wynthea's Sherlock Holmes, UD; Wynthea's Can Be, CD and Wynthea's Ace of Diamonds, UDX.

Preface

So much has happened in the German Shepherd world since 1988, when the last edition of my book was published, that I thought it was time for an update. My publisher agreed, and I have been researching the many facets of this wonderful breed for over a year in order to include all the new and wondrous activities available to German Shepherds and we who love them.

German Shepherd owners have more choices today than ever before in performance activities. The American Kennel Club and the German Shepherd Dog Club of America offer titles and incentives to those trainers who want to train their dogs to herd sheep. As impractical as it may seem, it is still fun to see how your dog will react when faced with anywhere from 5 to 100 sheep. These herding classes will be offered at the National.

Agility trials have come very much into vogue. Many handlers and dogs who are bored with Obedience competition find the Agility exercises fun and challenging. The AKC is offering titles for the different levels of expertise. The GSDCA is also offering incentives such as certificates and German Shepherd pins to those who win titles. And starting in 1996, an Agility Trial was offered at the National.

In Obedience the AKC is offering a UDX title for those dogs who have successfully qualified in ten shows in both Utility B and Open B. The GSDCA is offering a German Shepherd pin as an incentive.

A new Championship Title, CT, will be given to those German Shepherd Dogs who earn the three Tracking titles, TD, TDX and VST. This is really a challenge.

More people than ever are joining Schutzhund clubs. Many of the more open-minded Schutzhund enthusiasts realize that the dogs who are closer to the German Shepherd Conformation Standard make better Working Dogs. Top SV Conformation judges are coming to America frequently to conduct Breed Surveys, Courage Tests and Conformation Shows. These shows are as popular and well attended as some of the large AKC Shows. German Shepherd breeders in the United States, whose stock carries the top German bloodlines, are supporting these shows with their own American-bred entries, and German handlers are coming over to handle the dogs. The German judges are wholeheartedly supporting all the breeders who register their dogs with the SV. Some of the more prominent breeders are also showing their dogs in Germany. The GSDCA offered the B Schutzhund Class at the National in 1996. This was a first and a step in the right direction. It will be beneficial if the dogs are also registered with the SV since it is part of the Schutzhund program.

In this country some dedicated American breeders are taking a serious look at the German Shepherd Standard. As a result, we are seeing more dogs who are physically sound, who not only have beautiful side gaits but are also true coming and going. For many years the dogs being shown were too extreme and overangulated and a far cry from the German Shepherd described in our breed Standard. There are many beautiful German Shepherds in this country. If the majority of the American breeders will just realize we have an excellent German Shepherd Standard exactly the way it is, and adhere to it, they will again gain the respect of all German Shepherd fanciers.

Regardless of your own particular interest in the German Shepherd Dog, remember that this breed is capable of being many things to many people. Your love for the breed, therefore, should be as great and encompassing as the German Shepherd Dog Standard.

—Winifred Gibson Strickland

Acknowledgments

Grateful acknowledgment is made to the following people:

Dr. Otto Schales for his article "How to Read German Pedigrees."

The American Kennel Club for permitting me to publish its forms and quote from the *Rules Applying to Registration and Dog Shows*.

Walter Frost, Ph.D., and George W. Frost for their chapter on *Structural Analysis of the Ideal Forequarter, Body and Hindquarter*.

Gordon Garrett for his insights into early North American German Shepherd bloodlines.

Dr. George Wilson, III for his article on cancer.

Anne Due for furnishing statistical reports.

Georgia Bialk and Ron Strickland for their fine photographs.

The German Shepherd fanciers who sent me photographs of their beautiful dogs. (Your contribution is genuinely appreciated and of interest to German Shepherd owners everywhere).

Karin E. Wagner for translating Koer reports.

The German Shepherd judges who graciously took time off from their busy schedules to send me their commentaries: Dr. Morton Goldfarb, Ed Barritt, Mary Ellen Kish, George and Virginia Collins, Fran Ford and Ernest Loeb.

The prestigious Eastern Dog Club invited "Sergeant Preston of the Yukon" from the popular 1950s TV series to present the National Obedience Champion of 1953 Award to Winifred G. Strickland and her Hussan vom Haus Kilmark, UDT in a special ceremony at its show in Boston, Massachusetts.

Schafer

Introduction

In the years that followed the publication of my first training book, *Expert Obedience Training for Dogs,* I received hundreds of requests to write a book on the German Shepherd breed. Having bred, raised and trained German Shepherds for twenty years, I had accumulated a wealth of practical knowledge that I shared with anyone seeking advice and that I wanted to put into book form.

However, I had two important projects to finish before I could get to it. The first was to revise my *Expert* book because the American Kennel Club changed the Obedience Rules in 1969. The second concerned a completely different type of training book.

There had always been a desperate need for a trainer's manual to show the dog owner what an Obedience class should be like, how it should be run, exactly how the dogs should be trained and what should be accomplished each week. Such a book would describe in great detail and with vivid illustrations the right method and psychology to use to train dogs and conduct Obedience classes. The pathetically slow progress, due to inferior methods, made by many Obedience classes, as well as the grossly inhumane methods used by some instructors, prompted me to give my second book, *Obedience Class Instruction for Dogs—The Trainer's Manual,* priority over the breed book.

Although my interests in the fifties and sixties were primarily directed to conceiving a kind, fast training method based on the correct psychology, the dogs I owned throughout this period were progeny of the top producers of their day. I have always felt that an Obedience Dog should be a top representative of his breed. The German Shepherd was founded to be a utilitarian breed and is still bred for that purpose in Germany.

When these two books were published, I started a serious breeding program. My foundation bitch was a Youth Siegerin I bought in Germany. I was producing champions, and I now devote most of my time to the fascinating pursuit of breeding, training and showing my German Shepherds.

In writing a training book, I could sit down at the typewriter and let my thoughts pour out onto the pages, and I could get the illustrations with my own dogs. When writing a breed book, the material had to be obtained from dozens of sources. For instance, some of the material for the "Origin" chapter I acquired in Germany, from Herta von Stephanitz, the daughter of the founder of the breed.

James Moses was handling one of my Shepherds, and I was so impressed with his skill and knowledge of the breed that I asked him if he would like to collaborate with me on this book. Jim shows and handles dogs practically every weekend and is in close touch with German Shepherd activities. His contributions to this book are very sound and his thoughts on the "Handling" and "Judging" chapters are excellent.

Gathering the factual material, plus all of the illustrations of the great German Shepherds, has taken a tremendous amount of time. It is very gratifying to have it completed and Jim and I hope you enjoy reading it.

chapter 1

The Origin of the German Shepherd Dog

The young German cavalry officer stood on the crest of the hill, deep in thought, and watched the sheepherder tending his flocks in the valley below. For three days every moment he could spare away from his regiment had found him studying and contemplating the pastoral scene below.

The sheep in this part of Germany were large and tough and appeared to be almost more than a match for the small dogs herding them. The sheepherder, none the less, dozed unconcerned under a nearby tree while his dogs kept constantly on the move watching over the sheep. They kept the sheep from straying into the clover field nearby, herded them together when carriages approached on the road and permitted them to scatter and graze when it was safe. The sheep, with their voracious appetites, were persistently straying too far afield and the dogs worked continually to keep them contained.

While the young man watched, fascinated, he envisioned a dog of medium size who could cope with the two different sized breeds of sheep found in Germany. He saw a dog who would be extremely intelligent, quick on his feet, protective if necessary, noble in appearance, trustworthy in character, physically sound so that he could work tirelessly all day long and born with an innate desire to please. A dog who could reason and be a companion to man.

As the young man's ideas crystallized, he came to the conclusion that he would breed such a dog and make it available to sheepherders all over Germany. When the farsighted cavalry officer, Max von Stephanitz, returned to his regiment, he promised himself that he would start a utilitarian breed of dogs that would be known as German Shepherds. And so it was, this day in the 1890s, that the idea of founding a new breed came into being.

For many, many years the Germans had used a wide variety of dogs to herd their sheep. There was no real consistency of type among them, other than that found within various strains in different parts of the country. Attempts to merge the strains into one distinct breed had been tried unsuccessfully, and all the sheepherding dogs had been placed under the category of Shepherds, no matter what their size, shape, ear carriage, coat length or color. There were a few All-Breed Shows, and there had been one attempt at a club, known as the Phylax Society. It failed because it did not have a sound foundation. It was based solely on its members' common interest in breeding dogs to resemble wolves, presumably hoping to cash in on their high market value.

Since the early days, dog shows had been held so that breeders could compare their dogs with others of the same age and sex. For dogs under two years of age, there were two male and two female classes, twelve to eighteen months, and eighteen months to two years. For adults over two years of age, there was one class for males and one for females. The twentieth century was to see a dramatic change in both the dogs and the dog shows.

Max Emil Frederick von Stephanitz was born in Germany on December 30, 1864. In school he excelled in French and his command of the language was so great that the audience who listened to his graduation recitation thought he was a Frenchman. When he finished school, he wanted to become a gentleman farmer, but he respected the wishes of his mother and became a career officer. He served with the Veterinary College in Berlin for a time, and the biological knowledge he gained there was of great value later when he applied it to the science of breeding dogs. The motto of the von Stephanitz coat of arms is one that Max seemed to heed all through his life—"Do right and fear no one."

It is said that his family was of the nobility and his career as a cavalry officer was a highly respected position in this society. In 1898 he was promoted to Cavalry Captain, a singular honor for a young man. Shortly thereafter, however, he was requested to leave the service because he married an actress, who, in those days, was considered below his social standing. It was an act of fate. Now he had the time to devote to developing the German Shepherd Dog.

He bought a beautiful estate near Grafrath and developed it the same year he founded the SV. In the ensuing years, he had two children, Herta and Otto. Otto became a gentleman farmer and was never particularly interested in dogs. His sister Herta, however, was always keenly interested in dogs and took an active part behind the scenes. When the *Sieger* (champion) Show became an international event, Herta could be found interpreting for the many foreign visitors who attended the show. Even today she devotes many hours of her time compiling reports for German Shepherd officials.

Throughout the 1890s Captain von Stephanitz had experimented with breeding dogs and had employed many of the ideas the English dog breeders were using in England. He was vitally interested in the Shepherd dogs because they were the true working dogs of that era. Down through the centuries, these dogs had developed exceptionally sharp senses and instincts, plus the predisposition to work. In 1899 he attended one of the small dog shows where he found and bought Hektor Linkrsheim. He immediately changed the dog's name to Horand von Grafrath.

Two weeks later he and a friend, Artur Meyer, founded the *Verein für Deutsche Schaferhunde*, (SV), and von Stephanitz became its first president. Artur Meyer became secretary and conducted the affairs of the club from his home in Stuttgart. Three Sheep Masters, two factory owners, one architect, one mayor, one innkeeper and one justice joined them as cofounders. And so it was that this illustrious group of men founded the club that was destined to become the greatest single breed club in the world.

Horand became the first entry in the newly founded SV Stud Book, with the number SZ1. He was, in fact, the first registered German Shepherd Dog. To gain some insight into the Shepherd qualities that most impressed von Stephanitz, one should know what he said about Horand, the dog who so completely won him over at their first meeting and whose type became the foundation on which the breed was built:

Horand v. Grafrath, SZ1.

Also, for the fancy dog enthusiasts of that time, Horand embodied the fulfillment of their fondest dreams; he was large, from 24–24.5 inches height of back, and even from the point of view of present conditions, a very good medium-size with powerful bones, beautiful lines, and a nobly formed head; clean and sinewy in build; the whole dog was one live wire. His character corresponded to his exterior qualities; marvelous in his obedient faithfulness to his master; and above all, the straightforward nature of a gentleman with a boundless and irrepressible zest for living. Although untrained in his puppyhood, nevertheless obedient to the slightest nod when at his master's side; but when left to himself, the maddest rascal, the wildest ruffian and an incorrigible provoker of strife. Never idle, always on the go; well disposed to harmless people, but no cringer, crazy about children, and always in love. What could not have become of such a dog, if only we had had at that time military or service training? His faults were the consequence of his upbringing and never of his stock. He suffered from a suppressed, or better, a superfluity of unemployed energy; for he was delighted whenever someone gave him attention and he was then the most tractable of dogs.

Beginning in 1899 the SV held an annual *Sieger* Show and the winners of the adult classes at this show were named the *Sieger* and *Siegerin* for the year. (The terms *Sieger* and *Siegerin* effectively translate to what would be considered an annual national Grand Champion in other forms of livestock in the United States.) Captain von Stephanitz was the judge of this event, and in this capacity was able to guide the breeding practices. Realizing the tendency of most breeders to breed their bitches to the current Sieger, in the years that followed, von Stephanitz was able, through his selection of the Sieger, to guide the breed's development as well as correct any faults that became too widespread. Whatever faults were too prevalent, or whatever divergence from correct working type was evident, he tried to counteract by choosing a dog who was without such flaws and would be least likely to pass on the fault. Because pedigrees were also examined at the show, von Stephanitz was able to gain more insight into the virtues and the flaws hidden in a dog's lines, whether or not the dog himself exhibited them, for these qualities would be passed down through his line. The judging of this Show took two days to complete and was taken very seriously. As always, the character and temperament of the dogs were an important part of the judging.

Captain von Stephanitz had a monumental task ahead of him. First he had to create an effective organization, which he did with unparalleled leadership and initiative. The Club Statutes and the Breed Standard were drawn up and it is due to his remarkable foresight and unquestioned knowledge that they are still valid today. He initiated the start of the first Stud Book because he felt the breed should be founded on hereditary research and not show wins. In the early days many of the Shepherd dogs were of unknown ancestry, but those with appropriate breed characteristics were bred and recorded, even though their pedigrees were partially unknown. At this time von Stephanitz decreed that all litters must be recorded and this provided

Captain von Stephanitz directing SV affairs from his office.

the basis for genetic recording. Because he managed the SV without interruption throughout the years, the Stud Book also served as a base for research work. As soon as it was possible, only purebred German Shepherds whose hereditary bloodlines could be proven were entered in the Stud Book—a ruling that is still in effect today.

Just a couple of years after the club was founded, Artur Meyer died. Von Stephanitz absorbed his work and moved the seat of the SV to Munich. This doubled his work and for the rest of his life he devoted himself to his family, the SV and the science of breeding dogs.

Under his direction the membership in the SV grew steadily, and it soon became necessary to form branches in various parts of Germany to handle all the work. It was a gradual albeit rapid growth, and additional branches were set up as the need arose. Newsletters were sent out to the members and it was partially through this medium that the membership was kept informed of their responsibilities. Von Stephanitz advised the breeders which dogs would improve certain lines and dictated to which bitches they should be bred. He also advised which combinations were not advisable and which dogs should not be used at stud. He decreed the maximum number of puppies a bitch should raise and began a system whereby Breed Wardens, appointed by the club, would inspect litters at birth. From this early period until death, he dictated breeding policies to German Shepherd breeders all over Germany.

At that time most of the breeders were idealistic and completely willing to follow his orders because they wanted the best for their breed. In fact, their willingness to comply to his orders largely accounts for the swiftness with which the heterogeneous sheepdogs were molded into a distinct and recognizable breed.

However, the SV organization did not always run smoothly. In the early years, breeders of luxury breeds strongly disputed the judgment of the SV that the German Shepherd was a working breed and must remain so. It was due to the single-minded attitude of von Stephanitz that he was able to assert his position and defeat the attempts of less dedicated persons to ruin the breed.

Captain von Stephanitz took up residence in southern Bavaria and it was here that he bred German Shepherds and studied them closely. Horand was bred very selectively to those bitches most similar in type to himself. His son, Hektor von Schwaben, became the second German Sieger, and Hektor's sons Beowolf, Heinz von Starkenburg and Pilot III headed the three most important Horand lines.

Using Horand as the basic form on which to base his concept of the new breed, von Stephanitz proceeded to mold the German Shepherd into the canine epitome of usefulness, intelligence and nobility. He decreed that as a working dog, the German Shepherd was to be bred for intelligence and the physical soundness suited for his work. Never was he interested in a dog's beauty for it's own sake, but only as it reflected and was derived from the sound working build of the dog.

Von Stephanitz soon found that the intelligence of the dogs waned if they were kept kenneled. Since the German Shepherd's character, intelligence and utility were of major importance, he devised Obedience contests to preserve these qualities in the breed. Only a limited number of dogs were required to serve with the sheepherders, so von Stephanitz looked around to find other ways for them to serve mankind. The Army scoffed at his ideas, but by giving several dogs to policemen, he was able to demonstrate their usefulness as police dogs. The police were most willing to cooperate when they found the dogs were genuinely useful in apprehending and deterring criminals.

To arouse competitive interest in the breed, the SV issued awards in certain fields. The greatest honor was the title "Herding Trials Sieger." Another award was given for special achievement in breeding. Training Trials were established with the cooperation of the police, awards were given and another means was found to demonstrate the usefulness of the German Shepherd breed to man. Only SV members were permitted to judge the trials and they had to serve an apprenticeship before they could actually judge. Of course, as the membership grew, the number of Breed shows also increased and the SV offered awards at these shows in all classes.

It was some time later that the Army recognized the dogs' usefulness and employed them, but it wasn't until World War I that they discovered how useful German Shepherds could be. They served as messenger dogs, helped to lay telephone lines, found and indicated the positions of wounded soldiers for the Red Cross, worked as sentry and guard dogs and signaled the presence of the enemy while on patrol duty.

Through the leadership of von Stephanitz, the SV grew to a membership of 57,000 by 1923. He was in absolute control of the organization and dictated all policies pertaining to the breed. When the breed became famous after World War I and unscrupulous breeders raised puppies just to sell to foreign markets, von Stephanitz put a stop to it. He introduced the *Koerung*, a survey in which the dogs were thoroughly examined, judged and recommended for, or excluded from, breeding. In this way he put a stop to indiscriminate breeding and was able to steadily improve the breed.

Back in the early 1900s it had been necessary to resort to carefully supervised, close inbreeding and linebreeding, in order to gain a more rapid uniformity of type. One of the prime examples of this kind of breeding was Roland von Starkenburg, the all-black Sieger of 1906 to 1907. He was out of Heinz von Starkenburg and had both Hektor von Schwaben and Beowolf (who was a grandson of Horand's on both sides) as grandsires. Roland also had as grandam on both sides Lucie von Starkenburg, who also had Horand blood.

Roland's son, Hettel Uckermark, was the foundation of the first black-and-tan Shepherds that came to America. Hettel, when bred to the incomparable brood bitch, Flora Berkemeyer, sired the famous "B" litter, which included Bella, Bianka and Bello v. Riedekenberg, who sired many Siegers and Siegerins. Flora is one female who must be included in a discussion of the breeding of this period. Because males have a longer productive life

1925 Ch. Klodo v. Boxberg

and are able to produce many more progeny over a period of time than the females can, they exert a greater influence on the breed. For this reason it is the male lines that are considered most important in the history of the breed. But Flora was a bitch who produced prepotent offspring in her litters by various studs, her most famous litter being the "B" litter. Flora's daughter, Bianka v. Riedekenberg, and her half brother, Alex v. Westfalenheim, also out of Hettel Uckermark, were bred and produced a dog who became one of the most outstanding sires of his day. This dog was the 1920 Sieger and U.S. Champion, Erich von Grafenwerth. Erich had a greater influence on the breed in the United States and Germany than any other dog of that period. His son, Klodo von Boxberg, and Klodo's son, Utz von Haus Schutting, are but two of his many famous progeny.

In 1925 von Stephanitz was confronted with one of those breed problems that creeps up gradually and goes unnoticed until it is suddenly, unmistakably evident. The German Shepherds being produced were becoming too leggy. They were losing the proper working proportion that von Stephanitz had been trying so hard to keep. The breeders who met with von Stephanitz before the 1925 Sieger Show agreed that something had to be done, and at this show von Stephanitz deliberately chose a dog who was a different type from previous Siegers. His choice, Klodo von Boxberg, was the first of the modern German Shepherds. Linebred on Hettel Uckermark and a son of Erich von Grafenwerth, he was lower stationed with a deeper, longer body, short back and an elastic, ground-covering gait. He was a dog of moderate size with a sound, fearless temperament. By the end of the year he had been imported to the United States, but not before he had sired his famous son, Utz von Haus Schutting, who was also later imported and left an indelible mark on Shepherds in both countries.

There had already been much activity in importing, breeding and showing German Shepherds in the United States. The first imports to the States arrived in the early years of the 1900s. These pre–World War I dogs, however, were not destined to be particularly influential on latter-day Shepherds.

After World War I, the popularity of German Shepherds in the States rose because von Stephanitz had prevailed upon the German Army and Police to use these dogs. American soldiers were able to bring back many tales of the Shepherd's courage, loyalty and intelligence. Movie-makers cashed in on the sudden popularity of the breed with films of Rin-Tin-Tin and Strongheart, and everyone wanted a dog like these two. Puppy factories sprang up everywhere. They were characterized by indiscriminate breeding practices which led to large numbers of Shepherds being produced with unsound temperaments and faulty construction.

Between 1918 and 1926, when the breed's popularity reached its peak, the puppy factories had to work fast to produce enough puppies to meet the great demand for dogs. But as these unsound puppies grew into adults, their bad dispositions began to work against the money-making schemes of their breeders. During this period many poor to mediocre specimens were imported

1906–07 Sieger Roland v. Starkenburg

1909 Sieger Hettel Uckermark

1920 Ch. Erich von Grafenwerth

and sold to people who only wanted the dogs for status symbols. After 1926 their sales fell off sharply. Not all people could put up with the dogs when they became either too big or too rambunctious. Also, Shepherds were receiving increasingly bad publicity because of the many unsound temperaments being produced and the ease with which their misdemeanors got into the newspapers. It was fortunate for the breed that this overpopularity came to an end, as the unscrupulous breeders were doing the breed much harm.

However, many serious American breeders were still conscientiously trying to produce top-quality dogs and were importing some of Germany's greatest German Shepherds. One of these was the 1920 Sieger, Erich von Grafenwerth, who was imported by Hamilton Farms in 1921 and who became American Grand Victor in 1922. He influenced the breed in both countries more than any other dog of his day. His son, the 1925 Sieger, Klodo von Boxberg, was imported to the States the same year. Before he left Germany, he sired Utz von Haus Schutting who was Sieger in 1929. Utz, like his grandsire Erich, was a dominant stud who had a tremendous influence on the breed. He was consistently able to pass on to his progeny the great qualities that made his sire, Klodo, the 1925 Sieger and the dog who began a new era for German Shepherds. Like their counterparts in Germany, the American Shepherds had become too leggy. Utz was himself heavy-boned and low-stationed, and with his ability to pass on these qualities, changed the appearance of the American dogs. Some people felt that he went too far the other way, but since he was used at stud so frequently, controversies over his influence were bound to arise. Utz blood was the craze at this time and he sired a number of Siegers, Siegerins, Grand Victors and Grand Victrixes. Von Stephanitz himself said of Utz, "the pictures of the various Klodo and Utz children and grandchildren show clearly how well their blood prevailed over that of the different mothers. Through all those sons, daughters, and grandchildren, goes one great leading line: a strong, efficient, deep and stretched serviceable bodybuild combined with nobility of appearance and uniform expression."

As we have observed, of all the hundreds of imports coming to the States in the twenties and thirties, only eight had any lasting influence. These are Erich; Klodo; Utz; Ch. Geri von Oberklamm, 1921 Austrian Sieger; his son, Cito Bergerslust, 1922 and 1923 German Sieger and 1924 U.S. Grand Victor; and later, Ch. Pfeffer von Bern, U.S. Grand Victor in 1937 and 1938 and German Sieger in 1937, probably the most bred to stud in the States up to that time. The other two in this list were Sieger and Ch. Arras a. d. Stadt-Velbert and Ch. Odin von Busecker-Schloss, a half brother of Pfeffer's (both being out of Dachs von Bern). Both of these last two dogs were excellent German Shepherds, but were used at stud much less than Pfeffer. Also, they were used more and were more popular in the western states, whereas the eastern Shepherds were inbred on Pfeffer.

In the meantime, in Germany, von Stephanitz continued to dictate policy and initiate sound breeding laws to safeguard his beloved German Shepherds.

1929 Ch. Utz vom Haus Schutting

1937 Sieger Pfeffer von Bern, 1937 and 1938 U.S. Grand Victor

Although the dogs became very beautiful in appearance, he never let the breeders forget that this was a utilitarian breed and that the character, temperament and intelligence of the dogs should be their first consideration. The membership of the SV continued to grow and it was a singular achievement that he managed the organization so efficiently.

In the 1930s Nazism began to spread throughout Germany like a cancer. There were many SV members who were Nazis and they tried to meddle in the affairs of the SV. They persistently used vile means to cut von Stephanitz off from his life's work, and when he resisted they threatened to send him to a concentration camp. He gave up, after having managed his SV for thirty-six years. One year later, on April 22, 1936, the anniversary of the foundation of his SV, Captain von Stephanitz died.

Captain Max von Stephanitz was a man with a vision who had the strength of character to turn the dream into a reality. Even his severest critics greatly respected him, for he accomplished what no one else has done. He had formed a breed from a sheepherder's dog and, through selective breeding, had molded the German Shepherd into man's most noble and versatile canine companion. Never content with just beauty or harmonious structure, he had instituted a ruling that all dogs shown must have Working degrees. This, plus their acceptance by the Police, Military and other organizations, ensured the dogs' future as working dogs. His SV organization is the largest breed club in the world. Without his extraordinary foresight, the breed would never have attained the heights it has today. Everyone, everywhere, who loves German Shepherds can thank one man, Captain Max von Stephanitz, for creating them.

Although there were relatively few good dogs left in Germany after World War II, the German breeders were able, with the breeding formula Captain von Stephanitz had left them, to start producing top-quality dogs within a few years. Many of these fine dogs were imported into the United States and have been instrumental in making the breed great in this country.

The ruling body of the SV has endeavored to carry on the work established by Captain von Stephanitz and the SV has continued to grow. They now have a membership of 100,000 plus. There are approximately 2,133 active local clubs that are located in small towns or cities where the members can train their dogs for Conformation or Schutzhund. Today there are twenty Landesgruppen branches in Germany that govern the regional clubs and communicate with their members. In 1995 there were 30,000 German Shepherd Dogs entered in the SV Studbook. The dogs that rate Excellent at the Landesgruppen shows are eligible to compete in the Annual Sieger Show.

Excellent programs have been instituted that will further the progress of the breed. In January 1971 the SV started tattooing German Shepherds. The right ear of each dog was tattooed and this has not adversely affected any dog's ear. When the dog is x-rayed the tattoo number is noted on the film so that no switches can be made. To be acceptable, X rays must be taken by designated veterinarians.

Captain Max von Stephanitz

Herta von Stephanitz and author Winifred Gibson Strickland.

Claus v. Haus Werle, SchH3, VA Select 1946–49

Cralo v. Haunstetten, SchH3, VA Select 1946–49

The Select award is only given to dogs with the "a" stamp normal. While it is not a requirement that the parents also have the "a" stamp, in practice, judges do not award a Select rating unless both parents have the "a" stamp.

Any German Shepherd competing for the Sieger or Siegerin title must have the "a" stamp, an earlier rating of Excellent, a SchH2 title and both parents must have the SchH1 rating.

Hermann Martin, highly respected judge and owner of the world-famous Arminius Kennels, was president of the SV from December 1982 until 1994. Due to illness he resigned and was named honorary president of the SV. However, he remained president of the WUSV (World Union of German Shepherd Dog Clubs) with more than 450,000 members worldwide. Peter Messler became president of the SV at that time. The members gave him an overwhelming vote of confidence by their support when he judged the 1995 Sieger Show.

Hermann Martin died shortly after the 1996 Sieger Show. He had been a Conformation judge since 1970 and his knowledge and guidance will be sorely missed by serious German Shepherd breeders everywhere. He had produced 206 German Shepherd litters that included three Siegers and many top VA dogs and bitches. These included: Sieger Canto von Arminius, SchH3, Double Sieger Quando von Arminius, SchH3, FH, IP3 and the 1996 Sieger, Visum von Arminius, SchH3, FH.

Trainer Patti Mullins and her Assistance Dog, Ch. Wynthea's Francis v. Hyjinx, demonstrate for Dr. Joyce McDowell how easily he can pull a wheelchair. Besides pulling wheelchairs, Assistance Dogs like Francis are taught to open doors at home or in public, retrieve dropped items, substitute for a crutch in walking, turn switches on or off, assist a fallen person to rise, decrease vulnerability to crime and maximize independence.

chapter 2

The German Shepherd Dog—
No Truer Friend

The German Shepherd is an extraordinarily versatile dog. When bred correctly he can be molded into the kind of dog his master desires him to be, whether this is just a family pet, a top Obedience worker, a beautiful show dog, a guard or sentry dog, a hunting companion, an attack-trained dog, a police dog, a guide dog for the blind, an avalanche rescue dog, a sheep or cattle herder, a canine member of a search-and-rescue team, a movie actor, a TV star or a brilliantly trained canine companion.

The fact that the German Shepherd is in fourth place in the number of dogs registered with the American Kennel Club attests to the popularity of the breed in this country. Because the German Shepherd is a multipurpose dog, the demand for puppies is high. As a show dog, very few other breeds of dogs can equal the majesty and nobility of a top show specimen, or match the beautifully smooth, effortless gait that is peculiar to the German Shepherd breed. It is possible to have a beautiful show dog who is highly trained, naturally protective of your home, possessions and family, yet has such a gentle character that he can be completely trusted with children or friends. An intelligently bred dog will be able to learn many things. The success or failure of the individual dog depends primarily upon his breeding, environment, care and training.

The accounts that follow are true stories of German Shepherds from all walks of life and in different parts of the world. Many of these acts of intelligence could be repeated by other dogs of this breed, for the true German Shepherd is a courageous dog with a natural instinct to protect and work for his master.

I have numerous accounts of German Shepherds who discovered fires and saved the lives of their owners by alerting them to the danger. The following heroic acts are typical of a normal German Shepherd's behavior in time of danger.

In Mendon, Massachusetts, a German Shepherd pulled a nine-month-old baby out of her playpen and took her outdoors before anyone else realized that the house was on fire.

In Cranston, Rhode Island, a German Shepherd saved the lives of an elderly couple by summoning a neighbor from next door to help them. The dog smelled smoke, but was unable to arouse the couple by barking or to open their door by scratching on it, so he pushed open a back door and ran next door to the neighbor. There he barked madly until the neighbor opened his door. Then the dog led him back to his own house where the neighbor was able to help the couple to safety. In this instance, the shed that adjoined the house was consumed by flames, but the rest of the house was saved.

One morning I was typing away in my room on the second floor, with my Shepherd, Topper, curled up at my feet. He seemed to become uneasy after a while and I could sense him walking around the room. Finally, he

Joll helps to harvest the peaches.

barked sharply, and I looked up from my work; at this, he went to the door and jumped up and down, flashing a message to me with his eyes. I got up immediately, opened the door, and found the hall full of smoke. I dashed downstairs to the kitchen, which was very thick with smoke, found a toaster about ready to self-destruct, grabbed it with a towel and threw it out in the backyard. Later I found that the children had left toast in the toaster, gone outdoors for some reason, and had completely forgotten about the toast. The wooden cabinets above the toaster were very hot and blackened from the fire, and the varnish had burned off them. If Topper hadn't smelled the smoke and warned me, it would have been a serious fire.

Some time ago I trained and handled a German Shepherd called Shadow who won very high scores in Obedience Trials. While earning his CD, CDX and UD degrees, we won many top honors such as Highest Scoring Dog in Trial, Highest Combined Score, numerous First Place awards and a Perfect 200 score. Later he was given to a policeman, Officer Robert Hanacek, who gave him further training in police work. In May 1969 at the United Police Canine Association Seminar, Shadow won second place for overall obedience, agility, scent, and criminal work. He competed against thirty-eight police dogs from federal, state and local police organizations. He was retired from the canine police force when he was nine years old and went to live with his friend, Officer Hanacek. A few months later he saved the lives of his master and family by waking them up during the night when their house was on fire.

German Shepherds have saved lives in many ways. Dutch, a Shepherd owned by a family in Troy, Pennsylvania, saved the lives of two small boys who fell off a pier into icy water. He was chosen Dog Hero of the Year.

In June 1964 Lux, a three-year-old German Shepherd, helped his seventeen-year-old master escape from East Germany into West Germany. The dog attacked Communist guards and kept them from firing at his master. He then got across the border himself without injury.

German Shepherds are used very effectively to protect property and prevent vandalism in stores, museums, botanical gardens, government installations and other places. The Bronx Zoo uses them to patrol the grounds to protect the zoo animals.

In Finland a German Shepherd was trained to sniff out ore deposits. In competition with a prospector, the Shepherd found five times as many interesting rocks.

A friend of mine in Finland used his highly trained German Shepherd for still another purpose. During the last war, gas rationing was in effect, and in Helsinki long lines of people would queue up for taxicabs. This meant waiting for hours to get a ride home from work. My friend's Shepherd was used to riding home with his master, so it was not too difficult for him to learn to "Get the taxi" at his master's request. My friend would give his dog a note with his address on it and, upon command, his dog would race down the street to the front of the queued line, jump in the first taxi available, and give the note to the driver. The driver would then drive to the address to pick up the dog's master. No one in line ever argued with the big German Shepherd and he was able to save his master many hours of his valuable time.

Although German Shepherds are not bred to be hunting dogs, many people have used them in the field for this purpose. A friend of mine who had taught his dog the Novice and Open Obedience exercises in my Obedience classes took his German Shepherd duck hunting with him every fall. When he shot a duck, he would send his dog in to retrieve it and, whether it was on land or in the water, his dog would retrieve the game every time. The rest of the year the dog was a family pet.

A neighbor also used his dog for retrieving ducks and small game. His dog was trained to heel by his side when they were walking, stand quietly while he was aiming his rifle and race off to retrieve as soon as a shot was fired. This Shepherd also accompanied Jack on yachting trips, would jump overboard with him when they went swimming, and learned to climb the boat ladder himself to get back on board. This dog would jump off any diving platform or riverbank if someone would throw a stick for him to retrieve.

When I owned a summer camp on a lake, I taught three of my dogs— Hussan, Topper and Arry—how to save lives in the water. An unruly dog can injure someone by jumping on them while they are swimming. I taught mine to heel with me while I was swimming and if I tired I would place my hand on the dog's withers and he would pull me to shore. When lifesaving, the dog would hold the drowning victim's arm in his mouth and tow him to shore. German Shepherds are strong swimmers and love the water if they are introduced to it in a sensible way. Some people have even taught their dogs to aquaplane. Many people like to have their dog's companionship when they go fishing, and the dog will sit in the boat waiting patiently with them for hours.

German Shepherds are well known for their police work. They have been used for many years to track escaped criminals, help patrol troubled areas, and detect and hold suspicious persons. A policeman on night duty feels much safer with a trained dog by his side than he does patrolling the streets alone. A dog can smell or sense someone is lurking in the dark. Many lives have been saved by alert police dogs.

Toro, a canine member of the New Jersey police force, emerged as a hero of a massive hunt for a suspected killer. Police credit the dog with averting injury or death to scores of police and firemen who ringed a floodlit cornfield where the killer was hiding. Toro was sent into the high corn and captured and held the armed killer until the police arrived.

Many Shepherds have been successfully trained to find narcotics. There are numerous accounts in police files that indicate that large caches of narcotics were found only because a dog insisted they were there. Although the police had diligently but unsuccessfully searched an area, the dog's persistence encouraged them to continue the search until they found the cache. Shepherds

Melvyn Harker's "Rocky" being trained to work with bombs exploding nearby.

have been utilized for this work because of their keen sense of smell and their ability to work regardless of distractions.

In Philadelphia, the "Granny Squad" uses German Shepherds to help them apprehend petty criminals. Police officers dressed like women are sent into areas where purse snatching is a problem. A patrol car with a police dog in it follows them at a discreet distance, and as soon as the criminal snatches a purse from a "Granny Squad" member, the police dog is sent after him. These dogs work so fast the criminals are unable to elude them. The "Granny Squad" gives their German Shepherd Dog, Atlas, credit for twelve arrests for purse snatching. This alert dog was cited by the Chiefs of Police Association for his excellent work.

Thousands of German Shepherds have been utilized by the Military in the past ten years. Shepherds trained for scout duty in Vietnam have saved the lives of many hundreds of American soldiers. With their acute hearing, sense of smell and sharp instincts, scout dogs could be depended upon to warn their handlers of the presence of enemies, booby traps or snakes.

Some years ago my own dog, Topper, jumped across in front of me when I was reaching forward to pick some blueberries growing near a large rock. I jumped backward to avoid him and as I did so I noticed a four-foot snake slithering toward me. I didn't stay around long enough to find out whether the snake was a poisonous variety or not. I was just thankful that Topper had been keen enough to warn me to get back.

Selwyn Myers training South Africa's Ch. Bandit of Santiago to attack a gun position.

German Shepherds can be trained fairly easily to herd sheep and cattle. One sheep ranch in Rhode Island has bought four puppies from me over a sixteen-year period and each one has been taught to herd their sheep. Each new puppy served an apprenticeship with the older, trained Shepherd until he learned the rudiments of herding. Each puppy had a different bloodline, but all each one needed was his natural instinct, inherent intelligence, a sheepherding dog to copy and his master to show him what he wanted. The rancher always had one or two experienced dogs to show the young puppy the ropes.

Jim Patton in Gainesville, Florida, has taught his Shepherds to herd cattle as he works them on horseback. They bring the cattle in from the pasture whenever it is necessary, herd them into the corral and then return them to the pasture. The Shepherds make the work much easier and more enjoyable, and keep the cattle moving swiftly.

In Switzerland, German Shepherds have been utilized for twenty-some years to aid in the search for avalanche victims. Today, if necessary, the

Shepherds and their trainers are flown by helicopter to the disaster area, and with no visible clues, the dogs are able to locate the bodies of the buried victims. In many cases the rescuers are able to save the lives of the victims buried under the snow. An hour and a half is about the limit a person can live buried under an avalanche. Although most avalanche victims are found about seven feet from the surface, in Austria a dog found a victim buried under twenty-four feet of snow. Whether dead or alive, a person buried under the snow generates a vapor that rises to the surface and pinpoints his location to a keen-nosed German Shepherd.

In the state of Washington in 1961, the Search and Rescue Dog Association (SARDA) was headed by Bill Syrotuck. In 1971 Bill and Jean Syrotuck founded the American Rescue Dog Association (ARDA). Bill Syrotuck wrote a booklet that gave detailed instructions on how to start and maintain a Search and Rescue unit. He died several years later, but his legacy continues on.

Today Penny Sullivan is president of ARDA and anyone seriously interested in the American Rescue Dog Association can write to them at P.O. Box 151, Chester, NY 10918. The ARDA unit is prepared to give assistance at any time of day or night, in any kind of weather, in any terrain, or in any part of the world. The members do not receive any compensation for their efforts and pay all of their expenses out of their own pockets. If they receive a call for help from outside their state or country, it is expected that the people seeking assistance will pay the group's expenses

The ARDA unit has become expert in their search and rescue techniques. This unit and their German Shepherds have won national acclaim for their assistance in times of disaster. They have answered hundreds of calls for assistance, have saved innumerable lives and have found many missing people who would never have been found otherwise. When found, many of the missing people require first aid and the members of this unit are fully qualified to provide it.

Besides dog training, the handlers must gain proficiency in map reading, use of a compass, operation of a field-pack radio, survival techniques, first aid and evacuation procedures and must be physically fit. With a country as large as the United States, we should have a dozen highly trained rescue units. German Shepherds are preferred for this work for many reasons, the most obvious being their intelligence, willingness to work under adverse conditions and excellent scent work, strength and stamina.

Two-way radios are used to help direct the search, and quite frequently helicopters are required to transport the search party to the disaster area and to remove the victims to hospitals. Therefore, the dogs must receive a great deal of training to prepare them for any emergency. Besides avalanche work, their German Shepherds are ready to help in any emergency, including hurricanes, tornadoes, floods, train wrecks, airplane crashes, earthquakes and any disaster where people may be lost or buried under wreckage of some kind.

This Search and Rescue unit always works as a group and, once boundaries are established, each handler and his dog use a zigzag pattern to thoroughly search the area. The dogs are working on air scent more than ground scent, and this type of search work has proved to be much more efficient and successful than actual tracking. Tracking has its limitations because of the time element involved, the terrain and the weather, but the system used by

Layers of snow slide down the mountain, forming an avalanche.

Rangers discover a skier is buried somewhere under the avalanche.

Von Nassau's Bismark discovers the avalanche victim. Handled and trained by Jean Syrotuck, Bismark is considered America's first avalanche dog.

the Search and Rescue unit is effective even after a few days because the dogs are covering the whole area as a team. When they search an area, the victim is either found dead or alive or the searchers know there is no victim in that particular area.

The following account is typical of one of this unit's rescue missions and illustrates the efficiency and selflessness of the handlers, and the usefulness and intelligence of their German Shepherd Dogs. A boy was reported missing on Mount Si, Washington, and was last seen by his companion at 11:30 A.M. near the summit. Mount Si is a rugged mountain with an elevation of 4,167 feet and a base elevation of about 400 feet. On the west and north sides it rises in sheer rock faces which can be scaled or descended only by experienced climbers. A five-mile trail winds up its south side in a series of steep grades and innumerable switchbacks. On the east and southeast, two major drainages drop down the mountainside, quite steeply in several places.

Contour maps were carefully studied, and it was concluded that the most logical route for the boy to travel would be the two drainages. That night, at 10:00 P.M., four dog-and-handler teams were dispatched to those areas. They worked throughout the night in chilling 10-degree temperatures,

In remote areas handlers and their dogs are transported by helicopters.

Searching the ruins.

Search and Rescue members Wynthea's Tiki, CD and her owner-trainer Chuck Wooters, about to find a lost person during a simulated practice search.

Searching the river. Many Search and Rescue teams practice diligently all year round to retain their efficiency.

while thirty-miles-per-hour winds howled around the summit making the chill-factor at this time −40 degrees. The teams kept in radio contact and at 2:35 A.M. one of them reported finding a track in heavy snow in one of the drainages. At 4:06 A.M., in another drainage, one of the handlers and his dog found the missing boy at approximately the 1800-foot level. The boy had injured his knee and was extremely cold, but other than that was in good condition. He was given warm nourishment and made comfortable while waiting for evacuation. Another mission successfully accomplished.

In Great Britain, during the blitz of London, German Shepherds (called Alsatians there) were incredibly helpful in finding victims buried under rubble and demolished buildings. After a bombing raid, the dogs would be taken out to search the ruins. Many persons owe their lives to these courageous dogs, and many families were able to recover the bodies of their loved ones because some trained dog was able to sniff them out under the debris.

If you think that you would be interested in doing some Search and Rescue work with your dog, let me give you a brief account of the training that I would suggest that both you and your dog acquire in the first year.

Let's assume that you have made up your mind and have bought a German Shepherd puppy. You purchased a puppy from a working line that is noted for producing excellent temperaments, sound characters and intelligence. The parents are OFA (Orthopedic Foundation for Animals) certified and both are worthy representatives of the breed.

The first four months, the puppy is taken everywhere with you so that he can become acquainted with the world. When the puppy is four months of age, you join an Obedience class so that he can get used to working around other dogs. As the puppy learns how to respond to commands with all the distractions these group sessions provide, you are learning how to read your dog. He learns how to sit and stay for three minutes, down and stay for five minutes and ignore all the other dogs in the process.

Outside of class he learns to retrieve his toys, ride quietly in your car, wait patiently while you run errands and take long walks with you. He learns to sleep in a crate, on his bed or wherever he is told. If the weather is warm, your puppy can learn how to swim at this age and can learn to ride quietly in a canoe.

By the time your puppy is eight months old he should know all the exercises in the Novice AKC Obedience class and you could compete with him in two or three sanction matches. At this point the puppy should be ready to compete in three Obedience Trials and earn his AKC Companion Dog (CD) title.

If you live near a park, take your puppy to the playground and teach him to climb the ladders and scoot down the slides on his tummy. Take advantage of all the equipment there so that your puppy will be willing to try anything. Always make everything fun for him so that he will love working and playing with you.

If you enjoy hiking or backpacking, take your puppy camping with you. He will enjoy this and you will find out if Search and Rescue work appeals to both of you.

In the interim you should take a first-aid course, learn how to use a compass properly and become proficient at using two-way radios. In your spare time you could study contour maps, as this knowledge will be valuable later.

By this time your puppy will probably be ten months old. He can now learn to retrieve a dumbbell. Once he learns this, he could then learn to retrieve it over a 24-inch jump. The important point here is for the puppy to learn to jump when you say "Hup." At this age he should learn how to jump into the water on command and quite possibly retrieve a pond toy from the water.

Now that you and your German Shepherd have learned so many things together, you will want to step back and decide if you want to go on and earn a few more Obedience titles. If Obedience competition is not for you, it is possible that Search and Rescue work will appeal to you.

The German Shepherd will continue to be everyone's idea of the perfect, all-round working dog, but not everyone should have one of these dogs. If a person can't give a Shepherd the care he needs, the companionship he craves or the training he should receive, I would suggest that he get a breed of dog that is satisfied with less attention. The German Shepherd Dog should be permitted to be part of the family and to serve a useful purpose. As such, he will fulfill his destiny.

chapter 3

Choosing a German Shepherd Puppy

In order to choose a German Shepherd puppy wisely, you should consider a few facts before you make the initial plunge. The place to buy a puppy is from a reputable breeder who specializes in German Shepherds. He has spent many years, and many thousands of dollars, establishing his name and excellent breeding stock. You can take advantage of a breeder's experience and knowledge and buy a puppy that will be a credit to the breed. A reputable breeder will stand behind his stock and be as eager as you are for the puppy to turn out well.

Don't make the mistake of buying a puppy from a puppy mill, a pet shop or a backyard breeder, as they have no interest in the breed and are only interested in the money they can make on the sale. Not all of these puppies can be registered, and it is doubtful that you could ever obtain any accurate information about the puppy's ancestry, let alone see these ancestors for yourself. It is also questionable whether you will get a healthy puppy or, just as importantly, one that will remain healthy. All puppies are adorable when they are tiny. Don't let your heart overrule your common sense.

Even though you may have to shop around, find a conscientious breeder who believes that good nutrition, good care and clean kennels are all necessary and vital in order to produce strong, sturdy, healthy puppies. The breeder who doesn't skimp on food but provides the puppies with a well-balanced diet that includes plenty of lean meat is doing his best to safeguard the health of his stock and build up their resistance to diseases.

Good care means more than cleaning up after the puppies. The puppies should be raised intelligently and should be tested in many small ways so that the breeder can tell you which puppies have shown an unusual amount of intelligence, which are more agile, which move the best, et cetera. It also means that a lot of time is spent with the puppies to develop their personalities and to help them socialize with strangers and other puppies. Good care includes gaiting the puppies each day so that the breeder can note their progress, and it might, depending upon the age of the puppies, mean early conformation or obedience training. When training young puppies, the handler should make certain that the puppies have fun and enjoy the lessons. Only a breeder with experience, knowledge and the proper facilities can give his puppies the care they need.

It is equally important that the puppies and their quarters be kept clean. Puppies kept in a small area will be filthy unless their bedding is changed two or three times a day. Puppies who run and play in their own excrement will be hard to housebreak. The ideal setup is a puppy house that is clean, dry, and warm, with an adjoining large, fenced-in area where they can play. This type of arrangement encourages the puppies to housebreak themselves at a very early age.

Know exactly what you want when you go looking for a puppy so that you can tell the breeder whether you want a pet, an Ovedience Dog, a puppy that will make a good bitch later on or a top quality show puppy. You can get a very handsome puppy for a pet, Obedience Dog or brood bitch with the same top bloodlines as the show puppy. A breeder rarely gets a litter, even when it is very uniform, that is all of top show quality. Most of the time a breeder will have two or three puppies in the litter that he will sell for pets. Pet stock will include puppies that have a fault or faults that might exclude

Cool it!

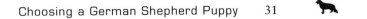

Wynthea's puppies learn to housebreak themselves with this type of housing.

"This is the life."

them from competition in the Conformation ring. These puppies will make wonderful pets and give you a lifetime of pleasure and devotion. However, don't delude yourself into thinking that because your puppy has excellent bloodlines, you can make him a champion or a great producer.

If you want an Obedience Dog, get one that has already shown signs of being unusually intelligent. But, don't get just a pet—buy a puppy that could do some Conformation winning. You are going to spend more time training your dog than the person who buys a top show puppy. Your initial investment will be very small compared to the amount of time and money you will spend training and caring for your dog in the years ahead. By purchasing a quality puppy in the beginning, you will be able to realize a return on your original investment by way of stud fees or the sale of puppies. And, equally important, you will have the feeling of pride and joy that comes with owning a beautiful German Shepherd. Whenever you take your dog into the showring, you can be assured that he is a worthy representative of the breed. To us the pleasure of observing a top-quality puppy develop into a beautiful, mature German Shepherd is worth the purchase price alone.

When choosing a puppy for both Obedience and Conformation, you will have to be careful where you look, for many breeders will not sell their top-quality stock to Obedience people. They erroneously feel that the puppy will be ruined. It is possible to buy a puppy for this dual purpose, but don't buy a top show-quality puppy if you have no intention of showing and finishing it in Conformation. It is unfair to the breeder to neglect showing a dog that could be an asset to the breed and a credit to its breeding.

Remember, it costs no more to take care of a beautiful show puppy than it does a mediocre specimen, or one that is advertised in your local newspaper for a comparatively low price. The price you pay, or the quality of your puppy, is of no consequence to your veterinarian. The fee for a veterinarian's services and medicine is the same for all dogs. If you intend to take care of your puppy properly you will have to give him a well-balanced diet, which means good food and supplements, so feeding a top-quality puppy will not cost you any more. Even though the initial cost of a good-quality puppy is higher, you will not have the medical problems or heartaches you might encounter with a puppy raised without the proper care.

The breeder will be able to show you the dam and sire of the puppies as well as give you pertinent information about many of the dogs in their pedigree. If it is a repeat breeding, the breeder may be able to show you a dog from the first breeding or may have pictures to show you. He can give you a good idea of what your puppy will look like when he is mature. Notice whether the sire and the dam of your puppy are friendly but reserved. The parents should be in good condition, clean, healthy, with clear bright eyes and glossy coats. However, expect the dam to lose her coat after she has weaned her puppies. The puppies will usually take after their parents in type, appearance and temperament when they are mature.

Leyenda's Starsky of Alkarah, owned and bred by Karin E. Wagner, a first-place winner at his first match show at three months. As an adult, Ch. Leyenda's Starsky of Alkarah, ROM, ROMC became an American and Canadian Best in Show winner.

Color is a matter of choice. A top-quality puppy can be any color, provided he has enough pigment. Faded-out tans and grays are undesirable, and white is a disqualifying color.

If you are undecided whether to buy a male or a female, be assured that either will be equally affectionate, protective, intelligent and trainable. The male is larger and weighs about ninety pounds when mature. The female is about three-quarters the size of the male and her size appeals to many people. She will be in season twice a year and should be confined at this time. If you are worrying about a male roaming the countryside looking for bitches in season, perhaps you shouldn't get a Shepherd. These dogs should not be permitted to run free, but should be trained to stay on your own property. Better yet, they should have a large fenced-in area in which to exercise. How large? Half an acre or more will do nicely. Nearly all the Shepherds I have trained were males because I love their size and nobility. Jim's personal choice would be a typey little bitch. Base your decision on your own personal taste, or make your choice when you see what the breeder has available.

You should be very cautious when buying your first puppy as you will have it for many years, and you will probably spend a considerable amount of time and money on it. You will learn more about German Shepherds during the dog's lifetime than you will with any others that might follow. If you are a novice interested in breeding German Shepherds we would advise you to

The author's Tell v. Frei-Aike UD at four months, showing his Schutzhund spirit and his willingness to take "a full bite."

"To the Victor belongs..."

Tell, at six months
Sire: V-Frei vom Hirschel, SchH3, FH
(Litter brother of Dbl. Sgr. Fanto)
Dam: V-Aike vom Kirschental, SchH1, HGH (daughter of Dbl. Sgr. Uran)

get a really good bitch with excellent bloodlines, one with a proven producing line behind her. By purchasing a puppy from a breeder who is consistently producing puppies that are sound mentally and physically you can get a fast start in the right direction. You can learn more about German Shepherds by watching a correct puppy grow up than you can if you observed 100 pet puppies. In studying the puppy's pedigree you should only be concerned with the first three generations; and the breeder who has spent many years perfecting his strain will be happy to tell you about them.

If all the puppies in a litter from a proven producing line seem identical in size, type and overall top quality, we call it a uniform litter. It is always wise to choose a puppy from a litter of this kind because any puppy you select should be able to reproduce quality if he is bred wisely. Because we think it is so important, I feel I should reiterate—buy a good puppy with excellent bloodlines from a proven producing line.

Buying a puppy is always a gamble because of the many risks involved. It is highly unlikely that a top breeder would guarantee that a puppy would become a breed champion. Even though the bloodlines are excellent, the puppy may never develop the potential that was so evident at seven weeks of age. He may become ill, be involved in a freak accident, be injured in some way or fall short of greatness for some other reason. You might have to raise a half dozen puppies before you get the show dog you desire. This could take several years to accomplish and, in the interim, you will spend a sizable amount of money. This risk doesn't exist when you buy a mature dog, because you can see what you are buying.

As to the choice between an American-bred puppy or a puppy with 100% German bloodlines, this has always been a controversial subject. I would suggest that you see the parents to get an idea of what your puppy will look like when he matures or whether you like their temperaments. Always remember that temperament, character and intelligence are just as important as conformation and far easier to predict. If you plan to train your puppy in Obedience or Schutzhund work, consider a puppy with German conformation bloodlines. These puppies have many generations of courageous working dogs behind them who are sound in temperament and character, and they are beautiful. If you request a pet, and pay a pet price, you will get a puppy that has some type of fault that will prevent him from winning in the Conformation ring. If this puppy is a cheerful, outgoing, intelligent, handsome little fellow, you will have a happy life together.

You might be able to find a mediocre litter of puppies and purchase the one beautiful puppy in it. And it is quite probable that there have been no notable producers on either the dam's or the sire's side. Although you are sorely tempted to take her home you should remember that your bitch puppy can only produce what is behind her. It is quite likely the price of the two bitch puppies from the aforementioned litters may be about the same, but money should be no object in procuring a top-quality bitch, as a major part of your life, and later success, are involved here. *These two puppies could start out seemingly equal in conformation, but as they mature, the excellent producing bloodline will manifest itself in the finished product.*

If you are purchasing a pet, you can take him home anytime after he is seven weeks old. The breeder will have decided at this point whether certain puppies from a litter will be designated as pets. Whether you take delivery of the puppy when he is seven weeks of age or twelve will have little, if any, effect on the puppy. The age of the puppy is not as important as his early care and environment. If the puppy is already acquainted with the world, kept under conditions that will encourage clean toilet habits and is mentally sound, he will have no problem adjusting to a new home. It is only the shy, neurotic, unhealthy or sequestered puppies that will have difficulty adjusting to their new surroundings.

Many people are of the opinion that you should not own a German Shepherd unless you have a large yard where your dog can run every day. If you have a home in the country, suburbs or city, it is safer for your dog to have a fenced-in yard where he can play and exercise. The peace of mind you will have knowing that your dog is safe from harm will far outweigh the cost of a fence.

On the other hand, it is not absolutely necessary for a German Shepherd to have his own plot of real estate. A German Shepherd is unique, he is what I call a people dog. He prefers to be with his people. He will be happy if you permit him to share your way of life whether it is a home in the country or an apartment in the city. He can adapt to any lifestyle, in any country or any climate. What is most important to your Shepherd is that he be allowed to be with you as much as possible.

Wynthea's Sailor, a German Shepherd, has shared a New York City apartment, two blocks from Central Park, with his owner DeTroy Kistner, from the time that he was seven weeks old. At that age DeTroy would tote him all over the city in an L. L. Bean bag while she shopped or visited friends. Far from being deprived, this city dog had many advantages. He took long walks and played in the park every day. As he grew up he met dozens of people who were smitten by his charm and exuberant personality. If he and DeTroy were out for a walk, one of these New Yorkers would remember him and want to pet him. He knew all of the cab drivers, doormen and tradespeople in the area and they would call to him whenever they saw him. For Sailor, it was a friendly, small-town atmosphere in the big city.

At the park he learned to swim and play in the fountains, climb the ladders in the playgrounds and cruise down the slides on his tummy, chase the squirrels, ride on the carousel, exchange greetings with the carriage horses and meet dozens of doggy friends. He became a very well adjusted, courageous, well-mannered city dog. Beneath his easy-going manner, he had also inherited the instinct to protect his owner if need be. Generations of highly trained protection dogs were in his background. A definite plus that any puppy-buyer should consider.

At four months, Sailor finds it great fun to cruise down the slide on his tummy.

Sailor emerges from a swim in the fountain.

At eight months, he stops to exchange greetings with his friend Chadwick, the carriage horse.

The suggestions we make in the remainder of this chapter refer to puppies three months of age. If you want a puppy for a pet, it is important that you choose one that will have an excellent temperament and be in good health. If you want an Obedience Dog, you should look for the same things, plus a puppy that is above average in intelligence. But if you want a top-quality puppy that you can show in Conformation, a bitch puppy you can use for breeding purposes, or a puppy you can show in both Conformation and Obedience, you should choose your puppy with the following things in mind.

One of the most appealing features about a German Shepherd puppy is his outgoing, aggressive inquisitiveness. He is completely unafraid and eager to make all the advances and investigate everything and everybody. Sometimes his exuberance and friendliness can overwhelm a stranger and he has to be restrained from making an uninhibited demand for affection. Puppies have a way of ganging up and taking sides against each other and sometimes one puppy in a litter may seem subdued and quiet as a result of this treatment. Take this puppy away from his rowdy friends and you will find him to be very friendly in a dignified way. A puppy like this will assert himself as soon as he gets a family of his own and will display all the courage and fortitude one expects of a German Shepherd.

Don't confuse the quiet puppy with a shy one. The latter is afraid of people, new locations, noises and strange objects at this age and is a pitiful thing to behold. Don't waste your sympathy or money on him, for, if you owned him, you would always be ashamed of his cowardly behavior. A puppy who has a poor temperament at this age should be put to sleep for he will turn out to be mentally unsound. He will always be unhappy and unable to face life's vicissitudes. Many times we hear the excuse that poor temperament in an individual dog was caused by poor early environment. We feel that a basically sound German Shepherd will overcome the environment problem. Breeders who hold on to puppies of unsound temperament because they are beautiful in structure are only hurting themselves and the breed. This is an inherited trait that could be passed on for generations to the detriment of the breed.

When choosing a puppy, remember that good temperament is the first requisite. Don't consider buying a German Shepherd without it. Even when some puppies have good temperaments at three months of age, there is still a chance that they will become shy later on unless you get them out in the world to meet strangers and visit new places.

The next thing you should notice is the health of the puppies. Whatever your reason for buying a puppy, you should be sure that the puppy is healthy. He should look sturdy and move easily and surely. The puppy should look solid, as if he were fed properly. Puppies fed a high-protein diet look solid, lean and fit. A puppy shouldn't have his ribs showing even though he has a big tummy; if he does, you should suspect that he has worms. A puppy shouldn't be too heavy, for this could adversely effect his back. His coat should be clean and he should smell good. You can often detect a sick puppy by the way he smells, a condition difficult to describe but easy to recognize when present. If a puppy has runny eyes, it might be from tonsillitis or some other illness, or the eyes could be irritated from weed seeds or straw, et cetera. His eyes should be bright, his nose moist and his skin clear. He should not have red splotches or pimples on his tummy. He should not be scratching and biting himself; if he is doing this, you should suspect he has fleas or lice.

A male puppy should have his testicles down at this age. A breeder might want to keep a very promising youngster, even though his testicles aren't down, if he thinks this condition will eventually correct itself. However, if you are paying a good price for a show puppy, it isn't worth the risk.

Check the coat of the puppy; if he is going to have a long coat, the fur will be long around his ears and on his tail. A long coat or curly coat detracts from the dog's appearance and is a fault.

A puppy may have his ears down at this age, but you shouldn't be alarmed about it. Most puppies have them up by the time they are four months old while some put them up at five weeks. However, you would certainly want your puppy's ears to be up by the time he is six months old. If the puppy's ears are set high on his head, they will go up sooner than those of the puppy with heavy ear leathers set lower on the sides of the skull. The puppy's eyes should be dark with a pleasing expression. They should be almond-shaped and should not protrude from his head.

The puppy's bones should be solid and hard and his forelegs should be very straight, sturdy and strong. If they are curved, or if the hind legs are bowed, it is a sign of rickets. An inadequate diet causes the soft, spongy bone which leads to this malformation, but as the dog matures the bone will become hard. If the knuckles are large, the puppy will have good bone; as he grows older he will lose these big joints and they will no longer be noticeable. Unknowledgeable people become alarmed and vociferous when they see a German Shepherd puppy's knobby knees. This is normal for this breed, so do not let them upset you. The puppy should be up on his pasterns; if he was not, you could suspect a vitamin deficiency. His feet should be compact, with thick pads and dark toenails.

Notice the puppy's teeth. He should have a scissors bite (the top teeth overlap the bottom teeth) or he could be slightly overshot. In either case he should end up with a correct bite. The puppy who is undershot (the bottom teeth extend beyond the top teeth) has a serious problem and this type of bite will not correct itself.

The males and females are about the same size at this age but you will notice the heads of the females are more feminine. Don't prejudge the litter by thinking the largest pup is the best. This is not necessarily true.

The most important thing to look for is angulation at both ends. A correct puppy should be heavily angulated at this age, for he will lose most of it when he is older. A puppy with very little rear angulation, who is well up on his legs, will grow up to have practically no angulation, and when he is moving he will kick up behind. This is a serious fault and is very displeasing to the eye.

A puppy with a good, long, upper and lower thigh might have loose hocks when he is small, but this doesn't mean that he is cow-hocked. Watch the puppy going away from you and notice whether he single tracks (puts one foot down in front of the other), for if he does he will move true behind. When he stands he may have his hocks together because of all his angulation; as he grows older this will correct itself. The cow-hocked puppy will single track with his hocks, not his feet, and this is a serious fault. The puppy should have a nice long curvature of stifle, with short hocks.

The length of the puppy should be the overall length; that is measured from the prosternum to the buttocks bones. It is desirable for the puppy to have good breadth of forequarter, a short back and loin and good breadth of thigh. The best way to tell about croup at this age is to watch the puppy when he poses naturally. If it has a nice slope now it will improve with age. Here is where it is important to know the individuals in back of your puppy. If they have good croups, your puppy most likely will also.

His hindquarter should look as strong as his forelegs and when he moves he should take strong, fluid steps. When he is in motion, notice how close he keeps his feet to the ground. The correct mover will keep both his front and back feet close to the ground. Many people think it is very cute to see a puppy lifting his feet high off the ground like a hackney pony but this is very incorrect. Watch the puppy when he is moving off-leash as this is the only way you can get a true picture of his structure. Observe him playing and moving in a large, fenced-in area. Notice how far forward he reaches, and how far he follows through. Don't have someone show you how the puppy moves on leash. A puppy who is pulling on-leash can be very misleading and will hide many faults. When puppies are shown in the breed ring under knowledgeable judges, they will have to gait on a very loose leash.

At twelve to fourteen weeks the puppy's hair lies close to his body and you can tell quite a bit about his structure at this time. Remember, the puppy will develop more forechest and greater depth of body as he matures. To choose the puppy with the best shoulders, study them as they are moving together. The puppy who reaches out the farthest and keeps his feet closest to the ground should be your choice. Your puppy should have a short, strong back and show no dip, or roach, while moving or posing.

Most young puppies carry their tails high, but they shouldn't curl them over their backs, nor carry them in a curl or a hook when they are standing. When the puppy is posed, his tail should be relaxed in a slight curve, like a sabre.

The breeder will give you a diet for your puppy, a list of the inoculations he has had, and those he will need. You should receive the puppy's AKC registration form, and a four-generation pedigree. If the breeder can't supply you with the registration certificate and the pedigree, don't buy the puppy.

Wynthea's Jack of Hearts at six weeks of age.

Wynthea's Jack of Hearts, UDX, at two years of age, owned and trained by Winifred Gibson Strickland.

The majority of people find it more difficult to choose a puppy than an adult dog because they find it hard to visualize the puppy a year or two later. We hope this chapter will make the choice easier for you. If you still need help, you can always rely on the integrity of the breeder.

Can. Ch. & OTCH. Joll v. Summerland, UD, imported from Germany and owned by author Winifred Gibson Strickland.
Sire: V-Alf v. Appenhainer Forst, SchH3
Dam: V-Erla v. Summerland, SchH3

chapter 4

Choosing a Mature German Shepherd Dog, American-Bred or Import

A German Shepherd is full grown when he is ten months old, but he is not mature until he is about two or three years old. An exceptionally promising puppy might be able to pick up some winning show points while still a puppy, but this is very rare. A young dog could finish his Championship before he is two years old, but he would have to be an exceptionally good mover and his structure near perfect, for he would be competing against dogs that are fully mature. You often have one youngster in a litter that matures early, never goes through an awkward age and always seems well balanced. It is this youngster who will gain his Championship when he is around eighteen months of age, while his brothers and sisters must wait for maturity in order to win any points. So, when we speak of a mature dog in this chapter, we mean one that is fully developed structurally and mentally.

If you are interested in obtaining a German Shepherd as a pet or an Obedience Dog, it is better to buy a puppy or a youngster so that he can become adjusted to your way of life and develop his character, personality and habits to suit your taste. If a puppy or youngster is outgoing and possesses a good temperament, it doesn't matter whether you buy him at seven weeks or seven months, for he will adjust to his new surroundings very quickly. The only question here is whether the puppy has been socialized and is acquainted with the world.

If you are buying a mature dog because you want one that is housebroken, trained and well mannered, be sure to find out how to handle the dog yourself. When we sell a trained dog, we give the new owner a lesson with the dog so that he will learn the correct way to handle him, use the right signals and give the same verbal commands, with the correct intonations, that we have used to train him. Once the new owner learns how to control his dog, the relationship between them will be very harmonious and his dog's adjustment to his new home will be made easily.

Whether buying a show dog or a companion, American-bred or import, you must realize that a mature dog will cost a great deal more than a puppy. In the case of a show dog, be prepared to spend thousands of dollars if you want to buy a good one. The price will be determined by the dog's show career, or potential, his producing ability and his bloodlines.

Buying a show puppy is always a gamble because of the many risks involved. He may never develop the potential that was so evident when he was a puppy; he may become ill, be involved in a freak accident, be injured in some way or fall short of greatness for some other reason. You might have to raise half a dozen puppies before you get the show dog you desire. This could take several years to accomplish, and in the interim you will spend a sizable amount of money. This risk is gone when you buy a mature dog, for you can see what you are buying.

Some people are limited in the number of dogs they can keep at one time. If they purchase a promising puppy, it is quite possible that he may never reach his full potential, but they will have become so attached to him that they will refuse to part with him. If this happens, very often they end up with a houseful of pets, while a sincere and dedicated potential dog owner, who loves the breed and who might have become an ardent fancier, is lost.

Some older people who want to take up the hobby of raising and showing German Shepherds are very interested in starting out with one or two mature dogs. They want to skip the time it takes to raise puppies, and avoid the uncertainty connected with raising potential show dogs from each litter. They can enjoy immediate success with good, mature dogs and raise puppies while campaigning the older dogs. It is an excellent way to get started fast and enjoy the thrill of winning dog shows.

As to the question "American-bred or German import?", this has always been a controversial subject. Many people are not objective—they are 100 percent for or against imports. In the pedigrees of the majority of our top American show dogs and producers, you will find German imports back in the fifth or sixth generations. In this country two main lines go back to the German dogs Axel von Deininghauserheide and Rolf v Osnabruckerland. Both Grand Victor Lance of Fran-Jo, who was bred and owned by Fran and Joan Ford, and Bernd vom Kallengarten, who was imported and owned by Ernest Loeb, are from these lines. These two dogs produced a great number of Grand Victors, Victrixes, Champions and ROM progeny. Hundreds of their descendants have become breed champions. By extensive inbreeding and linebreeding throughout the years, many of these beautiful champions have spectacular side gaits who look beautiful when posed. Unfortunately, in this process the temperaments and characters of the dogs have suffered. Too many of the show dogs are very poor coming and going and the trend in the past few years to breed for extreme angulation is contrary to our German Shepherd breed standard. If good imported dogs are used wisely, they will continue to exert a positive influence on American-bred German Shepherds.

When a German import has been shown in the breed ring in Germany, he will acquire a *Koer* report. Even if he is not old enough to have one, you will be able to find information about his parents.

This document is an individual breed survey and the examiner who conducts it gives a brief but complete description of the dog. The Koer report contains factual information about one particular German Shepherd Dog such as the dog's name, pedigree, breeder, owner, Koer Class rating and training degrees. The greater portion of the report contains a very detailed analysis of the dog while he is in motion and when he is standing at ease. The dog's weight, measurements, size of bone, color, feet, coat, teeth, eyes and all of his other physical aspects are all described in great detail. A complete report of equal significance is given on the dog's character and temperament, his reaction when agitated, his aggressiveness and sharpness under pressure and his response to his handler's commands. Each Koer report concludes with a recommendation, or warning, to be considered when breeding this dog. One can appreciate how helpful it would be to have a book of factual, unbiased Koer reports handy when one had bitches to breed. It would take much of the guesswork out of breeding dogs. When a German import has been shown in the breed ring in Germany, he will acquire a Koer report. Even if he is not old enough to have one, you will be able to find information about his parents. However, we must always remember that some Germans, like some Americans, do not interpret the Standard through strictly impartial eyes.

Not only are German dogs in demand in other countries such as Japan, France, Italy, et cetera, but many wealthy Germans are now buying the top dogs in Germany through their agents there and are showing them as a hobby. Frequently, the German imports go to people in other countries for much higher prices than most Americans will pay. With such a great demand for top show dogs, the prices in Germany have spiraled way above the dogs' true value. A buyer would have to be very prudent to purchase a top German show dog at a reasonable price. In spite of this, most of the top German dogs can be bought for a high price, although they become more expensive each year. These top dogs can bring their owners quite a sizable revenue from stud fees, as their services are in demand by breeders in neighboring countries as well as in Germany. Often, a top show and stud dog will be sold after the demands for his services have slackened and the breeder has enough of his bloodlines to carry on his breeding program. By this time the dog will be too old to do much winning in the American showring. If you can find a top show dog, our advice is to go ahead and buy him, regardless of his place of birth.

We feel, and many knowledgeable people agree, that the overall depth of quality in the United States is equal to that of any other country, including

Germany, and that American breeders are second to none. There are many beautiful dogs being produced in the United States that could win in Germany under knowledgeable German judges, providing, of course, that the dog shown had a complete and perfect set of teeth, correct ear and tail carriage, was courageous, had an impeccable temperament and character, had a Schutzhund 3 title, would release on command, had the "a" stamp and was demonstrating his value as a producer.

If you have your heart set on an American show dog, observe the youngsters at Specialty shows who are competing in the twelve- to eighteen-month-old classes. If one particular youngster appeals to you, watch his progress at two or three shows. Pay careful attention to the way he acts, not only in the ring where he is being double handled, but outside the ring where you can approach him. Is he winning his classes? If you are starting out, be sure that the dog you admire has a good, strong temperament and is very sure of himself. Expect him to be politely friendly. It is quite possible that such a dog would be for sale if the owner knew that you would seriously campaign the dog. Be willing to take the advice of the breeder, hire a competent handler, and be ready to accompany the dog to shows. You could easily spend a few thousand dollars, so insist on full ownership.

The situation abroad, particularly in Germany, is somewhat different. There, practically all breeders will sell their dogs if they can get their asking price. Hundreds of Germans raise German Shepherds for the express purpose of making extra money. When you travel in Germany, you will find Shepherds being raised in the most unlikely places. The dogs are confined to small spaces such as behind a barber shop, a restaurant, a laundry, a butcher shop, a bakery or some other place of business. If more room is needed, the owner might keep dogs in some makeshift kennel on the edge of town. Although most of the dogs are confined in small pens, the owners generally see that their dogs get plenty of exercise. It used to be the practice for German breeders to own only four or five dogs so that they could give them the personal attention that German Shepherds require. Some breeders would farm out their bitches and give the family who cared for the bitch a small remuneration in exchange for this service. Now there are quite a few breeders in Germany who are raising Shepherds on a large scale and can point to quite a number of dogs in their string. A German bitch is not permitted to take care of more than six puppies. If there are more, the local breed warden will help the breeder find a foster mother to care for the others.

The German people spend much more time with their puppies and young dogs than do most American breeders. Dogs are allowed to go almost everywhere, including stores and restaurants, and this makes it easy for the owners to socialize them. In Germany, practically every small town has a clubhouse, complete with training area and kennels, where many of the members keep their dogs. They meet there every night of the week to train their dogs and care for them. They condition their dogs from the time they are very young puppies to develop their protective instincts. When a German Shepherd Dog has this type of training and socialization, any temperament problem that arose would be one of heredity and not of environment.

At the Sieger Show in 1995, all of the dogs and bitches selected for the Utility classes had to pass a strict courage test in front of 30,000 spectators. This test is done on unfamiliar ground with a helper unknown to the dog. Dogs that fail this test cannot receive a high rating. If they pass, they go back to their classes and the judge very carefully studies the anatomy, the construction and the character of each dog. In this respect the judge observes each dog during the gun steadiness test. The character of the dogs is of utmost importance in Germany. It is true that the German dogs have much stronger temperaments and better characters than our American-bred dogs. It is now a rule in Germany that dogs who are judged for the distinct-courage and fighting-spirit test must release on command in order to get a VA rating. Dogs with distinct courage and fighting spirit who do not release are placed at the end of the V (*Vorzüglich*) group.

On the whole however, the German dogs are renowned for their excellent character, temperament and mental soundness. I have found that the German breeders will settle for nothing less than perfection where their dogs' mental fitness is concerned. If you have never had the pleasure of living with a handsome German Shepherd with a 100 percent sound temperament and faultless character, and who is just naturally courageous, you owe it to yourself to find one. Once you have experienced living with a German Shepherd who has such a superb personality, you will never want to settle for anything less.

During my visits to Germany, I have always been impressed with the attitude the Germans have regarding their dogs' working capabilities. They are always proud to show off their dogs and demonstrate their working ability. If a German breeder has a good show dog, it is to his benefit to train and show him in order to compile an impressive record for him. Sooner or later someone, who will be able and willing to pay the stipulated price, will buy him. However, even the dogs I have seen in German homes who are not of top show caliber are trained to work. I have yet to visit an American breeder that can show me any trained champions. We just don't train them. At this time there are very few American breeders who are interested enough in their dogs' intelligence to earn UDX Obedience titles with them.

Some people want to buy an imported dog for the wrong reasons. They think there is an aura of glamour to owning a dog from abroad. If they pay a reasonable price for a dog over there and are talked into thinking he is a show dog, they can be completely disillusioned when they start showing him here in the Conformation classes. He could easily end up out of the ribbons. A German dog could be rated V1 a few times at small German shows because the competition was poor. Those ratings would mean very little on the American show scene.

This young American-bred bitch, Select Ch. Helmic Delaine T was shown at the 1995 GSDCA National Specialty in the twelve- to eighteen-month bitch class. She was ten days over one year old on the day. She won her class, then Winners Bitch for five points. The next day she was awarded Select #6, which is quite an honor at the National. Three months later she had won four more majors and her Championship. This could only happen in America. She is bred and owned by Michael J. and Helen L. Peak, and handled by Bill Tank.

Today there are quite a few Americans across the country who have bought very good German dogs from top German bloodlines. These are handsome dogs with excellent temperaments who could excel in Obedience, Schutzhund, tracking, agility and herding. Many deserve to win at AKC all-breed Conformation classes where the emphasis should be on soundness. This is the type of German Shepherd who will appeal to the general public.

Because of the growing popularity of Schutzhund training in this country, there are a few German imports that are being brought over here who have poor conformation and are very aggressive in the sense that they are overactive. These importers advise newcomers to the sport that they should have "hard" dogs. Dogs that can "take" the type of training they will give them. They denigrate Germany's many beautiful VA (Select) dogs and bitches in an attempt to brainwash potential buyers and trainees. These so-called overactive dogs with high prey drives are purchased in Germany for very little

At the 1994 GSDCA National Specialty, Select Ch. Kismet's Heart Throb won the twelve- to eighteen-month dog class, and Winners Dog for five points. Later he was awarded Select #12—a considerable honor for a youngster. In 1995 at the GSDCA National Specialty, Heart Throb was named Maturity Victor and won Select #2. He was Select #5 in 1997. He is a credit to his proud breeders Maryellen Kish and Karin Wagner and is owned by Robert and Maryellen Kish. He was handled by Patti Breault.

and sold to gullible buyers for far more than they are worth. The new owners don't realize that these high-energy dogs prefer to be active and discover they can't cope with them in their homes as pets. These importers care nothing about the German Shepherd Standard but perpetuate their own mistakes by breeding these dogs. The emphasis is on bite work alone. American breeders and beginners who see these German imports are turned off. They never see Germany's great dogs like Double Sieger Uran v Wildsteiger Land, SchH3, FH; Sieger Eiko vom Kirschental, SchH3; Double Sieger Fanto vom Hirschel, SchH3; Sieger Ulk vom Arlett, SchH3; Sieger Zamb von der Wienerau, SchH3 or dozens of other magnificent German Shepherds. These Select German Conformation Dogs are also top Working Dogs who lived in the homes of their owners and could be called pets. Schutzhund trainers tell their trainees to keep their dogs in kennels when they are not working. The person who buys a dog to have as a companion takes a dim view of this advice.

Today there is a growing number of knowledgeable Schutzhund people who realize that a German Shepherd with the correct conformation, according to the Standard, is better equipped to handle any kind of work. Schutzhund clubs are inviting top German breeders and judges to conduct breed surveys and Conformation shows. These shows are becoming so popular that it is possible in the foreseeable future that they will attract larger German Shepherd entries than our large AKC Specialty Shows. I believe that Schutzhund training is a great sport. In fact, I like it so much I have five Schutzhund titled dogs, all of whom have beautiful conformation, are from top German conformation bloodlines and have earned German sheepherding titles.

A few years ago I attended a large Breed Survey and Conformation Show held by a very active Schutzhund club. The judge was Walter Martin, owner of the world-famous Wienerau Kennels in Germany, who has bred 363 litters that included some of the finest German Shepherds in the world, all of whom excelled in Schutzhund work. The majority of the people who supported and attended this show were ardent Schutzhund enthusiasts who had little genuine interest in the Conformation classes. Nevertheless, Herr Martin rated, classified and critiqued each of the Conformation entries. At the end of the show, when Herr Martin was summarizing the two-day event, he pointed out that the dogs bred for correct conformation made better Working Dogs. He reminded the Schutzhund enthusiasts that they wouldn't have their sport if it wasn't for the German conformation breeders.

If you do not feel qualified to choose a dog yourself, take someone with you who is knowledgeable about the breed. Or, buy a dog from someone who is noted for their integrity. If you decide to buy an imported dog, check the credentials of the importer. If you are dealing with strangers, have them sign a contract before you send the money. Be sure to obtain and study the pedigree and photo of any dog you plan to purchase. If there is a large sum of money involved, insist upon seeing the dog on video. It is a gamble buying a dog from Germany if you don't know the seller and haven't seen the dog.

If you are going to buy a mature dog for show or breeding purposes, you should have a very thorough understanding of the German Shepherd Standard. In order for the dog to win in the American showring or produce top-quality puppies, it must be close to the Standard in conformation. Show wins are not enough either—the dog must have good breeding because his true worth will be measured by what he can produce. To be able to get your investment back, whether it is a dog or a bitch, American-bred or import, the dog you purchase should be a good producer.

Generally, in this country German Shepherds are handled on a tight six-foot lead with the dogs pulling as hard as they can. When German Shepherds are judged in this fashion, it puts too much emphasis on their mental attitude and willingness to double handle, and not enough on their structural qualities. The majority of dogs that look good this way fall completely apart when viewed on a loose lead. Fortunately, many of the highly qualified American judges insist on judging German Shepherds for a short period on a loose lead.

I was favorably impressed with the way the dogs were shown in breed at the 1995 GSDCA National Specialty. The dogs had been superbly trained to pull out and to pose, they were all in beautiful condition and the handlers didn't crowd each other to hide their competitors' dogs. The handlers had their dogs out at the end of the leads and most of the time the leads were slack. It was a great show to watch, as you could always see the dogs gaiting out in front. Having just returned from attending the German Sieger Show that had drawn over 2,051 entries, it was a shock to find the total number of entries in the whole show at this National was 343, about the same number as just one of the German classes.

At the Sieger Show in Germany today, the German handlers show their dogs on six- to eight-foot leads and the dogs are judged at a trot for about two hours. At the end of this very lengthy period in which the dogs have been subjected to a hard physical and psychological test, which includes another gun test, the dogs are turned over to their owners or trainers. Now the dogs are judged on their stamina, perseverance and liveliness as they are required to trot off-leash by the sides of their owners or trainers. The dogs who maintain their trot without breaking their gait, regardless of how fast the owners run, bring loud cheers from the crowd. There is no way to hide a dog's faults when he is off-lead like this. It is not only a test of endurance, it is a remarkable example of discipline and obedience.

Each year at the Sieger Show, one or more of Germany's top VA or V dogs are sold to someone from another country for six figures. Despite the fact that this sorely depletes the breeding opportunities of those that are left behind, the German breeders continue to maintain a standard of excellence in their breeding programs. I believe they should be given great credit for this. Where would we be if most of our top producers were sold to other countries? One determining factor here is that all German judges and registrations are controlled by the German parent club, Verein für Deutsche Schaferhunde, (SV). If they have a breed problem and wish to correct it, they can make new rules and regulations without consulting another organization for approval. For instance, if they wish to eliminate a problem, such as splayed feet, they can refuse to register dogs with splayed feet as unacceptable for breeding. In the United States, the American Kennel Club has control over registrations and allows white German Shepherds, who are disqualified according to our Breed Standard, to be bred and registered.

We are not going to delve too deeply into the subject of structure and gait at this time. I would suggest that you be very well versed with our chapter on the German Shepherd Standard (chapter 32) before you go out to buy a dog. This chapter offers a very detailed explanation of the Standard, plus drawings and photographs, to make the account very clear. If you are sincerely interested in becoming more knowledgeable about this breed, we suggest that you start by reading and rereading this chapter.

The first thing to look for is good temperament, since a German Shepherd without it is worthless. It must be a very hollow victory for the owner when a Shepherd of dubious character and unsound temperament wins a Championship or becomes Grand Victor. This can and does happen occasionally.

A mature German Shepherd should be reserved but friendly and permit strangers to approach him without showing any trace of fear, shyness or aggressiveness. If the dog has been part of the family, he will have formed an

Ch. Altana's Mystique, born May 5, 1987, was bred by Maureen Charleton, sold to Jane Firestone and campaigned by James Moses. She became the top-winning dog of all breeds of all time. She won 275 Bests in Show, 455 Herding Group Firsts and 30 German Shepherd Specialties. She never had puppies.

attachment to them and it will take him two or three months to feel at home with his new owner. If he has a good temperament, he will be polite to his new owner and try to please him, but his thoughts will stray to his former home. He will make the transition more quickly if his new owner treats him kindly and considerately.

The kennel dog who has never actually formed an attachment for any one person will find it easier to adjust. However, if this dog suddenly takes to his new master, he will go through a period when he appears to be very shy and reserved. It is just that he loves his new friend and is not interested in meeting or making any new friends for fear they will interfere with the relationship he enjoys with his new master. Since he is basically sound, he will be his old, outgoing self after a few months, when he feels his position is secure.

Temperament is inherited, so try to see the sire and dam of the dog you plan to purchase. It will tell you something about your dog's disposition and character.

A person with a practiced eye, or one who has a sound knowledge of the breed, can tell at a glance whether the dog is worth considering or not. Many of the things we will discuss here will be evident at first glance.

If the dog has that intangible quality called nobility, you will want to keep your eyes on him and be very eager to see him move and pose. Watch the dog while he is gaiting off-leash in a paddock, or a yard, so that you can see how he moves, and notice how he looks when he poses by himself in a natural manner. If you are alone, take the dog for a walk on a loose leash so that you can study and evaluate him. If someone is showing the dog on leash, insist that he be shown on a loose leash so that you can appraise him. To earn his American Championship, this dog will be shown under knowledgeable Specialty judges who will insist that the dog be shown on a loose leash. This is the time when the dog must look structurally correct while standing at ease or moving at a slow trot. Never buy a dog when it is strung up on a tight lead and made to move at a very fast pace. This would be "buying a pig in a poke." Many structural faults can be covered up at this time, and many experts in the breed are fooled when they see a dog shown by himself in this manner. It is easier to judge dogs in competition by comparing them, for one dog shown by himself will always look better than he is.

At first glance you should know immediately whether it is a dog or a bitch. A male should give you the impression that he is strong, fearless and masculine. A female should give you the impression that she is graceful, agile and feminine. Both should appear to be alert, friendly, intelligent and healthy. The eyes should be dark and almond-shaped. The dog's teeth should be checked to see if he has a scissors bite, and the correct number—which is forty-two.

When moving, the dog should seem to glide smoothly and effortlessly, and while gaiting he should not break his stride. He should take long steps, but this long reach should be accomplished by scarcely lifting his feet off the ground, either when reaching forward or following through. Don't be fooled by the dog who lifts his feet high off the ground while gaiting, like a hackney pony. This is flashy but very incorrect. His back should remain firm with no apparent sag or roach to mar his topline. As he moves, you should notice that he is higher at the withers. His tail should be held low like a sabre. The dog's ears should not flop up and down while moving.

When posed, the dog should be very definitely higher at the withers, with a back that slopes gradually to the tip of his tail. His feet should be well arched and he should stand with feet parallel, without teeing in or teeing out, although a dog can be excused for teeing out slightly providing he moves true. His ears should be erect with the correct ear carriage. Check the dog's testicles while he is posed to be sure that both are down. Some German dogs refuse to allow anyone to check their testicles because their trainers hurt them in order to force them to be aggressive; avoid these dogs. Approach the dog and test his reaction when you talk to him and pet him. He should be reserved but friendly, and his disposition and personality should be apparent while you are observing him.

To sum up, a good German Shepherd Dog is a good German Shepherd Dog regardless of his country of origin.

Ch. Wynthea's Bruce, II, UD
Sire: GV Ch. Caesar von Carahaus, RO
Dam: Wynthea's Jolie Valiant
Owners: Winifred Gibson Strickland and Dr. George White

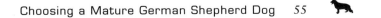

It was love at first sight when the author watched Double HGH Siegerin Pelli vom Kirschental, SchH1, win her title for the second time in Germany. Wynn bought her on the spot and brought her home to the States.

1968 Siegerin Betty vom Glockenland, SchH3
Sire: Black vom Lambertzeck, SchH3
Dam: Sonja vom Glockenland, SchH2
Breeder-Owner: Wilhelm Zeitzen

How to Read German Pedigrees

The SV pedigree (*Ahnentafel*) and registration certificate is a sheet of paper, either white with a greenish tinge or pink in color, 16⁵/₈ by 11³/₄ inches, which is folded in the center, resulting in four pages, 8⁵/₁₆ by 11³/₄ inches. The pink pedigrees are the *Koerzucht Ahnentafeln* and are issued only when the sire as well as the dam of the dog have been *angekoert* (surveyed and recommended for breeding).

The first three pages give information about the particular dog. On page 4 is space to record transfers of ownership (*Eigentumswechsel*) and the rest of the page gives general printed information about breeding rules and regulations.

The upper half of page 1 contains the name of the dog, sex (*Geschlecht*), type of coat (*Haarart*), color and markings (*Farbe und Abzeichen*), special characteristics (*Besondere Kennzeichen*), day and month when whelped (*Wurftag*), year of whelping (*Wurfjahr*), name of breeder (*Züchter*) and his address. The linebreeding (*Inzucht*) is listed, as well as the names, colors and markings of the littermates (*Geschwister*). Furthermore, there is a supplemental remark (*Erläuterungen*) about the size of the litter (*über Wurfstärke*), which will state, if there were more than six puppies raised, how many were nursed by a foster mother and how many by the dam.

Six lines of small print in a rectangle point out that this is a pedigree certificate (*Urkunde*) in the legal sense (*im juristischen Sinne*) and that those who falsify such a pedigree will be prosecuted. It also states that the pedigree belongs to the dog and that it must be turned over to the new owner when the dog is sold.

Next follows the space for remarks (*Bemerkungen*) and for the signature (*Unterschrift*) of the breeder (*Züchter*), certifying that the statements above are correct (*für die Richtigkeit vorstehender Angaben*).

On the bottom of page 1 there is a narrow rectangular area across the page which gives the registration number (*Nr.*) of the dog, the volume (*Band*) of the stud book (*Zuchtbuch*) where he has been entered and the date the pedigree was issued. It also states that the SV has examined the pedigree and certifies it to be correct. The SV stamp is in the lower right-hand corner.

On the upper right-hand corner of page 1 is the "a" stamp if the dog's hips have been certified normal. This information is also recorded on the lower right-hand corner of page 3.

Also at the top right-hand corner of page 1, space (*Raum*) is provided to enter survey remarks (*Koervermerke*). Such a remark might read, for example, *Angekoert 1960/61/I*, which means that the dog was surveyed, placed in Survey Class I and is recommended for breeding for the years 1960 and 1961. In the fall of 1961, he must be presented again and the *Koermeister* may then extend the recommended period for up to another four years, until the dog reaches the age of eight years. If the dog is in particularly good condition at the age of eight years, he may be presented again and the *Ankoerung* may be extended for one additional year. He has to be presented again each subsequent year to get further extensions, which are always limited to one-year periods.

Dogs in *Koerklasse* I are of the highest quality and are "especially recommended for breeding," while dogs in Koerklasse II are "suitable for breeding." This means that dogs in Class II have one or more structural faults that are compensated for by other qualities, such as bloodlines or performance in utility work. A dog in Class II may be presented again the following year if the owner believes that he has improved and may be worthy of a Class I rating.

Pages 2 and 3 (the inside of the *Ahnentafel*) contain a four-generation pedigree of the dog, from his parents (*Eltern*) through his great-great-grandparents (*Ur-ur-gross Eltern*). There is considerable space provided for information about the parents and grandparents of the dog. This includes color and markings (*Farbe und Abzeichen*), survey reports (*Koerberichte*) of all six dogs, *Zuchtbewertung* (ZB), which means "highest rating obtained in the Open class (*Gebrauchshundklasse*) at a Conformation Show" and a description of the littermates (*Geschwister*) of each of these six dogs, which states their names and training degrees, whether surveyed and their highest show rating, if any.

On the right-hand margin of page 3 are explanations (*Erläuterungen*) of abbreviations and symbols (*Abkürzungen und Zeichen*). An asterisk (*) preceding the name of the dog means that he was angekoert (surveyed and recommended for breeding); ZB means Zuchbewertung, i.e., rating received at a Conformation Show. There follows a set of twenty-three abbreviations denoting Farbe und Abzeichen (color and markings). Next come twenty-one training degrees (*Ausbildungs Kennzeichen*) under sixteen category headings and finally the seven different ratings (*Bewertungs Noten*) that are issued at shows and trials. Some of the terms are obvious, such as "gr" (*grau*) for gray, "M" (*Maske*) for mask, "S" (*Sattel*) for saddle and "L" (*Läufe*) for legs. The abbreviation "Pf" (*Pfoten*) denotes feet, whereas "F" (*Fang*) stands for muzzle, "s" (*schwarz*) for black, "g" (*gelb*) for tan and "A" (*Abzeichen*) for markings. If you read the letter combination "sg," it means the color is black and tan (*schwarz und gelb*); "sgA" means black with tan markings (*schwarz mit gelben Abzeichen*); "sgrg" stands for black and gray with tan (*schwarz grau mit gelb*), while "sggr" would mean black and tan with gray; "sgrl" is black with gray legs; "sbAM" reads black (s) with brown markings (bA) and a (black) mask (M). The colors are listed in order of predominance, "grg" means gray with some tan, "ggr" means tan (*gelb*) with some gray (*grau*).

Among the training degrees, those most often found are SchH (*Schutzhund* or Protection Dog) degrees, which are, in order of increasing accomplishment, SchH1, SchH2 and SchH3, and the FH (*Fährten Hund* or Tracking Dog) degree. These degrees are somewhat similar to our Obedience degrees in so far as basic Obedience of the type taught in the United States is included.

The rules for the trials leading to these four degrees are described in a small (forty-three-page) booklet issued by the SV. The examination for each of the three SchH degrees consists of three parts: Obedience (*Unterordnung*), Protection work (*Schutzdienst*) and Tracking (*Nasenarbeit*); each of these parts count maximally 100 points, so that a perfect score would be 300. To obtain a degree, the dog must get a total score of not less than 210 and not less than 70 points in each of the three parts of the examination. Minimum age for the SchH1 trial is fourteen months; for SchH3 and FH trials, only dogs twenty months or older are admitted. To be eligible for a SchH2 (or SchH3) trial, the dog must have obtained (at the trial for the previous degree) a rating of Good or better for Protection work (80 to 89 points out of a possible 100). All degrees are given with a rating. Nonpassing scores are 0 to 179 (unsatisfactory or *ungenügend*), and 180 to 209 (faulty or *mangelhaft*). Passing scores are 210 to 239 (satisfactory or *befriedigend*); 240 to 269 (good or *gut*); 270 to 285 (very good or *sehr gut*); and 286 to 300 (excellent or *vorzüglich*). The highest possible score in an FH trial is 100, with 70 to 79 being satisfactory, 80 to 89 good, 90 to 95 very good, and 96 to 100 excellent. After a dog has passed a trial, he receives a certificate granting him the degree and listing score and rating for each division and for the total. If both parents and all four grandparents of a dog hold Training degrees, the stamp Leistungszucht (breeding from dogs with training accomplishments) is affixed to the pedigree.

In addition to the SchH and FH degrees after the name of a dog, one finds the letters AD in the Koer book as well as in advertisements. The letters stand for *Ausdauerprüfung* (Endurance Test) and merely mean that the dog has passed this test, which is a prerequisite for Ankoerung. AD is not a Training degree and is not permitted to be listed as such, according to SV rules. In this Endurance Test, the dog trots next to a bicycle for a total of twelve-and-one-half miles with a speed of not more than nine-and-four-tenths miles per hour and a rest period of ten minutes at the halfway mark. The test must be carried out during the cool hours of the day and concludes with a few simple Obedience exercises as well as a check on the physical condition of the dog.

The last part of the column on the right side of page 3 explains the rating symbols as follows: VA = *Vorzüglich Auslese* (Excellent Select Group); V = *Vorzüglich* (Excellent); SG = *Sehr Gut* (Very Good); G = *Gut* (Good); Ausr. = *Ausreichend* (Satisfactory); M = *Mangelhaft* (Faulty); Null (or U) = *Ungenügend* (Unsatisfactory). The rating VA is only issued at the National Specialty Show and is obtained by about five or six males and about the same number of females. This rating was introduced in 1938 when the Sieger and Siegerin titles (Grand Victory and Grand Victrix) were abolished and was retained when the Sieger and Siegerin titles were introduced again in 1955. The idea behind an Excellent Select class was that it permitted several dogs and bitches of equal quality to be in the limelight as top specimens of the breed, instead of just one male and one female. It was done to prevent breeders from rushing to just one male (the Grand Victor) for breeding in the naive and mistaken belief that this was the sure road to easy breeding success.

Just as it is done at the Obedience Trials, there is also issued at each Conformation Show a certificate for each dog, giving his name, et cetera, and his rating. The letter abbreviations of the rating are usually followed by a number (at least for the leaders of each category) such as V-1, V-2, V-3, and so forth, indicating that, for example, a particular animal was rated "Excellent in sixth place" or V-6.

There are three main classes at German shows for either sex (there is no intersex competition): *Gebrauchshundklasse* (Open) for dogs two years and older with a training degree who have already received a rating of "Excellent" (*Vorzüglich* or V) at a local show, or a rating of not less than "Very Good" (*Sehr Gut* or SG) at a regional show, or at an earlier *Hauptzuchtschau* (National Specialty Show). The *Junghundklasse* is for dogs or bitches from eighteen to (but not including) twenty-four months of age. No previous rating of "Very Good" is required. The *Jugendklasse* is for dogs and bitches from twelve to (but not including) eighteen months of age. No previous rating of "Very Good" is required.

In 1995 the prerequisites for the V-rating were somewhat more severe as far as missing teeth are concerned. Now dogs must possess a complete, perfect set of teeth.

Dogs or bitches considered for the rating "Excellent-Select" (*Vorzüglich Auslese* or VA) may not receive this rating unless they are either surveyed (*angekoert*) or have a training degree of not less than SchH2, and unless both parents have training degrees. Dogs admitted for the second time into Selection Class V must possess a training degree of SchH3. They must also display distinct courage and fighting spirit and release on command in order to obtain the coveted VA ratings. Dogs with distinct courage and fighting spirit who do not release may be awarded the V (Vorzüglich) rating and positioned

Ch. Vax von der Wienerau, SchH3, FH, KK1a
Sire: Irk vom Arminius, SchH3 (Sire of Dbl. Sgr. Uran)
Dam: Eika von der Goritzenquelle, SchH2

Owners George and Virginia Collins imported Vax from Germany and he became their fiftieth AKC Champion. They bred their imported bitches to imported males such as the great GV Ch. Bill vom Kleistweg, SchH3, ROM, and GV Ch. Troll vom Richterbach, SchH3, ROM, combining the Axel Deininghauserheide blood with the R-litter Osnabruckerland. This combination is the basis for the best producing bloodlines in Germany to this day.

V1-Vedor vom Wildsteiger Land, SchH3, FH, IP3, KK1a
Sire: V-Rony v Arminius, SchH3
Dam: V-Mausi v Wildsteiger Land, SchH1
Owner: Tracy Bullinger-McCulloch

Rasse-Echtheitszertifikat

Herausgegeben vom Verein für Deutsche Schäferhunde (SV) e. V., gegründet 1899
Gründerverein der Rasse und für den Standard Deutscher Schäferhunde zuständig

Anerkannt von	**Verband für das Deutsche Hundewesen e. V.**	**Fédération Cynologique Internationale**	**Weltunion der Vereine für Deutsche Schäferhunde**

Körzucht-Leistungszucht-Ahnentafel

für den Deutschen Schäferhund   Tom vom Adlerweg

Geschlecht: Rüde **Haarart:** stockhaarig
Farbe und Abzeichen: schwarz,gelbe Abzeichen

Besondere Kennzeichen:
Wurftag: 06. MAERZ   1987   **Tätowier-Nr.** M-E 8726
Wurfjahr: NEUNZEHNHUNDERTSIEBENUNDACHTZIG

Züchter: Karl Reuter
Anschrift: Steinstr.7, 6806 Viernheim

Inzucht auf:

Flora Königsbruch (5-5)
Canto Arminius (5-4)
Quanto Wienerau (5-5,5)
°Cäsar Arminius (4-)-
Canto Arminius (5-4)°

Geschwister:

Tango sgA/
Tell sgA/
Tanni sgA/
Tina sgA/
Toska sgA/

Erläuterung über Wurfstärke: 3,3

Die Verwendung der Ahnentafel und der Eintragungen in ihr, die Anfertigung von Abschriften, Auszügen oder Übernahme in andere Zuchtbücher ist nur mit ausdrücklicher Genehmigung des SV zulässig. Eintragungen und Einstempelungen in die Ahnentafel dürfen nur vom Zuchtbuchamt des SV vorgenommen werden. Ausgenommen hiervon sind die Eintragungen der Eigentumswechsel und über Aushändigung der Beurteilungs- und Bewertungsnoten sowie Einstempelung der HD-Röntgenstelle. Die Ahnentafel hat nur Gültigkeit, wenn sie vom Züchter eigenhändig unterschrieben ist, sie gilt als Urkunde im juristischen Sinne. Wer Unrichtiges (Falsch) oder mit solchen Mißbrauch treibt, wird vom SV strafrechtlich verfolgt. Die Ahnentafel ist der schriftliche Nachweis über Rassereinheit, Name und Abstammung des Hundes. sie gehört somit zum Hund und ist beim Verkauf dem neuen Eigentümer unbedingt auszuhändigen. Beim Eingehen des Hundes ist sie an das Zuchtbuchamt einzusenden.

Bemerkungen:

Für die Richtigkeit vorstehender Angaben: (Unterschrift des Züchters)

Eintragungs- und Prüfungsbestätigung: Der oben bezeichnete Deutsche Schäferhund ist in das Zuchtbuch für Deutsche Schäferhunde (SZ) eingetragen worden. Die Ahnentafel wurde ausgefertigt vom **Verein für Deutsche Schäferhunde (SV)**, Mitglied des Verbandes für das Deutsche Hundewesen (VDH) und der **Fédération Cynologique Internationale (F.C.I.)**. Die Abstammungsangaben sind nachgeprüft, und ihre Richtigkeit wird hiermit bestätigt.

Das Zuchtbuchamt des SV
i. A.

SZ Band 87 SZ Nr. 1697598

Augsburg, den 09. JULI   1987

Neugestaltung gültig ab Januar 1984

Pedigree

I. Eltern	II. Groß-Eltern	III. Urgroß-Eltern	IV. Urgroß-Eltern	Abkürzungen und Zeichen
Vater: Jury von der Neuzenlache SZ: 1633670 SchH3 FH °1987-98 "a" ZUERKANNT ZB: V **Farbe und Abz.:** sg **KB:** Mittelgroß,mittelkräftig. In sehr gutem Verhältnis aufgebaut,typvoll,trocken, fest,Hoher Widerrist,gute Rückenlinie,gute Kruppen-länge und -lage,sehr gute Winkelungen der Vor- und Hinterhand,sehr gute Brustverhältnisse,korrekte Front. Geradetretend,sehr raum-schaffende Gänge,kraftvoller Nachschub,freier Vor-tritt.Wesen sicher,Härte, Mut und Kampftrieb ausge-prägt;läßt nicht ab. **Geschw.:** Jonny sg/°Joll sg SchH3,V/ °Jutto sg SchH1,SG/ Jenny sg SchH1,V/ Jutta sg/	Uran vom Wildsteiger Land SchH3 FH "a" ZUERKANNT SZ: 1526684 °Lebenszeit sgA ZB: V-A **KB:** Großkraft- und gehaltvoll,sehr gutes Erscheinungs-bild,sehr gute Allgemeinfestigkeit,Hoher Widerrist, fester Rücken,bei guter Lage genügende Länge der Kruppe,sehr gute winkelungen der Vor- und Hinterhand, korrekte Front,ausgezeichnete Brustverhältnisse,Hinten und vorne geradetretend,raumschaffende,bodengewin-nende Gänge.Sicheres Wesen, Härte,Mut und Kampftrieb ausgeprägt,wA 85!typvolls ausgewogen!Läßt ab. **Geschw.:** Ulen sgA/Ully sgA SchH1, SG/Utz sgA/ °Ulte sgA SchH2,V/Ulme sgA SchH3, V-A/Ursula sgA/ Ulme von der Neuzenlache SZ: 1486637 SchH3 FH "a" ZUERKANNT °Lebenszeit ZB: V-A **KB:** Mittelgroß,sehr ausdrucksvoll,gutes Gepräge,gute Ge-baudharmonie,guter Widerrist,guter Rücken,gute Ge-samtfestigkeit,Vorne und hinten sehr gut gewinkelt, gute Brustanlage.Sehr gute,geraumige Gänge.Härte,Mut und Kampftrieb ausgeprägt.WA 84!Läßt ab. **Geschw.:** Ulfe sq/SG/ Umsa sq/ Urfa sq/ Ursa sq/ Uta sq/	°Irk von Arminius SZ: 1437161 SchH3 FH IP3 °Palme vom Wildsteiger Land SZ: 1478659 SchH2 °Apoll vom Haus Tigges SZ: 1381702 SchH3 °Perla von der Neuzenlache SZ: 1429373 SchH1	°Pirol von Arminius SZ: 1381397 SchH3 °Dunja vom Wellachtal SZ: 1312041 SchH3 FH °Nick von der Wienerau SZ: 1386415 SchH3 °Fina vom Badsee SZ: 1405181 SchH3 FH °Cäsar von Bergischen Tal SZ: 1277393 SchH3 FH °Panja vom Zollgrenzschutz-Haus SZ: 1308525 SchH2 °Kay vom Sürenhelder See SZ: 1334541 SchH3 FH °Flanke vom Haus Beck SZ: 1239975 SchH1	**Farbe und Abzeichen:** **Ausbildungs-Kennzeichen:** **Bewertungsnoten:** **Stempel HD-Tierarzt:** **HD-Befund:**
Mutter: Fenja vom Monsato SZ: 1622037 SchH1 °1987-98 "a" ZUERKANNT ZB: V **Farbe und Abz.:** sg **KB:** Mittelgroß,mittelkräftig. In gutem Verhältnis aufge-baut,trocken,fest,Hoher Widerrist,etwas kurze Krup-pe,gute Winkelungen und Brustverhältnisse,korrekte Front.Geradetretend,sehr raumgreifende Gänge.Wesen sicher,Härte,Mut und Kampftrieb ausgeprägt,läßt ab. **Geschw.:** Falko sgA/ °Farro sgA SchH3 IP3,V/ Feger sgA/ Ferro sgA/ Fee sgA SchH1,V/	Tell vom Großen Sand SZ: 1523173 SchH3 "a" ZUERKANNT °Lebenszeit ZB: V-A sgAM **KB:** Großkraft- und gehaltvoll,durch ausgespro-chene Trockenheit und Festigkeit ins Auge fallend, guter Ausdruck,sehr gutes Gepräge,guter Widerrist, betonter Widerrist,gute Gesamtfestigkeit,fester Rük-ken,sehr gut gewinkelte Hinterhand,genügend lange Krup-pe.Korrekte Front.Raumgreifende,ausgreifende Gänge.sehr kraftvolle Gänge aus festem Rücken.Wesen sicher,Härte,Mut und Kampftrieb ausgeprägt. WA 86!Läßt nicht ab. **Geschw.:** Tasso sgAM/°Terry sgAM SchH3/Tim sgAM SchH3 ZH1/ °Tom sgAM SchH3,V/ Troll sgAM/ Tina sgAM SchH3,V-A/ Ricki von der Burgmühle SZ: 1505472 SchH2 "a" ZUERKANNT °Lebenszeit ZB: SG **KB:** Gut mittelgroß,sehr ausdrucksvoll,kräftig,harmo-nisch,guter Widerrist,fester Rücken,Kruppe könnte etwas länger sein.Gute Lage,gute Winkelung der Oberarms. korrekte Front,sehr gute Winkelung der Hinterhand. Kraftvolle,geraumige Gänge. Wesen sicher,Härte,Mut und Kampftrieb ausgeprägt.WA 86!Läßt nicht ab. **Geschw.:** Rando sbA SchH2/ Reza sbA SchH2,G/ Rocco sbA SchH2/ Rondo sbA/SG/ Ronny sbA ZH3 FH/	°Sonny vom Badener-Land SZ: 1391803 SchH3 °Jenny vom Großen Sand SZ: 1427244 SchH3 °Jupp vom Haus Loverich SZ: 1434005 SchH3 °Lassy von der Burgmühle SZ: 1439081 SchH2	°Canto vom Arminius SZ: 1277394 SchH3 °Luna vom Eldechsbrunnen SZ: 1249649 SchH3 °Lasso di Val Sole SZ: 1378829 SchH3 °Lidl vom Heiligenrech SZ: 1308367 SchH3 °Reza vom Haus Beck SZ: 1341149 SchH3 °Ute vom Haus Loverich SZ: 1347576 SchH3 °Liborius vom Liborius Brunnen SZ: 1313718 SchH3 FH °Topsy vom Lauerhof SZ: 1343667 SchH2	

The Ahnentafel, or SV pedigree, gives a great deal more information about the German Shepherd it describes than the dogs in its family background.

at the end of the V-Group. The Sieger or Siegerin title can only be awarded to a dog or a bitch from *Koerklasse* 1A (surveyed and especially recommended for breeding, free of hip dysplasia).

Dogs and bitches three and one-half years or older must be *angekoert* (surveyed) in order to be considered for the rating "Excellent" (*Vorzüglich* or V), but dogs from other countries are exempt from this requirement. The highest rating to be awarded in the *Junghundklasse* and *Jugendklasse* is "Very Good" (*Sehr Gut* or SG).

There is another set of letters seen in connection with imported dogs, namely CACIB, which means *Certificat d'Aptitude au Championnat International de Beauté*. When a judge issues a CACIB card to a dog, he expresses the opinion that the particular animal seems worthy to him to obtain the International Championship title. He certifies, in other words, the suitability (aptitude) of the dog for this title. The CACIB is only awarded at selected International shows that have been approved by the FCI (*Federation Cynologique Internationale*). The SV is a member of this International organization. Only one male and one female of a breed may obtain the CACIB at a CACIB show.

The International Championship title is awarded by the FCI after a dog has won two CACIBs in two different countries under two different judges. One of the CACIBs must have been won either in the country where the breed originated (Germany) or in the country of the owner. The second requirement is that the dog must have participated in a recognized trial in his country with at least five dogs taking part, and this trial must include a Temperament Test, Obedience, a Tracking Test, and Examination for Absence of Gunshyness. The dog must obtain not less than 75 percent of the theoretically possible score, i.e., not less than 225 points if this was a SchH1, SchH2 or SchH3 trial, and he must place first, second or third. The owner of the dog must apply to the FCI for the title—it does not come automatically—and he must submit the necessary documents to prove the validity of his claim. This may be done in stages by submitting each CACIB when received to the FCI, which will check it and return it together with a rather ornamental-looking card. This card certifies the validity of the CACIB, gives particulars as to the name of the dog, date of the show, name of judge, et cetera, and has space in front for a photograph of the dog.

Naming and Registering Your German Shepherd Dog

This chapter is included in our book for the sole convenience of the Shepherd owner who is having difficulty finding a name for his puppy. The names listed below could be combined with the owner's kennel name in any combination he prefers. When you register a dog with the American Kennel Club, you cannot use more than twenty-five letters for his name. According to the AKC regulations, the new owner has the right to name his puppy if it is being registered for the first time. Once a dog has been registered with the American Kennel Club, he will keep that name and registration number for the rest of his life.

If you have bought your puppy from a famous kennel, you will probably want to include the kennel name in your dog's registered name. Since the kennel owner is undoubtedly proud of his stock, he will be pleased to permit you to do so. A breeder who prefers to name his own puppies can make certain the names will never be changed by registering all the puppies in the litter individually. This costs the breeder considerably more money, but it assures him that the puppies will be registered under the names he has chosen.

We name each of our new litters with a different letter of the alphabet and, regardless of the number of puppies in the litter, their names all begin with the same letter. If the puppies are sold when they are very young, the new owners are given the chance to name their puppies. If we keep a litter until it is over four months of age, I generally name and register the puppies individually. This way I can teach the puppies to respond to their names at an early age.

FEE: $18.00

Effective July 1, 1991 litter applications must be received within six months of the date of whelping. Fee subject to change without notice. Do not send cash.

LITTER REGISTRATION APPLICATION

DO NOT WRITE IN SPACE ABOVE

To register a litter born in the U.S.A. out of an AKC registered female and sired by an AKC registered male of the same breed. Mail with fee to:

THE AMERICAN KENNEL CLUB, 5580 CENTERVIEW DRIVE SUITE 200, RALEIGH, NC 27606-3390

PLEASE READ REVERSE SIDE BEFORE COMPLETING APPLICATION

**PRINT IN CAPITAL LETTERS ONLY – USE INK
ONLY THIS ORIGINAL FORM WILL BE ACCEPTED**

BREED   **PLACE OF BIRTH OF LITTER: CITY**   **STATE**

Indicate number of living dogs in this litter on the date this application is submitted to AKC:

MALES   FEMALES   Date of birth of Litter: (Use Numbers)   MONTH   DAY   YEAR

AKC Champion Title (if any)   REGISTERED NAME OF SIRE   Other AKC Titles (if any)   AKC NUMBER OF SIRE

AKC Champion Title (if any)   REGISTERED NAME OF DAM   Other AKC Titles (if any)   AKC NUMBER OF DAM

SEC. A. OWNER OF SIRE ON DATE OF MATING COMPLETES THIS SECTION.

Name of Owner of SIRE   FIRST NAME & INITIAL   LAST NAME

I CERTIFY that the above-named Dam was mated to the above-named Sire and that the Sire was owned or co-owned by me on the date of mating.

Place of mating (check one): ☐ U.S.A. ☐ FOREIGN (Print country _____).

SIGNATURE of Owner or Co-Owner of Sire   Date of Mating: MONTH   DAY   YEAR

SEC. B. OWNER (OR IF LEASED, LESSEE) OF DAM ON DATE OF BIRTH OF LITTER COMPLETES THIS SECTION.

Note: If ownership of Dam changed while Dam was in whelp, SEC. C below must also be completed.

Name & Address of Owner (or if Leased, Lessee) of DAM

FIRST NAME & INITIAL   LAST NAME

STREET ADDRESS

CITY   STATE   ZIP

Please check one box.
☐ I witnessed the mating
☐ I did not witness the mating

Please check one box.
THIS LITTER IS A RESULT OF:
☐ a natural breeding
☐ artificial insemination
SEE REVERSE SIDE FOR INSTRUCTIONS

Co-Owner (If any) of DAM   FIRST NAME & INITIAL   LAST NAME

I apply to register this litter and CERTIFY that I was the Owner, Co-owner, or Lessee of the above-named Dam on the date of birth of the Litter, and that this Dam was not mated to any other dog during her season. I further CERTIFY that all of the representations on this application are true. I agree to comply with AKC rules and regulations. I have read the "Notice" and instructions on the reverse side of the application.

SIGNATURE of Owner, Co-Owner or Lessee of Dam

SEC. C. DO NOT COMPLETE UNLESS OWNERSHIP OF DAM CHANGED OR LEASE TERMINATED WHILE DAM WAS IN WHELP.

Note: Before completing, carefully read instructions on reverse side.

Owner (or if Leased, Lessee) of DAM on Date of Mating   FIRST NAME & INITIAL   LAST NAME

Co-Owner of the DAM on Date of Mating   FIRST NAME & INITIAL   LAST NAME

Please check one box.
☐ I witnessed the mating
☐ I did not witness the mating

I CERTIFY that I was the Owner, Co-owner, or Lessee of the above-named Dam on the date the Dam was mated to the above-named Sire. I CERTIFY that the Dam, while in my possession, was not mated to any other dog during her season.

SIGNATURE of Owner, Co-Owner or Lessee of Dam

AKC Litter Registration Application (first side only)

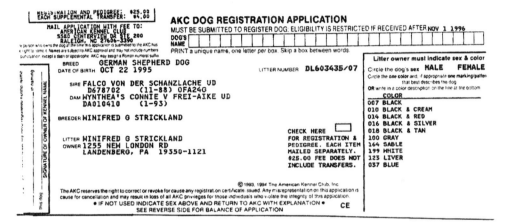

AKC Dog Registration Application (first side only)

AKC Registration Certificate (first side only)

AKC APPLICATION FOR REGISTRATION
OF DOG IMPORTED INTO U.S.A.
OWNED BY RESIDENT OF U.S.A.

Mail To: **THE AMERICAN KENNEL CLUB, 5580 Centerview Drive, Raleigh, NC 27606-3390**
Attention: Foreign Registration Department

Please Read Before Completing Application

INSTRUCTIONS

A dog whelped outside of the United States of America may be eligible for registration in the AKC Stud Book when imported into the U.S.A., **provided —**

(A) the imported dog is of a breed eligible for individual registration in the AKC Stud Book;

(B) the imported dog was registered in its country of birth with the registry organization designated on AKC's Primary List of Foreign Dog Registry Organizations before it was exported from its country of birth;

The list of countries and registry organizations whose Pedigrees are generally acceptable is contained in the pamphlet entitled AKC SPECIAL REGISTRY SERVICES. A copy of this pamphlet may be obtained without charge.

(C) The Pedigree for the dog issued by the foreign registry organization contains at least three generations of ancestry, establishing that each dog in the three generations was of the same breed and registered in its country of birth with one of the registry organizations on the Primary List. Each dog named in the three generations must be identified by its registered name and registration number. This Pedigree must also include the record of transfer to the U.S.A. importer;

A Pedigree issued by a foreign registry organization named in AKC's list is not automatically acceptable for AKC registration of the dog represented by the Pedigree. Each Pedigree will be examined in order to determine whether it is acceptable under the policies and regulations established by the Board of Directors of The American Kennel Club.

(D) the owner who applies to register the imported dog is a resident of the U.S.A.

An Application To Register An Imported Dog With AKC when completed, notarized and submitted must be accompanied by the original official foreign Pedigree. If the dog named on the application was imported from CANADA, the **original unrestricted Canadian Kennel Club Certificate of Registration** reflecting the ownership of the person applying to register the dog in the AKC Stud Book must be submitted in addition to the three generation CKC Pedigree.

The application must include a separate certification from each person or firm through whose hands the dog has passed, whether as owner, importer, dealer, agent, on consignment, or otherwise, certifying that the dog was delivered by him is the same one described in the application and that the dog was delivered by him directly to a named person or firm on a specified date.

Two (2) color photographs, providing close-up front and side views of the dog in a standing position, are required. The photographs should be no smaller than 3 x 4 inches in size.

THE FEE TO REGISTER AN IMPORTED DOG IS $25.00. DO NOT SEND CASH.

(Registration Fee subject to change without notice.)

A Registered Name Prefix may not be added to the registered name of an imported dog. Dog must be registered with the same name under which it was registered in its country of birth.

Titles earned in other countries by a dog imported into the U.S.A. are not shown on Registration Certificates or Certified Pedigrees issued by The American Kennel Club.

If there are any unusual circumstances connected with the importer's acquisition or importation of the dog (as when a bitch is left with the breeder abroad after being purchased, to be bred to a foreign stud dog before being shipped to the U.S.A.; or when the dog was not imported into the U.S.A. directly from its country of birth) the importer should explain all the circumstances, giving full details including dates, names and addresses, in the space provided for EXPLANATION on the last page.

IMPORTANT NOTICE

The American Kennel Club reserves the right to correct or revoke for cause the registration of this dog. Any misrepresentation on this application is cause for cancellation and may result in loss of all AKC privileges.

THE FOLLOWING MUST BE SUBMITTED TO AKC:
1. Completed and notarized application.
2. Original foreign 3-generation Pedigree.
3. Original foreign Registration Certificate (when applicable).
4. Two color photos.
5. $25.00 Registration Fee.

ORIGINAL DOCUMENTS WILL BE RETURNED VIA FIRST CLASS MAIL, UNLESS ACCOMPANIED BY THE CERTIFIED MAILING FEE OF $5.00.

<table>
<tr><td>
**PRINT IN CAPITAL LETTERS
ONLY—USE INK**
</td><td>
┌─ OFFICE USE ONLY ─┐
</td></tr>
</table>

PLEASE READ INSTRUCTIONS ON FRONT PAGE BEFORE COMPLETING.

SECTION I: DOG IDENTIFICATION

Must be completed by person(s) who imported dog into U.S.A.

DOG'S NAME
AS SHOWN ON   COUNTRY
FOREIGN PEDIGREE .... OF BIRTH ....

BREED .... SEX ....

DATE OF BIRTH ....   DOG'S COLOR
               Month   Day   Year   & MARKINGS ....

SIRE ....

DAM ....

BREEDER ....

From whom did you DIRECTLY
acquire the dog — Full Name .... Date of purchase ....
                                                  Month   Day   Year

Complete Foreign Address ....
                               Street   City   Country

Was the dog—Shipped to you   Did you bring the dog
          from abroad? .... OR with you into the U.S.A.? ....
                        Yes or No   Yes or No

          Date dog left its   Date dog arrived
          country of birth .... in the U.S.A. ....

Signature(s) of importer(s) ....

Printed name(s) ....

Address: ....
          City   State   Zip

COLOR PHOTO PRINT OF DOG IN A STANDING POSITION CLOSE-UP FRONT VIEW	COLOR PHOTO PRINT OF DOG IN A STANDING POSITION CLOSE-UP SIDE VIEW

When completed and submitted this application becomes the property of The American Kennel Club

AKC Application for Registration of Imported Dog (first and second sides only)

The following list will help you to select your German Shepherd's name.

ABBE	BAR	CARET	DAWN	ELEGANCE
ACE	BARDA	CARIN	DEENA	ELF
ADA	BARON	CARMEN	DELEGATE	ELGA
ADMIRAL	BARRY	CAROLE	DELIGHT	ELKA
ADOLF	BASCO	CAROUSEL	DELMA	ELKO
AFRA	BEATRICE	CARRO	DEREK	ELLA
AIDA	BELINDA	CASAR	DERRY	ELLY
ALAN	BELLA	CASSANDRA	DESIRE	ELSIE
ALEX	BELLE	CAUETCH	DEWET	ELYSIAN
ALEXIS	BENZA	CHALLENGE	DIANA	EMBER
ALF	BERN	CHANTILLY	DICK	EMMA
ALICE	BERND	CHARLIE	DIEDRE	EMMELINE
ALLADIN	BERRO	CHARM	DINAH	EMO
ALVINA	BESSIE	CHIEFTAN	DINO	ENCORE
AMBER	BETTY	CHRISTEL	DISE	ENNO
AMOR	BEVERLY	CHRISTY	DIXIE	ENSIGN
AMOS	BIANKA	CID	DOLF	ENVY
AMY	BIFF	CILLY	DOLLY	ERICA
ANDREA	BINKA	CINDERELLA	DOLORES	ERICH
ANGEL	BLANKA	CISSY	DONAR	ERNA
ANJA	BLAZE	CITO	DONNA	ERNIE
ANKA	BLONDIE	CLASSIC	DORA	EROS
ANNA	BOB	CLAUDIUS	DORIAN	ESKO
ANNE	BOJA	CLAUS	DORN	ESTA
ANTHONY	BONNIE	CLEVE	DOTTIE	ETU
APACHE	BRANDO	COCHISE	DOUGLAS	EVELYN
APOLLO	BRANDY	COLETTE	DROLL	EVIE
APRIL	BRAX	CONDOR	DRUSILLA	EXX
ARABELLA	BRETT	CONTESSA	DUCHESS	FAITH
ARCHER	BRIAN	COOKIE	DUFFY	FALCON
ARKO	BRIDGET	CORPORAL	DUSTY	FALK
ARMIN	BRITTA	CRALO	EBONY	FALKO
ARNO	BRIX	CRITIC	ECHO	FANCY
ARO	BRUNO	CURT	ECSTASY	FANNY
ARRAS	BUFFI	DACHS	EDA	FANT
ASTA	BURMA	DAEL	EDDIE	FARAH
ASTOR	BUSTER	DAGO	EDIE	FARO
ATTILAS	CAMELOT	DANCER	EDMUND	FASHION
AUGUST	CAMEO	DANDY	EDNA	FAVOR
AVA	CANDICE	DANKA	EFROM	FAWN
BALDUR	CANDY	DASCHA	EGON	FAX
BAMBI	CAPPY	DASHER	EIFER	FEATHER
BANNER	CAPUCINE	DAVID	ELAINE	FEE

FELICIA	GISA	HILDA	IVILLA	KARIN
FELS	GLENN	HOBO	IVISSA	KARLA
FERD	GLITTER	HONDA	JACK	KARU
FERDL	GLORIA	HONEY	JAHN	KASPER
FIELD MARSHALL	GLORY	HONEYBUN	JALK	KASSY
FIREFLY	GNOLA	HORAND	JAMBOURRE	KATHY
FLAIR	GOCKEL	HORST	JANICE	KATIE
FLAME	GO-LIGHTLY	HRUSKA	JANNETTE	KATJA
FLICKA	GOLDIE	HUMORESQUE	JARA	KATRINA
FLINT	GRAF	HUSSAR	JASMINE	KAZ
FLIRT	GRECCO	IAN	JEAN	KELLY
FLORA	GREIF	ICANDRA	JELL	KENA
FLORET	GRIMM	ICARNE	JENNIFER	KENO
FLORUS	GUNDA	ICRON	JENNY	KIDD
FORTUNE	GUNDO	IDA	JENO	KING
FRACK	GUSTAF	IDEARE	JESS	KIRA
FRANK	GYPSY	IDYL	JESSICA	KLAUS
FRANZ	GYVA	IGO	JESTER	KLEO
FRÄULEIN	HALLA	IGOR	JET	KLODO
FREDA	HALLE	IKE	JETHRO	KNIGHT
FREDDIE	HANNAH	IKO	JEWEL	KOLEX
FREIA	HANNIBAL	ILKO	JEZEBEL	KONSTANCE
FRIAR	HANSOM	ILLA	JILL	KONSTEN
FRIGGA	HARMONY	ILLUSTRIOUS	JOANNE	KOPPER
FRITZ	HAROLD	ILSA	JODO	KORA
GAIETY	HARRAS	ILSE	JODY	KORNO
GALAHAD	HARRY	IMAGE	JOLA	KORPORAL
GALAXY	HASSO	IMIMI	JOLIE	KORRY
GALLANT	HAZEL	IMMI	JONNY	KOSAK
GAMBLE	HEATHER	IMMO	JONQUIL	KOSTA
GARRY	HEDY	IMP	JORY	KÖNIG
GAUSS	HEIKO	INA	JOSÉ	KRISTA
GEMINI	HEIN	INCA	JOSEF	KRISTY
GENGIS	HEINZ	INDEED	JOYE	KURT
GENRY	HEKTOR	INDIA	JUDD	LADY
GEORGE	HELD	INDIGO	JUDGE	LAFAYETTE
GEORGIA	HELEN	INGDING	JUDY	LAIRD
GERDA	HELMA	INGO	JULES	LANA
GERI	HENRY	INGRID	JULIE	LANCE
GERMAINE	HERBIE	INSPECTOR	JUNE	LANG
GERO	HERMAN	INVADER	JUPITER	LARK
GERRY	HERMANE	IONA	JUPP	LASSIE
GERTRUDE	HERO	IPELLA	KAISER	LASSO
GIA	HERTA	IPHIS	KANA	LAURA
GILLY	HEX	IRENE	KANDACE	LAUREL
GINA	HEXE	IRIS	KANDY	LEAH
GINGER	HILARY	ITOL	KANNAH	LEE

LEGACY	MIA	NOEL	OTTO	QUAKER
LELANI	MICHAEL	NOLA	OVATION	QUALITY
LENA	MICKEY	NORA	OVERA	QUALRA
LENNY	MIKE	NORBERT	OWEN	QUASAR
LEO	MILLIE	NORDRAAK	OZELL	QUASHA
LETTY	MINDY	NORITA	PACETT	QUASS
LEX	MINX	NORMA	PADDY	QUASSA
LIBERAL	MIRANDA	NORSE	PAGEN	QUELL
LIDO	MITCH	NOX	PALADEN	QUELLA
LILLY	MITZI	NULLA	PAMELA	QUERRA
LINDA	MOLLY	NUZUM	PANCY	QUEST
LINUS	MONDAY	NYX	PANDORA	QUIBBLER
LOBO	MONTY	OBSERVER	PANDY	QUIBLA
LOCH	MOREY	OCCASION	PASCHA	QUIDA
LONNIE	MORGAN	OCCULT-ONE	PATIENCE	QUIDD
LORD	MORO	OCUNA	PAUL	QUIDIA
LORNA	MOXIE	ODANA	PAX	QUIDO
LOU	MOZART	ODIN	PEARL	QUIESCENCE
LOXY	MUSKET	OFFA	PEDRO	QUILLA
LUCIE	MUTZ	OFILLY	PEGGY	QUILLAN
LUCKY	NADJA	OGDEN	PENNY	QUINN
LUDWIG	NAIDA	OLANA	PERLE	QUINTON
LULU	NALCO	OLGA	PERRO	QUITTA
LUNDEEN	NANCY	OLIVE	PETER	QUIVER
LYDIA	NANDO	OLIVER	PETITE	QUIVERA
LYNN	NANNETTE	OLIVIA	PETRA	QUIX
LYON	NAPPS	OMANA	PFEFFER	QUIXA
MAC	NARDISS	OMAR	PHAEDRA	QUO
MÄDCHEN	NARVIK	OMEN	PHANTASIE	QUOLLY
MAGEE	NATASHA	ON-TOP	PHANTOM	QUONTA
MAJA	NATCHEZ	ONA	PHIL	QUONTO
MALACHI	NAVAJO	OPEL	PIROL	QUOPANA
MARCUS	NEA	OPERATOR	PLATO	QUOPERLE
MARGIE	NEIDA	OPHELIA	POLA	QUORR
MARGO	NEIL	OPINA	POLLUX	QUORRA
MARIO	NELDRA	ORA	POLLY	QUOTAN
MARION	NELLIE	ORACLE	PRIMA	QUOTANNA
MARKO	NELSON	ORBY	PRINCESS	QUOTATION
MARITZA	NEMO	ORDIE	PRISCILLA	RABITT
MARY	NERO	ORMANDA	PRISSY	RACHEL
MASTER	NICKY	OSCAR	PROXX	RACHITA
MATADOR	NICOL	OSSY	PRUESS	RACKER
MEDO	NICOLETTE	OSTANA	PRYSE	RADAR
MELISSA	NIGHTWIND	OSWALD	PUNDIT	RADIANCE
MELODY	NIKKI	OTIS	PUNJAB	RAGGETY-ANN
MEREDITH	NITA	OTLAN	QHESTA	RAJAH
MERRY	NOCTURNE	OTORR	QUAKA	RAMONA

RAND	SCAMP	TIFFANY	UTRANA	VOSTER
RANGER	SCINTILLA	TIMOTHY	UTZ	VOX
RAPTURE	SCORPIO	TINA	UVALI	VOYAGER
RAQUEL	SEBASTIAN	TINSEL	UVAN	WACO
RASCAL	SENSATION	TOBY	UVANE	WAGGLES
RAY	SENTRY	TOM	UVENUS	WAGNER
REAGAN	SHAWNY	TORRO	UVERA	WALE
REBEL	SHERLOCK	TOSCA	UVIA	WANDA
REGINA	SHILOH	TRACY	UVINCE	WANDERER
REMUS	SHOWGIRL	TREU	UVOL	WANN
REVA	SIGBERT	TREVOR	VADRICH	WARBLER
REWARD	SIGNETTE	TROLL	VAGA	WARD
RHAPSODY	SIMON	TRUDI	VALE	WARDEN
RHEMBA	SINBAD	TRUTZ	VALET	WARREN
RICKY	SIREN	TUF-E-NUF	VALI	WARRIOR
RINGO	SMOKY	TUNTE	VALKYRIE	WATZER
RITA	SONNET	TYLER	VALLEN	WAXERA
ROCETTE	SONNY	UBRAXA	VALLERIE	WAYFARER
ROCKET	STAN	UDA	VANCE	WAYNE
ROGUE	STEFF	UDO	VANDA	WEAH
ROLAND	STELLA	UHLOR	VANITY	WEAVER
ROLF	SULTAN	UKON	VARGO	WEE-ONE
ROLLO	SUNSHINE	ULK	VARMA	WEIR
ROSE	SYLVIA	ULLA	VARSS	WELKA
ROSEL	TABOURET	ULTIMATE	VAUNTA	WELTA
ROSELLA	TAFFY	ULTRA	VEIT	WENDY
ROWINA	TAKLA	ULYSSES	VELLO	WHEEZY
ROXY	TAMARR	UMORRA	VENETIA	WHIMSY
RUBY	TAMMY	UMPIRE	VENNO	WHODOO
RUDY	TANGENT	UNA	VENUS	WIA
RUTZA	TANYA	UNCAS	VERA	WIGAND
SABLE	TARA	UNDERA	VERACITY	WILLETTE
SABRE	TARAS	UNDO	VERGA	WILLIE
SADIE	TARGET	UNEX	VERNA	WILLOW
SAGE	TARGO	UNICE	VETTA	WINDSONG
SALLY	TARNIA	UNIQUE	VETTER	WINSOME
SALVO	TASSIE	UPROAR	VEUS	WITZ
SAM	TATE	UPSHOT	VIA	WIXIE
SANDRA	TAWNEE	URBANA	VIKE	WIZARD
SANDY	TEDDY	URCHIN	VIKI	WIZARD
SANGUINE	TELL	URSA	VIKING	WOLFGANG
SANNA	TEMPEST	URSEL	VIRGINIA	WOTAN
SARAH	TEMPTOR	USEFUL	VIXEN	WYATT
SARGE	TEMPTATION	USHER	VOL	WYNLA
SATELLITE	TERSA	UTELL	VONDA	XACO
SAUCY	TESSY	UTMOST	VORKO	XADA
SAVIOUR	THUNDER	UDELLE	VOSS	XADEEN
				XALYCE

XAMBER	XEROS	YEGON	YOULINDA	ZIBU
XANDRA	XERTA	YELANN	YOUTESSA	ZINA
XANJA	XEUS	YELONA	YUDRIX	ZINETTE
XANNE	XINE	YEMBA	YULE	ZINNIE
XANTA	XIRA	YEMO	ZACO	ZION
XANTH	XLEX	YEOMAN	ZADDUS	ZISSY
XANTO	XLI	YERA	ZALTA	ZITA
XARCH	XTENT	YERO	ZANDA	ZITHER
XARDO	XTREENA	YERONN	ZANN	ZOE
XARRAS	XYLIE	YEROS	ZAREK	ZOLL
XCANDO	XZAR	YESTEL	ZCON	ZON
XCEED	XZARINA	YEUS	ZEDA	ZONA
XCELL	YACO	YIPPER	ZEDO	ZONIE
XCENTH	YADA	YIRA	ZEEBRIN	ZONK
XCENTRY	YADARRE	YLERTA	ZENA	ZORA
XEGON	YALTA	YLINDA	ZENDY	ZORRO
XELA	YANCE	YLONDA	ZENTA	ZSA ZSA
XELANE	YANTA	YLSA	ZENTER	ZSAZETTE
XELI	YANTO	YOKEL	ZETA	ZUDD
XEMBA	YARDO	YOLA	ZEUS	ZVA
XEMO	YARRASS	YONA	ZHIVAGO	
XENTO	YASHO	YONDER	ZIA	
XERNA	YASMIN	YONKA	ZIBETT	
XEROICA	YAX	YORGO	ZIBO	

The three registration forms that are reprinted in this chapter, with the kind permission of the American Kennel Club, are self-explanatory. If you have a litter of puppies you wish to register with the American Kennel Club, you should write and ask them to send you the Litter Registration Application, fill it out according to the directions on the back and return it to the AKC with the correct fee.

If, upon processing the application, they find you have given them the required information, they will send you as many individual blue registration forms as there are puppies in the litter. Each new owner should be given one of these forms for his puppy. However, the litter owner must be sure to fill it in and sign his name before presenting it to the new owner. The latter should also sign his name and address before sending it, with the fee, to the AKC. They, in turn, will mail the new owner a Registration Certificate that names him as the owner of the puppy.

If you have an imported dog you wish to register in the United States, you should request from the American Kennel Club the Application for Registration for a dog whelped outside the United States and Canada that is owned by a resident of the United States. Fill it out correctly and send it back to the American Kennel Club with the stipulated fee.

chapter 7

Housetraining

If you have just bought a German Shepherd puppy, you will want to know how to housetrain him. I believe this training should start immediately. The best method is to teach the puppy to go outdoors when he has to relieve himself. The length of time it takes to housetrain a puppy usually depends upon your determination to put up with the inconvenience of watching him constantly. A concentrated effort over two weeks is better than sporadic methods that may last for months. A puppy should be let out first thing in the morning (try to get up and let him out before he wakes up, for as soon as he is awake, he will want to relieve himself), after each meal, after he has been playing, after each nap and before he goes to bed for the night.

When you get your puppy home, give him a bowl of water; and when he has had all he wants, take him outdoors so that he can relieve himself. Wait until he does, then praise him and take him back indoors. Thereafter, when you let him out, take him back to the same spot and give him some command such as "Hurry up." Use the same words each time so that the puppy will associate the act with the words. Months or years later, if you travel with your dog, he will understand what you want when you tell him "Hurry up" in a strange place.

Many people make the mistake of confining a puppy in their garage or basement and permitting the puppy to relieve himself in these places. Besides the fact that the owners are forcing their puppy to practice dirty habits, they are also harming his temperament by shutting him off in a room by himself. Temperament will be discussed in another chapter.

If you work all day and must leave your puppy alone, you might prefer to break him on newspapers. In this case, start him off in one room with newspapers covering the whole area. When he gets used to soiling the papers, which will probably take two or three days, gradually reduce the papered area until only one square of newspaper remains. The puppy will still go over to it. This arrangement will work at night for the puppy who is trained to go outdoors in the daytime. For this little fellow, wait until he is reduced to one square of newspaper for several nights, then do not put any down. Try to get up earlier than your puppy does each morning and he will soon learn to wait for you to let him out. Puppies entirely broken to newspapers sometimes refuse to go outdoors when they get a little older and when you yourself are tired of this whole procedure. If this is the case, take a soiled newspaper outdoors, and when your puppy decides to use it, slip it away from him. Once he has soiled the ground, take him back to the same place each time.

If you notice your puppy circling and sniffing the floor, he probably wants to go out. If your puppy makes a mistake, be sure to clean the spot thoroughly with some all-purpose cleaner. If there is any odor left, the puppy will feel it is permissible to return to the same place to relieve himself. When he soils the floor in your absence, take him over to the spot, saying in a disgusted tone of voice, "What did you do? Shame. Go out." Besides being trained, he will learn the word "out." Eventually, he will look at the door and whine if he needs to go out or if the word "out" is mentioned. If a puppy accidentally soils a rug, I clean it immediately, before it stains, with a foamy rug cleaner, let it dry, then vacuum the residue.

It will help with the puppy's training if you will take his water away from him at 5:00 P.M. A very young puppy has difficulty going through the night without relief. If he should get up during the night and soil the papers, don't scold him. The average puppy is anywhere from twelve to fourteen weeks old before he can go from 10:00 P.M. to 6:00 A.M. comfortably. For the older puppy who is slow in going through the whole night, tie him to your bed; if he has to relieve himself, he will whine and ask you to let him out. Another method is to tie him to a radiator or some other stationary object, with a four-foot leash or light chain. A puppy rarely soils his bed, and this prevents him from straying far enough to feel comfortable.

Summing up, the simplest way to housetrain your puppy is to watch him constantly for a period of at least two weeks, and take the time to take him out whenever necessary.

German Shepherd puppies are naturally clean, providing they have had the right start in life. Puppies that are raised in kennel runs or small pens develop dirty habits because they are used to sleeping and playing in their own excrement. It is extremely difficult and time-consuming to housetrain such puppies.

People who buy Wynthea puppies are pleasantly surprised when they find their puppies are easy to housetrain. This is not just luck. It is the way they are trained from the time they are two weeks old. From the time they are born, we talk to them so that they will know the sound of our voices. As soon as they are given solid food, at three weeks of age, they get used to hearing a cheerful, inviting voice calling them to dinner, "Puppy, puppy, puppy."

The puppies stay in their whelping box for four weeks. After that they are permitted to explore the area outside their box. They get used to curling up with their mother on a blanket on the floor, but at night they are all in the whelping box again. After five weeks of age, when the weather is pleasant, they learn to follow their mother to a grassy paddock some 150 yards from the nursery. At first they try to follow their mother, but there is always one or two who will make a pit stop, or pause to investigate a weed, who will need a little guidance. Gradually, they are trained to follow my voice when I call, "Puppy, puppy, puppy." Indoors their run is divided into two sections by a guillotine door. If for some reason, such as inclement weather, they stay indoors, I find that they will instinctively keep their blanket clean and go to the outside area of their run to do their business. They get a new blanket frequently so that it always smells fresh and clean. By the time they are seven weeks old, they are all following at heel, happy to go for a long walk around my property. They will also come when called from a distance of fifty or more yards. I have always believed in training dogs by communicating with them. It all starts right here.

If you just have one or two dogs, it is a good idea to teach them to go to one particular place in your yard to relieve themselves. If you partially fence in an area about twenty-by-twenty feet square and insist that the dogs use this place for their toilet, they will get into the habit of doing so, and the rest of your yard will be clean. Although watching that the dogs use this portion of the yard every time they relieve themselves will take a little vigilance on your part, it is worth every minute of the time you allot to it. Your yard will be free of stools and the grass and shrubbery won't be killed as a result of your dogs wetting on them. If this area is covered with sand, sawdust or small stones, you can keep it free of worm eggs by removing some of this material with each stool. Keep a large pail of extra sand, sawdust or small stones in this section so that you can replenish it each day. If you contribute five or ten minutes to this chore each day, you will keep your yard beautiful, and the one small drawback to owning a dog will be eliminated.

The training method is the same for the apartment dweller in the city who has to teach his dog to use the curb. It is just a matter of taking the dog back to the same place until he forms a habit of going to that spot. This dog owner should take a small shovel, hoe and paper bag along and remove his dog's stool from the street. If every dog owner in the city would clean up after his dog, the city would be a much cleaner place to live.

Ch. Caraland's Limited Edition, OFA
Breeder-Owner: Jack Newton

chapter 8

Grooming, Raising and Caring for a German Shepherd

THE IMPORTANCE OF DAILY GROOMING

A healthy German Shepherd does not have any body odor and his coat will stay glossy if you give him a balanced diet and groom him daily. The diet will be mentioned later in this chapter and is extremely important to your dog's well-being. Cleanliness is as important to your dog's general health and well-being as a good diet. Your dog should be brushed or combed every day. Even though it may appear unnecessary, it still should be done. Dust particles, skin scales and dead hair accumulate and make the dog want to scratch to get rid of them. If he scratches, he may do so too vigorously and break the skin, thus leading to skin infections.

Make it a practice to groom your dog at the same time every day. By doing so it will become a good habit, and when this happens, you will not consider it a chore. I prefer a metal comb with medium-sized teeth and a boar-bristle brush with the bristles surrounding a single nylon shaft. You may have to clean these grooming tools several times during the same grooming session. If your dog's coat is dusty, you might want to go over it with a damp, artificial chamois. You will find that this type of chamois is indispensable. I keep one in my car and another in my grooming bag at all times to rub over my dog's coat if necessary. It is also a big help in removing dog hairs from your own clothes. Just rinse it in water after each use and store it damp in a closed container. That way it won't dry out.

If you are grooming a puppy, start by having him sit in a corner. Press down on his rear to make him sit, and then quickly brush his neck, shoulders and chest. If he gets up, caution him with the command, "No, sit," in a pleasant tone of voice. When the brushing is finished, have the puppy stand, and show him how to do this by supporting him with your hand under his stomach. Then quickly brush him again to center his attention upon the act.

Brush his back, sides and hindquarters. If he moves, caution him to "Stand," and then pause and say, "Stay." Do not use a wire brush on a puppy.

The puppy will learn quickly what is expected of him, and he will absorb the four words, "No," "Sit," "Stand" and "Stay." By the time you are ready for formal training, you will have accomplished a great deal. When the puppy responds nicely, talk to him and praise him for his good behavior in a pleasant tone of voice. Use any of these commands whenever it is necessary so that the puppy will really understand their meaning, and be quick to show him what any command means. This applies to mature dogs as well.

HOW TO GIVE YOUR DOG A BATH

Dogs do not need many baths in the course of a year. Still, there may be times when it is necessary. If they should soil their coats, whether in winter or summer, give them a bath. In washing any dog, the important things to remember are to rinse his coat thoroughly with clear water, dry it just as thoroughly and make sure that he is warm and away from drafts.

In my home I have a special room where my dogs are groomed. They have their own bathtub that is raised up off the floor so that we don't have to bend over to wash them. Two cement steps have been built against the far end of the tub so that the dogs can step into the tub. There is a telephone shower attached to the wall and this is just the greatest thing for bathing dogs that I have seen. It is a glorified hose attachment that resembles a telephone and, when it is not in use, it hangs up out of the way like a phone. The hose is made of flexible chrome tubing to match the rest of the fixtures.

I bathe my dogs one at a time, and since German Shepherds are too heavy for me to lift, I have taught them to step into the tub. I did this by lifting their front paws into the tub, saying, "Hup," and then lifting their hind legs in. With a little urging, I soon had them stepping in themselves by just saying, "Hup." Of course, I praise them a great deal, letting them know the instant they start to get the idea that they are really clever.

Whenever a dog has a soiled coat, he should get a bath. Use a very mild shampoo, work a rich lather into the dog's coat and leave it on for ten minutes. This will also kill any fleas present. If the dog has any kind of skin problem, use a medicated shampoo prescribed by your veterinarian, rub gently and leave the lather on the coat for ten minutes. Then, completely rinse it all out with lukewarm water. It is important to get every bit of soap out of the coat. When rinsing the dog's head, be careful to protect his ears so that no water gets into them. A good way to do this is to insert large cotton balls in the ear opening before starting the bath. Do not wash the inside of the dog's ears with soap and water. Dampen a wad of cotton with alcohol or hydrogen peroxide and clean the dirt out of the ears gently and thoroughly. After you clean the ears, if you find some red, sore areas, spread a light film of Panolog™ ointment over these places. Do not forget to examine your dog's ears at least once a week. If dirt and wax are allowed to build up, it could be most uncomfortable for your dog and may lead to a painful, chronic condition.

Winter or summer, after my dogs have had a bath I blow-dry them. I use an Air Force Commander™ two-speed dryer. If you have a German Shepherd, you owe it to yourself and your dog to get such a dryer. While blowing the coat dry, you can see any cuts, bruises, fleas or ticks. A German Shepherd has a very dense undercoat and blow-drying the dog in this way will blow out all the loose hair. It is terrific to use when the dog is shedding. You will have very few, if any, dog hairs on the furniture or carpets if you use one of these dryers. And on top of all this, you should use it because it makes your dog look absolutely gorgeous. Finish grooming him by running the comb over his coat ever so lightly.

A very young puppy, an old dog, a pregnant bitch or a sick dog should be given a sponge bath rather than a soaking wet bath in a tub. Their resistance is low and they could easily catch cold if they had a tub bath. Keep them in a warm place, and groom their coats by rubbing them with a damp cloth that is kept clean with repeated rinsings. Get them thoroughly dry by using plenty of towels. If, after you have bathed a dog, you let him lie on a large beach towel, you will find that it will absorb a great deal of the water. It is rarely necessary to bathe a German Shepherd. The daily brushing will keep him clean.

NAILS

Your puppy's toenails should be cut every two weeks or as often as it is necessary to keep them short. If they are permitted to grow unattended, they become unsightly, cause the puppy's toes to spread apart and may cause lameness. Up to the time the puppy is two months old, you can use a special type of scissors made for this purpose. These scissors are very sharp and cut the nails very quickly and efficiently.

There are two ways to cut a puppy's nails so that he will not be aware of what you are doing. I carry a small puppy in the crook of my left arm and cut his nails as I am walking. He is so interested in looking around, he doesn't notice that his nails are being cut. When the puppy is a little older, my daughter holds the puppy and attracts his attention by talking and petting him while I cut his nails. If you are all alone, you could place him on a table, hold him with your left arm and cut his nails with your right hand. Talk reassuringly to the puppy so that he won't be upset. If you cut his nails frequently, you won't have to remove very much nail to keep them short. A problem arises when you forget about them, suddenly notice that they are too long, and try to cut them back short all at once. When this happens you might accidentally cut into the quick and cause the nail to bleed. Don't panic. Just dab a little coagulant powder on it to stop the bleeding. Talk soothingly to the puppy

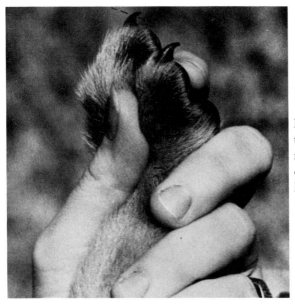

Hold your dog's foot and toe firmly when you cut his nails. Cut off the portion indicated here by the dotted line.

as you hold the paw gently but firmly, and place a tiny bit of the powder on the bleeding nail. The bleeding will stop immediately. Alum will also stop the bleeding.

The older dog should have his nails cut regularly. Dogs kept on cement rarely need to have their nails cut as they wear them down a little each day. If you have neglected to cut your dog's nails for some time, don't cut them short all at once or they will bleed and the dog's toes will be sore for several days. Either have your veterinarian give him a sedative while he cuts his nails, or you cut a little off every few days until they are short again. Each time you cut them, the quick will recede until eventually they are back to normal. Have your dog sit while you cut his nails, and clip off just the portion of the nail that extends beyond the quick. After the nails have been cut, file them off smoothly with a dog file, a strip of coarse sandpaper, a coarse emery board or a file from your workbench. If you have made a nail bleed, do not file it for several days, as it will be tender.

Some dogs object strenuously to having their nails cut but do not mind having them filed. The simplest way to file a mature dog's nails is to do it while he is lying on his side. Have your dog lie down flat on his side, scratch his tummy or chest to get him to relax, then file away. Most dogs will go to sleep while you file their nails if you talk to them. Hold the nail firmly between a finger and thumb as you grasp the paw firmly with the same hand, then file with the other. To file it down fast, go sideways, then, to finish it off smoothly, file in one direction, down toward the dog's pad.

Do not cut your dog's toenails on the day that he is being shown at a dog show. It is quite possible that one nail will bleed and be tender, and a lame dog will be excused from the ring. Do cut them two or three days before the show, however, so that his feet will look well groomed.

One dog may get neurotic about having his nails cut, while another will become very rebellious when he sees the nail clippers appear. Over the years I have clipped the nails of dozens and dozens of German Shepherds and all were very pleasant about it except two. They were both in a class by themselves and will never be forgotten. The first Shepherd was rough and tough. He wasn't afraid of any other dogs and delighted in catching them off guard and knocking them down if they were foolish enough to get close to him when they were playing. As a protector he was fearless, and as a jumper he would scale a seven-foot wall and jump down without giving it a thought. But lift his foot to cut his nails and he would let out such a blood-curdling scream that you would freeze to the spot. The clippers just had to touch his paw and he would go into his act of jerking his paw and screaming at the top of his lungs. At first it was somewhat unnerving until I decided on a course of action. I put all of the other dogs outdoors so they wouldn't witness the scene and get nervous about having their own nails cut, closed all the doors and windows so the neighbors wouldn't hear the commotion and misinterpret it and went to work. My daughter held his leg firmly while I quickly cut all his nails despite his vocal protestations. It was always the same story, and each time I had finished he would race around the room wagging his tail, smiling sheepishly but apologetically at us. He was just a big, tough, lovable sissy.

The other Shepherd was a 100-pound Troll son who was normally well mannered and agreeable. Trimming his nails had never presented a problem until he became three years old and then one day he rebelled. It wasn't a short skirmish, but a long battle of wits that lasted until he was twelve years old, when he finally mellowed and gave in resignedly. I couldn't use a file—when he saw one he wanted to walk right up the walls—so it was the nail clippers or nothing. I finally found I could get the job done if I straddled him and had someone hold his leg steady and his mouth closed, while I clipped his nails. He became very suspicious if I opened the drawer where the nail clippers were kept and would go and hide in a corner and fold all his legs under him like a deer. When I did attempt to pull one of his legs from under him, a tug-of-war ensued, with him fighting and rolling over or submitting and jerking his foot away at the last second. When he was about seven years old, Susan and I were attempting to cut his nails when guests arrived. We were always able to cut his nails, it just took ten times as long as it did with the other dogs. The men in the party were kidding us about how ridiculous it was that we couldn't hold our own dog. So we made a little wager that the four of them plus the two of us would have a hard time. After struggling ineffectually for several minutes, they gave up in defeat and admitted it was impossible to hold 100 pounds of squirming, fighting, clawing, struggling dog. He rebelled at having his nails cut, but he rebelled even more when someone tried to hold him forcefully. Thereafter, I used the psychological approach, letting him think I trusted him. I clipped his nails all by myself, and would straddle him in a corner, hold his paw under his chin, cut a nail when he least expected it and kept up a verbal barrage to counteract his own. He never bit anyone in his life, but he was often sorely tempted to bite me when I cut his nails. With each nail I clipped, he would growl and roar and show his teeth trying to frighten me, and his deep-throated growls would bounce off the walls like thunder. Perhaps when he was twelve he finally realized I wasn't going to be intimidated and decided to accept his fate.

If you have a rambunctious dog who objects to having his nails cut, you can muzzle him, tie him on a short chain and go to work. If you do it this way, don't be surprised if he objects more strenuously each succeeding time.

While we are on the subject of feet, there is one more grooming suggestion I would like to mention that will make your dog's feet more attractive. A dog with a splay-foot, an abnormally long foot or a large foot with good pads, may have hair growing out over his toes that makes his foot seem even longer. To correct this impression, it is wise to trim the hair back so that his toenails show. This will make his foot look shorter and neater.

If you are taking your dog to a dog show or an Obedience class that is conducted indoors on a slippery floor, carry a small bag of rosin in your grooming bag. Before you start training, or before you go into the ring, pat your dog's pads lightly with the rosin bag and it will help him to maintain his footing.

TEETH

Your puppy will start to get his first, or "milk," teeth when he is about two and one-half weeks old. As he grows older he will test them out frequently. These teeth are sharp and it is wise to teach the puppy not to nip or bite while he is playing. Provide him with some hard rubber toys and some raw beef marrowbones during this period and later when he is getting his permanent teeth. The action of chewing on these hard things will loosen the baby teeth and force them out. If you notice a loose baby tooth, try to push it out while you are playing ball or tug-of-war with your puppy. You can loosen it at this time without him being aware of what you are doing. The baby teeth have no long roots, but they are pretty sturdy while they last. Often, a canine baby tooth will hold fast while the second canine is growing out alongside it. If it doesn't become loose after a week or so of pushing it in different directions a few times a day, get a small pair of pliers and pull it out. The permanent canine tooth should be out halfway before you attempt this, for, nine times out of ten, the permanent tooth will dislodge the baby tooth if you give it a chance. However, if you think the permanent canine is growing in crooked because of the baby tooth, you may prefer to have your veterinarian remove the milk tooth.

The teething period, when the permanent teeth come through the gums, may be any time from the fourth month through the ninth. Some bloodlines are slower in this respect than others, and some bloodlines seem to have weird tooth problems that are troublesome to the youngsters but straighten out when they pass the puppy stage. The two- or three-month teething period can be hard on some puppies as their mouths and gums become very tender and sore, and they may feel out of sorts. A bleeding gum caused by a loose tooth can be painful and the puppy may suffer a loss of appetite until it gets better. Don't insist upon training him to show his teeth for the Conformation ring while he is experiencing discomfort with his teeth or he will take a permanent dislike to this practice. Be patient with him and his mouth will heal by itself.

Not all puppies have the same number of baby teeth and it isn't particularly important, providing they get the correct number of permanent teeth. A small puppy appears to have many empty spaces along the sides of his mouth, but these should all fill in when he gets his second teeth. He should have forty-two permanent teeth: twenty in the upper jaw, and twenty-two in the lower. The six small teeth in front, upper and lower, are the incisors; the large fangs on either side of these are called the canines; and the teeth along the sides of the jaws are called the masticating molars. The teeth should meet in a scissors bite in which part of the inner surface of the upper teeth meets and engages part of the outer surface of the lower teeth. An even bite is undesirable as the teeth will wear down from constantly hitting each other. A dog's mouth is considered overshot when the upper incisors protrude over the lower. When a puppy is overshot, this bite will correct itself when he matures if the fault is not too pronounced. The teeth of a puppy who is undershot, the lower teeth extending beyond the uppers, will not improve with age.

The puppy's system is forming enamel for his permanent teeth during his early life so it is very important that he be fed a high-protein diet with a balanced combination of calcium, phosphorus and vitamin D. A siege of sickness accompanied by high temperatures may result in discolored and pitted permanent teeth. These are sometimes referred to as "distemper teeth," although they could result from some other sickness. The administration of tetracycline before a puppy's second teeth are in has been known to discolor them. If these second teeth are unsightly, the dog will not be able to do much winning in Breed, but they will be strong enough to be useful to him during his lifetime.

Now that your puppy has his second teeth, you should make it a habit to clean or brush his teeth two or three times a week. At first, wrap a soft washcloth that has been moistened in a solution of one-half of a cup of lukewarm water, a pinch of salt and one-half of a teaspoonful of baking soda around your index finger. Gently rub your puppy's teeth with this cloth in circular strokes making sure to rub both the inside and the outside surfaces. When he is a little older you can get him used to a soft toothbrush. Now you can clean his teeth with a bacteria-controlling dentrifice you can buy from your veterinarian. It has a taste the dog's like. If you give your dog lots of praise and hugs he will look forward to getting his teeth cleaned. Just don't use tooth-paste made for humans, as it might upset your dog's stomach.

There are two precautions you should take to insure sound, healthy teeth for your dog, besides providing him with good food and balanced supple-ments. Don't let your dog get into the habit of chasing stones or playing with them. The dogs get so excited and eager to chase them that they either break their teeth or wear the enamel off them.

On one of my trips to Germany to buy myself a dog, a friend of mine over there highly recommended a three-year-old Shepherd who had several V-ratings and was currently winning at shows. We went to see him, and I watched the dog moving and posing off-leash and was impressed with his gait and his structure. His temperament was excellent, and he seemed very alert and responsive to commands. I was just about to say I would take him when his owner threw a large stone and told his dog to *"Bringen."* The dog sped after the stone so quickly that it dawned on me that this was a little game they had played before. When the dog returned, I examined his teeth and, sure enough, the canine fangs were all broken in half and the other teeth were worn down very badly. As much as I liked the dog, I knew he couldn't become an American Champion. However, with his fine ancestry, I thought he would be able to produce, so I offered his owner an amount that was less than his asking price, but he refused the offer. After all, he was still able to win in Germany. Thereafter I noticed many German dogs with worn teeth and I suspect they were permitted to play with stones. Some German trainers teach a dog to race out on command by first teaching him to retrieve a stone. Later, they just give a signal and the dog races away expecting to hear the stone fall ahead of him. This teaches a dog to race out on command, but if the dog is fast, he may catch the stone and his teeth will be worn down or broken in the process.

The second precaution is to keep your dog's teeth clean. You can give your dog one large hard biscuit daily, or a beef marrow bone once a week, to aid him in removing tartar from his teeth. You can brush his teeth and gums with a toothbrush and toothpaste, or equal portions of baking soda and salt. Tartar builds up on a dog's tooth and, besides being unsightly, it can cause gum problems. To remove the tartar from your dog's teeth, use a tooth scaler you can get from a dog-supply house, have your dog lie down with his head on a towel and scrape the tartar off his teeth. You will have to bear down hard to remove it near the gums but it will chip off in small pieces. Let your dog bite down on a wooden dowel while you work on his back molars and it will save your fingers. If you clean your dog's teeth at regular intervals, you will always know the exact condition of his teeth and gums. Your dog will not object to having his teeth cleaned if you are very gentle with him and do not stick your fingernails or scraper in his gums or pinch his lips.

Joll had a freak accident that involved one of his canine teeth and the fact that he was highly trained and responsive to commands was the prime reason we were able to save his tooth. I am, and have always been, a strong advocate of dog training. The obvious reasons are that training makes dogs well mannered, well adjusted and easier to live with; but the important factor appears when an emergency arises and the dog responds with a display of intelligence and understanding that is nothing short of admirable. I am mentioning this incident because it might happen to your dog some day and you could presumably save his tooth if you followed the right course of action.

Joll had been left alone in the house for a few hours, and when we returned I didn't notice anything wrong with him, so I went ahead and made dinner. He always lies down near me, and while we were eating I noticed him licking his lips and investigated to see what was wrong. I was horrified to find that his upper canine tooth had been pulled out of its socket and was hanging intact in a piece of his gum. The gum itself was ripped open and bleeding and he had been licking this when I noticed him. I immediately called a dentist friend of mine, Dr. Jack Sokoloff, and made arrangements to meet him in the city at my veterinarian's office.

I took a piece of cotton and soaked up the blood that was welling up in the hole, put the tooth back in it and held Joll's mouth closed. During the twenty-mile ride to the doctor's office, a good friend drove the car while I held Joll's head in my lap and watched him carefully to be sure he didn't dislodge his loose tooth.

At the veterinarian's office, Joll was given a general anesthetic to put him out while Jack worked on his tooth. He cleverly made a brace for him out of wire and acrylic and held it in place by firmly wiring it across the gums of his upper front teeth to his other canine tooth. Then he sewed up the torn, jagged gum and repaired that damage.

Jack was optimistic enough to think that the brace would work if Joll would keep it in his mouth. This sort of accident happens to people occasionally and the results are quite successful, but it is easier to anchor a brace on a human being since the adjoining teeth can be used for this purpose. With a dog, the teeth next to the canine teeth are so small that they are of no use in holding a brace. It was a long stretch from the loose canine tooth to the other, but it was a gamble I wanted to take for Joll.

The veterinarian thought differently, however, and stated quite bluntly that it wouldn't work, but he would be glad to see us try. He said it wouldn't last overnight. He went on to tell us that he saw dozens of dogs each year who had knocked out their canine teeth, but in all cases the teeth had been broken off and he had to pull the rest of the tooth out and try to repair the damages. He thought it was extremely unusual for a canine tooth to come out in one piece and thought it must have received one heck of a blow to knock it out that way. He said that a dog was very different from a person in the respect that he wouldn't tolerate anything like a brace in his mouth. He said he would paw and work at the foreign object until it came off. He had

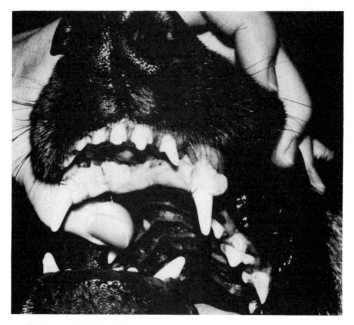

Joll's brace holding his canine tooth in place.

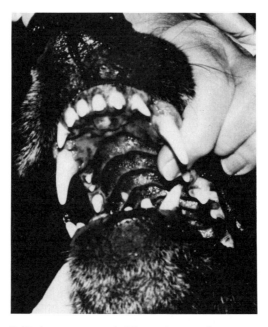

Joll's brace removed. His canine tooth now as good as new.

had many experiences with such things and found they never worked out satisfactorily. Undaunted by his remarks, we were determined to give it an honest try.

The next morning Joll started to regain consciousness and felt the pain in his jaw. The long vigil began, one of us staying with him constantly to watch him and see that he didn't injure himself. So I devised some soft booties made of old socks for Joll to wear on his front feet so that he wouldn't scratch his tooth out with his dew claw. I taped them on with masking tape so that they would be easy to replace. The veterinarian had given us some tranquilizers for Joll so we started off by giving him two every six hours. On the third day he seemed to be fighting the drug to stay awake so we eliminated them in the daytime and just tried them at night. He would wake up in the middle of the night, half-conscious and ready to tear his muzzle off. The tranquilizers were making him edgy, the opposite effect that we wanted, so we stopped them entirely. He preferred to be aware of what was going on and could handle the situation and the discomfort in his stride. After one week we took the booties off and explained that he wasn't supposed to scratch his face. He would look at us with his big, expressive, brown eyes and you could see he understood what we meant. If he forgot at any time and lifted his paw to his muzzle, we would just have to say, "No, Joll," and he would sigh and put his paw down.

He must have been sorely tempted to scratch his nose because the top of it and one whole side of his muzzle were very swollen, the brace across the roof of his mouth had enough play in it to be annoying and he couldn't close his teeth in a tight scissors bite because the brace prevented this. But the occlusion was excellent, and the gums had started to heal.

The first three days he was on soft foods, but after that he ate his ground beef and softened kibble. Eating bothered him more than anything because the brace was always in the way, but he gradually regained his appetite. I would keep Joll's brace clean by rinsing it with a water pic to remove the food particles. Every once in awhile, Joll would come to one of us and bare his teeth while pushing his tongue against his brace as if to say, "See, I've got something stuck." So we would clean it for him and he would be pleased.

After the third week we found that we could leave him alone and trust him not to disturb his brace or scratch his muzzle. He knew that we were trying to help his sore tooth and he was very cooperative. It was very simple to communicate with him because he was highly trained. At this time Joll had to go back to see his dentist for a checkup. After wagging his tail at his friend, he climbed up into the dentist's chair and laid his head on the headrest. He knew why he was there and very good-naturedly permitted Dr. Sokoloff to look at his teeth and tighten his brace. He didn't need an anesthetic because he was well-mannered and responsive to commands.

As the pain subsided, he began to want to play with his toys again, but we couldn't chance him loosening his tooth. I would explain, "No, drop it, you've got a sore tooth." He'd look at me understandingly and drop the toy.

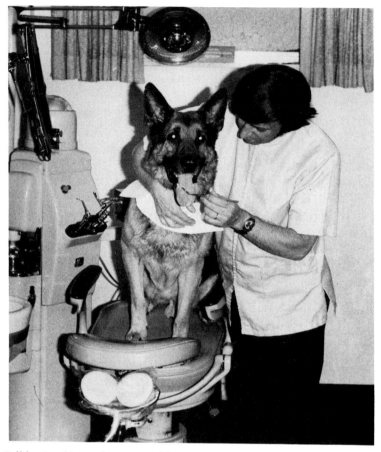

Joll having his tooth examined by Dr. Jack Sokoloff.

Joll had kept his brace intact for 10 weeks when he came to me one night and bared his teeth and started to push against his brace with his tongue. So, I said, "Do you want me to take it out?" Joll got all excited and turned around in little circles, then I got a small pair of wire-cutters, cut the wires that held the brace and removed the whole piece. It bled for a minute or two, but Joll was so happy to get rid of it that he went racing around the house showing all the other dogs what had happened. Today his tooth is strong and firm, and looks as good as new. He plays with his toys as if nothing had happened and we are very grateful to Dr. Sokoloff for using his ingenuity to save Joll's tooth.

EARS

A German Shepherd puppy's ears are rarely ever erect before he is five weeks old. Most puppies put them up when they are about three months old, but it is an individual thing and not predictable. The new owner, who is raising his first German Shepherd puppy, is sometimes alarmed at the various positions the puppy's ears assume. One may go up one day and the other two weeks later. They often form a hood over the puppy's head, or one may lie on top of his head while the other stands up straight and stiff. Watching a Shepherd puppy's ears go up is part of the fun of owning a Shepherd, as it can be most amusing and endearing.

However, don't be too complacent about it, as I once was, and let your belief that his ears will go up by themselves carry you beyond his fourth month without doing something about it. I raised, trained and showed Shepherds for years and never encountered any ear problems. Then, years later, during a period when I lived in the city and was unable to raise my own Shepherds, I bought a show puppy with excellent bloodlines. A few months later, when people would meet our puppy and express their doubts about his ears, I would reply, "Oh, I'm not worried about them, they'll go up." This remark is now a family joke.

At six months of age the puppy's ears were still down, so I contacted the breeder who suggested I take him to someone she knew who was good at taping ears. We took the puppy back six or seven times to have them taped, but in the end, only one ear stood erect. The experience was costly and hard on all of us. The method that was used involved taping the outside of the ears with adhesive tape, and often taping the two together over the puppy's head. The puppy's ears became very raw and sore and I was always doctoring him to prevent them from becoming infected. By the time he was eight months old nearly every method of ear taping had been tried on him. His

Normal ear carriage for puppies.

ears had practically no hair left on them and he had become very sensitive about them. I decided to let nature take its course, the puppy had had enough. Even if the ear had gone up, he would have passed this fault on to his off-spring, so he was given to a friend who wanted a pet.

I learned a lot from that experience, and in the years that followed, when I again became active in breeding Shepherds, I used a method to make ears stand erect that proved to be very successful and caused the dogs no discomfort. I have since been able to help many people who had dogs with ear problems.

If a puppy's ears are not up at five months, I believe it is wise to put them up for him so that he will get the feel of holding them erect. I have seen a puppy with his ears down actually shake his head to keep them down when one went up. This puppy should have his ears held up until he has got the feel of holding them up constantly. Then he will continue to do so himself.

If, at five months of age, the ear is half up, tipped slightly, tipped back or up one day and down the next, it needs help. If it is supported at this time, it will not become a problem. It is so simple to train the ear to stay erect that it seems wiser to do this than wait and perhaps be sorry later.

The method I use needs no tape. Someone must hold the puppy's head so that he will be absolutely still and quiet. Then, I swab the ears with a piece of cotton that has been moistened with alcohol, and I remove any wax or dirt. Next, I take a large sponge hair roller and insert a blunt pencil, eraser end first, through the hole. I spread 3M Super Weatherstrip 08001 all over the roller with a small piece of cardboard, and let it dry for about two minutes. I wear rubber gloves while doing this as it is very sticky.

Holding the ear very erect, the roller, with a small piece of cotton on one end, is placed in the dog's ear just above the knobs. The sides of the ear are quickly wrapped around the roller so that they meet, or slightly overlap, depending upon the size of the ear. And I hold the ear gently but firmly until the roller adheres to the ear. Remember to remove the pencil.

It is so very lightweight and so comfortable for the dog that he doesn't think about it. Leave it in the ear for about two weeks. When it starts to loosen by itself take it out.

Do not try to support a dog's ears if they are red or sore. Spread Panolog™ ointment on the irritated parts once a day until healed.

Your puppy's ears should be cleaned regularly with a small wad of cotton moistened in alcohol. To clean around the small knobby areas, use a swab stick moistened in alcohol. By checking your puppy's ears frequently, you can notice whether they are clean and healthy. If they should look red or swollen deep inside, it is possible he has a fungus infection. Your veterinarian can give him some medication for this and it is a good item to keep on your dog shelf. If the condition is advanced before you notice it, your dog will be shaking his head and rubbing it on the furniture, et cetera. It can become quite painful if not treated in the early stage. Occasionally a dog will

Insert roller and cotton in ear; the pencil will facilitate holding it while it dries.

The ear is wrapped around the roller.

get mites in his ears and this is something your veterinarian should treat. It is another problem that should be treated promptly.

LONG COATS

Many times a very young puppy will have a long, fluffy coat, but when his second coat comes in, the fur will lie flat and smooth, except for the area around his ears, which will look shaggy. If the dog is a pet, you can improve his appearance by clipping the hair with thinning shears, being careful to make it look natural. If you take your time and trim or thin out the unwanted hair, the dog will have a much neater appearance. There is nothing you can do for dogs that have really long coats. These dogs should be castrated and sold as pets. They will not do any winning in the Breed ring, but can be shown as Obedience Dogs. If they were bred, this fault would show up in their offspring.

THE GROOMING BAG

If you plan to attend dog shows, or travel extensively with your dog, it is a good idea to have a grooming bag in your car that contains articles you might need. I am listing a number of articles you might want to include in such a grooming bag.

Supplies for Obedience Handlers

Extra leash and collar

Extra dumbbell

White gloves

Scent discrimination articles

Large towel or bed to lie on

Towels

Dog toy

Bottled or home water

Small bowl

Treats for rewards

Flea stick and spray

Folding chair and umbrella

Kaopectate

Plastic cleanup bags

Supplies for Conformation Handlers

Extra leash and collar

Crate and space blanket

Comb and rake

Dryer

Cleanup plastic bags

Spray bottle

Folding chair

Grooming spray

Kaopectate

Bottle of water and bowl

Flexi lead or thirty foot leash

Towels

Dog toy

Alcohol and cotton swabs

Bait

Umbrella

Nail clippers and Quik Stop

Roll of paper towels

MAKE YOUR DOG A PART OF THE FAMILY

I have always thought that owning a German Shepherd required a certain kind of responsibility that is above and beyond mere dog ownership. It isn't like buying a hound and keeping it in the back yard until the day you take it hunting. A German Shepherd requires a special kind of care and understanding. You should be prepared to let him be part of your family, take part in most of the activities and educate him to be well mannered. These dogs can't develop their full potential if they are chained in a back yard, locked up in a garage or basement or shut off in a room. Too many people buy a German Shepherd Dog and do just this. It is the worst thing that could happen to a Shepherd. This dog is bred to be a companion dog in every sense of the word, and if you want to realize your dog's full potential, you should let him be a member of your family.

TEACHING YOUR DOG TO RIDE IN A CAR

Whether you pick up your new puppy at the airport or a kennel, let him ride on the seat with you when you drive home. This early association with you will start him off feeling secure and wanted. Let him sit next to you on the seat and have a small towel on your lap in case he should drool or throw up. Most puppies ride very well the first time they are in a car, but you will be happier if you are prepared for the unexpected. Start his training immediately, don't let him wander around the car, but make him lie down and be quiet. Pet him and talk to him conversationally so that he will relax and enjoy the ride. If he can snuggle up to you, he will be happy. If you force a dog to ride in a carton or keep shoving him down on the floor, he will associate riding in a car with something unpleasant, and the next time you want to take him in the car, he will become apprehensive and get carsick. Car sickness is not always motion sickness—often the dog is actually so uneasy and nervous that his saliva glands start overworking and he can't help drooling.

You can teach a dog to enjoy riding in a car by reassuring him in a soft tone of voice and petting him the first few times you take him with you. Don't let him bury his head in back of you in a cowardly fashion, insist that he lie down with his head up in an alert manner. If he is so relaxed that he wants to take a nap, that is good for him.

When the puppy gets home, let him relieve himself in the yard before taking him into the house. He will probably want a drink after that. If you keep his water dish in the same place all the time, he will be happier. Dogs are creatures of habit and they like to know where they can get a drink, eat their dinner or go outdoors. When training the puppy to do his business outdoors, it will be easier for him to learn if you take him out the same door each time. When he is housebroken, it won't make any difference.

TEACHING YOUR PUPPY TO STAY

I think it is a good idea to teach a puppy what "Go in your bed" means. There will be many times when you will not want him underfoot, and there will be other times when he might like to retire to the privacy of his own corner. You can provide him with a small rug or bed, and teach him to go to it and stay there while you are busy. I use a beach towel as a bed because it is easy to launder—folded in half for puppies and opened up full length for the large dogs. You could use a dog crate for the same purpose and let your puppy get used to sleeping in it. Most dogs like a crate in the house as it is natural for them to prefer to lie under something like a table, desk, et cetera, as this gives them a sense of security. Thousands of dollars of repair bills would be saved if puppy owners would teach their dogs to stay in their crates for a couple of hours when they are left alone. I've had hundreds of calls from people who owned dogs that were being destructive and wanted to know how to control them. You either have to teach the dog to behave himself when he is left at home or in the car, or you should keep him in a strong crate where he can't do any damage.

Some puppies and youngsters like to try out their teeth on anything that is close to them. The puppy teeth are quite sharp and one can get some nasty scratches if the puppy is permitted to do as he pleases. I would suggest that you give the puppy a sharp tap on his nose with your hand every time he tries to bite something. He will learn in two or three lessons if you are quick enough

Tom learns to stay in a crate.

to show him you are displeased. Tapping a dog with your hand will not make him hand-shy, but try to tap him while he is in the act, such as when biting. He should be petted whenever he is being good.

We don't permit dogs to get up on the furniture, but we do hold puppies on our laps so they can be petted. When they get bigger, they seem to understand that they are not supposed to climb on the furniture by themselves.

THE EXERCISE AREA: TEACHING YOUR DOG THE BOUNDARY LINE

If you own a German Shepherd, you should fence in your yard, or at least a portion of it, so that he will have a place to exercise. The fenced-in area should be as large as possible; ten feet by forty feet should be the minimum size. You could keep two German Shepherds in that area very nicely. The ideal size, of course, would be a 100-foot-square paddock with many shade trees. Dogs love to lie under trees, so if there are none on your property, you should provide shade for your dog. This is extremely important. If you build a doghouse, be sure that the dog can get up off the ground on some type of platform that is shaded from the sun. He shouldn't, either, have to lie on ground that is damp or cold. A dry bed of straw should be provided in cold weather.

If you don't fence in your yard, you should thoroughly train your dog to stay on your own property and respect the boundary lines. This can be done by walking the property lines with the dog on-leash and jerking him back when he steps over the line. This training will take two or three months and you will have to keep testing the dog to see if he has reached the point where you could trust him to stay in the yard if should there be any distractions. Have someone outside the family try to coax your dog to leave your yard, have a child ride a bike past your yard or ask someone to run their dogs on the adjacent property. If your dog stays in his own yard despite these distractions, then he will stay there 95 percent of the time. Just remember that the one time your dog does leave your property might be the time he gets run over and killed.

German Shepherds should never be permitted to run free as this is just inviting trouble. It is surprising how many people still have the mistaken idea that a large dog should be allowed to roam free. These people give their dogs little or no training because they want them to be "themselves." What they mean is that they don't want to accept the responsibility of caring for a dog. Because of this attitude, most communities now have leash laws to protect the dogs and the neighbors' property. If a dog owner really loves his dog he won't want it to run free because it might be poisoned, be stolen and sold to a laboratory for experimental purposes, get in a dog fight and be injured, meet a bitch in season and be shot by her irate owner, pick up worms in someone's yard, get run over by a car or destroy someone's property. If a person doesn't want to take care of his dog, he shouldn't own one.

Ch., Twice Select, Can. Ch. Omega's Allegro, ROMC, OFA
Breeders: Joseph, Frank and Clary Douwes
Owners: Lew and Debi James and Mary Quinlan

A German Shepherd should never be tied on a chain as this makes him overly aggressive. Anyone who keeps his dog on a chain, or confined in a run, should watch him often enough to know what is going on. A dog, so restricted and unable to defend himself, is often tormented by children and this sadistic teasing goes unnoticed by the owners. Then the day comes when they discover their dog has taken an intense dislike to children and they are at a loss to understand why. Many dogs with good dispositions have been ruined by this kind of irresponsible treatment, and the German Shepherd breed has been unjustly slandered.

DIET AND FEEDING

A diet for pregnant bitches and young puppies can be found in chapter 29, "Breeding German Shepherds." There are as many different diets for dogs as there are different breeds, and many breeders have very strong opinions on the subject. The one basic truth that should apply to any dog-feeding program is that the diet should be well balanced. Human beings who are interested in maintaining their health are able to eat well-balanced meals with an infinite variety of meats, vegetables, fish, fruit and dairy products. Dogs, on the other hand, must accept whatever they can get. The owner should give them something nourishing and palatable that agrees with them.

There are several dog food companies that have excellent dry dog foods on the market. These dry biscuits come in various sizes from a meal and a small bite size, to a large kibbled variety. The manufacturers claim that their dry dog foods are so well balanced in protein, carbohydrates, minerals, et cetera, that dogs will thrive on this food alone. I have seen a good number of hunting dogs that were kept in excellent condition on dry food only. However, I have always felt that German Shepherd dogs required fresh meat in their daily diets, so we add this to their dinners.

We feed our adult dogs first thing in the morning so that they will be content the rest of the day. If a dog is being shown in Obedience, staying home or going on a trip, the morning meal is best for him. The Obedience Dog will not get pangs of hunger just about the time he has to perform in the ring, and will keep his mind on his work. If a dog is being shown in Conformation, however, he should not get fed until that evening. A heavy meal might slow him down, make him feel sluggish, or make his tummy bulge out. He should have a lean, fit appearance for the Breed ring. It is a big chore feeding a large number of dogs and it is more practical to feed them in the morning so that the feeding dishes, as well as the runs, can be cleaned early in the day.

In our case, the dogs are fed early in the morning, then they spend the rest of the day outdoors in large paddocks. With a supply of fresh water and fresh air, they are happy to stay outdoors all day exercising themselves. I believe that fresh water should always be available to dogs so that they can drink it whenever they want it.

I suggest you feed your dog a good grade of kibbled biscuit (my dogs prefer the bite size, and it is easy to mix) and mix this with lean ground beef. My very active dogs get one pound of beef daily and those who are less active get one-half pound. To this mixture I add a good vitamin supplement and then add enough water so that the dinner is moist and will mix easily. Many good vitamins are made in tablet form, as is brewer's yeast, and my house dogs enjoy them so much they get them as rewards for tricks. When I give out tablets, I ask them to sit up, shake hands, catch or some such thing. The dogs learn their tricks very quickly with competition so keen.

Many dry dog foods expand to three times their size when water is added. The dog that eats a large, dry meal is in danger of getting bloated because this food will expand in his stomach. I believe the dog owner who feeds dry food should take the precaution to give his dog two smaller meals a day and withhold water for an hour after he eats. I feed my dogs an all-natural dry food that does not expand in water, and contains no soybean meal, dyes, chemicals or preservatives.

For variety, buy several chickens when they are on sale, boil them until the meat falls off the bones, remove all the bones, cut up the meat into small pieces (including the skin, liver, heart and gizzard) and mix this with the kibble, using chicken broth instead of water. This is a nourishing meal that is high in protein. Another time you could give your dog canned or fresh filleted fish.

We go to a poultry farm to buy eggs for the dogs and by getting those that have blood spots in them we get them very cheap. We are able to give them eggs four or five times a week and this is another source of protein that is very nourishing and tasty. We hard-boil the eggs and mix them in the dinners so that the dogs can't pick them out. Raw egg whites are not good for your dog, so give him cooked eggs.

If you find that your puppy is *growing too fast,* cut down on the protein. Feed a dry kibble that is low in protein, add fresh ground beef or cottage cheese without supplements.

My house dogs are crazy about various fruits and vegetables and they all get them as treats every day when these things are being prepared for our meals. By eating these snacks, the dogs are getting added vitamins and minerals that are good for them. They will eat the clean parings from apples, carrots, broccoli, turnips, potatoes, beans and cabbage. A new dog who joins the group will just watch the first time the parings are handed out, but the second time around, he quickly acquires a taste for them because the others are so eager to get them that he doesn't want to miss his turn.

Some dogs throw up a small amount of greenish-yellow fluid every once in awhile, and this will worry you if you don't understand why they do it. It is a bile secreted by the liver and delivered to the small intestine at that point where the food leaves the stomach. It contains salts and enzymes essential for digestion. Occasionally, a mild spasm will force some of this fluid into the stomach which irritates the lining and may cause regurgitation. Heavy infestation of worms in the small intestine might do it, and if this is the case, the dog should be wormed. Dogs who vomit this type of fluid who do not have worms should be fed twice a day as this will normally clear it up. If the condition persists, you should have your dog examined by your veterinarian.

It is very easy to take care of German Shepherds. If you train them to behave when they are three months of age, they will be no bother to you. They don't need fancy diets, just sensible, high-protein meals. Grooming is very simple as they require no clipping, and the exercise you give them each day will keep you both fit and feeling great.

HOW TO PICK UP YOUR PUPPY

There is a correct way to pick up a German Shepherd puppy so that he is comfortable and his hindquarters are supported. If he is very small, place your right hand between his front legs, under his body, while you balance his hindquarters on your wrist, and press him gently against your body. Use two hands to lift a larger puppy; your left hand should support his front end while the right supports his hindquarters. Place both of his front legs over your left arm

Left: To carry a puppy with one arm, press his body against yours as you cradle his hindquarter under your right arm, and place your right hand under his chest to hold him firmly. *Right:* Place the puppy's front paws over your left arm while you support his hindquarter with your right arm and hand.

while you support his rear with your right hand and arm, and lean him against your body. You can carry him with one arm by placing your right hand between his front legs to hold him firmly, and pressing his body against yours as you cradle his hindquarters under your right arm.

The handler should raise his right hand quickly to where the puppy can see it, give the verbal command, "Down," and pull the puppy down with his leash.

Susan Birch with April O'Neal of Wynthea's Gem, AKC-CD, HT, CGC, SchH1, UKC-CD, and Sgt. York of Wynthea's Gem, AKC-CD, HT, CGC, TD, SchH3, AD, UKC-CD. (AD is an endurance test in which the dog must gait for twelve miles at an average of eight to nine miles per hour with two fifteen-minute rest stops. At the end of this period, he must show that he is in good physical condition by doing a simple Obedience exercise. This is one of the requirements for a breed survey).

chapter 9

Preliminary Training

TEACHING YOUR DOG NOT TO BITE

Teaching your dog to be gentle when he is using his teeth and mouth will not lessen his effectiveness as a watchdog or protector, but will make him aware of his strength and show him how to control it.

This training should start when he is a puppy. As you will find out, puppies have very sharp teeth and even an accidental encounter with them can hurt. A young puppy likes to exercise and experiment by chewing on anything within reach. If your puppy tries to bite your hands or ankles, you should say, "No, no biting," and give him a sharp tap on his nose. I say sharp tap because a person may be timid about tapping a puppy and hardly touch him. This encourages the puppy to start nipping at his owner's hand. A timid, hesitant correction is worthless and makes a fresh puppy more aggressive. One good tap that the puppy can feel will stop him from biting, and further corrections may not be necessary. Puppies learn very quickly to respect the people who correct them. The correction should be repeated if the puppy has a lapse of memory. Once your puppy has shown that he understands how you expect him to behave, you will be able to correct him verbally by saying, "No biting."

You will be able to use this command any time the puppy is testing his teeth—if he is biting someone else, chewing the rung of a chair, nibbling on a sofa, chewing on a slipper or trying out the armrest in the car. This training will help him to understand that chewing is forbidden.

The owner who encourages his puppy to bite and play rough is fostering bad habits. This puppy will grow up to be uncontrollable; he will become very bold and aggressive and a hazard to have around. Dogs that are permitted to grow up unchecked become so unruly that the family finally has to either try training the dog themselves, or take him to a professional trainer. In either case, the dog will resent the handler's attempt to correct him, and force will have to be used to teach him manners.

The Shepherds that are passed on from one home to the next are those who are so uncontrollable that the owners can no longer tolerate them. It is so much simpler for everyone if the owner will train his puppy while he is very young, easy to handle and eager to please.

Teach your puppy to be gentle by offering him a piece of food with your fingers. If he snatches the food, say, "No, ouch." If he continues to grab for it, give him a tap on his nose with your fingers, and then offer him the food again saying, "Easy," in a soft tone of voice. If he takes it gently, praise him. Repeat this lesson over and over again. After a lesson or two, you will note that if you say, "Easy," and pause for a second before giving the food to him, he will be gentle. This is a valuable lesson that can be learned easily and early, and the puppy will retain it.

A variation of this lesson will be very useful from time to time. For instance, if you are playing with a toy and the puppy gets excited and starts to bite, just say "Easy," softly. If he has learned his food lesson well, he will relax and play gently.

TEACHING YOUR DOG NOT TO JUMP UP

It is easy to teach a puppy or a dog not to jump up on you if you are consistent in giving effective corrections. When the puppy or grown dog jumps up on you, quickly bang your knee into the dog's chest with enough force to throw him off balance. As you do this you should say, "No jumping," in a disapproving tone of voice. Don't shout at your dog; it is the tone of voice that is important.

If you have a tall, very leggy dog, you may find it impossible to catch him with your knee because he is holding his long legs way out in front of him. In this case, give him a quick shove with the bottom of your foot and knock him off balance. Don't kick him. When you own a dog, you learn to have very fast reflexes, and this is one instance where you will need them.

Puppies and dogs that jump up on you are only looking for attention and it is up to you to give it to them. If, when you enter a room, your puppy dashes over to greet you, bend over to pet him. If you simply stand where you are, he will probably want more of a greeting from you; and speaking to him is not enough—he wants to be petted. Remember that this display of affection is one of the ways your puppy will show that he loves you, and your affectionate response will assure him of your devotion. Dogs are gregarious creatures and enjoy your company. Don't be surprised if your dog greets you with the same abandon with which he greeted you only a few minutes ago, it is a compliment.

If your puppy jumps on your friends or strangers when they come to visit you, another method must be employed. Since you could hardly expect anyone else to use the knee method to prevent the puppy from jumping up on them, it is up to you. Have the puppy on a leash when a caller comes to the door, and as the puppy starts to jump up on him, jerk it back off balance and say, "No, easy," to him. It is best to have a choke collar on your puppy at this time. The collar should not be heavy and it should fit properly. Ask your friend to reach down and pet your puppy while you hold him quietly.

I like to have my dogs jump up on me when I command them to do so. If you want to teach your dogs to do this, encourage him to stand on his hind legs and place his front paws against you by saying, "Up," and tap your shoulders with both hands. If your dog jumps against you too heavily or roughly, bump him in the chest with your knee. Encourage him to try again, and when he leans against you lightly, praise him with your voice and pet him. Here is another opportunity to use the word "Easy."

I started training one very bright, affectionate puppy that I own, and whenever he had learned something I would say, "Good boy." He would be so pleased that he would jump up quickly and put his front legs around my waist and squeeze. I would give him a little hug, put him down and go on with the lesson. He got to be a big dog and still does this unless I say, "Good boy, stay." It is his way of expressing his happiness and affection and he is such a smart, willing worker that it is a pleasure to give him a little hug. He is fast to return to position with the word "Heel," but is so full of exuberance that he needs to be permitted to do this occasionally while we are practicing so that he can blow off some steam.

TEACHING YOUR PUPPY TO LIE DOWN

Lying down on command and/or signal is one of the basic commands that every puppy should be taught. It is simple to teach a puppy this command and, once the puppy understands it, his owner will use it hundreds of times.

Clip a leash on your puppy's collar, stand in front of him with the leash in your left hand, and when you raise your right hand quickly to where the puppy can see it, give him the verbal command "Down," in a quiet tone of voice, and pull the puppy down with his leash. As soon as the puppy is down, you should quickly pet and praise him in a pleased tone of voice saying, "Down, good, down, good." If necessary, apply a little pressure to the puppy's withers to hold him down while you are stroking him. When the puppy is down, he should be told to "Stay," and you should leave him, walk to the end of the leash and turn to face him. If your puppy gets up, you should quickly return to him saying, "No, down, stay," and put him down again. You may have to repeat this several times until the puppy understands what you want him to do, but he will soon be lying down when he sees your hand signal or hears the verbal command "Down."

Quite frequently, a handler will give his dog a "down" signal that his dog couldn't possibly see, then he wonders why the dog is being stubborn. The handler should never hold the down signal behind his dog's head. He should raise his hand quickly and hold it in front of the dog's nose where it is visible to him. Many times in the beginning, it is wise to repeat the down signal a second time by raising the hand quickly. The handler should not give a downward sweep several times with his hand, as this would be incorrect. It is much better to repeat the correct signal.

If you tell your puppy to lie down when he is in the same room with you, be sure to make him do so even though you have to go up to him and quickly pull him down with his collar as you give him the down signal with your right hand. When the puppy lies down, be sure to pet and praise him in a very pleased tone of voice. By enforcing your command, even though you do so kindly and quietly, your puppy will soon learn to respond to your signal or command the first time you give it.

TEACHING YOUR DOG TO RIDE IN A CAR

When you take your puppy for his first ride, he will be much happier if he can cuddle up next to you on the seat. It will give him a sense of security and make this first ride a pleasant experience. Have an old blanket or towel handy in case he drools or is sick. Hundreds of puppies take to riding the first time they are in a car and are never sick, but many others get used to riding only by countless short trips. As they get accustomed to the car's motion, the excursions can be gradually lengthened. Keep a window or two open so that the puppy will have plenty of fresh air.

It is a good idea to teach the puppy to sit quietly in the car right from the beginning. Dogs that dash from one window to the other, or that jump from the front to the back seat, or those that are allowed to bark, soon become a nuisance and a driving hazard. If you want your puppy to ride in the car, it is up to you to make him behave. Have someone else drive the car while you correct the puppy. Every time he stands up say, "No, sit," and make him sit by pushing his rear down. When he sits, praise him quietly. This will probably have to be repeated dozens of times but it is worth it to have a well-mannered dog.

If you have a station wagon and want to teach the puppy to ride in the back, place a thick, nonskid rug on the floor so that the puppy can dig into it with his paws and prevent himself from sliding. There is nothing quite so frightening for a puppy as to ride in the back of a station wagon that is covered with a slippery rubber mat; it gives him a sense of insecurity because he can't stop himself from slipping and sliding whenever the car starts, stops or turns a corner.

Today minivans have become very popular and all dogs seem to love to ride in them. Your canine passenger can either sit up on one of the seats, or he may prefer to sit on the floor next to you while you are driving. If you want your dog to be quiet in the car, just teach him to sit next to you on a seat or on the floor. He will feel very secure if you pet him and talk to him quietly during these lessons.

To teach an older dog to ride in a car, follow the same routine, unless you have a dog that is actually afraid of cars. In this case you must gain his confidence. First, you should put him on-leash and give him the idea that something special is going to happen by asking in a pleasantly excited tone of voice, "Do you want to go for a ride?" Step into the car with him, or lift him in if he is stubborn, and have him sit on the seat with you for ten minutes, talking to him and petting him. Repeat this the second day, and on the third day try it with the engine running.

Keep this up for a week, and then try it while you back the car out of the garage; park it in the yard for ten minutes, and then drive back in the garage. Be sure to keep talking to your dog, reassuring him and praising him. This slow method is the easiest and brings the best results. When you have worked up to a two-mile ride around the block, you can gradually increase the ride to ten miles. If you plan to drive more than fifteen miles, it is a good idea to give your dog some car-sickness pills an hour or so before starting. It will probably be many weeks before he is actually a good rider, but it will be worth the effort to have the pleasure and protection of his company.

Teach your dog to sit by the car and wait for your command to get in. Also, after a ride, have him sit patiently inside while you step out and until you have given him the command "Out." Everyone appreciates a well-mannered dog, and a few minutes' practice each time he goes for a ride assures you of owning one.

If you take your dog on a long trip, be sure to carry his water dish along. Dogs get thirsty more often than we do. It is also a good idea to carry a container of water from home for your dog, as often a change of water will give your dog diarrhea. If your dog eats a certain kind of food, take a supply along with you so that you won't have to substitute a new kind that might upset him. Keep a short leash and a thirty-foot leash in the car at all times. You never know when you may need them on a trip. If you should stop to exercise your dog, always put him on a leash.

If you have a dog that barks madly when he is in the car, it is fairly easy to stop him. Purchase a water pistol, and squirt him in the face with it whenever he barks, saying, "No barking." If this doesn't work, have someone drive your car while you sit next to your dog. When he barks, give him a good clop under the chin as you say, "No barking." Two or three good clops will calm him down and make him listen.

I am often asked whether I would recommend a crate for a dog that rides in a car. I personally do not like my dogs to ride in crates. I prefer to teach them to be well mannered in my car so that they can enjoy the freedom of it. I have a four-door car and have had a bench made that is upholstered and is like an extension of the back seat. I cover it all with a heavy throw rug that can be washed. My dogs are very happy with this arrangement.

Crates have become popular due to the fact that professional handlers use them for each of the dogs they transport and recommend them to their clients. It is a practical way to carry untrained dogs and, when several are being transported at the same time, it is also the safest way. A dog owner who owns show dogs that have had no training finds it is easier to carry them in crates rather than train them. One dog can be left in his crate in the car while another is being shown. He doesn't have to worry about the dog chewing the upholstery in his car, or getting into mischief while he is gone. A dog will generally be more alert in the Breed ring if he has been kept in a crate prior to the time his class is judged. Crating untrained dogs will also lessen the danger of them fighting among themselves.

If you prefer to have your puppy or dog travel in a crate, first get him used to it in your home. The easiest way is to give your puppy his meals in the crate. Just as dogs like to lie under a desk or table, if you leave the crate door open, the puppy will soon decide it is a good place to relax. Buy the puppy a large wire crate so that he can use it when he is full grown. If you put a soft dog bed in it, he will like it even more and eventually regard it as his den.

If you plan to do any traveling by air with your dog, it is wise to get him used to a crate so that he won't object to traveling in one should the day come when he has no choice. Bitches being shipped airfreight to stud dogs are sent in crates and spend several days in them. It is therefore wise to train them to accept this situation gracefully.

TEACHING YOUR DOG TO STAY ALONE: AT HOME OR IN YOUR CAR

Once your puppy is housebroken and is trusted enough to be allowed the freedom of the house, it is time to train him to stay alone. By this time he will have been taught not to chew on anything that does not belong to him and will have developed a conscience.

Begin by leaving him in a familiar room that can be shut off from the rest of the house. Be sure to leave his toys in the room. Leave him for only a few minutes the first time, and gradually increase the time as he behaves. When you leave him say, "Wait."

If he scratches the door, open it quickly and tap him with your hand, saying, "No, shame," hesitate a few seconds then say, "Wait," and leave him. Stand near the door the first few times so that you can correct him quickly if you hear him being naughty. Repeat this as often as necessary. Eventually you will be able to leave the house, bang the door so the puppy hears you leave, wait outdoors for ten minutes, then return and praise him if he has been good. You are inviting trouble if you leave a puppy who has been allowed the freedom of the house shut up in a room for several hours. There are very few puppies who will behave themselves without some previous training.

If you do not want your puppy to get up on the furniture in your absence, do not allow him up while you are there. If it is entirely his idea, set some mousetraps on the furniture and cover them with a dishtowel (to avoid injury) before you leave. When he tries to sneak up on the chair or sofa, the loud snaps will scare him off.

It is easy to teach a dog to stay in a car, since he loves the car so much he is happy to wait in it. Leave two or three windows partly down so that he will have plenty of fresh air. Always park your car in the shade in the summer if you leave your dog in it as it becomes as hot as an oven, even with the windows open a little. If you have the one dog that resents being left alone in the car, you will have to leave him for short periods of time while you hide and watch him. As soon as he starts to misbehave, run back to the car and scold him. When he realizes you will correct him for misbehaving, he will learn to wait patiently.

TEACHING YOUR PUPPY TO WALK ON-LEASH

If you purchase a puppy at about seven weeks old, fit him with a lightweight five-eighths-inch nylon or cotton buckle collar. He should wear this type of collar until he is about fourteen weeks old. His next collar should be a fat, round nylon choke collar that is also lightweight. This collar is very comfortable for the puppy to wear. It is important that you get the right size for your puppy. To form a collar, just slip the cord through one of the rings, and draw it all the way through to the other ring. When the collar is pulled snug around the puppy's neck, there should be three inches left over including one ring. If you need to put license and rabies tags on the collar, put them on the buckle collar. The choke collar can be used when you start his training. I do not ever recommend chain collars, as they are too heavy and cut the coat. If you prefer chain, try the lightweight German collars called "fur savers."

If you have more than one puppy and you let them play together outdoors, remove their collars as they might become entangled or get them caught in some way. Many weird and tragic accidents have occurred as a result of a dog getting his collar snagged on something. Many dogs have hung themselves by catching their collars on fences, water spigots and dead tree branches. Such accidents can be avoided if you are aware of the danger.

I prefer a soft, pliable leather leash, one-half inch wide by five feet long. It is easy on the hands and can be folded easily to fit in a pocket. The puppy will feel no pressure on his neck from this type of leash. Never use a chain leash on your puppy or dog.

When walking on a leash the first few times, a puppy may pick up the leash and carry it in his mouth. This makes it much more fun for him, so don't correct him. He shouldn't be permitted to bite or chew on the leash. Hold the leash in your left hand, and try to keep the puppy by your left side. If he moves over to the right side, guide him back gently and pet him with your left hand. By reaching down and petting him occasionally as you walk along, and by calling him back to you when he runs out to the end of the leash, you will be able to keep him near you. If you practice in your back yard, a ten-minute lesson should suffice.

Some puppies fight the leash in every way they can. A puppy may sit and refuse to budge when he realizes he is on a leash. Have the leash clipped to the dead ring on the collar and if he refuses to move when you coax him, give him a little jerk to his feet. When he starts moving, go with him and let him pull you as far as he wishes. A stubborn puppy will keep sitting, or stand and plant his feet and refuse to move. If you jerk the puppy when he is being stubborn and pet him when he is near you, he will begin to walk a little. Some puppies will dash to the end of the leash and start jumping and bucking in the air. When they start having a tantrum like this, go to the puppy and hold his leash short as you walk along and try to keep him by your side. His lesson should be very short. Stop occasionally to pet him and talk to him. It might take two or three short lessons for this puppy to decide to walk along with you, but each lesson will find him more willing to comply. Puppies do better on-leash when they are away from home, for they don't want to be left alone in a strange place and will therefore hurry along to stay with you.

chapter 10

Tricks to Teach Your Puppy

Tricks are fun to teach, enjoyable for everyone to watch and beneficial for your puppy to learn. Most dogs love to show off, and whether you have an Obedience Dog, a pet or a show puppy, this initial step that teaches him to be a showman will be good for his ego and help him to develop his personality. The more you teach your puppy the more self-assured and confident he will become. If you teach him the following tricks, it will help him become more responsive and alert to commands.

The more exercises you give your puppy that will help him to develop mentally and physically, the better off he will be. This is an excellent way to introduce new commands and signals to him that will be utilized many times later on, and most of these tricks will help him to become more coordinated and agile.

When teaching your puppy some of these tricks, it is wise to offer him food as an inducement. Puppies are very fond of tidbits, and if they are rewarded with a dog cookie or a piece of meat, they will be eager to try something new. This applies to puppies, as they become bored very easily and the food will hold their interest until they have learned the trick. Later, when your puppy is older, he will be happy to do the tricks for praise alone.

SHAKING HANDS

This is a very simple trick and your puppy can probably learn it in one or two lessons. Start by having your puppy sit in a corner; he is less likely to walk away. As you offer your hand to your puppy say, "Shake hands," and touch his right foreleg. If your puppy doesn't raise his paw, lift it yourself. Repeat this until your puppy understands what you want. To make it easy, as you offer your right hand, gently shift your puppy's weight over onto his left side by pushing his shoulder gently with your left hand. As soon as your puppy lifts his paw, take it firmly but gently, praise him and give him a piece of meat.

ROLLING OVER

Rolling over is excellent therapy for tense, nervous dogs. If they can be persuaded to relax by doing this exercise, formal training will be much easier.

Begin by having your puppy sit, then have him lie down and next push him over flat on his side. When your puppy is lying flat on his side, say, "Roll over," making a circular motion to the right with your right hand. At the same time, grasp your puppy's paw in your left hand and help him to roll over. Once he has rolled over, say, "Roll back," and help him to do so as before.

When your puppy has mastered this, you can vary the trick by saying, "Roll over and over and over," and then, "Roll back, and over and over." Eventually, you can give your puppy the verbal command and the hand signal without helping him at all. Be sure to give him a piece of meat every time he rolls over and back. If he knows he will be rewarded, he will be more eager to do it. Be sure to make a big fuss over him when he does it right.

SITTING UP

Sitting up teaches a dog to sit squarely on his haunches, and the dog that can sit up is less likely to sit crooked later on. In the Obedience ring, your dog will be penalized if he sits crooked.

This will be fairly easy to teach your dog, but it may take him one or two weeks to learn how to balance himself alone. When you practice, have your puppy sit on a rug or floor that is not slippery. Position him in a corner and persuade him to sit up by holding a choice piece of meat just out of reach above his nose. When your puppy sits up, give him the food, and then praise him. Soon he will be doing this the moment you say, "Sit up," and hold your hand above his nose.

Once he learns to sit up in a corner, bring him out into the middle of the room. Place his tail straight out behind him as it will help him maintain his balance. Some puppies have trouble in the beginning, so to help your puppy balance, have him give you his right paw which you take in your left hand. At the same time, hold a piece of meat over your puppy's nose with your right hand, and using his right paw as a lever, try to get him to sit up straight as you gradually withdraw your left hand. The trick is to withdraw your hand at the precise moment that he is able to maintain his balance without any support whatsoever. If you succeed in getting him to balance himself every time he sits up, even though it is only for a second or two, you will find that his skill will improve with practice. Eventually you will be able to have him sit up and stay on command, while you step back and take his picture.

Help your puppy to balance himself by gently holding one or both paws.

SAYING HIS PRAYERS

This trick follows the last and is easily learned. Once a puppy has learned to sit up, he will naturally come over to you if you are eating something and beg for a piece. If you are sitting down, he will sit up and place his paws against you. This is the position he should be in to learn this trick.

Say, "Stay," to your puppy, and gently push his head between his paws. Hold it there for a minute until you say, "Amen." Then praise your puppy and give him a piece of meat. Your puppy will learn this by repetition.

Holmes, my old Caesar son who is twelve years old, has a passion for ginger snaps. If he notices me getting the cookie box, he will come over and start saying his prayers. He will bow his head and hide his eyes for a whole minute or two until I say, "Amen." He will keep repeating this until the cookie box is put away. It is impossible to refuse him some ginger snaps when he does this trick. It is no longer an easy feat for him to balance on his arthritic hind legs, and when I praise and reward him he feels very proud and pleased with himself.

CATCHING A BALL

Dogs do not generally have good eyesight, although I have known several exceptions to this rule. My firm belief is that if you teach your dog to catch a ball, he will watch for it so intently that the exercise will be beneficial for his eyes. Topper became so adept at catching a ball that anything else in the air fascinated him. He would sit in the yard and watch a hawk circling in the sky, a plane passing overhead or birds flying by. These innocent periods of watchfulness gave his eyes much-needed exercise and now, as he is going into his thirteenth year, his eyesight is still good. One of the prescribed exercises for nearsightedness is to look at an object close to you and then at a distance. Since dogs are notoriously nearsighted, this trick is an excellent way to improve your dog's eyesight.

Start in your home, since your puppy will not be so apt to run away with the ball. I must caution you first not to use a ball that is too small for your particular dog; he may swallow it or get it caught in his throat. The exercise is perfectly safe, provided the ball is small enough to be caught and large enough not to be swallowed.

Have your puppy sit, then get him interested by pretending to throw the ball. Do this several times, and then throw it directly into your puppy's mouth saying, "Catch it." Your puppy may let it hit him on the nose a couple of times before he gets the idea of catching it. When he does succeed, praise him, take the ball and try it again. Remember to have him sit each time you throw the ball. If you make this fun, your puppy will soon be catching the ball and bringing it back to you each time for another try.

Once he has learned the trick in the house, move the game outdoors. This is a very good way to exercise your puppy with very little work for you. A dog who will retrieve a ball in your yard will generally retrieve a ball floating in the water. The first time you try it, be sure to throw it near shore where your puppy simply has to wade in to reach it. As he gets used to retrieving from the water, you can gradually throw the ball farther out. Swimming is excellent exercise for dogs, and retrieving makes it fun. Many busy people, who do not have time to walk their dogs, find that retrieving a ball gives them sufficient exercise.

BACKING UP

Once your puppy has learned to catch a ball, you can teach him to back up. If you have made it a point to have your dog sit and wait for you to throw the ball, he now understands the word "Sit." When your puppy brings the ball to you, wave him back with your right hand saying, "Go back," and after he takes several steps back say, "Sit." When he sits, throw the ball. If your puppy does not understand immediately, walk into him and push your knees against his chest, gently forcing him to step back. Wave him back at the same time so that he will learn to go back on your hand signal. After he has backed up several paces, say, "Sit, stay," return to your *original* position and throw the ball. Always praise your dog. Repeat the whole procedure until your dog will back up on either your verbal command or hand signal.

Joll loved to jump, so I taught him this trick.

Joll with the author, Winifred Gibson Strickland.

Joll executing a thirteen-and-one-half-foot broad jump at a height of four feet. He started thirty feet back from the hurdle in order to get enough momentum to clear it.

Joll and I have combined a few of these tricks to make retrieving more interesting. When he brings me a ball or a toy, I tell him, "Go back," which he does with quite a flourish, and then I tell him to "Sit." Next I ask him to "Sit up, and stay," and while he is sitting up I throw the ball to him and he catches it. Sometimes I vary the act a little by asking him, "Do you want to say please?" He then paws the air in a most appealing way and I throw the ball to him. It is all in fun. I enjoy playing with him, and he loves to perform.

JUMPING

There will be many times in your dog's life when it will be practical and advantageous for him to jump when ordered to do so. Whether the occasion calls for him to jump into the back of your station wagon or jump up on a table to pose for a Best in Show picture, it will be desirable for him to respond to the verbal command "Hup."

You can start your puppy when he is about seven months old, but never jump him over thirty inches until he is over eleven months of age. A German Shepherd is a heavy dog, and the strain of jumping repeatedly would be hard on his shoulders, back and hindquarters. Have your jump set at two feet at first, run up to the jump, say, "Hup," and jump over it with your dog. He will learn faster if you jump with him the first few times. If your dog balks at the jump, lift him over with the leash the next time you run up. Soon he will be jumping by himself as soon as you run up to the jump and say, "Hup." Next teach your dog to jump by himself. Have him sit about six feet from the jump, and tell him to stay while you take a position behind the jump. Say, "Come, hup," and clap your hands over the jump, beckoning him toward you. Keep his attention focused on a point higher than the jump so that he will clear the hurdle.

When your puppy has learned to clear the solid jump on command, try the same routine with the bar jump. Next, have someone hold the bar while you teach your puppy to jump over it. From here it is an easy step to teach him to jump over a short bar. Any time he refuses, simply lower the bar until he is jumping it consistently and then start raising it again.

If you would like to teach your dog to jump through a hoop, start with one that is about thirty inches in diameter. When he is proficient at jumping through this, you can teach him to jump through a hoop twenty inches in diameter. You should hold the hoop steady without lowering it. Once you lower the hoop for your dog, he will expect you to do this every time he jumps. It is a sign of inferior training or jumping when the handler moves the hoop; the idea is to teach the dog to jump through the hoop without touching it, at whatever height it is held.

Another version is to teach your dog to jump over your arm when you hold it out straight to your side. I have also taught several of my dogs to jump through my arms by forming a circle with them. This is one of the many ways you can have fun with your dog and give him exercise at the same time.

When you stop, hold the leash in your right hand, near your left side, then reach down and make the puppy sit. Praise and pet him.

Early Obedience Training

The perfect time to start obedience training your puppy is when he is four months old. At this age he is very receptive and will try to please, just for the sake of pleasing. If he receives an adequate amount of praise and petting, he will learn his lessons more quickly than an older dog. At this age he has an open mind, and if he can be trained to do all the right things, he will not acquire any bad habits. Because the puppy has not acquired any bad habits, he will understand the lesson that much sooner. There is never the defiance one sometimes gets from an older dog, and any opposition the puppy gives is short-lived.

You must always be aware of the fact that you are training a puppy and show an extra amount of patience and understanding. You should always let your puppy know that you love him, and give him a sense of security so that he will develop complete confidence in you and be unafraid. The puppy who trusts his owner will be kind and understanding, and is the puppy who will be eager to learn and willing to work. This is the opportunity you will have to teach your puppy to respect and trust you. Once you earn your puppy's trust, you must strive to keep your relationship harmonious.

An independent puppy will become a well-adjusted dog. The puppy who would rather stay with his littermates than associate with human beings, who cries without cause or who wants to run and hide because he is shy will become neurotic if he is not corrected when he is young. This puppy should be trained when he is four months old. If you will just spend a little time each day training your puppy, he will turn out to be a well-mannered, well-adjusted dog.

There are still people who are advising others to wait until their dogs are a year old before training them. This poor advice has ruined a great number of good dogs. People who wait a year to train their dogs are in for a lot of grief. The dogs by this time are wild and unruly, and the bad habits they have acquired will be hard to break. It is possible to train a dog at any age, but the longer you wait the more strict you must be and the harder it will be on your dog and you.

Occasionally one hears from a dog owner the plaintive cry, "I wouldn't train my puppy so young. I want him to enjoy being a puppy." This naive remark comes from a well-intentioned person who doesn't know what he is talking about. Contrast the little untrained monster who cannot be left alone in the house because he chews anything in sight and ends up either getting a licking or being locked in a room alone, usually in the basement or garage, with the trained youngster who is learning to be well mannered and is taken everywhere with the family because he is such a good puppy. Which puppy is enjoying life—the wild, uncontrolled puppy who gets in everybody's hair, or the puppy who is getting acquainted with the world? Because the latter is being trained, he is enjoying every minute of being a puppy and his privileges are endless. The joy he spreads is contagious, and everyone greets him with a smile and wants to pet him. He grows up to be a beloved member of his family with his place in life secure. The untrained dog, however, very often becomes a burden and an unwanted responsibility and is passed along from one family to another until his luck runs out.

When you train a puppy, you should be much more demonstrative and uninhibited than with an older dog. During the early stages of his training, you should bend over frequently to show your puppy where he should be and pet him when he is close. You should be willing to forget yourself and concentrate all your thoughts and attention on your puppy. Besides teaching your puppy to be obedient, you must keep your puppy happy and encourage him to work. Since not everyone has the temperament to train a puppy, you should honestly appraise yourself, and if you find you consider training him a chore, you should let someone else in the family do it.

The method you use to train a puppy is very important, and the one I describe here is one that I have conceived and practiced with all my own puppies. This method will appeal to the overwhelming number of people who love their dogs and who realize that a dog who has been trained with intelligence and understanding will always win over the dog who has been subjected to cruelty to force him to work. Whatever the temperament of the puppy, training will be good for him, providing the experience is always a pleasant one. Even though minor corrections will have to be given throughout the lesson, the puppy should have fun while he is learning. This training method will give your puppy self-confidence and he will become very self-assured and alert.

You should train your puppy ten or fifteen minutes at a time during the first few weeks. The first lesson should be spent teaching your puppy to heel and sit automatically, and to stay and come. The puppy should be wearing a thick nylon choke collar and the leash should be clipped to the dead ring. I prefer a web leash made of nylon and cotton because it is very light. If your puppy keeps slipping his collar off his head, clip the leash to the choke ring. Have the puppy sit by your left side every time you begin his training session. Give your puppy's name and the command "Heel" and start walking. If the puppy just sits there, give him a little jerk, tap your left leg in front to show him where you want him, and repeat his name and "Heel" in a firm but pleasant tone of voice. If your puppy tries to forge ahead or go off to the side, jerk him back with just enough force to bring him back. It doesn't take much of a jerk to teach a puppy to heel; his neck is tender and a small jerk will suffice. Reach down and pet your puppy when he is by your side. Laugh and talk to him so he will think you are having fun. When making an about turn, pivot to the right while remaining in the same place, don't wander in a small circle to make a turn, and don't stand and wait for your puppy to catch up for he must learn to stay with you. When making a left or right turn, both of which are like right angles, jerk your puppy as you say his name in a persuasive tone of voice, tap your leg to show him where he should be, and praise him when he is by your side. The leash should always be slack except for that brief moment when it is jerked. A puppy is always very interested in voices and odd noises, and you should use your voice continually to keep your puppy alert and his attention focused on you.

When you stop, you should switch hands on the leash, grab it with your right hand, hold it near your left side and reach down with your left hand to guide your puppy into a straight sit. The puppy, at this age, can be taught to sit automatically if he gets a push or a quick tap on his croup. A combination of both should be used during the heeling routine. All the puppies that I have trained have learned to sit automatically during the first fifteen-minute lesson. When the puppy starts sitting automatically, you should always have your hand down near your puppy when you stop, so that you can guide him into a straight sit or pet him, or both.

A big fuss should be made over the puppy who sits automatically. If he gets up and climbs on you when he is praised, he can be excused. He should be petted and praised and then made to sit again quickly. This is one of the differences between training an older dog and a puppy. The puppy should be allowed to express himself and then the lesson should continue immediately.

Your puppy may try all sorts of tricks, depending upon his temperament and personality. Almost anything a puppy does is cute, but you should be firm and make your puppy obey the first time you command him to do something. Even though you are guiding your puppy, or petting him, your puppy must do what he is told. When you make turns, your puppy should receive a quick, small jerk, as you remind him to "Heel," and immediately let the leash go slack. By talking to him, showing him how to stay close and repeating his name and the word "Heel" frequently, you can soon teach your puppy to keep up with you.

It is so easy to correct a puppy at this tender age that I must warn you not to be too rough with him. German Shepherds grow very quickly, and if

Hold the lead taut, give the puppy a stay signal as you say "Stay" softly.

When your puppy comes to you, place one hand under his chin as you guide him into a straight sit.

When the puppy comes in and sits automatically, hold him gently under the chin as you praise and pet him.

you are not familiar with the breed, you might forget that the large German Shepherd by your side is just a baby. Although he seems huge and very heavy to you now, you must remember that you are training a puppy and be patient with him. Most German Shepherd puppies are highly intelligent and very sensitive and respond to kindness by learning their lessons quickly. Harsh treatment dulls their spirits and makes them cowed.

Spend the last half of the first lesson teaching your puppy the recall exercise. With your puppy sitting in front of you, hold the leash taut in your left hand behind your puppy's head. Give your puppy the stay signal by gently placing your right hand in front of his nose as you give him the quiet command, "Stay." Your puppy will probably try to get up and follow you when you step back, but the taut leash will keep him in place. This should be repeated whenever the puppy tries to move, and you should repeat the words, "No, stay," each time you put him back. When your puppy stays for a second or two, you should try to step back and let the leash go slack.

At first your puppy may be quite stubborn. If he persists in getting up, you must hold the leash taut, give the command, "No, stay," push the palm of your right hand against your puppy's nose firmly but not roughly and then hold your hand a few inches in front of your puppy's nose. If your puppy tries to jump up, you should place your hand on your puppy's chest and quickly push him into a sit; all the while you should be talking softly, "Now stay, stay. That's it, stay." When your puppy has decided to stay, he may turn his head to the side pretending to look at something. This is just a ruse and you should not repeat the stay command as long as he remains in one place. As soon as it is practical, you should step back to the end of the slack leash and, if necessary, continue to hold the stay signal out to your side where your puppy can see it. In the beginning you will have to repeat the verbal command "Stay," and show your puppy the stay signal many, many times.

After the puppy has stayed in place a few seconds, you should call your puppy by saying his name and the word "Come." If your puppy doesn't respond immediately, you should give his leash a little jerk. When your puppy starts toward you, you should praise him exuberantly, quickly guide him into a straight sit and pet him. Puppies will learn to sit when they come in to their handlers in a very short time; in fact, they will probably accomplish this during their first lesson. To accomplish this you must always remember to praise your puppy as he is coming in; when the puppy is close, you should hold him gently under the chin or by the skin around his neck and with the other hand gently guide him into a straight sit. The puppy should be praised and petted immediately. The puppy that is started this way will enjoy learning the recall and will respond quickly.

The puppy that jumps up when he reaches his handler should be made to sit quickly with the command "No, sit," and then praised when he is sitting. The next few times your puppy comes in, he should be told to sit when he is fairly close. You should be ready to bend over quickly to pet your puppy and guide him into a straight sit. You must learn to make the corrections quickly and smoothly so that your puppy is doing the right thing only a second after doing something wrong. His praise should come swiftly even though you have gently forced him to do it correctly. Since your puppy is never permitted to do anything wrong, he will remember the times when he was praised and will associate the praise with the correct things he did.

The first lesson should end with a long sit-stay exercise. The puppy should be made to stay on a long sit for twenty seconds or so the first time. Eventually, in the lessons to follow, you can increase the time to two minutes. You should practice this exercise two or three times during the first lesson. If it is necessary, hold your hand signal out to your side where your puppy can see it and repeat the "Stay" command.

When you return to your puppy after a long sit-stay, hold your leash in your left hand with your arm extended, walk by your puppy's left side, behind him, and into heel position. The leash will remain on your puppy's right side all of this time. Your puppy should not move when you return to stand by his side. At first, when you return, you should do so quickly before your puppy has a chance to move. Then, when you are back in heel position, you should reach down and pet and praise him. This is all you should work on the first few lessons.

Your puppy can learn many things at a very early age by the different tones of voice you use and by the different inflections you give your words. He may not understand your new word commands until you have repeated them over and over, but he will instantly recognize your different tones of voice. He will soon learn to recognize words when they are used in the form of a question. This is especially true when an act is performed each time a question is asked. Here are a few examples:

Do you want to go out? (As you go to the door.)

Do you want your dinner? (As you pick up the puppy's dish.)

Do you want a drink? (As you turn on the faucet.)

Do you want a cookie? (As you take the cover off the cookie jar.)

Do you want to go for a walk? (As you pick up his leash.)

If you repeat these questions and go through the motions a great number of times, your dog will soon learn to understand all the words. At first, upon hearing a question, he will look at you expectantly, and may wag his tail with anticipation. Later he may speak, and still later he may bring you his dish or leash. When your dog's training is completed, you can sit in your living room and ask any of these questions, and your dog will reply by acting out the answers. So, at first, when you ask your dog questions, use a pleasantly excited tone of voice and emphasize the last word of the question.

When you use the word "No" to correct your dog, lower your voice, making it sound authoritative and firm. When reprimanding your dog, lower your voice and draw out the words, *"S-h-a-m-e. Ba-a-a-d do-o-o-o-g."*

The tone of voice that is most important in training is the one you use when you praise your dog. Make it gay and full of good spirits. Include a laugh here and there, and be sincere, for a dog can spot insincerity easily. Put on a little act for his benefit, for this is his real reward for being obedient. Put your heart in your voice and watch your dog respond.

If you give commands to your dog in actual training, use a moderately pitched, pleasant voice that is both firm and authoritative. There is absolutely no reason to shout at your dog if he is working near you. A dog's hearing is at least sixteen times better than that of a human being. With such acute and sensitive hearing there is no excuse for you to speak to your dog above a moderate tone. If you wish to attract his attention, clap your hands, say, "Sssssst," or call him by name. Even at a distance, raise your voice just enough to be heard above the crowd.

If you find yourself continually shouting at your puppy, it would be better to turn him over to another member of your family for training, since you are probably temperamentally unsuited for the job. If you find yourself confronted with a problem, your puppy seems to be getting stubborn and you find yourself shouting at him, stop. Repeat a simple exercise the puppy knows and understands, praise him, then stop for the day. Always end the day's training on a pleasant note. You will accomplish more the next day when you both are rested. By yelling at a dog in a rude manner, some handlers expect to command the dog's attention, but in so doing they eventually lose their dog's respect. It is an insult to a dog's intelligence to expect him to respond to this crude method. Contrast this type of handler with one who asks his dog to heel in a pleasant, quiet tone of voice. The quiet handler, in setting a standard of perfection, would by contrast alone expose the loud handler's imperfections.

When handling your puppy or dog, be gentle, make a companion of him, talk to him as you would to a friend—conversationally. You won't spoil him by doing this but will gain your dog's respect. Your dog will be your best friend if you just consider his feelings at all times. If you train him with patience and establish a mutual feeling of companionship, he will be eager to work just to please you. A well-trained dog will execute any command perfectly, even if the order is given in a whisper. Gentleness and smoothness of handling can be acquired only through constant practice.

After you have practiced for about a week, you may add the "long down" exercise to the others. If you have taught your puppy to lie down, just leave him, walk out to the end of the leash, turn and face him, place your leash on the ground and step on the end of it. After one minute you may return to him the same way you did on the long sit exercise. If you have not taught your puppy to lie down, you will find it explained in chapter 9, "Preliminary Training," under "Teaching Your Puppy to Lie Down." You should practice this exercise until you have succeeded in teaching your puppy to go down on signal or voice command. In the weeks to come, you should gradually increase the time that he stays down until he is remaining in position for five minutes.

Give your puppy a down signal as you say "Down."

When you practice the long sit and the long down exercises each day, get in the habit of folding your arms in front of you. This will help your puppy distinguish between this and the recall exercise and will give you a more comfortable stance.

About the third week, start incorporating a "finish" with your recall exercise. It is much easier to teach a puppy to do the finish than it is to teach an older dog.

Start by having your puppy sit directly in front of you. Hold your leash in your left hand, palm down, about a foot from your puppy's collar. Keep your right foot stationary while you take one step back with your left foot. As you step back, put most of your weight on your left foot, give your puppy a jerk and say, "Joll, heel." Always give your puppy's name first, before the command. The jerk should be big enough to propel the puppy past your left side, at which point you should turn him toward you and let him take the step or two that will bring him into heel position. Now you should switch hands on the leash; hold the leash in your right hand over near your left leg, as you guide and help the puppy sit straight. Praise him in a very pleased tone of voice.

Remember to jerk your puppy back; do not pull him back on a tight leash or he will dislike the exercise. The jerk will teach him to move fast, and to go far enough back so that he can turn and step into heel position. After you have practiced several times with your puppy, try guiding your puppy back past your side with a slack leash. He will probably follow the leash around and into heel position. If he stops short, jerk him back so that he will learn to go far enough back in order to turn and sit straight at heel position. Don't continue to jerk your puppy back each time when it is unnecessary. Do not practice this exercise too much at first or your puppy will start anticipating the finish. Eventually your puppy should be able to go to the heel position when you give the verbal command or the hand signal, which is simply swishing your left hand and arm back by your left side.

The "stand for examination" exercise should be introduced about the fifth week. By this time your puppy will understand the stay signal and will be sitting automatically. Walk forward with your puppy and give him the stay signal and verbal command, "Stay," when you notice your puppy lining up his front feet. You can get your puppy to do this by holding him on a short, taut leash with your left hand, quickly giving him the stay signal and verbal command, "Stay," and stepping forward to the end of the leash. If your puppy starts to move, show him the stay signal and hold it out where he can see it as you repeat the "Stay" command.

After a few seconds, you should return around your puppy, as you do when you return to him on the long-sit exercise, and caution him to "Stay." When your puppy understands this portion of the exercise, the next phase is to drop your leash on the ground way out in front of him when you leave him. After a few seconds, return and examine your puppy by running your right hand over his head, back and hindquarters. Puppies like this attention and will move unless cautioned to stay. This is not a difficult exercise and your puppy will learn it through repetition.

You should never jerk on the leash when you give the stay signal to your puppy as this would make him sit. Using a taut leash will restrain him and help him to learn what is required. Once the puppy has learned this, you can teach him to stand in the same manner on a loose leash. If your puppy attempts to take another step, you should say, "No, stay," and place his leg back in line with the other, or have your puppy take one more step so that he would again have his front feet in line with each other. You should make it clear to your puppy that the stay signal means he is not supposed to take another step.

If your puppy should sit at any time when he is being trained to stand, you should lift him up on his four feet by placing your forearm under his tummy. Never lift him by his fur, his skin or his tail. During the time that your puppy is learning this exercise, he should also be taught to get up and stand on the verbal command "Stand." This will take considerable repetition, but your puppy will learn the verbal command if you make him stand each time you command him to do so. Eventually your puppy will stand when you give him the stay signal and you will be able to practice the exercise both on- and off-leash.

As soon as your puppy is heeling nicely, you should try changes of pace in your heeling routine. Try going very slowly and then suddenly change to a brisk pace, which is a normal pace. Keep your puppy by your side by talking to him and patting the front of your left leg with your hand. Later try a fast

The finish. Hold the leash taut in your left hand about a foot from your dog's collar.

When you say, "Joll, heel," jerk him back past your left side, as you step back with your left foot.

He should turn in toward you, and, as he does, bring your left foot back in line with your right. The leash should be slack at this point.

Tap your dog to make him sit.

He sits.

Immediately pet and praise your dog.

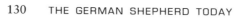

The advanced way to hold the leash.   Heeling with a loose leash.

Keep plenty of slack in the leash when your puppy is coming to your hands.

The author, Winifred Gibson Strickland, with her internationally famous German Shepherds, whom she trained and handled: Margelen's Chieftain, UDT (Topper) on the right, and Hussan v. Haus Kilmark, UDT, on the left.

Topper was the National Obedience Champion of the United States in 1950, 1951 and 1952. He also won Highest Combined and Highest Single Score in Show at the GSDCA National Specialty Shows in 1951 and 1952 with First Place Scores of 195, 200, 198 and 199$^{1}/_{2}$. Topper's sire was the 1941 and 1944 GV Ch. Nox of Ruthland, his dam was Ch. Diedre of Longworth (from famous "D" six-Champion litter).

Hussan was the National Obedience Champion of the United States in 1953, and a close runner-up in 1952 and 1954. He won fifteen perfect scores in two years. He also won Highest Combined Score at the GSDCA National Specialty Show in 1954 with two First Places of 197$^{1}/_{2}$ and 200. He earned Highest Single Score in Show at this trial and also the 1953 Show. Hussan, when shown in Breed before he retired, earned 11 points and two Majors of 4 points each. He was a grandson of two great German dogs who were each VA Select for four consecutive years, Claus v. Haus Werle and Carlo v. Haunstetten.

In conjunction with the above awards, the Verein für Deutsche Schaferhunde (SV) honored the author with a special citation extolling her "excellence in dog training." She was also presented with a gold medal, an honorary membership in the SV and a year's subscription to the SV magazine which included a special article about her.

pace, which is running, then change back to the normal pace. Regardless of the pace you are going, your puppy should be taught to heel with precision; this means he should keep his shoulder even with your left leg. This can only be accomplished by practicing with him and it is quite possible that it will take several months to perfect his heeling.

Teach your puppy to do the figure-eight exercise around two posts. The posts could be two people, two dogs, trees, chairs or whatever is available. The idea is to teach your puppy to heel with precision without lagging, forging or bumping into you. You should make a game of this exercise so that your puppy will enjoy it.

As the weeks and months go by, you should teach your puppy to heel on a very slack leash and gradually control your puppy with just your voice. At this point, you should remove the leash and practice working without it.

Winifred Gibson Strickland with her German Shepherd, Alf v. Kroppelberg, UDT (Arry), whom she trained and handled. They are being presented with a Special Dog World Award at the prestigious Westchester Kennel Club Show as President Len Carey looks on. Gustave Schindler, at right, imported Arry from Germany.

Arry, in just one year, 1954, earned his UDT in twenty-three weeks, with an average of 199 points, and passed Tracking twice—the finest record made in Obedience history; earned seven perfect scores of 200 points each; and was named the National Obedience Champion of the United States. Also shown in Breed by Winifred, he won a Major and other points. In Germany Arry was rated V (Excellent) in Conformation.

Wynthea's Roger, UD
Sire: Ch. Wynthea's Bruce, II, UD
Dam: Wynthea's Little Sister
Breeder-Owner: Winifred Gibson Strickland
Judge: Philip Warner
Roger earned his CD, CDX and UD in nine months.
He won twenty-two First Place Awards.

If you have trained your puppy correctly, the removal of the leash will have no effect on your puppy's work. He will enjoy walking and be happy to stay by your side.

There is no reason why you shouldn't expect your puppy to work with as much precision as an older dog will. It is up to you to insist upon perfection. A puppy can learn to sit straight if he is reminded often enough. The puppy should not be punished for sitting crooked, but he should be shown and guided into a straight sit with the admonition "Sit straight." After several weeks he will sit straight upon hearing the verbal command.

You should practice recalls on-leash until your puppy is coming in and sitting straight in front of you consistently. Next, let your puppy practice the recalls dragging his leash. If you leave your leash by your puppy's side or down his back, he will not trip over it. Remember, it is extremely important to praise your dog when he responds to your call. If your puppy runs away, go after him, get the leash, run backward to the place where you were originally standing and as you do so jerk your puppy two or three times and each time say, "Come." This simple correction will teach your puppy not to run away.

As soon as you can trust your puppy, you should do long recalls, about fifty feet. The last step is to practice recalls off-leash. If you have worked up to this point gradually, you will have no trouble at all. The difficulty arises when a handler takes his puppy off-leash before he is ready. If this happens, you will have to put him back on-leash and start all over again.

You should not allow your puppy to go past you when you call him. If he attempts this, you should say, "No, come," and either give him a small jerk to the front or clap your hands to entice your puppy to come to you. Your puppy should be taught that "Come" means to take a position directly in front of you and nowhere else. If this point is made clear from the beginning, your puppy will form a good habit of sitting straight in front of you. As with everything else in training dogs, it is up to the handler to teach his dog good working habits.

chapter 12

Teaching Your Puppy to Retrieve

When your puppy is three or four months old, you can teach him to retrieve a ball or a toy by rolling it about twenty feet away from you, telling him to "Get the ball" and coaxing him to bring it back to you. If you make exaggerated gestures before you throw it, you will arouse his curiosity and it will be a natural impulse for him to run after it. By clapping your hands and calling your puppy by name, you should be able to coax him to bring the ball back to you. He should be petted and praised when he does so. If you play with him in this manner, he will soon learn to retrieve his toys. However, this is no guarantee that he will retrieve a dumbbell on command.

When your puppy is five or six months of age, you can teach him to retrieve a dumbbell. The first step is to teach him to grasp the dumbbell and hold it. You should have your puppy on-leash, and as you hold it in your left hand to restrain your puppy from moving, you should hold the dumbbell by the end and place it in front of your puppy's nose with your right hand. As you command your puppy to "Get the dumbbell," press the dumbbell against his mouth and with your left hand, slip the puppy's mouth open by placing your two fingers in behind the puppy's canine teeth. Then order your puppy to "Hold it," while you stroke him on the nose and under the chin. After a second remove the dumbbell and praise your puppy in a very pleased tone of voice.

I have found that after a few attempts a puppy will open his mouth and take the dumbbell. Since puppies seem more eager to hold onto the dumbbell than do older dogs, it is an easy step to run backward once the puppy has taken the dumbbell and call him. As your puppy runs to you with the dumbbell, you should praise and guide him into a straight sit in front of you while you say, "Hold it," and, after a second, "Out," and then you take the dumbbell.

You should work on this exercise for a week or until your puppy is doing it well. The next step is to throw the dumbbell six feet away and run up to it with your puppy, encouraging him to "Get the dumbbell." You should hold up one end of the dumbbell or wriggle it back and forth to arouse your puppy's interest and entice him to pick it up. If this is done gradually, your puppy will be quite willing to get it. If he should get stubborn about picking it up, you should hold his head down near the dumbbell and make him take it by holding one end of the dumbbell off the ground and wiggling it. By making it easy when he gets stubborn, he will soon be willing to pick it up every time. You should make your puppy get it every time he is told, even though you may have to give him a little help. This should not be practiced very long; nothing is gained by forcing a puppy to work when he is tired. I have found that ten minutes is long enough. A puppy can be taught to retrieve willingly in three weeks or less, so there is no need to make the lessons tedious.

The last part of the exercise is done in the following sequence, and, as your puppy responds, he should progress from one step to the next. With your puppy still on-leash, throw the dumbbell about ten feet from you. Give your puppy the command, "Get the dumbbell," and run up to the dumbbell with him. Immediately as he starts to pick it up, back up quickly, stand and let your puppy come to you while saying, "Good boy, come," in a pleasant tone of voice. Guide him into a straight sit and pet him, then take the dumbbell and pet him again. When he is doing this quite well, repeat the whole procedure, but just take a few steps forward toward the

Wynthea's Shiela, an eight-week-old puppy, retrieving dumbbell.

Teaching a puppy to retrieve on a loose leash.

dumbbell and let him go the remainder of the distance alone, dragging the leash. Gradually decrease the number of steps you take toward the dumbbell until you are just taking one big step toward it. You may have to run half-way to the dumbbell with him occasionally, but he will gradually begin to go out by himself. When the day comes when you feel he should go out by himself, don't take that one step toward the dumbbell when you command him to "Get the dumbbell," but grasp the leash and jerk him toward it if he just sits there. If your puppy is heavy, you may have to take a small step forward as you jerk him in order to maintain your balance. Once he realizes that he has to go out after the dumbbell or be jerked, he will run out after it. Let him drag the leash when he runs out to the dumbbell, retrieves it and brings it back. Keep the leash on him until you feel that you can trust him to stay with you. You will accomplish nothing, and in fact encourage him to be disobedi-ent, if you take the leash off too soon and permit him to run away with the dumbbell once he has picked it up. I'm sure it will seem very cute to you at the time, but once you let your puppy get away with such mischievous acts, he will get out of hand. Puppies are quick to take advantage of a situation, and they enjoy the excitement associated with disobedience. It is a grave mistake to train a puppy in such a way in which you foster disobedience. When your puppy is consistently retrieving the dumbbell each time that you throw

Falco v.d. Schanzlache, UD, and his owner-trainer Winifred Gibson Strickland checking out a good book. At eighteen months of age, Falco, a grandson of Double Sieger Uran v. Wildsteiger Land, SchH3, FH, earned his CD, CDX and UD within five months with a 195 point average.

it, you may take him off-leash. Be sure to praise him when he picks it up so that he will be anxious to bring it back to you.

Over the years, retrieving has been considered a difficult exercise to teach a dog. However, this is only true in those areas where intelligent instruction was not available. Instructors were using ineffective and often cruel methods to teach a dog to retrieve, and as a result of this the dogs were poorly trained, if at all.

The training method I have conceived is very simple and direct. It is the fastest yet most humane way to obedience-train a dog, and anyone using it should be able to get all three AKC Obedience titles in less than one year. I have trained several dogs with this method who got their CDs, CDXs and UDs in six months with scores of 197 points or higher.

If you are interested in further obedience training, you will enjoy my book *Expert Obedience Training for Dogs*. This book is very complete and covers my method of training from the beginner's first lesson through the most advanced training work, including Tracking. All the exercises are fully illustrated as well as explained in great detail.

chapter 13

The Obedience Training Class: Tracking and Agility

Once you have given your puppy some early obedience training, you may want to take him to an Obedience class where he will get more exposure. The classes offer you the opportunity to work your dog with other dogs in a group. It is good experience for him to work alongside the other dogs if he is taught to watch his handler and pay little or no attention to the dogs and people around him. Some dogs may be timid with strange dogs, or people working around them, and class work is especially good for them. The long sit, long down and group-examination exercises can be practiced as a group exercise, and show conditions can be simulated to make the routines more realistic. Any routine that prepares a dog for show competition is worthwhile.

Obedience classes can be very interesting, challenging and gratifying if the instructor is qualified to teach. If the handlers are congenial, you become as interested in the progress of their dogs as you do your own. When the Obedience Trials are attended by several members of the same training school, it is exciting to watch the dogs and their handlers in actual competition. Many times a well-trained dog will react adversely in the ring because he senses his handler's nervousness. Certain class routines will help the handler to overcome these periods of uncertainty and give him confidence and poise. A good class is invaluable in giving the handler and his dog experience that will be very beneficial to both of them.

Please note that I said good class, for there are classes that could do your dog more harm than good. The classes should not have more than twenty students unless there are one or two assistants to help the instructor. A highly qualified instructor can handle forty trainees with an equally able assistant. You don't find many instructors of this caliber, so your best bet is to watch a class in progress before you join it. Notice these things: Does the instructor notice handler errors and point them out to the handler and the whole class? Does he instruct the handlers to pet and praise their dogs whenever they deserve it? Does he insist upon perfection? Does he appear to be thoroughly familiar with the AKC regulations? Is he considerate of the dogs and the handlers? Do the routines have a practical value? Does he keep his class under control at all times? Does he enforce the "No barking, No whining, No fighting" rule? When he demonstrates with a dog, does he use a humane training method that is obviously effective? Does he use a formula of praise, patience, firmness and understanding?

Avoid any classes that encourage the trainees to train their dogs with force. Avoid instructors who recommend the use of throw chains, spike collars, rubber hoses, shock collars, loud intimidating voices, whips or any such

At first each handler holds the stay signal where the puppy can see it.

A class practicing the long down exercise with the leashes on the ground.

devices. Don't condone acts of cruelty such as stringing a dog up in midair, pinching a dog's toes or ears to teach him to retrieve, kicking dogs or any other inhumane treatment. There is no point in letting your dog be ruined when there is an excellent training method readily available.

If Obedience classes are inferior or nonexistent in your area, I suggest that you train your dog with the help of my book, Expert Obedience Training for Dogs, and/or my video tapes. My book will explain everything in great detail and is fully illustrated. My three video tapes cover every level of training. My first video for beginners and novice handlers will show you exactly how to train your new puppy, or an older dog, by communicating with him. One can earn a Companion Dog (CD) title or teach the dog to be well mannered by following the simple, commonsense instructions.

The intermediate video tape will show you how to teach your dog the Open exercises. This demonstrates how to gain more control off-leash in teaching the precision heeling, fast sits, drops, finishes, retrieving, jumping and more, so that your dog can earn a Companion Dog Excellent title. It makes the advanced Obedience work very easy and helps you eliminate costly mistakes. The transition from one level to the next is so smooth that it makes dog training more fun than you can imagine. If you are showing in Breed, this method will enhance your dog's personality.

The Utility video tape will show you how to earn a Utility (UD) title in the shortest possible time. I conceived this training method so that dogs can avoid problems and make rapid progress from one level to the next without wasting time. I have repeatedly proved that it works, by earning 182 Obedience titles with dogs of all ages, American-breds and German imports. Once your dog has mastered the Novice exercises, try showing him in Obedience sanction matches where you can participate in the group exercises.

TRACKING

If you belong to an Obedience class or group, you will find it great fun to teach your dogs to track. Class members should learn how to lay tracks. By helping each other in this way, everyone will benefit from the experience.

German Shepherds love to track, and they are good at it. In fact, I would venture to say they are better at it than any other breed. My dogs and I earned five Tracking titles. During that period I was the first person in America to earn two tracking titles at one trial with two dogs. This was really very elementary and I mention it because it focused my interest on my dogs' natural ability. Several years later I tried all manner of tracking experiments with my German Shepherd, Joll. He was unbelievably good at everything we tried. His real skill surfaced when he combined his uncanny instincts with his scenting ability.

German Shepherds never seem to be too young to track. One puppy that went to live in Florida earned his Tracking title at seven months of age.

Nor are they ever too old. On September 10, 1995, CT Sea Lair's Raggedy Ann, UDTX, an eleven-and-one-half-year-old German Shepherd, was the first dog of all breeds in this country to pass the new AKC Variable Surface Tracking test (VST). She is owned, trained and handled by Darlene Ceretto. By earning all three training titles, Ann was the first German Shepherd Dog to be awarded the Champion Tracker title, CT. This team certainly deserves a great deal of credit for this major accomplishment.

Ann had been tracking on variable surfaces for two years, so just ten days after the AKC Tracking Trial authorization, this talented German Shepherd, piloted by her happy handler, became the first of 139 breeds to win the new titles. I expect that when you read this you will be as proud of this team as I am. This is not just because they were the first in the country to earn this difficult title, but because Ann was eleven and one-half years young, and Darlene had faith in her. Ann's sire is Ch. Hoheneichen's Magnum, ROM. Her dam is Asta of Fran-Jo, by GV Ch. Aspen of Fran-Jo, ROM ex GV Ch. Lor-Locke's Tatta of Fran-Jo.

If you enjoy walking or jogging with your dog, you could make good use of your time by teaching your dog to track. You will both get lots of fresh air and plenty of exercise. And you will love it. If you practice three or four times per week, you will be ready for a Tracking Test in three or four months.

THE REQUIREMENTS FOR A TD TEST ARE AS FOLLOWS:

1. The track shall be at least 440 yards and not more than 500 yards in length.
2. The length of each track leg shall be at least fifty yards.
3. The scent on the track shall be not less than thirty minutes nor more that two hours old.
4. A total of three to five turns shall be used, including both left and right turns.
5. The dog should find the article at the end of the track.

THE REQUIREMENTS FOR A TDX TEST ARE AS FOLLOWS:

1. The track shall be at least 800 yards and not more than 1,000 yards in length.
2. The length of the track legs shall be at least fifty yards.
3. The scent on the track shall not be less than three hours or more than five hours old.

4. A total of five to seven turns, including left and right turns, shall be used.

5. At least three turns shall be right turns.

6. No part of the track may be within fifty yards of any other part of the same track.

7. No part of the track shall be within seventy-five yards of any other track.

8. There will be two cross tracks.

9. There shall be at least two obstacles. An obstacle being a fence, stream, bridge or lightly traveled road.

10. Four articles will be used that are about the same size as a glove. One at the beginning, one at the end and two some distance apart in between.

THE REQUIREMENTS FOR A VST TEST ARE AS FOLLOWS:

1. The track shall be at least 600 yards and not more than 800 yards in length.

2. The track shall have a minimum of three different surfaces, such as vegetation, concrete, asphalt, gravel, sand, hard pan or mulch.

3. The length of each leg shall be at least thirty yards.

4. The track shall be plotted using different surfaces and scenting conditions as afforded by the terrain.

5. The scent on the track shall be not less than three hours or more than five hours old.

6. Turns shall be on various surfaces as dictated by the terrain, with at least four and not more than eight turns on the track, including both left and right turns.

7. No part of the track shall be within fifty yards of any other track.

8. Tracks may be laid along the sides of buildings and fences, and through buildings with two or more openings or open-sided, such as breezeways, shelters or roofed parking garages.

9. There shall be four articles. The first at the start, the next two at wide intervals directly on the track, the last at the end of the track.

The dog who earns all three Tracking titles shall be called a Champion Tracker (CT).

If you are seriously interested in tracking, send to the American Kennel Club for the very helpful booklet *AKC Tracking Regulations,* which is sent free on request for individual copies.

Darlene Ceretto working a Variable Surface track with her German Shepherd, CT Sea Lair's Raggedy Ann, UDTX, VST.

Ann holds the last article she found at the finish of her Variable Surface track. Ann was the first dog of all breeds to pass this test.

Ch. Hoheneichen's Baretta Avalon, CD, TC, TD
Owner: Jan July.
Photos courtesy Jan July.

AGILITY

Agility Trials will appeal to dog owners who find Obedience competition calls for too much precision and control. Since all dogs enjoy racing around and jumping, handlers will find it is easy to encourage their dogs to try these jumps. Back in the 1960s when I conceived a set of exercises that included Agility jumping, the spectators, as well as the handlers, loved every minute of it.

There are several Agility classes in which dogs can perform. To furnish an idea what it is like, I will just discuss the Novice class. This class will include the following:

1. The **A**-frame measures approximately five feet, six inches at the apex. The boards are about nine feet long and about four feet wide. It is a nonslip surface that is slatted every twelve inches.

2. The dog walk consists of three boards twelve inches wide by eight feet long. The center board is thirty-six inches above the ground. The entrance and exit ramps have nonslip surfaces and are slatted every twelve inches.

3. The seesaw measures approximately twelve inches wide and eight feet long, and is mounted on a fulcrum about twenty-two inches high. It must have a nonslip surface.

Falco loves to climb the barrier jump, stand there and use it as a vantage point to watch Wynn train her other dogs.

4. The pause table is three feet square and twenty-four inches high. This is a five-second pause exercise.

5. The open tunnel measures approximately twenty-four inches in diameter and is ten feet long. It is set in a curve or at an angle so that the dog cannot see the end of the tunnel from the entrance.

6. The closed tunnel entrance is approximately twenty-four inches in diameter. The tunnel should be rigidly supported for about three feet and measures approximately twelve feet overall. It is constructed of dark material, such as nylon rip-stop that the dog cannot see through. The exit is flared and approximately ninety-six inches in circumference. The tunnel may be lightly fastened or weighted to the ground.

7. The solid jump is four feet wide and twenty-four inches high.

8. The bar jump is four feet wide and twenty-four inches high.

9. The tire or window jump is twenty-four inches high. The inside measurements of the window jump are twenty-four by twenty-four inches.

10. The standard AKC broad jump may be used. The four boards set to forty-eight inches.

11. The double oxer jump is two bar jumps set twelve inches apart and twenty-four inches high.

12. The double bar jump contains a series of three ascending bars in a 45-degree angle. It is twenty-four inches high with bar heights of twelve inches, eighteen inches and twenty-four inches The bars are twelve inches apart.

chapter 14

Conformation Training for Puppies and Young Dogs

Conformation training for puppies should start when the puppies are about ten weeks old. The first thing to consider is the correct type of collar. You should never use a narrow collar on a young puppy as it will cut into his tender, little neck. I believe that chain choke collars are too heavy for young puppies. If you put one of these on a small puppy, he will lower his head, then run and hide under the nearest piece of furniture. If you want him to wear a chain choke collar, he should only wear it for five to ten minutes at a time until he gets used to it. A heavy collar on a young puppy is depressing to him. The wide, round nylon collar is best for a puppy because it is so light-weight that he won't mind wearing it. He may scratch his neck a few times because it feels a little strange to him, but he'll get used to wearing it very quickly. A soft, well-oiled, leather buckle collar that is five-eighths of an inch wide is fairly comfortable for a puppy to wear all the time, even when he is learning to gait. The collar should fit low on his neck and he can pull against it like a little harness.

When a puppy is wearing a choke collar, don't leave him for any length of time as he might catch it on something in your absence and hang himself. He might even get his leg caught in it if he were to scratch himself.

When we have a litter or two of very promising, show-quality puppies, we start their conformation training when they are nine weeks old. I prefer to start their training on a Simplicity show lead that is made of grosgrain ribbon, five-eighths of an inch wide. One end of the lead is a loop that you slip over the puppy's head to form a collar, and the size is controlled by an adjustable clip that permits you to tighten or enlarge the collar simply by pressing on it. The puppy will not be choked by this type of collar, and it is short enough so that you can drop it occasionally and let the puppy drag it. These leads are so lightweight that the puppies never object to them, and I have found that it is the easiest way to get a puppy used to wearing a collar.

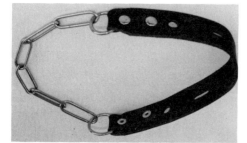

This is the ideal collar to teach your puppy or dog to pull out for conformation training. It fits low on his neck and encourages him to pull against it. Start using it for this purpose when he is three months old.

Keep the collar low on the puppy's neck so she will not form a "goose neck." Wynthea's Nancy.

When Joan and I take five or six puppies out to train them, we put the Simplicity show leads on four of them and let the puppies pull us to our orchard which is one-quarter of a mile away. The first time a puppy is on-leash he may balk and sit down, so we drop the leash and let the puppy drag it. He is eager to follow his friends and therefore will hurry to keep up with us. A puppy will often grab another puppy's leash and walk along holding it in his mouth. This gets the puppies used to countless little tugs which they ignore. When we arrive at the orchard, the puppies want to run around and play under the shady trees so we let them drag their leashes. This helps them get used to something dragging in back of them, and often a puppy will step on his own leash, or that of another puppy, and it is excellent training for them to get used to these tugs. A puppy shouldn't become discouraged or sensitive if he feels his leash being tugged or tightened, or if another puppy steps on it and he is jerked to a stop. When he sees that it is another puppy near him, he will forget the incident immediately and continue on his way. We switch the leads on the puppies so that each one will receive this training while he is out with us. We keep toys in the orchard and let the puppies play with them there

The author giving Wynthea's Heather a gaiting lesson.

so that they will remember this pleasant experience when they are put on-leash. They get a snack to eat on their return to their own paddocks, and after a week the puppies are very eager to pull on-leash, and they learn very quickly that food will be waiting for them. One can observe the conformation, temperament and intelligence of the individual puppies when they are trained every day. After puppies have had the lead-training for about two weeks, we then try it out on the sidewalks in town. We find that the puppies are quite willing to pull out ahead, particularly if another puppy is leading, so we take turns letting each puppy be in front. It doesn't take them long to learn that they can pull as hard as they want, and they soon take advantage of it.

If you use a choke collar on your puppy that is too large, tie a knot in it near the dead ring so that the collar will not be able to choke the puppy. A choke collar that tightens when the puppy starts to pull could easily frighten him. We use a nylon choke collar on a puppy when he is over four months of age, but always clip the leash to the dead ring. You will need several different-sized collars as your puppy will grow out of them very quickly. To determine the correct size for your puppy, pull the collar snug on his neck and measure the collar you have left over. It should be three inches.

If you just have one puppy, enlist the help of someone in your family to train the puppy to pull on leash. Have him walk briskly ahead of you, calling to the puppy, so that the puppy will want to pull to catch up with this person. Every once in awhile this person should stop and pet the puppy and/or give it a food tidbit. This will make the puppy eager to pull at the end of the leash and he will get used to you walking behind him. Eventually, the puppy will be willing to go out to the end of the leash and pull, even when you take him out alone.

In the beginning, if there is no one around to help you, just put the puppy on-leash and follow him wherever he goes. Let him get used to the leash being taut, and after a week or two he will be willing to go wherever you choose to guide him. Don't make the training sessions too long or the puppy will get overtired and take a dislike to the leash.

The first few times you introduce a puppy to a leash, you should make it a short, happy occasion. If he balks or sits down, coax him to follow you by using a pleasant tone of voice, tap your leg to show him where you want him and reach down and pet him. Keep talking and encouraging the puppy as you are walking. If you start training him early, you will find it easier to control him when he is mature.

After a few weeks, when your puppy is used to pulling, you can practice posing him. As the puppy becomes accustomed to pulling on-lead, be certain that you always let the puppy precede you. If he should slow down, adopt a pace that is slower than his so that you will still be following him. When he stops, be sure the leash is very loose; there should just be pressure on his collar when he is moving out.

The Germans teach their puppies and dogs to pull out, like this. Rings are set up on clubhouse grounds and the club members practice frequently. The puppies get in the habit of pulling out while they are young, and learn to gait next to the rope and take corners automatically. With this system used at shows, the judge can see each dog clearly, and handlers learn to stay in line. Spectators get the opportunity to study each entry.

When the handlers want to practice posing their dogs, they step into the ring. The rope is ten inches from the ground.

Many puppies will carry their heads lower than their withers. If you try to raise the puppy's head with the leash, the puppy will fight it and end up carrying his head even lower. Get your puppy interested in playing with a toy or a stick, then let him carry it while he is moving on-leash. This will get him to carry his head higher, and, once he forgets he is on-leash, he will acquire the habit of doing so. Another way to get him to lift his head is to feed him small bits of meat while he is walking on-leash beside you. Another method is to bounce a ball directly in front of your puppy and he will lift his head to watch it rolling ahead of him.

The next step is to teach your puppy to stand for examination in a show pose. We do this by alternately walking the puppy into a show stance one time, then posing the puppy by hand the next. It should be a fleeting stance the first few times, as the puppy may be very stubborn about it. Just praise, pet and encourage him with your voice so that he thinks it is a game. At first, examine his teeth and bite while he is sitting, then try it while he is standing. Remember that he will be cutting his second teeth and his gums may be tender and swollen. If you do not hurt him, he will not object. While handling a male puppy, examine his testicles as this will be done at every show. After a few weeks of training, you will find that your puppy can be walked into a show stance by gently placing one hand under his chin and pulling him forward until his left hind leg is stretched back in the show stance. When his front feet are directly in line under him, give him the command, "Stand, stay," and lift his head. This will make him stay where you want to pose. Get the puppy used to being handled; this means that you will place his legs in the position of a show stance and run your hands over his body as if a judge were examining him. You will have to be very patient with your puppy at this time. Don't expect him to learn this quickly, and don't expect him to be as well trained as an adult dog. Always remember that he is just a puppy. If you lose your patience and speak harshly to him, he will lose the sparkle that makes a happy show dog.

Another way to teach a puppy to stand for examination is to bait him with food, such as cooked liver. Have your puppy standing in front of you when you give him a tidbit. Don't give him anything when he is sitting, or jumping up on you, and don't let him pick anything up off the ground. You don't want him to pick up food in a show that some other handler has dropped. When the puppy gets used to taking it from you when he is standing, you can start training him to bait for it. This means that you will offer the puppy the meat as you move back slowly, and when the puppy is in the show stance you want, lift the bait up high and command him to "Stand, stay." Make him hold this pose for a few seconds before you give him the meat. The more you practice with your puppy, the longer he should be taught to hold the pose.

In order for a German Shepherd puppy to develop his full potential, he should be socialized. You must take him out into the world and let him meet strangers, visit new places, and hear, see and smell the sights and sounds outside his own home. If you keep your puppy in your kennel, you should let

Hand-setting puppy's hind leg.

Kolbrook's Allez France at three months.

Select Ch. Kolbrook's Allez France, ROM, at 22 months. Breeder-owner, Ann Brogden.

him visit in your home frequently so that he can become familiar with everything that goes on. A puppy with a good temperament will act timid until he has had some worldly experiences. The puppy who is very friendly but who has never been away from home, will seem backward (green) when shown the first couple of times. This is not shyness but a natural tendency to be cautious in a new environment. Judges should be more friendly and tolerant when examining puppies. Kennel dogs who never go anywhere except to shows have very poor personalities. They never get the chance to develop their characters and personalities. If you have a good puppy, get him out into the world; you can warp his personality by neglecting him. However, a dog with an inherited temperament problem will always be basically unsound, no matter how much time you spend working with him. German Shepherds should be a part of family life, so let them share yours.

Sanction Matches are very good places to start your puppy's show career. Don't worry about winning, but concentrate on teaching your puppy how to gait and pose. It should be an exciting, enjoyable experience for him, so don't act nervous and convey your feelings to him. Be relaxed and let him be a puppy, talk to him and pet him when you can. If he has a good time in the showring, he may become a natural showman, the type of dog that everyone would like to own. Show him just often enough so that he benefits from the experience. Many people show their puppies so often that the puppies become bored and, later, when they are shown as adult dogs, they have no interest in gaiting or posing.

The show careers of many promising German Shepherd puppies have been ruined by incorrect training or no training at all. If your puppy's early experiences in conformation training and showing are fun for him, he will become

Ch. Wynthea's Julie, CDX at eleven months of age
Sire: Ch. Dot-Wall's Vance, ROM, CD
Dam: Bess of Wynthea, ROM
Breeder-Owner: Winifred Gibson Strickland

Ch. Brentaryl's Nevada Woodside, ROM, at seven months of age with owner, Carlyn Rose.

a well-adjusted, well-trained dog, alert, full of fire and eager to move. The judge you show him under will have but a short time to evaluate your dog's structure while posed or in motion, so he must be shown at his best in order to be appreciated. A dog's attitude and willingness to move may be the deciding factor between first and second place. Perhaps, some day, the judges will place more emphasis on correct structure and coordinated movement rather than how fast a dog will move. In the meantime, be prepared by training your puppies at an early age to be alert, willing and happy movers. The top-quality puppy who shows with fire and animation will become the dog who will be hard to beat.

During the Courage Test, Ulk von Arlett lets go of the sleeve, backs into a sit and guards the helper upon hearing his handler yell, "Aus". Ulk had taken a full bite.

Tens of thousands of spectators from all over the world watch the judging at the Sieger Show each year.

chapter 15

The Sieger Show

Anyone seriously interested in German Shepherds owes it to himself to attend at least one Sieger Show. There is nothing comparable to it in the Shepherd world and you have to attend it in person in order to appreciate the difference between this and all other dog shows.

Over the years the German Sieger Show has been held in at least fifteen large cities in Germany. Mannheim, Frankfurt, Bremen, Karlsruhe, Munich and Hamburg have hosted the show more often than the other cities. Each year the show is held in a large soccer stadium that has additional fields within the compound large enough to accommodate tens of thousands of people. Parking is outside of the stadium grounds.

In 1995 the Sieger Show in Hamburg drew 2,051 class entries. The Progeny Groups (*Nachkommengruppen*) were well represented by 1,330 dogs and bitches. In addition to all this, there were forty-nine Kennel Groups competing.

Competition becomes keener each year in the Progeny Groups. In the 1995 Sieger Show, there were forty-seven Progeny Groups ranging in size from twelve progeny of a lesser-known stud, to ninety-one progeny for the 1995 Sieger Ulk von Arlett, SchH3. The judging of the Progeny Groups shows which of the often-used stud dogs has produced good or not so good progeny. It also shows which good points and bad points have been inherited by their offspring and what to look for in future matings of these dogs. A family member leads his Group and carries a large placard that gives the stud's name. Although most of the stud dogs precede their Groups, it is not necessary in this class that they be shown. They have been shown at previous shows and the public knows them. But now is the time to see if the confidence shown in them has proved to be right, and breeders can learn if they have helped to improve the breed.

This is a three-day show, and in Germany the dogs are judged in three main classes only. The dogs and bitches are judged separately and do not compete against each other as they do in the United States. The young dogs do not compete against the adult dogs, so they have a Junghundklasse for young dogs and bitches which is divided by sex and is limited to Shepherds eighteen to twenty-four months of age. The Youth Sieger and Youth Siegerin will be chosen from these classes and will reign for one year until the next Sieger Show. There are also classes for more youthful Shepherds called the Jungendklassen, for dogs and bitches between the ages of twelve and eighteen months. The highest rating awarded in any of the youth classes is Sehr Gut (SG), meaning "very good." Another class is the Sonderklasse Herdengebrauchshund for dogs and bitches who are actively engaged in herding sheep. An HGH Sieger and Siegerin title is awarded in this class.

While several of these classes are being judged in various fields, the Courage Tests for the Adult Dogs are being held in a large fenced area the size of a football field. Half this field is for the dogs and the other half is for the bitches. The handler, who has his dog on-leash, walks onto the top part of the field and stops. At a nod from the judge, the handler removes the leash and orders his dog to heel. As they approach a blind, the helper (a tall, muscular assistant wearing leather overalls and a tough, padded sleeve) suddenly jumps out, gesticulating wildly. The dog at this instant attacks the helper, bites his padded sleeve (with a full bite) and hangs on until his handler commands him to let go ("Aus"). The handler then holds his dog, who is more than eager to continue this game, while the helper jogs about 200 feet across the field, turns and runs toward the dog, who is released at this moment. The helper yells and waves his stick in an attempt to intimidate him. The courageous dog races toward the helper, propels himself at the sleeve when he is within six feet, bites the sleeve with great vigor and enthusiasm and hangs on to it until his handler yells, "Aus," at the top of his voice. The fact that the dog is hit with the stick a time or two doesn't deter him in the least. When he lets go of the sleeve, he sits and barks, staring at the helper until his handler runs up, puts him on-leash, gives him a well-earned pat and praises him. Then, as they walk off the field together, the handler smiles approvingly while his Shepherd prances happily by his side, looking back at the helper several times with a pleased, "I showed him" expression. The bitches are particularly expressive in this regard and are great fun to watch. Once the dogs have been tested for their courage, they can go back and rejoin their class.

The crowd, which numbers in the thousands, loves these tests, and applauds and cheers with great gusto when the dogs are courageous. However, they are just as quick to groan if a dog hesitates or shows any sign of timidity. The latter is seldom seen. Courage is an important facet of a German Shepherd's character. A dog must be highly courageous and of sound character to protect his handler from a sudden unexpected assault, then leave his side to pursue and attack a helper who is a great distance from him. This test is much more difficult in the presence of thousands of spectators where the atmosphere is charged with excitement and the surroundings are strange to the dog.

In 1995 dogs with pronounced fighting spirit couldn't get the VA rating unless they would release. Dogs with distinct courage and fighting spirit who did not release could be awarded the vorzüglich (excellent) rating and would be positioned at the end of the V Group. Dogs with fighting spirit present can no longer get the V. Dogs that get the grade nicht genugend (not enough courage) will be put at the end of the "SG" Group as a unit.

In January 1996 the Courage Test was changed. Now the handler must have more control of his dog. During the initial test, the helper will step out of the blind and threaten the handler. The dog must immediately attack the helper on his own or on one verbal command. He must take a full bite on the sleeve and at a signal from the judge the handler will call "Aus." The dog must sit and guard until the handler goes up and releases him.

Now the handler and his free-heeling dog will go to a center point indicated by the judge. The handler may hold his dog by the collar but the dog must sit calmly by his side. The dog is to remain in this position until given the command to attack. If the dog appears restless, points will be deducted from his score. The handler must not stimulate the dog. The second helper leaves a hiding place about seventy-five paces from the handler and crosses the field in a normal manner. The handler orders the helper to "Stand still." The helper ignores the order and makes a frontal attack on the handler. The judge immediately signals the handler to release the dog to stop the attack, and the handler sends his dog with one command. The dog must show an energetic, firm, full, secure and calm grip. When the dog has a grip, the helper will briefly press the dog and than cease the aggression on a signal from the judge. The dog will not be hit with the stick. The dog should release independently, or upon one command from the handler, then guard the helper. The handler will then walk to the dog at a normal pace, tell the dog to sit, then leave the field with the dog heeling free by his side. In training dogs it is considerably more difficult to obtain this kind of calm control, but you can be sure that the German trainers who are the best in the world will find a way to do it.

Out in the fields, a small tent has been erected in each ring with tables and chairs for the judge and his assistants. In case of rain, each secretary will have a sheltered area to take notes and compile the data that the judge gives him after examining each dog. This efficiency in handling the paperwork provides the judges with an accurate record of each dog which they refer to when making their classifications. At the end of the show, this enables the SV to distribute a list of all the class winners, as well as the numerical ratings and classifications of all the dogs shown.

The classes at the Sieger Show in 1995 were very large. The judges evaluated each dog posed, the dogs' teeth were examined and counted, the males' testicles were checked and the anatomy of the dogs was studied. The judge watched each one gait. Then he would take about forty dogs at a time to compare them. Next he would watch five as they were coming and going. Each group of dogs was tested for gun steadiness. This judging, evaluating and grading went on for two full days and into a third.

It is interesting to take a few minutes away from the show and visit the many fascinating shops and stands on the show grounds. There you will find all kinds of items related to German Shepherds that you will not see anywhere else. Postcards, calendars, jewelry, clothing, dishes, bric-a-brac and other collectibles are all offered for sale. Top quality Schutzhund equipment is available, as well as trailers for transporting dogs, dog foods of all kinds and some of the best leather leashes made in Germany.

While the judging of the various classes was in progress outside in the fields, the spectators were standing six or seven deep around the rings, cheering for their favorite dogs, double handling or taking pictures. The classes were so large that the judging went on all day. Friends or families of the dogs would race around the ring outside the rows of spectators, calling their dogs' names and waving. If they yelled loud enough, the dogs would hear them and this proved to be enough of an inducement to keep them trotting.

Eventually the judges finished their classes and the presentation ceremony for the top groups of Young Dogs and Youth classes was made inside the

1995 Sieger Ulk von Arlett, SchH3
Sire: VA5 Yago vom Wildsteiger Land, SchH3, FH
Dam: V-Dolly von Arlett, SchH2
Breeder: Margit van Dorssen
Owner: Mathijs van Dorssen

stadium. The records that are compiled for the Adult Dogs during the course of the preliminary judging will determine the dog's order of entry into the ring on Sunday afternoon. Then the dogs will enter the stadium in the order in which they were classified.

It is the custom for the president of the Verein für Deutsche Schaferhunde (SV) to judge the *Gebrauchshundklasse Rüden* (Utility Dog class), and the vice president to judge the *Gebrauchshundklasse Hündinnen* (Utility Bitch class). Peter Messler, who became president of the SV in 1995, judged the dogs.

Once the judge has studied the anatomy, construction and character of the dogs, the judging begins. The functioning of the bones and the muscles, the firmness of the ligaments and the joints, rhythm of movement, the strength and the perseverance as well as the liveliness are now carefully tested and are of very great importance to the judge. All of the dogs present are subjected to a hard physical and psychological test. For more than two hours, the dogs are studied and classified down to the last entry. There is no doubt in your mind that it is the dogs who are being judged and not the handlers.

In 1995 there were 376 dogs competing in the Gebrauchshundklasse Rüden. There were 288 bitches competing in the Gebrauchshundklasse Hündinnen. As the preselected groups filed into the stadium, there ensued a long period of gaiting, posing, tests for coming and going and gun steadiness tests. At about this time, the judge examined the pedigree papers of the VA dogs he had selected, to be sure that each one had the "a" stamp and that the

The Progeny Groups were judged in the stadium.

VA5 1991 Yago vom Wildsteiger Land, SchH3, FH
Sire: 1988 Sieger Eiko vom Kirschental, SchH3, FH
Dam: V-Quina von Arminius, SchH2
Breeder-Owner: Martin Gobl

1988 Sieger Eiko vom Kirschental, SchH3, FH
Sire: 1984, 1985 Sieger Uran vom Wildsteiger Land,
    SchH3, FH
Dam: VA Xitta vom Kirschental, SchH3, FH, IP3
Breeder: Karl Fuller
Owners: Karl Fuller and Martin Gobl

1984, 1985 Sieger Uran vom Wildsteiger Land, SchH3, FH
Sire: V-Irk von Arminius, SchH3, FH, IP3
Dam: V-Palme vom Wildsteiger Land, SchH2 (Dam of Sgr. Quando v. Arminius)
Breeder-Owner: Martin Gobl

V-Palme v. Wildsteiger Land, SchH2
    (Litter sister of 1982 Siegerin Perle v. Wildsteiger Land,
    SchH3)
Sire: V-Nick von der Wienerau, SchH3
Dam: VA-Fina v. Badsee, SchH2
Breeder-Owner: Martin Gobl

The winners appeared on television during the 1995 Weltsieger Show.

number corresponded with the ear tattoo. The final test came when he took five dogs at a time to test them off-leash. In most cases the owner, or the dog's trainer, would come into the stadium to handle the dog. At the judge's direction, the dogs were taken off-leash and commanded to fuss, (heel). The owners would race around the stadium as fast as they could go, with their dogs trotting beside them without breaking their stride. This was an exciting spectacle to watch as the owners tried valiantly to keep up with their dogs. However, with an incredible burst of speed, Ulk von Arlett and his handler left everyone far behind. There was no doubt in anyone's mind, Ulk had earned the Weltsieger (World Champion) title that day.

Shepherd breeder Walter Martin died the night before the 1996 Sieger Show. The next day when people heard this news, they were both shocked and saddened. He was only sixty-three years old. In his lifetime he had bred 363 German Shepherd litters under his kennel name of von der Wienerau. He had a great many VA dogs over the years, which included 1965 Siegerin Landa v. d. Wienerau, SchH2, FH; 1992 Sieger Zamb v. d. Wienerau, SchH3; 1992 and 1994 Siegerin Vanta v. d. Wienerau, SchH3; and 1995 Siegerin Nathalie v. d. Wienerau, SchH3, FH, IP3.

I met Walter in the 1960s at his kennel, where he showed me Quanto v. d. Wienerau. Quanto was an important link in a chain of great producers. Through his descendants he produced seven German Siegers, including Quando von Arminius, Uran v. Wildsteiger Land, Eiko v. Kirschental, Ulk v. Arlett, Jeck vom Noricum, Zamb v. d. Wienerau and Visum von Arminius.

Breeder Hermann Martin died two weeks later, and the world had by then lost two of the most knowledgeable breeders of this century. Like the German Shepherds they produced, their fame was international. The breeders in every country in the world respected their expertise. Throughout their lives they had stressed one fact, "A German Shepherd is a working dog, if it is not a working dog it is not a true German Shepherd."

Once the decisions were made and the winners announced, the Sieger and top VA dogs were presented with their trophies with all the pomp and

In 1996 Jane Steffenhagen's vom Steffen Haus Kennels was the first German Shepherd kennel from the United States to have an entry in the Kennel Group at the Sieger Show. Her beautiful Bravos vom Steffen Haus, SchH3, was the first American-bred dog to present a Progeny Group at the German Sieger Show. He presented thirty-four of his progeny.

In 1995 the *Zuchtgruppen* (Kennel Groups) who gradually filled the stadium were most impressive. Despite the fact that the dogs had been competing for three days, they were full of spirit when they marched onto the field.

ceremony of an Olympic event. The same held true for the Siegerin and the top VA bitches. It is at this point that the photographers rush in to take photos of the new World Sieger, for this is a show that is of great interest all over the world.

When the field was cleared, the Kennel Groups marched onto the field in their colorful outfits. The handlers and their dogs paraded six abreast as one member of each Group, carrying their kennel placard, preceded them. Each Group wore suits of a different color. The handlers had their dogs in heel position and the Groups all marched with precision as they paraded around the stadium several times. It was an absolutely beautiful sight to watch. The SV president, Peter Messler, was the judge of this event, and he studied each of the forty-eight Groups very carefully. This was a very important contest, for many of these kennels raise the finest German Shepherds in the world. They were judged on similarity of type, color, size and overall quality.

In 1995 and 1996 the top two kennels that won these prestigious awards were:

First—Zwinger vom Wildsteiger Land

Second—Zwinger von der Noriswand

In 1997 Zwinger von der Noriswand came back to win first among the Kennel Groups.

It is interesting to note that in 1996 the Wildsteiger Land Kennels won this honor for the eighth time. Herr Martin Gobl, owner of this kennel, has told me that it is as great an honor to win this contest as it is to win the Sieger title. He bred the famous Double Sieger Uran v. Wildsteiger Land, SchH3, FH, who is recognized as having been the top producer in Germany for twenty years. He also co-owned Sieger Eiko vom Kirschental, SchH3, FH. Every year since 1979, when he co-owned VA Fina v. Badsee, SchH2, his kennel has produced top VA dogs and bitches. One of his brood bitches, V-Palme vom Wildsteiger Land, SchH2, produced two Double Siegers, Uran and Quando v. Arminius, SchH3, FH. Her sister was Siegerin Perle vom Wildsteiger Land, SchH3. There is no question that Zwinger vom Wildsteiger Land is one of the top German Shepherd Dog kennels in the world.

GERMAN SIEGERS

Year	Sieger	Sire and Dam
1899	Jörg v. d. Krone	Sparwasser Strain Nelly
1900, 1901	Hektor v. Schwaben	Horand v. Grafrath Mores v. Plieningen

Year	Sieger	Sire and Dam
1902	Peter v. Pritschen	Horand v. Grafrath Lotte v. Klosterfeld
1903	Roland v. Park	Sgr. Hektor v. Schwaben Flora I v. Karlsruhe
1904	Aribert v. Grafrath	Audifax v. Grafrath Sigrun v. Grafrath
1905	Beowulf v. Nahegau	Beowulf Walpurga v. Nahegau
1906, 1907	Roland v. Starkenburg	Heinz v. Starkenburg Bella v. Starkenburg
1908	Luchs v. Kalsmunt Wetzlar	Graf Eberhardt v. Hohen Esp Minka Barbarossa
1909	Hettel Uckermark	Sgr. Roland v. Starkenburg Gretel Uckermark
1910	Tell v. d. Kriminalpolizei	Sgr. Luchs v. Kalsunt Wetlar Herta v. d. Kriminalpolizei
1911, 1912	Norbert v. Kohlwald	Beowulf v. Kohlwald Sgrn. Hella v. Memmingen
1913	Arno v. d. Eichenburg	Sgr. Tell v. d. Kriminalpolizei Diana v. d. Blosenburg
1914–18	No titles awarded	
1919	Dolf v. Düsternbrook	Luchs Uckermark Dorte v. Riedekenburg
1920	Erich v. Grafenwerth	Alex v. Westfalenheim Bianka v. Riedekenburg
1921	Harras v. d. Jüch	Nores v. d. Kriminalpolizei Lora Hildenia
1922, 1923	Cito Bergerslust	Geri v. Oberklamm Goda v. Mundtsdorf
1924	Donar V. Overstolzen	Orpal v. Grünen Eck Blanka v. d. Urftalsperre
1925	Klodo v. Boxberg	Sgr. Erich v. Grafenwerth Elfe v. Boxberg
1926	Erich v. Glockenbrink	Gundo Isentrud Dolli v. Glockenbrink
1927	Arko v. Sadowaberg	Cuno v. Wohwinkel Afra v. Jahnplatz
1928	Erich v. Glockenbrink	Gundo Isentrud Dolli v. Glockenbrink
1929	Utz v. Haus Schutting	Sgr. Klodo v. Boxberg Donna Z. Reurer

GERMAN SIEGERS

Year	Sieger	Sire and Dam
1930, 1931	Herold a. d. Niederlausitz	Otlan v. Blaisenberg Burga v. d. Lämmerherde
1932	Hussan v. Haus Schutting	Sgr. Utz v. Haus Schutting Cora v. d. Sennhutte
1933	Odin v. Stolzenfels	Curt v. Herzog Hedan Bella v. d. Jagdschloss Platte
1934	Cuno v. Georgentor	Bero v. d. Deutschen Werken Afra v. Georgentor
1935	Jalk v. Pagensgrüb	Erich v. Pagensgrüb Gudrun v. Pagensgrüb
1936	Arras a. d. Stadt Velbert	Luchs of Ceara Sgrn. Stella v. Haus Schutting
1937	Pfeffer v. Bern	Dachs v. Bern Clara v. Bern
1938–54	No titles awarded	
1955	Alf v. Nordfelsen, SchH3	Axel v. Deininghauserheide Carin v. Bombergschen Park
1956	Hardt v. Stuveschacht, SchH2	Rolf v. Osnabruckerland Amala v. Stuveschacht
1957	Arno v. Haus Gersie, SchH3	Edo v. Gehrdener Berg Delia v. Walburgitor
1958	Condor v. Hohenstamm, SchH3	Arko v. d. Delog Asta v. d. Jacobsleiter
1959, 1960	Volker v. Zollgrenzschutz-Haus, SchH3	Harry v. Donaukai Perle v. Zollgrenzschutz-Haus
1961	Veus v. d. Starrenburg, SchH3	Alf v. Nordfelsen Ilsa v. d. Starrenburg
1962	Mutz a. d. Kuckstrasse, SchH3	Condor v. Hohenstamm Mori v. Gieser Waldchen
1963	Ajax v. Haus Dexel, SchH3	Bodo v. Tannenbuch Amsel v. Haus List
1964	Zibu v. Haus Schuetting, SchH3	Donar v. d. Firnskruppe Niobe v. Haus Schuetting
1965	Hanko v. Hetschmuhle, SchH3	Witz v. Haus Schuetting Eva v. d. Hetschmuhle
1966	Basko v. d. Kahler Heide, SchH3	Sgr. Zibu v. Haus Schuetting Nixe a. d. Eremitenklause

Year	Sieger	Sire and Dam
1967	Bodo v. Lierberg, SchH3	Vello zu den Sieben Faulen Betty v. Eningsfeld
1968	Dido v. d. Werther Königsallee, SchH2	Zibu v. Haus Schuetting Frigga v. Salzufler Ring
1969, 1970	Heiko v. Oranien Nassau, SchH2	Alf von Convent Cilly von Oranien Nassau
1971	Arras v. Haus Helma, SchH3	Tom v. Haus Solms, SchH2 Dixi v. d. Rokokoperle, SchH1
1972	Marko v. Cellerland, SchH3	Kondor v. Golmkauer Krug, HGH Cilla v. Hünenfeuer, SchH1
1973	Dick v. Adeloga, SchH2	Quanto v. d. Wienerau, SchH2 Asta v. d. Modauquelle, SchH1
1974–77	No Sieger titles awarded, only Excellent Select	
1978	Canto von Arminius, SchH3	Canto von der Wienerau, SchH2 Frigga v. Ecclesia Nova SchH1
1979	Eros von der Malvenburg, SchH3	Lesko Grubenstolz, SchH3 Anke Grubenstolz, SchH2
1980	Axel von der Hainsterbach, SchH3	Lasso di Val Sole, SchH3 Paet Blue Iris, SchH1
1981, 1982	Natan von der Pelztierfarm, SchH3	Quax v. Bubenlachring, SchH3 Frigga v. Bottwarstrand, SchH2
1983	Dingo von Haus Gero, SchH3	Caesar von Arminius, SchH3 Britta von der Malvenburg, SchH2
1984, 1985	Uran von Wildsteiger Land, SchH3	Irk von Arminius, SchH3 Palme vom Wildsteiger Land, SchH3
1986, 1987	Quando von Arminius, SchH3	Xaver von Arminius, SchH3 Palme vom Wildsteiger Land, SchH3
1988	Eiko vom Kirschental, SchH3, FH	Dbl. Sgr. Uran v. Wildsteiger Land, SchH3, FH VA Xitta vom Kirschental, SchH3, IP3, FH, HGH
1989	Iso vom Bergmannshof, SchH3, FH	Dbl. Sgr. Quando von Arminius, SchH3, IP3 Nora vom Bergannshof, SchH1
1990, 1991	Fanto vom Hirschel, SchH3	VA Tell vom Grossen Sand, SchH3 Ica vom Haus Reiterland, SchH2
1992	Zamb von der Wienerau, SchH3	VA Odin v. Tannenmeise, SchH3, FH Ica von der Wienerau, SchH2
1993	Jeck vom Noricum, SchH3, FH	VA Odin v Tannenmeise, SchH3, FH Anett vom Noricum, SchH3

GERMAN SIEGERS

Year	Sieger	Sire and Dam
1994	Kimon v. Dan Alhedy's Hoeve, SchH3	VA Mark vom Haus Beck, SchH3 Candy v. Dan Alhedy's Hoeve, IP1
1995	Ulk von Arlett, SchH3	VA Yago v. Wildsteiger Land, SchH3, FH Dolly von Arlett, SchH2
1996	Visum von Arminius, SchH3, FH	Jeck vom Noricum, SchH3, FH Ratta von Arminius, SchH2
1997	Lasso vom Neuen Berg, SchH3	Folemarkens Jasso, SchH3, IP3, BHP1 Eike vom Neuen Berg, SchH2

GERMAN SIEGERINS

Year	Siegerin	Sire and Dam
1899	Lisie v. Schwenningen	Basko Wachsmuth Schafermadchen v. Hanau
1900	Canna	Parents unknown
1901	Elsa v. Schwaben	Carex Plieningen Fides v. Neckarursprung
1902, 1903	Hella v. Memmingen	Beowulf Nelly Eislingen
1904	Regina v. Schwaben	Beowulf Sgrn. Elsa v. Schwaben
1905	Vefi v. Niedersachsen	Beowulf Nelly v. Eislingen
1906	Gretel Uckermark	Beowulf Hexe v. Hohen Esp
1907	Hulda v. Siegestor	Sgr. Roland v. Starkenburg Adelheid v. Siegestor
1908	Flora v. d. Warthe	Sgr. Roland v. Starkenburg Julie v. Brenztal
1909	Ella v. Erlenbrunnen	Dewett Barbarossa Sgrn. Hella v. Memmingen
1910	Flora v. d. Kriminalpolizei	Sgr. Luchs v. Kalsmunt Wetzlar Herta v. d. Kriminalpolizei
1911, 1912	Hella v. d. Kriminalpolizei	Sgr. Tell v. d. Kriminalpolizei Fanny v. d. Kriminalpolizei

Year	Siegerin	Sire and Dam
1913	Frigga v. Scharenstetten	Horst v. Boll Adelheid v. Scharenstetten
1914–18	No titles awarded	
1919, 1920	Anni v. Humboldtpark	Alex v. Westfalenheim Helga v. Riedekenburg
1921	Nanthild v. Riedekenburg	Jung Tell v. d. Kriminalpolizei Bella v. Riedekenburg
1922, 1923, 1924	Asta v. d. Kaltenweide	Sgr. Erich v. Grafenwerth Flora v. Öringen
1925	Seffe v. Blasienberg	Caro v. Blasienberg Wanda v. Blasienberg
1926	Arna a. d. Ehrenzelle	Claus v. d. Fürstenburg Hidda v. Flandersbach
1927	Elli v. Fürstensteg	Baron v. Borkhofen Annerl v. Morteltal
1928, 1929	Katja v. Blasienberg	Samson v. Blasienberg Anni v. Glasienberg
1930	Bella v. Klosterbrunn	Erich v. Geisenhof Boda v. Westfalenplatz
1931	Illa v. Helmholtz	Alf v. d. Webbelsmannslust Dea v. Helmholtz
1932	Birke v. Blasienberg	Baron v. d. Deutschen Werken Eiche v. Blasienberg
1933	Jamba v. Haus Schutting	Sgr. Hussan v. Haus Schutting Sonja v. Haus Schutting
1934	Grete v. d. Raumannskaule	Dux v. Haus Schutting Gisa v. Godorf
1935, 1936	Stella v. Haus Schutting	Sgr. Hussan v. Haus Schutting Flora v. Hils
1937	Traute v. Bern	Bodo v. d. Brahmenau Vicki v. Bern
1938–54	No titles awarded	
1955	Muschka v. Tempelblick	Arno v. d. Pfaffenau Nandl v. d. Stuveschacht
1956	Lore v. Tempelblick	Berusko v. Tempelblick Elfi v. Tempelblick
1957	Wilma v. Richterbach	Axel v. d. Deininghauserheide Hexe v. Richterbach
1958	Mascha v. Stuhri-Gau	Brando v. Tappenort Werra z. d. Sieben-Faulen

GERMAN SIEGERINS

Year	Siegerin	Sire and Dam
1959	Assja v. Geigerklause	Casar v. d. Malmannsheide Blanka v. Sandbachdamm
1960	Inka Grubenstolz	Brando v. Tappenort Werra z. d. Sieben-Faulen
1961	Assie v. Hexenkalk	Fero v. Emsschleuse Cora v. d. Malmannsheide
1962	Rike v. Colonia Agrippina	Unfried v. Colonia Agrippina Forma v. Colonia Agrippina
1963	Maja v. Stolperland	Marko v. Boxhochburg Werra v. Osnabruckerland
1964	Blanka v. Kisskamp	Mutz a. d. Kuckstrasse Iris v. Walienhof
1965	Landa v. d. Wienerau	Jalk v. Fohlenbrunnen Dixie v. d. Wienerau
1966	Cita v. Gruchental	Cello a. d. Forsthausstrasse Mira v. d. Balinger Bergen
1967	Betty v. Glockenland	Black v. Lambertzeck Sonja v. Glockenland
1968	Rommy v. Driland	Kay v. Hexenkolk Cilly v. Helfriedsheim
1969	Connie v. Klosterbogen	Dido v. d. Werther-Konigsalle Farah v. d. Starrenburg
1970	Diane v. d. Firnskuppe	Ajax v. Haus Dexel Ulli v. d. Firnskuppe
1971	Kathia v. d. Rheinliese	Nick v. Dreimarkenstein Hexe v. d. Rheinliese
1972	Katinka v. d. netten Ecke	Olden v. Asterplatz Exa van de Croonstadt
1973	Erka v. Fiemereck	Canto v. d. Wienerau Druxi v. Silberbrand
1974–77	No Siegerin titles awarded, only Excellent Select	
1978, 1979	Ute von Trienzbachtal, SchH3	Hero von Lauerhof, SchH3 Otti von Trienzbachtal, SchH3
1980	Dixi von Natoplatz, SchH3	Rondo von Ecknachtal, SchH3 Birka von der Holledau, SchH1
1981	Anusch von Trienzbachtal, SchH3	Arras von der Gruber-Hölle, SchH3 Otti von Trienzbachtal, SchH3

Year	Siegerin	Sire and Dam
1982	Perle von Wildsteiger Land, SchH3	Nick von der Wienerau, SchH3 Fina von Badsee, SchH2
1983	Tannie von Trienzbachtal, SchH3	Irk von der Wienerau, SchH3 Otti von Trienzbachtal, SchH3
1984, 1985	Tina von Grossen Sand, SchH3	Sonny v. Badener Land, SchH3 Jenny v. Grossen Sand, SchH3
1986	Pischa von Bad-Boll, SchH3	Irk von Arminius, SchH3 Birke Filsperle, SchH3
1987	Senta von Basilisk	Quando von Arminius Gora von Basilisk
1988	Ronda v. Haus Beck, SchH2	Dbl. Sgr. Uran v Wildsteiger Land, SchH2, FH Janka vom Konigsadler, SchH3, FH
1989, 1990	Inka von der Eichwaldhutte, SchH3	VA Gundo vom Trienzbachtal, SchH3, IP3, FH Kina vom Trienzbachtal, SchH3
1991	Yolli vom Kreuzbaum, SchH3	VA Odin vom Tannenmeise, SchH3, FH Katy von Arminius, SchH1
1992	Vanta von der Wienerau, SchH3, FH	Sgr. Zamb von der Wienerau, SchH3 Xandra von der Wienerau, SchH3
1993	Palie vom Trienzbachtal, SchH3	VA Yago vom Wildsteiger Land, SchH3, FH Puste vom Trienzbachtal, SchH3
1994	Vanta von der Wienerau, SchH3, FH	Sgr. Zamb von der Wienerau, SchH3 Xandra von der Wienerau, SchH3
1995	Nathalie von der Wienerau, SchH3, IP3, FH	Sgr. Zamb von der Wienerau, SchH3 Xandra von der Wienerau, SchH3
1996	Quena vom Haus Sommerlade, SchH3	Karo v. Tweelerland, SchH3 Gipsy du Village le Plus Long d'Alsace, SchH1
1997	Connie vom Farbenspiel, SchH3	Eros von der Luisenstrasse, SchH3 Daggi vom Farbenspiel, SchH2

These German Shepherd Dogs are being judged as they herd 400 sheep onto the road, keeping them out of the fields of corn.

chapter 16

Sheepherding Trials in Germany

The Annual Grand Champion Sheepherding Trials that are held in Germany are the same today as they were in the days of Captain von Stephanitz. The trials cover all the problems a sheepherding dog might encounter during the course of a day's work. The German Shepherds who take part in these tests are actual sheepherding dogs, and they work with their own masters who are sheepherders. The terrain, which is flat farm country with dozens of fields separated by hedge rows, is strange to the dogs. The sheep are also new to the dogs, so the trials are a good test of each dog's sheepherding ability. The dogs' scores are based upon their individual skill, as well as their teamwork, in herding the sheep quickly and efficiently under different conditions.

On one of my most recent trips to Germany, Joan and I had the opportunity of attending a typical Champion Sheepherding Trial. I had seen a sheepherding test in the United States and had not been impressed with the work because the small dogs that were used were trained to respond to whistles, loud commands and exaggerated signals. The dogs had been trained to work at a distance with the use of shock collars, and this type of force-training requires practically no skill and very little native intelligence. I didn't realize, therefore, what a treat we had in store for us.

The judges who were officiating at the trials were very gracious and gave us permission to photograph and take movies of the work. We noticed two flocks of sheep, 400 in each flock, that were penned in two different fields. One flock was used for the two morning tests, and the other flock for the two afternoon tests. The sheep had been confined in the enclosures for one day and were hungry by the time the trial started. Hungry sheep can be stubborn and contrary, since they would rather stop and eat grass than move along willingly.

The sheepherder's outfit was very picturesque, albeit practical. His large brimmed hat and long flowing cape were attractive and kept the sun and rain off him. He wore knickers, boots, a bemedaled vest that sparkled in the sun and a harness strapped across one shoulder to which he attached the dogs' leashes. This arrangement kept his hands free when his dogs were on-leash. He carried a long staff with a small spade at one end. The purpose of this spade was to throw a clump of dirt in the path of the sheep to stop them from moving forward.

The sheepherder walked up to the pen with his two dogs and in an almost inaudible tone of voice told them to lie down across the entrance while he removed the two gates. The two dogs stretched out in front of the gates in a casual manner and ignored the sheep unless one stepped near the entrance. He would then merely glance in its direction and the sheep would stand still.

The herder quietly instructed his dog to jump into the pen. As he quickly herded all the sheep into that half of the pen that incorporated the gates, the bitch worked on the outside and repeatedly dashed at the sheep to keep them from crowding against the fence, which could easily collapse. By thus squeezing them out of the pen, they herded the flock out into the field. The herder, meanwhile, was backing up in front of the sheep, motioning them to come toward him.

As they moved down the entire length of the field and up onto a narrow dirt road, the dogs kept the flock in a compact group. The herder very rarely gave a signal to his dogs, but when he did he merely lifted one arm slowly to give the direction. He never whistled, and when he spoke to his dogs it was always in a soft, low tone of voice. His dogs worked the whole time and kept the sheep moving by dashing at them, pretending they were going to nip them. The sheep were continually stopping to bite clumps of grass, jumping into the culvert or adjoining field to grab some clover or trying to lag behind to graze, and it took constant vigilance on the part of the dogs to keep them all

At the Annual Championship Trial, Karl Fuller precedes this large flock of sheep while his two German Shepherd Dogs, ignoring the spectators and cars, herd them along the side of the road, out of harm's way.

contained. Despite the fact that the dogs were constantly on the move, they were always glancing at the herder ready to acknowledge and respond to his signal should he give one.

The sheep took a dogleg into an adjoining field and the dogs took up positions on either side of the flock to see that they made a left, and then a right-angle turn without losing any continuity of movement. Between the two of them, the sheep just seemed to flow in a controlled stream of woolly bodies with bobbing black faces and ears. It was a beautiful picture to watch.

One-third of this field was barren and the other two-thirds was planted in clover and vegetables. The hungry sheep spied the clover and tried to make a dash for it, but the dogs were completely in control of the situation. One Shepherd kept the herd contained while the other prevented any of the sheep from nibbling on the clover. They moved them down the entire length of the field without letting the sheep get out of their control. Then they took the sheep over a hard surface road, down a 200-yard dirt road and over a bridge into a large pasture. Here the flock of sheep was permitted to scatter and graze.

When the sheep started to graze, the sheepherder softly called his Shepherd bitch to him, clipped the leash to her collar and instructed her to lie down by his side. He watched the sheep grazing and, once in a great while, signaled his dog to go farther to the right or left. He always used just one signal with his arm and each time the dog responded immediately and willingly. During this period when the sheep were grazing, the dog moved continuously at a fast trot back and forth around the perimeter of the field. We were told by an official that ordinarily the dogs travel fifty miles a day when they are herding sheep. The dogs were in excellent physical condition and structurally were very good representatives of the breed.

After about twenty minutes, one of the judges gave the sheepherder the signal to start back. The sheepherder then unleashed his bitch and gave his dogs the command to take the sheep out of the field. They rounded them up in a couple of minutes, herded them over the small bridge, down the dirt road, around the corner and onto the hard-surface road. As the dogs were herding the sheep along the road, a small truck approached at thirty miles an hour and the dogs quickly herded the sheep onto the right side of the road out of harm's way. The truck turned around and came whizzing past the flock again, but the dogs had kept them over on the side, out of the way of traffic.

The sheep were moved in a compact group back to the starting point and were herded back into the pen. The sheepherder again had his dogs lie across the entrance while he replaced the gates, and then he gave each dog a generous amount of praise and petting. The dogs were very happy and it was obvious they enjoyed their work and loved their master.

The dog still had to pass the Courage Test, and at this point the "heavy" approached the sheepherder, who had his dog on-leash, and raised his stick as if to strike him. The dog immediately lunged at the attacker, ready to defend his master. Needless to say, the dog passed this test.

At the end of his test, the dog must demonstrate his courage and his ability to protect his master, the sheepherder.

Being a perfectionist in the art of dog training, I am extremely critical of the way dogs are trained. I know they can be trained with compassion, gently and humanely. They can be taught to respond to soft-spoken commands and short signals. The German Shepherd is limited in his capacity to learn only by the intelligence of his trainer.

It was a memorable experience to watch such superbly trained German Shepherds in the hands of expert trainers. There is nothing more beautiful than seeing the quick response of a highly trained dog who is eager to please his master. One has but to attend one such trial to understand why von Stephanitz instituted regulations to protect his breed from outside interference.

In every field of endeavor, there is always one person who stands tall above the rest. Karl Fuller, owner of the Kirschental Kennels, is such a person. Karl raises sheep and he and his wife, Marion, raise German Shepherd Dogs, and they excel at both. The Annual Grand Champion Sheepherding Trial (Hauptpreishütenfür-Herdengebrauchshunde) is held in Germany every fall. Karl and two of his German Shepherds, not necessarily the same ones each year, have competed in many of these trials over the years. He has won the Grand Champion Award (the Golden Ship) ten times. This, in itself, is a major accomplishment, but it is just half the story.

The dogs and bitches that Karl trains to herd sheep in competition have very good conformation. His German Shepherds have won the HGH Sieger title six times, and the HGH Siegerin title eight times. His Kirschental Kennels have produced many top V and VA German Shepherds including VA Nanni vom Kirschental, SchH3, and VA Xitta vom Kirschental, SchH3, IP3, FH, HGH, who produced seven V progeny in one litter. Then there was Sieger

Karl Fuller, at home, holding one of the ten Golden Ship Awards he has won at the Annual Grand Champion Sheepherding Trials.

VA Xitta vom Kirschental, SchH3, FH, IP3

Eiko vom Kirschental, SchH3, FH, a great producer who was co-owned with Martin Gobl. He was considered one of Uran's finest sons.

Each winter when the grazing land becomes scarce at home, Karl Fuller would move his 1,000 sheep to new pastures. He would be accompanied by his three German Shepherds, two who would do the herding and one as a spare in case another got sick or tired. It takes them one month to make the journey on foot, for it is about eighty miles. They go through small towns,

Karl Fuller and his two German Shepherd Dogs herd his sheep along a stream and through the woods. This is one portion of their eighty-mile trek to grazing lands in Frankfurt. It will take them one month to cover the distance in each direction.

Two weeks later, Karl Fuller is pictured with his 1,000 sheep on the outskirts of a town. He and his dogs have been subjected to all kinds of weather on their journey. Karl is a sheepherder and loves his work. There are very few sheepherders left in Germany as the younger people feel the work is too hard.

large cities, over big bridges, tramp through fields and woods, up hills and down, in all kinds of weather, until they reach their destination. At any time it was an amazing feat, but in this day and age it is a most remarkable, unbelievable journey. Surely Capt. Max von Stephanitz is smiling down on them.

chapter 17

Schutzhund Trials

Schutzhund Trials have been held in Germany since the early 1900s and are open to civilians as well as the police. In this country individuals who had purchased trained German Shepherds from Germany attempted to give their dogs refresher courses so they wouldn't forget the work they had learned. Nevertheless, prior to 1972, Schutzhund training similar to that in Germany has never been popular in this country, and people who wanted to train their dogs turned to the Obedience Trials that are sanctioned by the American Kennel Club.

Joll carrying a four-pound German dumbbell.

In the late 1950s Gernot Riedel and a few friends formed the Peninsula Police Canine Corps in San Mateo, California. This was America's first Schutzhund training club and he worked tirelessly to introduce and develop the Schutzhund sport in America. It had long been an international sport where trainers and their dogs competed against each other. He was determined to bring Schutzhund training to the attention of as many German Shepherd owners as he could. Some time later he was appointed to run the GSDCA Schutzhund program. However, this didn't last when he found that the differences between him and the GSDCA Board were too great. At that point the United Schutzhund Clubs of America (USA) was formed.

Riedel was the first Chairman of the USA's Breed Advisory Committee (1983–1991). He molded the Breed Registry Program and phased in the Conformation system as it is known today. He wanted to be known not only as a Schutzhund advocate, but also as a German Shepherd Dog breeder. At one time he had campaigned his ROM bitch in AKC shows. One of his greatest accomplishments was the establishment of the first American Sieger Show in 1990. This show was a combination of Conformation and Schutzhund that stressed both physical and mental soundness with particular emphasis on Courage Tests. He always worked for and encouraged the improvement of the German Shepherd Dog breed in this country. He not only confronted the GSDCA board, but also the anti-Conformation faction of his own USA Schutzhund Clubs. He tried to make both groups look at the breed the way it must be seen: not entirely structure without working ability, nor entirely working ability without sound conformation. He would be especially pleased that the entries in the USA Sieger Show have increased each year and that the quality of the dogs has improved immensely.

He would indeed be proud of the over 200 Schutzhund Clubs across the USA. And all Americans can be particularly proud of the USA Schutzhund Team placings at the WUSV Championship in Europe. (The World Union of German Shepherd Dog Clubs). Following are some of the USA Team placings, and individual USA winners over the past several years.

USA Siegerin Jada vom Steffen-Haus, SchH2, USA Sieger Show
Sire: Double Sieger Fanto vom Hirschel, SchH3
Dam: V1 Quinte vd Burg Reichenstein, SchH2
Owner: Jane Steffenhagen

1987 FOURTH—St. Gallen, Switzerland

1988 THIRD—Münster, Germany

1990 SECOND—Waremme, Belgium
At this show Joan Elliott and Heiko won the Fourth Individual Placing.

1991 THIRD—Strasbourg, France
At this show Gary Hanrahan and Asko won the Second Individual Placing.

1992 FIRST—Linz, Austria
At this show Glenn Bennett and Buck won the Second Individual Placing. Gary Hanrahan and Asko won the Third Individual Placing after a tie.

1995 SECOND—Budapest, Hungary
At this show Randy Rhodes and Digger won the Second Individual Placing.

1996 FIRST—Turku, Finland
At this show Howard Rodriguez and Vanto won the Fourth Individual Placing.

The USA Schutzhund teams have shown the world that they are a formidable force to be considered in international competition. I would like to see the GSDCA acknowledge their accomplishments in some positive way.

This international competition at the WUSV Championship Trials, where the best dog-and-handler teams of all of Europe compete, is incredibly difficult. For instance, in 1995 two USA members consistently qualified in U.S. Trials. Randy Rhodes and his great Working German Shepherd, Digger, had an amazing winning streak at trial after trial with high scores. Then there was Rich Pastucka, a Pennsylvania Police K-9 handler, and his German Shepherd, Uras, who won 100 points in Protection at the North American Championship Trial. This gave him a place on the 1995 team. He and Uras won the "Triple Crown" by earning 100 points in Tracking and 100 points in Obedience in 1994 when they qualified for the SchH3 National.

Every year the teams seem to be faced with insurmountable problems because of conditions beyond their control; still they manage to hold their own in this world competition and continue to do well. In Budapest, Hungary, in 1995, despite some tough luck, the USA team won Second Place. Rich and Uras earned 97 points in Obedience and 98 in Protection. Later, in Tracking, when he was going for a 97 score, Uras ran into trouble on his very last turn. The field was extremely dry and with thirty seconds to the finish he couldn't find the last turn. He was given a very disappointing score of 67. Over 30% of the teams had difficulty in the Tracking phase because of the

Rich Patuska, a Police K-9 handler, and his dog Uras, are International competitors. They won the coveted "Triple Crown" award by winning 100 points in each of the three tests, Tracking, Obedience and Protection, at qualifying trials in this country in 1994 and 1995.

Randy Rhodes and his dog, Digger, taking the baby for a stroll. In 1995 they won Third Place at the WUSV World Championship Trials in Budapest, Hungary.

V1 Xcell vom Steffen-Haus, SchH2, (rated SG 20 at 1993 German Sieger Show)
Sire: VA Cimbo vd Burg Reichenstein, SchH3, FH
Dam: V1 Dhorne du Clos de Savoie, SchH2
Breeder-Owner: Jane Steffenhagen

way the track-layers made the turns. In the meantime Randy and Digger earned the excellent scores of 96+95+94 for a Third Place Individual Score of 285. Despite the fact that an individual team member has the heart-rending disappointment of an unexpected setback, this member puts it aside and gallantly supports the other team members. It is a well known fact that the camaraderie that exists between team members is the shining star that lights their path to success.

There are two Schutzhund teams in the United States that could compete on an international level providing the individual team members who were chosen had earned their qualifications at specific National trials. These are the USA Schutzhund and the GSDCA–WDA teams. Since the Working Dog Association is sponsored by the GSDCA, it has the right to vote in the World Union of German Shepherd Dog Clubs. The USA Schutzhund Club does not. The USA has over 200 Schutzhund clubs across the country and they have attracted over 4,000 enthusiastic members from all walks of life. Whether the members are intent upon competing at an international level in Schutzhund Trials or Sieger Shows, or simply join the clubs to work out with their dogs after a hard day's work, they have one common goal—to spend some prime time working with their dogs. Both groups were given the opportunity to get together in 1997.

In May 1997 the North American Sieger show was held in Bowling Green, Kentucky. It was sponsored by the GSDCA–Working Dog Association and hosted by the German Shepherd Dog Club of Southern Kentucky.

This was an SV-style Sieger Show and German Shepherd Dogs from all over the world were welcome to compete. There were even classes for American-bred dogs and bitches without working titles. The judges were internationally famous: Herr Rolf Fauser, SV Koermeister and Vice President of the SV; Herr Guenther Bauer, SV Koermeister; and our own Dr. Morton Goldfarb, SV and AKC Judge.

Many members of the WDA are also USA members and not only practice at the USA Schutzhund clubs but support their trials. There is a growing number of serious German Shepherd breeders in this country who carry some of the top German conformation lines. These breeders will continue to upgrade the quality of the German Shepherds in this country, both as Conformation Dogs and/or Working Dogs. A few of these breeders have shown that they are able to successfully compete at the Sieger Shows in both this country and Germany with their American-bred dogs. There is certainly room in this country for all of the different factions who believe their role for German Shepherds is best. If everyone concerned, directors and members alike, would give this subject some serious thought, they might discover that von Stephanitz was right in fighting for the total German Shepherd Dog.

In 1983 the GSDCA decided to become more involved and formed the German Shepherd Dog Club of America–Working Dog Association. It sponsored the first Schutzhund Qualification Trial, which was held in Farmer City, Illinois. Since then teams who are most qualified to compete on an international level have been chosen from the membership. The parent club donates between six and eight thousand dollars to pay the team members' expenses for the trip abroad, including their uniforms. As far as I could find out, no WDA teams have as yet won any of the first three placings in WUSV International Trials.

The Schutzhund Examinations and Titles, as they are known today, were conceived by the German Working Dog Federation, and all Working Dog

Xcell's sister, V1 Xtra vom Steffen-Haus, SchH1 (rated SG 34 at 1993 German Sieger Show) in a Jugendklasse of 345 entries. Breeder-Owner: Jane Steffenhagen

SG-2 Bravos vom Steffen-Haus, SchH3, (Junghundklasse Rüden) at the Sieger Show in Bremen in 1994.
Sire: VA Hoss vom Hasenborn, SchH3, FH, IPO3
Dam: V1 Dhorne du Clos de Savoie, SchH2
Breeder-Owner: Jane Steffenhagen

V1-Lars von Wilhendorf, SchH2 (SG16 Junghundklasse Rüden),
    at 1995 Sieger Show in Hamburg, with 249 entries in the class.
Sire: V4, Jello von der Wienerau, SchH3
Dam: Hilla vom Hasenborn, SchH3
Breeder: John Henkel
Owner: Ronald Harris

Gary Hanrahan and Asko. Placed Second and Third at two
WUSV World Ch. Trials. Gary also won five USA National
Championships.

Societies are consulted when changes in the rules are considered. The SV is a
member of this organization and a very dominant force in the application of
the Schutzhund rules. In 1995 in Germany, 45,600 German Shepherds participated in scheduled Schutzhund Trials. The SV sponsors an Annual

Bundessieger Show, which, like the Sieger Show, takes place in a different location each year. A great number of Germany's top dogs participate in this event.

Law enforcement agencies from all over the world send their officials to these trials to study the new training techniques. Since the Schutzhund Examinations are the foundation for all Police Dog and Search and Rescue work, they are held in nearly all the European countries. The Schutzhund movement has now spread to the Middle and Far East, South America and the North American continent.

The word *Schutzhund,* when literally translated, means Protection Dog. A correctly trained Schutzhund will protect his master and his property defensively. In other words, the dog should not be taught to be aggressive or a menace to society. I have had several SchH3 dogs that were expertly trained in all three phases of the Schutzhund work, yet were so gentle and well mannered that no one ever suspected they were protection trained.

I am frequently asked if I approve of Schutzhund training. I very definitely do believe in it, providing that only dogs with absolutely sound temperaments are used, that the dog is trained in Obedience and Tracking before the Protection work is started and that the right training method is used to control the dog. There are two schools of thought. Some people believe a dog should receive the Protection training first when he is less inhibited. It is quite possible that this type of thinking brought about the drastic changes in the VDH rules.

The VDH (*Verein für Deutsche Hundesport*) is the German National Dog Club and the keeper of the rules for Schutzhund trials. Effective January 1, 1996, the VDH rules went through a sweeping revision that effected every phase of the sport and added some new titles. New USA Rule Books reflecting all of these changes in detail are available from the USA office, 3810 Paule Ave., St. Louis, MO 63125-1718.

Before a dog competes for the SchH1, SchH2 or SchH3 titles, he must first pass the Companion Dog *Begleithunde*-B test. This test was included in the program at the 1996 GSDCA National Specialty. If you have a German Shepherd with a Utility or UDX title, you might be interested in competing in this class. For your information, the rules pertaining to this test are available from the address given above. The whole idea of this test and the revision of the Schutzhund rules is to provide more, if not absolute, control over the dogs. A well-mannered dog who is completely under control should be welcome anywhere.

chapter 18

Koer Reports of Famous German Dogs

VA—*Axel von der Deininghauser Heide,* SchH3, DPH
Sire: Immo vom Hasenfang, SchH2
Dam: Helma vom Hildegardsheim
Whelped June 2, 1946; surveyed October 10, 1948.
Linebreeding: None
Medium-sized, very good general appearance, good angulation. Confident. Height: 24.8 inches. Weight: 80 pounds. Color: Tan with black saddle and nice black mask on face.
Breeding advice: Not suitable for bitches with Arras Stadt Velbert, Onyx Forelienbach or Brando Heidelbeerberg blood.
The immortal Axel was one of the greatest producers in the history of the breed. His sons and grandsons were among the finest German Shepherds bred and they, in turn, have continued to produce a great depth of quality in their progeny. Axel was a beautiful dog with a faultless temperament and was the result of an outcross. A breeding miracle that rarely occurs, yet because it did, his lines click beautifully with others.

Sieger Alf vom Nordfelsen, SchH3
Sire: Axel von der Deininghauser Heide, SchH3, DPH
Dam: Carin vom Bombergschen Park, SchH1
Whelped July 23, 1949; surveyed August 26, 1951.
Linebreeding: Gockel von Bern (5-5)
Large, strong, long male with slightly yielding back, good angulation, confident, fearless. Heavy and substantial. Height: 25.2 inches. Weight: 88 pounds. Color: Tan with black saddle.
Breeding advice: Not suitable for large bitches or bitches with weak backs.

Holland and United States Grand Victor Ch. Troll vom Richterbach, SchH3
Sire: Axel von der Deininghauser Heide, SchH3, DPH, FH
Dam: Lende vom Richterbach, SchH2
Whelped May 31, 1953; surveyed July 24, 1955.
Linebreeding: None
This is a strong and substantial male, over medium-size, harmoniously built
　　with very good chest and excellent angulation. Fluid, reaching and pow-
　　erful gait, strong back. Lively temperament with excellent courage and
　　excellent defense reaction. Lively, alert, good natured and fearless. Height:
　　25.2 inches. Weight: 98 pounds. Color: Black and tan. Teeth very strong,
　　back very strong, depth of chest very good. The shoulder is very good,
　　but deviates slightly from correct position. Moves slightly narrow behind.
Breeding advice: Linebreeding on the C-litter vom Hain and especially on Fels
　　Vogtlandshof must be avoided under any circumstances.

VA—Jalk vom Fohlenbrunnen, SchH3
Sire: Vello zu den Sieben Faulen, SchH3, FH
Dam: Gunda vom Fohlenbrunnen, SchH2
Whelped March 19, 1957; surveyed July 23, 1961.
Linebreeding: Lex Preussenblut (4-4), Maja Osnabrücker Land (4-4),
　　Osnabrücker Land, Inda, Rolf, Rosel (3,5-3).
Large, medium-heavy male with strong back and good angulation. Good
　　appearance, very good gait. Good temperament with pronounced defense
　　reaction, lively, alert, fearless. Height: 25.0 inches. Weight: 86 pounds.
　　Color: Black with tan markings. Strong head, good jaws with scissors
　　bite and healthy, strong teeth.
Breeding advice: Recommended for all bitches with compatible bloodlines.

VA—Lido von der Wienerau, SchH3
Sire: Jalk vom Fohlenbrunnen, SchH3
Dam: Dixie von der Wienerau, SchH1
Whelped May 20, 1962; surveyed August 30, 1964.
Linebreeding: (Osnabrücker Land, Ina, Rosel-Rolf, 4,4-5).
Large substantial, long male with harmonious structure. Very good appear-
　　ance. Clean, reaching gait. Confident, pronounced defense reaction.
　　Lively, alert, good natured, fearless. Trotter-structure, long, medium
　　substantial. Height: 25.4 inches. Weight: 97 pounds. Color: Black and
　　tan. Very strong head, scissors bite, healthy teeth.
In motion: trotter, fleeting reaching gait, clean movement, strong back. El-
　　bows very good, pastern strong, hocks strong. Drive is effective. Good
　　natural temperament, alert, confident. Behavior in traffic is good; he is
　　not gun-shy.
Breeding advice: Suitable for all good bitches.

Irk von Arminius, SchH3, FH ("a" fast normal)
Sire: Pirol von Arminius, SchH3
Dam: Dunja vom Weilachtal, SchH3

Substantial, expressive, correct medium size, very good expression, good masculinity, hard and dry, good proportions. High wither, very good topline, good croup. Very good front and rear angulation. Ideal front with well-proportioned chest. Slightly tight coming, correct going away. Superb, uniform and far-outreaching side gait which is transmitted from a totally firm back, completes the overall picture of this type male. Sound temperament, hardness, courage and fighting instincts pronounced.

1984, 1985 Sieger Uran v. Wildsteiger Land, SchH3, FH ("a" Normal)
Sire: V—Irk von Arminius, SchH3, FH
Dam: V—Palme v. Wildsteiger Land, SchH2 ("a" Fast Normal), Dam of Quando.

Born March 12, 1981. Large, substantial and powerful, very good type, very good overall firmness. High wither, tight back. Good croup placement with just sufficient length. Very good front and rear angulation, correct front. Correct chest proportions. Correct coming and going, far-outreaching, ground covering side gait. Sound temperament, hardness, courage and fighting instincts pronounced. This magnificent Shepherd was considered the top stud dog in Germany for a twenty-year period.

V—Xaver von Arminius, SchH3
1986, 1987 Sieger Quando von Armi-
nius, SchH3, FH, IP3, ("a" Fast
Normal)
    V—Palme vom Wildsteiger
Land, SchH2
(Dam of Sgr. Uran)

Born November 18, 1981. Large, medium powerful, hard and dry, very typey male
with a high wither. Good topline and very good position and length of croup. Very
good front and rear angulation, correct chest proportions, correct front. He is correct
coming and going and has a very good ground-covering side gait along with powerful rear drive and good front reach. Sound temperament, hardness, courage and fighting
instincts pronounced.

V—Lasso vom Wiedenbrucker
Land, SchH3
VA Fedor von Arminius, SchH3,
born June 8, 1983
    V—Fee vom Weiherturchen,
SchH1

Dbl. Sgr. Uran v. Wildsteiger
Land, SchH3, FH
Sieger 1988 Eiko vom Kirschental,
SchH3, FH, ("a" Normal)
    VA Xitta vom Kirschental,
SchH3, IP3, FH

V—Kim von der Michaelswiese,
   VH2
VA Fando v. Sudblick, SchH3, ("a"
Fast Normal)
   V—Wiske v Sudblick, VHI

Dbl. Sgr. Quando von Arminius, SchH3, IP3, FH
VA Odin v Tannenmeise, SchH3, FH
("a" Normal)
   V—Hasel v Tannenmeise, VH2

VA Fedor von Arminius,
   SchH3
VA Mark vom Haus Beck, SchH3,
("a" Fast Normal)
   V—Quina von Arminius,
   SchH2
   (Sister of Quando)

V—Gundo vom Trienzbachtal,
   SchH3, IP3, FH
VA Jack vom Trienzbachtal, SchH3,
(noch zugelassen)
   Nixe vom Trienzbachtal, SchH1

VA Tell vom Grossen Sand, SchH3
Sieger 1990 & 1991 Fanto vom Hirschel, SchH3, ("a" Normal)
V—Ica vom Haus Reiterland, SchH2

VA Odin v Tannenmeise, SchH3, FH, Sieger 1993
Seiger 1992 Zamb von der Weinerau, SchH3 ("a" Normal)
Ica von der Weinerau, SchH2

Born March 7, 1987. Large, medium strong, dry and hard male with high wither, good topline and good placement and length of croup. He has very good angulation in forehand and rear, well let down chest and correct front. Coming and going he shows far-reaching gait with strong underdrive and free forehand.

VA Odin v. Tannenmeise, SchH3, FH, Sieger 1993
Jeck vom Noricum, SchH3, FH. (noch zugelassen)
V—Anett vom Noricum, SchH3

Born August 4, 1987. Medium large, very typey and developed, harmoniously structured male with very good body proportions. Good topline and very good length and placing of croup. Very good angulation of forehand and hindquarter, well let down chest and correct front. In motion he shows a very outreaching gait with a free forehand and functioning underdrive.

VA—Yago vom Wildsteiger
Land, SchH3, FH
Sieger 1995 Ulk vom Arlett,
SchH3, ("a" Fast Normal)
    V—Dolly vom Arlett, SchH2

Born January 28, 1990. Medium large, full bodied, medium strong, very expressive male. Altogether very dry, hard and well coupled. Correct proportion height to length. High wither standing and in motion. Well-placed hard back and well laid on croup with good length. Very good angulated hindquarter. Normal angulated forehand. Well-developed prosternum and long lower chest, correct front. Very correct movement. Outreaching, strong gait with functioning underdrive, free forehand and functioning transmission through the back.

Sieger 1993 Jeck vom Nori-
cum, SchH3
VA Cash vom Wildsteiger Land,
SchH3, ("a" Normal)
    V—Belli vom Wildsteiger Land,
    SchH1

Born November 10, 1990. Large, expressive, developed, medium strong male. High wither standing and in motion. Strong, well placed back, the croup has very good length, correct angulation in forehand and rear. Normal front, correct movement. Far-reaching, strong gait with functioning underdrive and free forehand.

German Terminology

GERMAN TITLES AND RATINGS

Angekoert   Recommended for breeding.

Koerklasse I   Especially recommended for breeding.

Koerklasse II   Suitable for breeding. Dog may have a structural fault, which could be compensated for by bloodlines or working qualities. May be resurveyed and reclassified at a later date.

(*)   This symbol before a dog's name means he has been surveyed and approved for breeding.

"a"   Dog's hips have been certified normal.

LG (*Landesgruppen Show*)   There are approximately 1,500 German Shepherd Dog clubs in Germany and these are under the jurisdiction of the fifteen Landesgruppen clubs. The LG Shows are larger than the local shows and the judging and rating requirements are stricter. Landesgruppen Sieger and Siegerin titles are awarded.

VA   Excellent Select title that is only awarded at the Annual Sieger Show (*Auslese Klasse*) Select Class.

V (*Vorzüglich*)   Excellent

SG (*Sehr Gut*)   Very Good

G (*Gut*)   Good

A (*Ausreichend*)   Sufficient

M (*Mangelhaft*)   Faulty

0 (Zero)   Failed

U (*Ungenügend*)   Unsatisfactory

CACIB   A European International Champion.

SchH (*Schutzhund*)   For dogs who have passed the examinations for Obedience, Protection and Tracking. The titles 1, 2, and 3 denote how advanced the training tests were.

AD (*Ausdauerprüfung*)   The dog passed an endurance test by gaiting about twelve miles at approximately eight to nine miles per hour. There will be two fifteen-minute rest stops along the way. At the end the dog will rest for fifteen minutes, be given a simple physical examination, and do an Obedience exercise to show he is in good physical condition.

Zpr (*Zuchtprüfung*)   Dogs who have passed a breed survey and are recommended for breeding.

HGH (*Herdengebrauchshund*)   Herding Dog

PH (*Polizer Hund*)   Police Dog

BlH (*Blinden Hund*)   Guide Dog for the blind

DH (*Dienst Hund*)   Service Dog

FH (*Fahrten Hund*)   Trailing Dog

SH (*Such Hund*)   Tracking Dog

   (*Sanitäts Hund*)   Red Cross Dog

KrH (*Kriegshund*)   War Dog

LawH (*Lawinen Hund*)   Avalanche Dog

GRH (*Grenzen Hund*)   Border Patrol Dog

MH (*Meldehund*)   Dispatch Army Dog

Leistungssieger   Working Dog Champion of the Year

Preishuten Sieger   Sheepherding Champion of the Year

GERMAN COMMANDS

Achtung   Watch

Aus   Let go

Bei Fuss   Heel

Bleib   Stay

Bleib sitzen   Stay sitting

Bringen   Fetch

Fass   Attack

Geh weiter   Go on

Gib Laut   Speak

Halten   Halt

Hopp   Jump

Komm   Come

Kriech   Crawl

Nein   No

Nimm   Take it

Pass auf   Watch out

Platz   Down

Setz   Sit

Such   Search

Voraus   Go out

Zur Spur   Trail

Zur Wache   Guard

GERMAN DOG TERMS

Abstammung Ancestry

Abzeichen Markings

Abzugen Offered, for sale or at stud

Ahnen Ancestors

Alter Age

Amme Foster mother

Apportierbock Dumbbell

Augen Eyes

Ausbildungskennzeichen Standard

Ausdruck Expression

Behaarung Coat

Belegt Bred

Besitzer Owner

Bewettung Qualification

Brustfieck Spot on chest

Decken, frei At public stud

Decktag Breeding date

Ehrenpreis Trophy

Ellenbogen Elbows

Eltern Parents

Fehlerhaft Faulty

Gang Gait

Geschlecht Sex

Geschutzer Zuchtname Registered kennel name

Gewinkelt Angulated

Geworfen Whelped

Grau Gray

Gross Large

Haar Coat

Hals Neck, throat

Halsband Collar

Hinterhand Hindquarters

Hinterlaufe Hind legs

Hitze Female in season

Hoden Testicles

Hohe Height

Inzucht Inbreeding

Jung Young puppy

Klein Small

Knochen Bone

Kopf Head

Kraftig Strong

Kruppe Croup

Kurz Short

Langhaarig Long-haired

Meldeschein Registration certificate

Nase Nose, muzzle

Oberschlachtig Overshot

Ohren Ears

Ptote Foot

Reinzucht Purebred

Rucke Back

Rute Tail

Sattel Saddle

Scheu Shy

Schulter Shoulder

Schwester Sister

Vater Sire

Vorderbrust Forechest

Vorderhand Forequarters

Vorderpfote Forepaw

Wesen Character, temperament

Winkelung Angulation

Wurfdatum Whelping date

Wurfmeldung Litter registration

Wurfstarke Size of litter

Ziminerrein Housebroken

Zwinger Kennel

"a" or "a" Zuerkannt-certified hips
"a" Normal Normal hips
"a" Fast Normal Certified near-normal hips
"a" *Noch Zugelassen* Certified still permissible

The "a" stamp itself is on the front or the back of the pedigree; the rating is given on the inside page, lower right hand corner.

Ch. Wynthea's Bruce, UD, OFA, giving his son some fatherly advice.

chapter 20

German Shepherds in the United States

The German Shepherd Dog Club of America was founded in 1913 with twenty-six charter members. In spite of this name, the American Kennel Club officially called the breed the German Sheepdog. At that time there were only about eighty-five German Shepherds registered each year with the American Kennel Club, and these were recorded as German or Belgian Sheepdogs in a nonsporting division. They did not have the groups as they do today. Shepherds were entered in the Miscellaneous class, and it was possible for one dog to become a Champion with very little competition, since the points were determined by the number of dogs of all breeds shown that day. The dogs in those early days had no influence on those that came along later. Research shows that the first German Shepherd to become a Champion did so despite the fact that it had one ear down.

With the advent of World War I, the American soldiers came back with glowing tales of the intelligence and heroism of German Shepherds. Many of the dogs they sent back, however, were bred in France and were inferior to those bred in Germany. One gray German Shepherd puppy was born in the trenches under fire and was later brought to America. Although he did not have the conformation to become a show dog, he was very intelligent, and in the hands of Lee Duncan he became one of the greatest dog stars of all time. His name was Rin-Tin-Tin and he became such a popular star that thousands of people wanted a dog just like him.

In those days if fifty dogs were entered in a show, half of these would be imports. Of the twenty-five homebreds, many of these would be puppies; the breeders would enter whole litters of puppies at the show as they brought big prices and there was always a demand for them.

In 1917 the American Kennel Club changed the name of the breed to Shepherd Dog and it wasn't until 1931 that they restored German to its name. During the war anything German was extremely distasteful to the British, so they named their dogs Alsatian Wolfhounds. They soon found this was a

mistake because the public tried to identify the dogs with wolves and erroneously believed they were a wolf cross. So the name was changed and for a
great number of years German Shepherds were called Alsatians in Great Britain. As time passed and breeders started importing some of Germany's excellent German Shepherds to strengthen or enhance the bloodlines in
their kennels, their love for the breed won them over. Now their German
Shepherd Dogs are acknowledged by their rightful name.

In 1923 the Shepherd Dog Club of New England was formed. The
members made a sincere effort to learn all they could about the breed and
preserve its good qualities. This organization filled the need for a club in that
area as people didn't travel very far to dog shows in those days. They worked
hard to present these dogs to the public in the most favorable way through
breeding, training and showing them properly.

The initial issue of the *Shepherd Dog Review* came out in January
1924. This magazine has endeavored to present articles of general interest
by knowledgeable fanciers and is considered the top breed publication in
its field in this country. It is now published and owned by the German Shepherd Dog Club of America.

At first the different areas had their own clubs, and each area seemed to
produce a different type of Shepherd. At that time traveling was difficult and
time-consuming as the roads were not very good and cars were not very reliable. Later, when the fanciers could travel with ease and take their dogs to
shows a great distance from their homes, the dogs became more similar in
type. Today fanciers fly their dogs to faraway shows and breed their bitches
to a popular stud dog, even if they have to fly them across the United States
to do it. This practice was impractical if not almost impossible in those days.

The Germans had their Breed Surveys and Critiques and these were
accepted as part of an educational process to further improve the German
Shepherd breed. In the 1920s and 1930s both the Shepherd Dog Club of
America and the New England Shepherd Dog Club invited well-known Shepherd experts from Germany to conduct Breed Surveys here. Each German
Shepherd was thoroughly evaluated as to size, gait, angulation, character,
mental alertness, physical soundness, et cetera. Each dog was evaluated as a
breeding force and, after the pedigrees had been studied and analyzed, the
correct choices of mates were named. Two volumes were completed from this
data and called *Breed Survey,* Volumes I and II.

Both German and English judges were brought over to officiate at many
of our Breed Shows. They were both honest and helpful in pointing out the
differences between the American-bred German Shepherds and those in
Europe. The dedicated American fanciers were anxious to preserve the
foreign-type German Shepherds and realized the importance of establishing
one universal type. Because of their sincere interest in the breed and their desire
to follow the advice of the German experts in caring, breeding and showing
their dogs, the German Shepherds in this country steadily improved.

After World War II, wealthy Americans bought the best German dogs and imported them to this country. Germany was in the throes of inflation and breeders were willing to sell their finest dogs in exchange for American dollars. Siegers, Siegerins and animals with the finest breeding and greatest potential were brought to America in a never-ending stream. With all these great dogs at the disposal of American breeders, it is a shame that their full potential was never realized. Over the years many genetically promising stud dogs have been ignored by the Fancy who flocked to more publicized studs. Many of these great dogs became pets and were just used at stud by their owners, so their true value as stud dogs was lost to the breed. However, not all the imports that arrived were of value. A large number of them were purchased by importers who bought them in Europe for a few hundred dollars each and sold them over here for thousands. The Germans were delighted to get rid of them, and the gullible new owners were equally pleased to purchase imported dogs, until they discovered the dogs were worthless as American show dogs and producers.

These were the years when the German Shepherd popularity was growing so fast that the demand for puppies exceeded the supply. Puppy factories owned by opportunists sprang up everywhere and these breeders were only interested in the monetary return. The type and temperament of the dogs they raised were of no concern to them. Consequently this craze finally reached a saturation point when the public discovered that ill-bred German Shepherds are also undesirable, unhealthy and ill-tempered. It became an era of bad publicity for "police dogs" and reporters callously blamed these dogs for everything and anything that occurred. The demand for German Shepherds came to an abrupt end.

Despite the sudden decline in its popularity, the sincere and dedicated breeders continued to do their best to breed the finest German Shepherds they could. It is due to these serious fanciers that the German Shepherd breed survived the exploitations of the backyard breeders.

Captain von Stephanitz was invited to judge the Morris & Essex show in 1930. His judging was extended to two days because he drew an entry of 271 Shepherds. He toured the United States and gave advice to all the fanciers who sought it. He had established breeding studies in Germany and his advice was invaluable. He and other German judges were particularly interested in judging the dog in motion. They preferred the smooth gait, long, ground-covering stride and dogs who were true coming and going. They looked for the harmonious dog with a strong back and dry bone with a rather flat contour, as compared to the round bone that tends to be spongy and is accompanied by large joints. They emphasized naturalness, soundness, balance and symmetry. They demanded health, endurance and mental stability.

The backyard breeders and commercialists of that day tended to ignore the advice of Captain von Stephanitz and other foreign experts to breed for the ideal German Shepherd. We have exactly the same problem today with many breeders ignoring the concept of a German Shepherd as called for in our Breed Standard. They forget intelligence and character and are satisfied to have a kennel full of "spooks," providing the structure and gait of the dogs will gain their championships.

The German Shepherds that were imported from Germany were highly trained in Obedience, Protection work and Tracking. The Germans had Schutzhund Trials in which their dogs could earn titles for being proficient in all three phases. Each of these titles, Schutzhund 1, 2 and 3, was progressively more difficult to earn. It was only natural that the Americans should continue this training with their imported dogs by conducting similar trials in this country. Eventually, other dog breeds were included in modified Obedience Trials, but the German Shepherd Dogs were instrumental in introducing Obedience into the United States.

In later years the Americans tried conducting their own Breed Surveys but they had a very limited amount of success, partly because of the way the Surveys were conducted, and partly because Americans do not wish to have their dogs criticized by people they think are no more knowledgeable than themselves.

The Critiques written by American judges proved unpopular because many unknowledgeable judges were either unkind or incorrect when they criticized the dogs. To be of value, a Critique should emphasize the good points of a dog and note comparisons between the placings. A dog should not be condemned for a fault that is due to his age, condition or attitude, since this could change with time. The unknowledgeable person or judge reading the Critique would take the criticism verbatim and consciously or unconsciously penalize the dog in his own mind. Such misunderstandings would hurt a dog's chances at future shows for it is a human frailty for one to repeat faults and ignore virtues.

Despite occasional internal problems within the club, the German Shepherd Dog Club of America continued to expand with the years. In 1949 it united with the Shepherd Dog Club of New England to form one group of dedicated fanciers. Since that time many worthwhile projects have been offered to the membership to further the interests of the breed. The Register of Merit System was introduced by Burr Robbins with the assistance of Marie Leary. It is designed to show breeders which shepherds are good producers; from that point, it is up to the individual breeder to do a little research to determine which bloodlines are compatible with certain ROM dogs and bitches. The Futurity and Maturity shows were initiated around 1950 and are now held in every section of the country. The Futurity Shows are a great means of determining which stud dogs are prepotent, how their youngsters develop and what bloodlines click together. The German Shepherd Dog Club of America sponsors the German Shepherd National Specialty Show and Obedience Trial every year. This is hosted by one of the regional clubs and a

Grand Victor, Grand Victrix and Obedience Victor are chosen and reign for one year.

The GSDCA offers the following Membership Benefits to those members who are in good standing, who achieve certain goals. A bronze, silver or gold pin and a certificate will be awarded upon completion of the following titles/degrees: Champion, Companion Dog Excellent, Utility Dog, Utility Dog Excellent, Tracking Dog, Tracking Dog Excellent, Variable Surface Tracker, Champion Tracker, Herding Started, Herding Intermediate and Herding Excellent. Only a certificate will be awarded for Companion Dog, Herding Tested and Pre-Trial Tested.

A Breeders Pin is awarded to the breeder of a conformation champion.

- A silver medal is awarded to an Obedience Trial Champion, or Herding Champion.
- Annual Training Achievement Award: Annual award to the sires and dams of German Shepherd Dog progeny who achieve AKC Obedience and Tracking titles and/or GSDCA–WDA Schutzhund degrees.
- Award of Excellence (AOE): It awards a combination of beauty and brains and addresses the "total dog concept." The requirements are:
    1. Dog must be a Champion.
    2. Dog must have earned the Select title at a National show.
    3. Dog must have an OFA certificate.
    4. Dog must have earned a regular AKC Obedience, SV or SV/WDA title.
    5. Dog must have passed the GSDCA Temperament Test.
- Dual Award Plaque: Breed and Performance Award
- Temperament Certificate: To promote good temperament
- Schutzhund Award Pins: For members of the GSDCA and WDA only
- Register of Merit Plaque: Dogs and bitches who have obtained a Register of Merit status

(In addition to the above, I suggest that the GSDCA offer a gold German Shepherd pin to be awarded to the member who owns the dog or bitch who wins the Obedience Victor title at the Annual GSDCA National Specialty Show. This is not an AKC title.)

There are many different factions in the United States who are raising and utilizing German Shepherd Dogs according to their own beliefs and purposes and who have absolutely no interest in the German Shepherd Dog Breed Standard. This is also true of the many people breeding German Shepherds for Schutzhund work or utilitarian purposes. If the dog can be trained to do the work and has a decent temperament, they are satisfied. It is my belief that

Ch. Stoneway's Uecker, FV
Breeders: Robert Eaton and Jane Kerner
Owners: John and Donna Schacht and Bob Eaton

there are thousands of German Shepherds in this country who are given loving homes and good care. The people who own them do not have the time or
interest to show them in any type of competition. They bought their dogs
because they love the breed and want to enjoy the intelligence, loyalty and
companionship these dogs provide.

If the Schutzhund USA Clubs continue to hold Breed Surveys and Conformation Shows that include courage tests, judged by some of Europe's
knowledgeable SV breed judges, this group will continue to influence hundreds of German Shepherd Dog owners. As of now they are continuing to
show the world that the USA Schutzhund teams are a force to be considered
in international competition. As long as they continue to hold USA Sieger
Shows each year, they will draw the people who believe in the total dog concept. Hopefully this will become an international event.

German Shepherd Regional Clubs

In 1996 there were 104 regional clubs in the United States and the number is gradually decreasing. The majority of these clubs hold annual German Shepherd Specialty Shows, and Sanction Matches, and some of the more active clubs sponsor two Specialty Shows per year plus Sanction Matches. Many of these clubs also hold Obedience Trials at their Specialty Shows and Sanction Matches but they are in the minority. It is the regional clubs that host the National Specialty Show and Obedience Trial and the Futurity and Maturity shows each year.

The German Shepherd Review is considered one of the finest breed publications in the country. It's published monthly and features the photographs of the winners at the GSDCA National Specialty Show, the Futurity and Maturity shows held throughout the country, breed statistics, Obedience news and various other articles on the German Shepherd breed. One must be a member of the parent club in order to get this magazine.

A club could hold three or four fun, multipurpose matches a year. All of the club members could learn how to be stewards in both the Conformation and Obedience classes. I have been to countless Specialty Shows where the stewards chosen to help the Obedience judge knew absolutely nothing about the rules. The same holds true for the stewards chosen to help the Conformation judge. Members should be encouraged to show their dogs in both the Conformation and Obedience rings at these informal fun matches so that they can get some firsthand experience. It could be either a rude awakening or an enlightening, fun-filled experience. In either case the point should be made that the German Shepherd Dog is a Working breed. By participating, one can remember rules and procedures that would ordinarily be forgotten by merely watching at ringside. Many clubs, such as mine, hold an Annual Awards Dinner where club members receive incentive awards for all titles they have won with their dogs during the year.

Each regional club has to give the GSDCA an $80 annual fee for providing certain functions. Whenever a regional club holds a Specialty Show, the parent club provides two handsome bronze medals. One is awarded to the Best of Breed winner and one to the High Combined Score team in Obedience. There are many advantages in belonging to a regional club that offers educational programs, shows and fun matches. Just getting to meet people who share your interests and goals is a big plus.

Many of these clubs present very interesting educational programs to their members each month. Breeders, veterinarians, obedience trainers, judges, handlers, geneticists and many others are invited to lecture at these meetings. Classes are given to show members how to handle a dog in the Conformation classes or train a dog in Obedience. Movies are shown in conjunction with a series of lectures to explain and illustrate the Breed Standard. Incentive awards are offered the membership for obtaining Obedience titles and Championship titles. Some clubs offer cash awards to members for breeding and showing the top winning puppies of the year in their club. There are many advantages in belonging to a regional club when they offer educational programs such as these. If you are interested in joining a German Shepherd club, contact one of the leading breeders in your area. He or she will tell you how you can join one.

Most of these clubs publish monthly or quarterly newsletters. Many of these contain extremely interesting articles pertinent to German Shepherds that were written by very knowledgeable people. So, besides the local news within the club, a member can read the minutes of the parent club meeting, a list of the new ROM sires and dams, a discussion about some new disease or some other topic of general interest. The parent club offers awards each year for the Newsletter of the Year and the Honorable Mention Winners. It is an incentive to the clubs to turn out better newsletters.

A German Shepherd dog club is as good as the members who run it. The most successful clubs are those whose members have very progressive ideas; offer interesting educational programs; and are very active in handling, training, showing, judging and breeding German Shepherds. New members can be persuaded to work hard for the interests of the breed and the club when the more experienced members set such a good example. The club that is governed by people who do nothing but hold dull meetings is sick and needs a blood transfusion. If you wish to join a German Shepherd club, be prepared to offer your services in some field of endeavor. The members who work the hardest and contribute their time and efforts are those that benefit the most. A progressive club is one that is always interested in promoting the German Shepherd breed.

Ch. Alkarah's Rolo
Breeder—Owner: Karin E. Wagner
Handler: Chip Rayner

1995 Select Ch. Welove Du Chien's R–Man, 1995 Futurity Victor, OFA
Breeders-Owners: William and Jane Kerner and Jeffrey Moebius
Handler: Kent Boyles

c h a p t e r 22

Futurities and Maturities in the United States

A Futurity is an AKC-sanctioned puppy match. No championship points are awarded, but it is a distinction to win one of the classes and an exceptional achievement for a puppy to be acclaimed Best in Futurity or Best of Opposite Sex in Futurity. These are National Match Shows that are held in nine regions of the United States and they draw large entries from all over the country. These Futurities are an excellent method of determining how well the leading German Shepherd Dogs in the United States are producing, not only in one specific region but throughout the whole country. They reveal what bloodlines click together and offer guidelines to students of genetics. It is primarily a breeder's show and should be of interest to everyone seriously interested in the future of the breed in America. The GSDCA does everything possible to make these shows fair and unbiased so that breeders will support the regional clubs with their entries. If the chosen judges base their decisions on the German Shepherd Standard and select mentally and physically sound dogs, the integrity of their placements will be exemplary.

If you are interested in obtaining the show directions and full particulars about the National Futurities and Maturities, write a note to: Corresponding Secretary of the GSDCA, Blanche Beisswenger, 17 W. Ivy Lane, Englewood, NJ 07631.

This distinguished threesome consists of (from left) Sel. Ch. 4x, Stuttgart's Sundance Kid, ROM, ROMC, OFA; GV Ch. Rio Valle's Nestle's Crunch, ROM, ROMC, OFA, CD, AOE, HIT; and GV Ch. Piper Hill's Polo, ROM, ROMC, OFA.

German Shepherd National Specialty Show and Obedience Trial

The German Shepherd National Specialty Show and Obedience Trial is sponsored by the German Shepherd Dog Club of America, Inc., and each year is hosted by a different regional club. This means that the show might be in California one year, Arizona the next, or some eastern state after that. The geographical location is changed each year to give the fanciers in different parts of the country a chance to participate. Being a National Specialty Show, people fly or drive to it from all corners of the nation and the Conformation and Obedience classes draw a total of about 900 entries. There are generally about seventy-five Champions competing for the Grand Victor and Grand Victrix titles, but it is possible for the titles to be given to a dog or bitch from the classes.

The National has grown tremendously since the first such show was held in 1918. This annual show is held in the fall and lasts for three days. The Obedience Trial consists of the regular classes, Novice A and B, Open A and B and Utility, as well as the nonregular classes, Graduate Novice and Team. The Obedience Victor title is awarded to the dog or bitch who earns the highest combined score in Open B and Utility, providing the dog has earned 190 or more points in each of these classes, with a combined score of not less than 385 points. In order to be eligible for the Obedience Victor or Victrix award, the handler of the winning dog or bitch must present it to an AKC Conformation judge who is present, to verify that the dog or bitch does not have any disqualifying faults as described in the AKC Standard for German Shepherd Dogs. Regardless of the AKC rules, spayed or neutered dogs who otherwise meet the Standard are acceptable.

The Conformation classes consist of the six- to nine-month and nine- to twelve-month age groups for puppies, twelve- to eighteen-month-old youngsters, Novice, Bred by Exhibitor, American-Bred and Open classes, and in each class the dogs and bitches are judged separately. After these classes are judged the Winners Dog and Winners Bitch are chosen.

The Futurity and Maturity Finals for dogs and bitches are also judged, and the subsequent winner of each group is called the Futurity Victor, Futurity Victrix, Maturity Victor and Maturity Victrix.

The Progeny Groups are of general interest. This is an excellent opportunity for breeders and the general public to see what American-bred stud dogs and resident imports are producing and to determine which bloodlines complement each other. Realistically, breeders and owners find it is just too difficult, or too expensive, to fly progeny great distances. Therefore, the progeny classes are very small and the results inconclusive. However, if the progeny who are competing in the various classes also support these groups, it is certainly worthwhile to study them. They should resemble their parents in general appearance and type and should have inherited their good characteristics. It should show which studs are producing good, or not so good progeny.

It has become a regular event to include a Passing Parade of Shepherd Greats. To be eligible for this class, the dog or bitch must be a Grand Victor, Grand Victrix, Obedience Victor, Obedience Victrix, ROM Sire, ROM Dam, Select Winner at a National Specialty Show, Obedience Trial Champion, Champion Utility Dog, Utility Dog Tracker, Utility Dog Excellent, Tracking Dog Excellent, Variable Surface Tracker or Champion Tracker. This is a very popular feature and it is always a pleasure to see the famous dogs on parade. Another feature is the Veterans class. This is a nonregular class for dogs and bitches over seven years of age.

A Temperament Test has been included for those German Shepherd owners who want to submit their dogs to a formal temperament test. Over the years it has become a popular feature, and now includes a gun test. Before the Best of Breed dogs and bitches enter the main arena, I would suggest that they be required to pass this test. Since the Grand Victor and Grand Victrix titles are not AKC titles, this could be a requirement.

A list of ten Conformation and ten Obedience judges selected by the Board of Directors of the GSDCA is mailed to the membership who cast their votes for the three persons they want to judge at the next National. The judge who receives the greatest number of votes is asked to judge Best of Breed in the Conformation classes, or Utility in the Obedience classes. The other judges who are chosen will be assigned the other classes.

The National Specialty is a licensed American Kennel Club show and the Conformation points and Obedience scores count as they would at any other show. The Grand Victor and Grand Victrix titles are awarded to the Best of Breed and Best of Opposite Sex winners. The Obedience Victor title is awarded to the dog who attains the Highest Combined Score in the Open B and Utility B Classes.

The National is the most prestigious show of the year and carries an aura of excitement about it. Many people start planning for it as soon as the judges are announced. They tentatively decide which dogs they will show, how they will get them to the show site, what strategy they will use during the year, who will show their dogs and many other specifics. Handlers are equally concerned with their ultimate choice of the dogs they will show for they could make thousands of dollars at this one show. If they handle the winners in some of the classes, their services will be in great demand in the future.

It is one of the most interesting shows to watch because of the depth of quality of the dogs being shown. However, it is one judge's decision as to who will be chosen Grand Victor or Grand Victrix and it is possible that he or she may not, through lack of knowledge or some other reason, choose the dog and bitch in the show who are most worthy of being named Grand Victor and Grand Victrix.

All German Shepherd superstars, new stars and superpets, with the sole exception of those dogs whose breeders and owners realize they won't have a chance under the chosen judge, will converge on the current show site with their owners, handlers and admirers. Each one has his own following that fervently hopes he or she will make the Select class, or more optimistically still, win the most coveted title of all, Grand Victor or Grand Victrix.

Even though the judge's choice of Select Dogs and Bitches and his ultimate selection of the Grand Victor and Grand Victrix may not agree with your own, you will be able to admire many, many fine Champions, thrill to the spectacle of seeing the stars of yesterday and look with anticipation at the young stars of tomorrow who might be shown in the Regular or Futurity classes.

A Tracking Test is held first thing in the morning. The tracking fields are generally located some distance from the show grounds, as the site has to be large enough to accommodate several tracks. If you don't have a car, the show committee will provide transportation for you and your dog.

A Herding Trial is now offered to those Shepherd owners who have been working their dogs with sheep. It is conducted according to the AKC rules so a dog could get a leg toward a title. As is the rule at AKC events, the dog must qualify three times in order to win a title. A Sheepherding Instinct test is also offered to any and all German Shepherds. This is still a novelty and dozens of people want to see how their dogs will react when faced with several sheep. It is a fun class and quite popular. The beginners who earn the Herding Instinct certificate are rightly proud of their dogs.

In 1965 I conceived a new set of Obedience exercises for German Shepherds with Utility titles. I named my jumping exercises "Agility" and they had a tremendous appeal to spectators and trainers alike. Shortly thereafter, when I judged Obedience at the National Specialty show in Arizona, these exercises were introduced as a nonregular class that included Agility jumping. This was a "first" for German Shepherd fanciers in the United States. Twenty-five years later, various people were experimenting with a set of jumping exercises using the name "Agility." It became so popular that the AKC devised rules and regulations for this new activity. Seven of my original

Agility jumps which I designed for exceptional Working Dogs are now offered in a very simplified form. The Dog Walk, Bar Jump, High Jump, Broad Jump, Window Jump, Barrier Jump and Long Jump. I expect that an Agility class will be offered to handlers at future National Specialty shows.

All these different events are offered to German Shepherd owners so that they can participate in one or more classes. Len and Kathy Steen were chairpersons of this event for many years. The volume of work to be done during the entire year before the actual show is mind-boggling. Besides the major task of exploring show sites and investigating hotels that *will* take dogs, there are dozens of important details to be handled to assure a smooth-running, efficient operation. The 1995 National was a good example of the professional way they handled this Specialty. Everything was done for the efficiency of the dogs being shown in Conformation. Stalls were provided for the dogs, water, hoses and outlets were made available so dogs could be washed and blow-dried. The two Obedience rings were conveniently placed outdoors on the cricket field and in my opinion it was an absolutely perfect setup. A rope had been set up eight feet from the ring ropes, which kept spectators at bay. This is a far superior arrangement than that of holding the Obedience classes indoors next to the Conformation classes with their entourage of loud, uninhibited double handlers. Specialty Shows that offer both Conformation and Obedience classes should take note. Both classes should receive *equal* consideration.

The last day is a very exciting one. The Obedience Victor is presented with the coveted award. The Agility winners and the Sheepherding winners are presented trophies in the main arena. Then one has the opportunity to see Champions from all over the country competing against each other. Many of these Champions have been promoted by advertisements in the *Review* and other publications, or by being campaigned extensively at dog shows by professional handlers during the year. It is extremely interesting to evaluate and compare all of these Champions. Regardless of your field of interest in German Shepherds, you owe it to yourself to attend a GSDCA National. A great deal of time and effort is extended to make it interesting to everyone concerned. If you love German Shepherds, you will enjoy it.

In 1996 the National Specialty Show was held in Lexington, Kentucky. It drew a total of 599 entries in Conformation including 108 Best of Breed entries. There were 165 entries in Obedience, including the entries in the nonregular classes. The Agility classes were offered three days in succession so one could earn a title at one show. The Sheepherding Trials were also open to beginners and advanced handlers and were very popular. The BH (*Begleithunde*) is the International Companion Dog degree. Although it was offered at the National, very few people had the opportunity to watch or participate. Hopefully it will be offered at all future Nationals. Despite the fact that it was bitter cold at this show, everything went according to schedule. All of the dogs enjoyed it.

I would like to see our National Specialty become an international event where dogs from other countries would compete, and where the American Best of Breed dogs would have a CDX title and a certificate showing they had passed a courage test. If they were all subjected to a hard physical and psychological test, it would raise the standard of German Shepherds in this country. If this were the case I am sure the top American Champions could meet the challenge.

The following are lists of the American Grand Victors and Grand Victrixes.

GRAND VICTORS

Year	Dog's Name	Sire and Dam
1918	Komet v. Hoheluft	Nero (Affolter) Erika Elberfeld
1919	Apollo v. Hunenstein	Ajax v. Hohenstein Liselotte v. Hannover
1920	Rex v. Buckel	Nores v. d. Kriminalpolizei Asta v. Gabelsburg
1921	Ch. Grimm v. d. Mainkur	Nores v. d. Kriminalpolizei Gustel v. Hoffstatt
1922	Ch. Erich v. Grafenwerth	Alex v. Westfalenheim Bianka v. Riedekenburg
1923	Ch. Dolf v. Dusternbrook	Luchs Uckermark Dorte v. Riedekenburg
1924 & 1925	Ch. Cito Bergerslust	Ch. Geri v. Oberklamm Goda v. Mundtsdorf
1926	Ch. Donar v. Overstolzen	Dutch S. Orpal v. Gruneneck Blanka v. d. Urftalsperre
1927, 1928, & 1929	Ch. Arko v. Sadowaberg	Cuno v. Wohwinkel Afra v. Jahnplatz
1930	Ch. Bimbo v. Stolzenfels	Wolf of the Hedges Meta v. Stolzenfels
1931	Ch. Arno v. Sadowaberg	Cuno v. Wohwinkel Afra v. Jahnplatz
1932	No title awarded	
1933	Golf v. Hooptal	Ch. Utz v. Haus Schutting Karin v. Cleve
1934	Ch. Erikind of Shereston	Dual Ch. Hettel v. Bodman Hamilton Cilla

GRAND VICTORS

Year	Dog's Name	Sire and Dam
1935	Ch. Nox of Glenmar	Ch. Utz v. Haus Schutting Ch. Jessica v. Hoheluft
1936	Award withdrawn	
1937 & 1938	Ch. Pfeffer v. Bern, ROM	Dachs v. Bern Clara v. Bern
1939	Ch. Hugo of Cosalta, CD	Ch. Utz v. Haus Schutting Ch. Hexe of Cosalta
1940	Ch. Cotswold of Cosalta, CD	Ch. Nox of Glenmar Lorain of Cosalta
1941	Ch. Nox of Ruthland, ROM	Ch. Pfeffer v. Bern Ch. Carol of Ruthland
1942	Ch. Noble of Ruthland	Ch. Pfeffer v. Bern Ch. Carol of Ruthland
1943	Can. Ch. Major of Northmere	Ch. Anthony of Northmere Can. Ch. Torga v. Hoheluft
1944	Ch. Nox of Ruthland, ROM	Ch. Pfeffer v. Bern Ch. Carol of Ruthland
1945	Ch. Adam of Veralda	Ch. Yip of Hobby House Ch. Olga of Ruthland
1946	Dex of Talladega, CD	Can. Ch. Major of Northmere Zaida v. Liebestraum
1947	Ch. Dorian v. Beckgold	Ch. Jeffrey of Browvale Blondy v. Hoheluft
1948	Ch. Valiant of Draham, CD, ROM	Ch. Nocturne of Grettamarc, CD Adelia of Draham
1949 & 1950	Ch. Kirk of San Miguel	Ch. San Miguel's Baron of Afbor, UD Ch. Judy of San Miguel
1951	Ch. Jory of Edgetowne, CD, ROM	Ch. Vol of Long-Worth Ch. Orpha of Edgetowne
1952	Ch. Ingo Wunschelrute, ROM	Arry v. Burghalderring Lona v. Aichtal
1953	Ch. Alert of Mi-Noah, ROM	Ch. San Miguel's Baron of Afbor, UD Ophelia of Long-Worth
1954	Ch. Brando v. Aichtal	Claus v. Haus Werle Wilka v. Aichtal

Year	Dog's Name	Sire and Dam
1955	Ch. Rasant v. Holzheimer Eichwald	Claudius v. Hain Udda v. Holzheimer Eichwald
1956	Ch. Bill v. Kleistweg, ROM	Ch. Hein v. Richterbach Adda v. Reiffeck
1957	Ch. Troll v. Richterbach, SchH3, ROM	Axel v. d. Deininghauserheide Lende v. Richterbach
1958	Ch. Yasko v. Zenntal, SchH3	Xanto v. Osnabruckerland Mina v. Gerstenberg
1959	Ch. Red Rock's Gino, CD, ROM	Ch. Edenvale's Nikki Kay of Ayron
1960	Ch. Axel v. Poldihaus, ROM	Axel v. d. Deininghauserheide Ch. Petra v. Richterbach
1961	Ch. Lido v. Meller Land	Brando v. Tappenort Jola v. Richterbach
1962	Ch. Yorkdom's Pak	Ch. Lido v. Johanneshauch Jutta v. Colonia Agrippina
1963	Ch. Condor von Stoerstrudel, SchH1, ROM	Bello v. Hollewinkel Birke v. Saturner-See
1964	No competition	
1965	Ch. Brix v. Grafenkrone, SchH3	Bar v. d. Weissen Pforte Tatyana a.d. Weingengend
1966	Ch. Yoncalla's Mike, ROM	Yoncalla's Mr. America Yoncalla's Colette
1967	Ch. Lance of Fran-Jo, ROM	Ch. Fortune of Arbywood Frohlich's Elsa v. GrunesTahl
1968	Ch. Yoncalla's Mike, ROM	Yoncalla's Mr. America Yoncalla's Colette
1969	Ch. Arno v. d. Kurpfalzhalle, SchH3	Fant v. Eichengarten Peggi v. Aichtal
1970	Ch. Hollamor's Judd, ROM	Ch. Yoncalla's Mike Fanchon of Edgetowne
1971	Ch. Mannix of Fran-Jo	GV Ch. Lance of Fran-Jo Hilgrove's Erle
1972	Ch. Lakeside's Harrigan	GV Ch. Lance of Fran-Jo Cobert's Melissa
1973	Ch. Scorpio of Shiloh Gardens	GV Ch. Mannix of Fran-Jo Waldesruh's Pud Shiloh Gardens

GRAND VICTORS

Year	Dog's Name	Sire and Dam
1974	Ch. Tellaheide's Gallo, ROM	Ch. Tellaheide's Enoch Baroness Bella von Friden
1975	Ch. Caesar von Carahaus, ROM	GV Ch. Mannix of Fran-Jo, ROM Aretha of Glentaner
1976	Ch. Padechma's Persuasion ROM	Zeus of Fran-Jo, ROM Ch. Padechma's Galaxie
1977	Ch. Langenau's Watson, ROM	GV Ch. Scorpio of Shiloh Gardens, ROM Langenau's Quessa, ROM
1978	Ch. Baobab's Chaz, ROM	Ch. Doppelt-Tays Hammer, ROM Ch. Pinebeach's Darlin
1979	Ch. Schokrest on Parade, ROM	Covy's Oregano of Tucker Hill, ROM Philberlyn's Rhoda of Marin
1980	Ch. Aspen of Fran-Jo	Quint of Shiloh Gardens Ch. Elfie of Fran-Jo, ROM
1981	Ch. Sabra Dennis of Gan Edan	Ch. Ozark of Gan Edan Fran-Jo's Dawn of Gan Edan, ROM
1982	Ch. Kismet's Impulse von Bismark	Ch. Marty von Bid-Scono Ch. Von Bismark's Dark Angel
1983	Ch. Sukee's Mannix	Ch. Tara Bella's Impresario Sukee's Windy
1984	Ch. Cobert's Trollstigen	Ch. Doppelt-Tays Hawkeye, ROM Ch. Cobert's Zephyr of Windigail
1985	Ch. Ossipee Caesar v. Clover Acres, CD	Ch. Clover Acres' X-Citation Spirit of Clover Acres
1986	Ch. Sequel's Senator v. Merivern	Ch. Sequel's Lonnie v. Glisando, ROM Knockout of Merivern, ROM
1987	Ch. Rio Valle's Nestle's Crunch	Ch. Stuttgart's Sundance Kid, ROM Dolmar's Megan of Springrock

GV Ch.& Can. Ch. Rio Valle's
Nestle's Crunch, ROM,
ROMC, OFA
1988 GV Ch. Piper Hill's Polo,
ROM, ROMC, OFA
Piper Hill's Kodachrome

Sel. Ch. Woodacre's Dakota,
ROM, OFA
1989 GV Ch. Bethesda's Tacoma of
Si-Don, CD, OFA, AOE
Mikah's Miracle by Prestige,
CD

Proven Hill's Obi Wan
1990 GV Am. & Can. Ch. Proven
Hill's Banker of Altana, OFA, ROM,
ROMC
Kolbrook's Favorite Decision

GV Ch. & Can. Ch. Rio Valle's
Nestle's Crunch, ROM,
ROMC, OFA
1991 GV Ch. Woodside's Nestle's
Quik v. Merwesteyn, OFA, ROM,
ROMC
Woodside's Chelsey v. Windi-
gail

Ch. Carmil's Stetson
1992, 1994 GV Ch. Campaigner's
Gatewood Uzi, OFA, ROM,
ROMC, OFA
Ch. Campaigner's Gatewood
Haganah, ROM, OFA

Ch. Earth Wind & Fire of Edan,
CD, ROM
1993 GV Ch. Bethesda's Earth of
Jada-Edan
Si-Don's Tenille of Bethesda,
ROM

Ch. Sandyhill's Paco Robanne,
HIC
1995 GV Ch. Inflight's Spencer v.
Sandyhill, OFA
 Kolbrook's Crooked Halo

Toro of Jeanden
1996 GV Ch. Stoneway's Uecker,
OFA
 DuChien's Ghia of Langenau

GRAND VICTRIXES

Year	Bitch's Name	Sire and Dam
1918	Lotte v. Edelweiss	Horst v. Boll Grete v. Nahetal
1919	Vanhall's Herta	Nero (Affolter) Oakridge Joma
1920	Boda v. d. Furstenburg	Alex v. Westfalenheim Clara v. Herkulespark
1921	Dora v. Rheinwald	Nores v. d. Kriminalpolizei Asta v. Gabelsburg
1922	Debora v. Weimar	Nores v. d. Kriminalpolizei Flora v. Weimar

GRAND VICTRIXES

Year	Bitch's Name	Sire and Dam
1923	Boda v. d. Furstenburg	Alex v. Westfalenheim Clara v. Herkulespark
1924 & 1925	Irma v. Doernerhof	Ch. Claus v. d. Furstenburg Elsa v. Walrube
1926	Ch. Asta v. d. Kaltenweide	Ch. Erich v. Grafenwerth Flora v. Oeringen
1927	Ch. Inky of Willowgate	Ch. Armin v. Pasewalk Richa v. Dusternbrook
1928	Ch. Erich's Merceda of Shereston	Ch. Erich v. Grafenwerth Hamilton Winnifred
1929	Ch. Christel v. Stimmberg	Ewald v. Haus Paland Afra v. Glockenbrink
1930	Ch. Katja v. Blasienberg	Samson v. Blasienberg Anni v. Blasienberg
1931	Ch. Gisa v. Koenigsbruch	Ch. Erich v. Glockenbrink Dina v. Vilsendorf
1932	No title awarded	
1933 & 1934	Ch. Dora of Shereston	Kim of Shereston Sprite of Shereston
1935	Ch. Nanka v. Schwyn	Ch. Utz v. Haus Schutting Anka v. Saliba
1936	Ch. Frigga v. Kannenbackerland	Reinulf v. Haus Schutting Tilla v. Hallerwald
1937	Ch. Perchta v. Bern	Dachs v. Bern Clara v. Bern
1938	Ch. Giralda's Geisha	Ch. Giralda's Dewet v. d. Starrenburg Giralda's Worthy
1939	Ch. Thora v. Bern (of Giralda)	Bodo v. d. Brahmenau Vicki v. Bern
1940	Ch. Lady of Ruthland, ROM	Ch. Pfeffer v. Bern Ch. Frigga v. Kannenbackerland
1941	Ch. Hexe of Rotundina	Kaspar v. Hain Alma of Rotundina
1942 & 1943	Ch. Bella v. Haus Hagen	Ch. Pfeffer v. Bern Ch. Hexe of Rotundina

Year	Bitch's Name	Sire and Dam
1944	Ch. Frigga v. Hoheluft, ROM	Ch. Nox of Ruthland Ch. Lady of Ruthland
1945	Ch. Olga of Ruthland	Ch. Pfeffer v. Bern Ch. Carol of Ruthland
1946	Ch. Leda v. Liebestraum, ROM	Ch. Garry of Benlore Lita of Dalric
1947	Ch. Jola v. Liebestraum, ROM	Ch. Garry of Benlore Zaida v. Liebestraum
1948	Ch. Duchess of Browvale	Ch. Nox of Ruthland Alma v. d. Aller
1949	Doris v. Vogtlandshof	Claudius v. Hain Barbel v. Haus Trippe
1950	Ch. Yola of Long-Worth	Ch. Keno of Long-Worth Elsa v. Saliba
1951	Ch. Tawnee of Liebestraum	Judo v. Liebestraum Vonda v. Liebestraum
1952	Ch. Afra v. Heilholtkamp, ROM	Armin v. Trilke Fenja v. d. Eifferburg
1953	Ch. Ulla of San Miguel	Judo v. Liebestraum Ch. Christel of San Miguel, CD
1954	Ch. Jem of Penllyn	Ch. Hussar of Maur-Ray Lou-Ed's Carus
1955	Ch. Sola Nina of Rushagen, ROM	Ch. Lorian of San Miguel, CD Ch. Simba v. Hagen, CD
1956	Ch. Kobeil's Barda	Ch. Ingo Wunschelrute Evida v. Grafmar
1957	Ch. Jeff-Lynne's Bella	Ch. Gernda's Ludwig Ch. Gretel v. Waidberg
1958	Ch. Tan-Zar Desiree	Ch. Xantos of Rocky Reach II Ch. Twilight of Mi-Noahs
1959	Ch. Alice v. d. Guten Fee, SchH1, ROM	Cent v. Hermannschleuse Fee v. d. Graftschaft-Hoya
1960	Ch. Robin of Kingscroft	Ch. Bill v. Kleistweg Elene of Allsbruck
1961	Ch. Nanhall's Donna	Ch. Field Marshall of Arbywood Ch. Bonnie Bergers of Ken-Rose
1962	Ch. Bonnie Bergere of Ken-Rose, UDT, ROM	Ch. Lake Trail Terrywood's Cito Ch. Ginger Girl of Long-Worth

GRAND VICTRIXES

Year	Bitch's Name	Sire and Dam
1963	Ch. Hessian's Vogue, ROM	Ch. Kurt v. Bid-Scono Hessian's Quella
1964	No competition	
1965	Ch. Mar-Sa's Velvet of Malabar	Ch. Ulk Wikingerblut Malabar's Lorri of Rocky Reach
1966 & 1967	Ch. Hanarob's Touche	Ch. Wilva Don's Faust Ch. Wilva Don's Schatz v. Thornoaks
1968	Ch. Valtara's Image	Ch. Bernd v. Kallengarten Valtara's Amber
1969	Ch. De Cloudt's Heidi, CD	Ch. Fritz de Cloudt Duchess de Cloudt
1970	Ch. Bel Vista's Solid Sender	Ch. Treu v. Wolfsstock Hessians Helene v. Bel Vista
1971	Ch. Aloha von Bid-Scono	Ch. Waldo v. Bid-Scono Kiela v. Bid-Scono
1972	Ch. Cathwar's Lisa v. Rob	Ch. Lakeside's Gilligan's Island Ch. Lorjo Donka
1973	Ch. Ro San's First Love	Elwillo's Rand Rosan's Bridgette
1974	Ch. Lor-Locke's Tatta of Fran-Jo	Ch. Eko-Lan's Paladen, ROM Fran-Jo's Kelly of Waldesruh
1975	Ch. Langenau's Tango	GV Ch. Mannix of Fran-Jo, ROM Ch. Langenau's Elude, CDX
1976	Ch. Covy's Rosemary of Tucker Hill, ROM	GV Ch. Lakeside's Harrigan, ROM Ch. Tucker Hill's Angelique, ROM
1977	Ch. Charo of Shiloh Gardens	Ch. Scorpio of Shiloh Gardens, ROM Waldesruh's Pia of Shiloh Gardens
1978	Ch. Jo-San's Charisma	Ch. Reno of Lakeside, ROM Covy's Bonita of Tucker Hill
1979	Ch. Anton's Jesse	Zeus of Fran-Jo, ROM Arnhild's Black Frost
1980	Ch. Lacy Britches of Billo	Zeus of Fran-Jo, ROM Just A Joy of Billo, ROM
1981	Ch. Anton's Jenne	Zeus of Fran-Jo, ROM Arnhild's Black Frost

Year	Bitch's Name	Sire and Dam
1982	Ch. Merkel's Vendetta	Ch. Merkel's Quaestor Merivern's Ms. Fortune v. Sierra
1983	Ch. Von Ivo's Blithe Spirit	Ch. Doppelt-Tay's Hawkeye, ROM Von Ivo's Shivaree
1984	Ch. Jeanden's L'Erin of Langenau	Ch. Doppelt-Tay's Hammer, ROM Langenau's Minx Renaissance
1985	Ch. Lynrik's Kristal	Shebland's Eldorado Camareigh Lynrik's Shanon of Winchester
1986	Ch. Dawnhill's Carli	Ch. Patrick-J of Lebenstraum August Keshua v. Pawn Hugel
1987	Ch. Howard's Magic Moment	Howard's Snakmaster Miklin's Wodin Cara Mia

Ch. Willow Dale's Admiral
1988 GV Ch. Sea Lair's Ciera, ROM
Sea Lair's Espiritu

Ch. Proven Hill's Up 'N Adam
1989 GV Ch. Altana's Kricket
Ch. Covy's Altana of Tucker
Hill

Ch. Amber's Stockbroker, ROM
1990 GV Ch. Amber's Rosie of
Bracewood
    Ch. Carolina of Bob-Lyn

Ch. Brentaryl's Gunner, ROM
1991 GV Ch. Brentaryl's West Side
Story
    Brentaryl's Mercy

Ch. Pete of Fran-Jo, ROM
1992 GV Ch. TR's Guinevere v.
Kenlyn
    Ch. Jerland's Rosalita v. TR

Ch. Hoheneichen's Flag
1993 GV Ch. Hoheneichen-Avalon
Chinadoll
    Ch. Avalon's Fancy Free

Leiter's Firecracker
1994 GV Ch. Leiter's Cross My
Heart
    Oakdale's Rosenthal

Ch. Pinebeach's Stars 'N Stripes,
ROM, OFA
1995 GV Ch. Jerr's French Pastry
Cross Timbers Chuey Clihu

Inflight's Fly So Free
1996 GV Ch. Inflight's Heaven Only Knows
Inflight's Hepburn Sandyhill

THE OBEDIENCE VICTOR TITLE

The German Shepherd Dog Club of America established a new title in 1968 for those dogs who earn the Highest Combined Score in the Open B and Utility B Classes at the National Specialty Show. The winner will be called the Obedience Victor and must meet the following requirements.

1. A combined score of not less than 385 points.
2. A score of not less than 190 in the Open B Class and in the Utility B Class.
3. Must have won a ribbon in an AKC Conformation Show and provide proof. This requirement was discontinued in 1994. Now the owner must present his Highest Combined Winner to an AKC Conformation judge who is present at the show to verify that the dog has no disqualifying faults according to the AKC Standard for German Shepherd Dogs. However, regardless of the AKC rules, spayed bitches and neutered males who otherwise meet the Standard are acceptable.

Over the years the location of the Obedience rings at the National Specialty has been less than ideal. I would suggest that the rings be located outdoors and away from the Conformation rings. If the show is held in a hot climate such as Arizona, or in frigid weather, the rings should be indoors. If the classes are held indoors, flash photos should be prohibited. At one indoor show a dog was momentarily blinded by a flash photo just as his handler was giving him a signal. He lost the OV title in that second. The 1995 National Specialty could serve as a model. The Obedience classes were held outdoors at that show in a perfect setting. The weather was ideal.

OBEDIENCE VICTORS AND VICTRIXES

1968	OV Heide von Zook, UD
1969	None
1970	OV Schillenkamp Duke of Orleans, UD
1971	OV Bihari's Uncle Sam, UD
1972	OV Ruglor's Reboza Von Zook, UD
1973	OV Brunhild of Ravenna, UDT, SchH1
1974	OV Kenilworth Lady Jessica, UDT
1975	OV Penny auf der Heide, UDT
1976	OV Natasha von Hammhausen, UD
1977	OV Herta von Hammhausen UD
1978	OV Indra von Hoheneichen, UD
1979	OV OTCH Johnsondale's Kool Kaper, UD
1980	OV Von Jenin's Link, UD
1981	None
1982	OV Martin's Kassel v. Lahberg, UD
1983	OV OTCH Wynthea's Tony, UD
1984	OV OTCH Wynthea's Scorpio of Lu-Jon, UD
1985	OV OTCH Gutes Liebchen von Haus Sagan, UD, TDX
1986	OV OTCH & CH. DeBrut's Butch Cassidy, UD
1987	OV Scotswd New Wave, CDX, TD, SchH3
1988	OV OTCH Scotswd New Wave, UD, TDX, SchH3, FH
1989	OV OTCH Sacheim Hills Natash, UD
1990	OV OTCH Vom Vilhaus Ram, UD
1991	OV OTCH Vom Vilhaus Ram, UD
1992	OV Kinderknoll's Deo' Favents, UD
1993	None
1994	OV OTCH Noonmark's Quincy Jones, UDX
1995	None

1983 OV OTCH Wynthea's Tony, UD with Wynn.

1996   OV OTCH Ashmead's Sizl'n Pyrotekniks, UDX, TD

Tony's Story—A Study in Courage

Tony had that fighting spirit that enabled him to defy all odds. At seven weeks, with Wynn's care he astounded his vet by recovering from a near-fatal parvo attack. At eleven months, ready for Novice competition, he was deliberately hit by a car that left him with four bad fractures and a badly bruised and battered body. In pain and unable to walk, he never lost his spirit and cheerful attitude and convinced his worried owner that he would be okay.

He was crated for six weeks while he received TLC along with the therapy his recovery required as his muscles had atrophied. The therapy he received every day came in the form of obedience training. Due to his broken bones, he would crab sideways instead of walking straight. It was physically impossible for him to perform a natural, straight sit. However, after his nurse worked with him patiently for several months, he returned to some degree of normalcy. The hardest thing he had to do was change his opinion of a straight sit and sit the way it pleased Wynn. Being such a good sport, with a 100% willing heart, he succeeded.

Shown in Novice competition from October 30 to December 20, 1982, though *not fully recovered,* he was "in the ribbons" every time with a 197+ average. From April 8 to May 7, 1983, he competed in Open A, scoring three Highs in Trial (HITs) including a score of 199.5 at the Philadelphia DTC Obedience Specialty in a field of 198 entries. He won five first-place awards.

Tony won his Utility title, plus an HCS award over the weekends of September 16 and 24, 1983. The GSDCA National Specialty was scheduled for the following weekend, at an indoor venue, and the Obedience Trial took place six feet from the Conformation ring. Tony earned first in Open with 197.5 and second in Utility with 197. Now at two years of age, he was the National Obedience Victor. In May 1985 he won his Obedience Trial Championship title, (OTCH). He was a proud, happy fellow; he would like you to

1984 OV OTCH Wyn-
   thea's Scorpio of Lu-
   Jon's UD
Owner-Handler: John
   Brooks

1986 OV OTCH & Ch. DeBrut's
Butch Cassidy, UD, TDX
Owner-Handler: Lori Nickeson

1987 & 1988 OV OTCH Scotswd New
Wave, UD, TDX, SchH3, FH, HC
Owner-Handler: Leonie Pulis

know how hard he tried.

1989 OV OTCH Sacheim Hills Natash, UD
Owner-Handler: Bill Carroll

1990 & 1991 OV OTCH Vom Vilhaus Ram, UD
Owner-Handler: Florence and Ed Wilson

1994 OV OTCH Noonmark's Quincy Jones,
 UDX, NA
Owner-Handler: Nancy Brayton

1996 OV OTCH Ashmead's
 Sizl'n Pyrotekniks, UDX, TD
Owner-Handler: Jean Rodoski

Dog Shows in the United States

A Sanction Match is a dog show for purebred dogs in which you and your dog can compete to gain experience and get the feel of ring competition. If you have a promising show puppy, it is a good idea to get him out to Sanction Matches so that he can gain valuable ring experience and be exposed to a dog show atmosphere while he is young. Match Shows are put on by dog clubs with American Kennel Club approval, are held for practice purposes only and no Championship points or Obedience credits are given. They are always unbenched, can be entered the same day as the show, and you may arrive any time before the scheduled closing time for entries, and if you wish, you may leave as soon as you have shown your dog. The bitches and dogs are judged separately and the classes usually consist of Puppy classes that are divided into age groups of three to six months, six to nine months and nine to twelve months. The Adult classes usually consist of two classes, Novice and Open. The Novice class is for young dogs over a year of age while the Open class is filled with mature dogs who have had some ring experience.

There are two kinds of Match Shows. Plan A is given by the club that is trying to get permission to hold a Point Show. The club publishes a Premium List and conducts the show like a Point Show although no points are given. Most of the matches are called B Matches and they are for practice and fun, with a very informal atmosphere. Most anyone who attends dog shows can tell you where and when the next Match Show will be held. Once you have entered a Match, your name will be on the club's mailing list and you will receive their Match notices thereafter.

Your Obedience Dog should have the experience of working in at least one Match before he tries competing at a Point Show. Even if you think he is ready, you may be surprised how poorly he works the first time he is out in public. He may be so busy watching the other dogs and staring at all the new sights that he will momentarily forget what you have taught him. And you might be nervous yourself if you have never been in the ring before. This is valuable experience you both need and can profit by. You will find the regular Obedience classes—Novice, Open and Utility—offered at these shows. If you are just beginning, you would enter the Novice A class. Many Match Shows also include nonregular classes in Obedience such as Sub-Novice (all the work is done on-leash), and Graduate Novice (a drop is included in the Recall exercise), and in this class the long sit and the long down exercises are done out of sight, as in the Open class.

Dog shows are licensed by the American Kennel Club and are permitted to give Championship points in the Conformation classes, and legs toward an Obedience title in the Obedience classes. It is possible in one day at an All-Breed Show that holds classes both in Obedience and Breed to gain points toward a Breed Championship and a qualifying score toward an Obedience title.

Dog shows are put on for the individual dog clubs by licensed superintendents, and are for purebred dogs only. A list of the coming shows is published in the dog magazines. The American Kennel Club compiles this list, and publishes it in their official magazine, *Purebred Dogs, The American Kennel Gazette.* You will find their address on your dog's registration certificate. The magazines will give the date of the show, the name of the club, the location, the superintendent and his address, or if the club puts on its own show, their secretary and his address.

If you write to any of the superintendents and ask them to put your name and address on their mailing list, they will be glad to send you Premium Lists for the coming shows. The Premium Lists will give you all the pertinent information about the shows such as the location, date, judges, prizes, closing date, classes, et cetera. You then fill out the form included in the Premium List that asks for your dog's name, breed, registration number, place of birth, birthday, sire, dam, breeder, class and your name and address, and send it back to the show superintendent with the stipulated fee. This varies slightly from show to show but is generally twenty dollars for each class. The closing date is about three weeks prior to the show, so you must plan to mail your entry early so that it will get there in time. A week before the show, you will receive an entry slip which is your admission ticket. A schedule will also be included that will tell you at what time the various Conformation and Obedience classes will be judged, your dog's catalog number and the number of entries in each class. If the show is benched, your entry slip will give your bench number.

Point Shows are held indoors and outdoors and are benched or unbenched. When they are benched, it is necessary to keep your dog in a stall when he is not being shown or exercised. Dogs of the same breed are benched together in adjoining stalls which are separated by partitions. Take a three-by four-foot rug for your dog to lie on so that he will be more comfortable. You will find a metal ring in the back of the stall and you may secure your dog to it by means of a bench chain. These chains are sold at all benched shows, and come in different lengths. At one time, practically all the dog clubs had a stipulation in their Premium Lists that the dogs must arrive by a certain time in the morning, and must stay until a certain hour in the late afternoon or evening. The handlers were warned that they would be penalized or fined if they didn't adhere to this rule. Fortunately, today, very few dog clubs cling to this old inequitable rule, which is extremely hard on the dogs and their owners. The most popular shows are those that permit the dogs to arrive ten minutes before the scheduled hour of judging and leave when they have been judged. One rule that still applies is that dogs must be kept on-leash at dog shows except when being shown in the Obedience rings.

Dog shows are an excellent sounding board for dog owners. Your dog may look beautiful to you and your friends in your own back yard because you have no other dogs with whom you can compare him. In a dog show he will be judged comparatively with other dogs of his own age and sex, and any structural flaws will be more apparent.

It is particularly beneficial to the owner or breeder if he can watch impartially while the dogs are being judged and benefit from the opinion of a judge who has a sound knowledge of the breed. It is only by exhibiting your dog in dog shows that you can get an accurate picture of your dog's good or bad points. It is only by comparing your dog against others of top quality and sound structure that you can truly evaluate him. If you make it a point to observe competent judges at various dog shows, you will gradually gain a more thorough understanding of the breed.

In the Conformation classes, a dog is judged against the Standard of his particular breed, and the judge determines which of the dogs present are the best representatives of this breed in type and temperament. The judge examines the dogs for soundness while they are gaiting and posing.

There are six regular classes in Breed—Puppy, Twelve-to Eighteen-Months, Novice, Bred-by-Exhibitor, American-bred and Open—and the sexes and they are judged separately with dogs preceding bitches.

The Puppy class shall be for dogs that are six months of age and over, but under twelve months, that are not champions. The age of a dog shall be calculated up to and inclusive of the first day of a show. For example, a dog whelped on January 1st is eligible to compete in a puppy class at a show the first day of which is July 1st of the same year and may continue to compete in puppy classes at shows up to and including a show the first day of which is the 31st day of December of the same year, but is not eligible to compete in a puppy class at a show the first day of which is January 1st of the following year. The first day of a show is considered to be the first day on which there is regular conformation judging.

The Twelve-to-Eighteen Month class shall be for dogs that are twelve months of age and over, but under eighteen months, that are not champions. The age of a dog shall be calculated up to and inclusive of the first day of a show. For example, a dog whelped on January 1st is eligible to compete in the class at a show the first day of which is January 1st of the following year and may continue to compete in this class at shows up to and including a show the first day of which is the 30th day of June of that year, but is not eligible to compete in this class at a show the first day of which is July 1st of that year.

The Novice class is for dogs six months of age and over, born in the United States or Canada, which have not, prior to the date of closing of entries, won three first prizes in the Novice class, a first prize in Bred-by-Exhibitor, American-bred or Open classes, nor one or more points toward their Championships.

The Bred-by-Exhibitor class shall be for dogs born in the United States or, if individually registered in the *American Kennel Club Stud Book,* for dogs whelped in Canada, that are six months of age and over, that are not Champions and that are owned wholly or in part by the person or by the spouse of the person who was the breeder or one of the breeders of record. Dogs entered in this class must be handled in the class by an owner or by a member of the immediate family of an owner. For purposes of clarity, the members of an immediate family are: wife, husband, father, mother, son, daughter, brother or sister.

The American-bred class shall be for all dogs (except Champions) six months of age and over whelped in the United States of America by reason of a mating which took place in the United States of America.

The Open class shall be for any dog six months of age or over, except in a member Specialty Club Show held only for American-bred dogs, in which case the Open class shall be only for American-bred dogs.

If your dog wins his class, he will then compete against the winners of the other classes for Winners Dog. It is the winner of this competition that will win points toward his Breed Championship. Next, the class winners plus the second-place winner must compete for Reserve Winners. For instance, if the Open Dog won Winners Dog, then the second-place Open Winner would be eligible to compete for Reserve Winners. Reserve Winners is awarded in case the Winners Dog is disqualified for some reason, such as an incorrect entry, which would make him ineligible for the class. The bitch classes are then judged and the Winners Bitch is chosen. Next, the Reserve Winners Bitch is selected. If the Winners Bitch has earned more points than the Winners Dog, he automatically gains the same number of points by defeating her.

If there are Specials entered (a Special is a dog that already has won enough points to gain his or her Championship), they will now compete against the Winners Dog and Winners Bitch for Best of Breed. If the Winners Dog or Winners Bitch is awarded Best of Breed, he or she is automatically awarded Best of Winners. If Best of Breed is awarded to an entered Special, then Winners Dog and Winners Bitch must compete for best of Winners after Best of Breed has been marked in the judge's book.

After Best of Winners has been awarded, the Best of Opposite Sex Winner should be selected. Eligible for this award are: Dogs of the opposite sex to Best of Breed that have been entered for Best of Breed competition; and the dog awarded Winners of the opposite sex to Best of Breed.

The dog that wins Best of Breed is now eligible to compete in his Variety Group. There are seven Variety Groups and a miscellaneous classification for currently unrecognized breeds. For instance, if you were the owner of a German Shepherd, he would be in the Herding Group. If by some good fortune you were to win First in this group, you could then show him with the winners of the other groups for the top honor, namely Best in Show. During this competition, if your dog were to win Best in Show over another dog that had picked up more points that day, this award would entitle your dog to the same number of points. The largest number of points that can be acquired at one show is five, and if you have a popular breed of dog this means that a large number of dogs will be competing against one another. A dog needs to gain fifteen points in order to become a Champion, but he must have won two major shows worth three or more points apiece under two different judges, and his total fifteen points should be made under three different judges.

The American Kennel Club has devised a Schedule of Points for twelve regions of the United States. Eight of these regions are each made up of a group of states, the ninth is California, the tenth is Alaska, the eleventh is Hawaii and the twelfth is Puerto Rico. This rating is based on the number of dogs shown in that area and is subject to annual review and change as the number of dogs in a specific breed increases or decreases. You will always find the latest Schedule of Points pertinent to the region printed in the dog-show catalog for the event.

In the Conformation classes, "A dog who is blind, deaf, castrated, spayed, or who has been changed in appearance by artificial means except as specified in the Standard for its breed, or a male who does not have two normal testicles normally located in the scrotum, may not compete at any show and will be disqualified."

In the Obedience classes, a dog who is castrated, spayed, a cryptorchid, a monorchid or a dog that has a fault that would prevent him from winning points in Conformation may be shown, for it is the dog's working ability and attitude that counts. It is a pleasure to live with an Obedience-trained dog when his good behavior is a way of life. It is even more rewarding to live with an Obedience-trained Champion.

Obedience Trials are held in conjunction with most All-Breed Shows. There are also Obedience Trials held separately that are sponsored by training clubs. The latter cater to the Obedience exhibitors and conduct efficiently run trials that feature regulation-size rings, close-cropped grass at outdoor shows, matting for indoor shows, efficient stewarding and an impressive trophy list.

There are three regular classes at an Obedience Trial: Novice, Open and Utility. The degrees that correspond with these classes are CD (Companion Dog), CDX (Companion Dog Excellent) and UD (Utility Dog). A perfect score in each of these classes is 200 points, and in order to qualify a dog must earn 170 or more points and more than 50 percent of each exercise. When you have received three qualifying scores in the Novice class under three different judges, the American Kennel Club will send you a Companion Dog certificate with the name of your dog and the title CD after his name. This makes it official, and you may now compete in the Open class whenever you are ready. You need the same number of qualifying scores to earn a Companion Dog Excellent or a Utility Dog certificate. Once you have the CDX title, you may continue to compete in Open B. When you earn the UD title, you may compete in both Utility and Open B. If you win First or Second Place in these classes, you may win points toward your Obedience Trial Championship. The number of points you win is determined by the number of dogs competing in the class. To win the OTCH, you need 100 points, a First in each class and wins under three judges. This title is comparable to a breed championship and denotes a top working dog. However, those who compete for an OTCH title soon discover that the rule that applies to Conformation does not apply to Obedience. In order to win points toward a Championship title in Breed, your dog does not have to compete against Champions. In Obedience he is forced to compete against Champions in order to win OTCH points. This is most unfair since handlers showing dogs with OTCH titles can continue to compete with the same dogs indefinitely.

The exercises and maximum scores in the Novice classes are:

Heel On-Leash and Figure 8	40	points
Stand for Examination	30	points
Heel Free	40	points
Recall	30	points
Long Sit	30	points
Long Down	30	points
Maximum total score	*200*	*points*

The exercises and maximum scores in the Open classes are:

Heel Free and Figure 8	40	points
Drop on Recall	30	points
Retrieve on Flat	20	points
Retrieve over High Jump	30	points
Broad Jump	20	points

Long Sit	30	points
Long Down	30	points
Maximum total score	**200**	*points*

The exercises and maximum scores in the Utility classes are:

Signal Exercise	40	points
Scent Discrimination Article #1	30	points
Scent Discrimination Article #2	30	points
Directed Retrieve	30	points
Moving Stand and Examination	30	points
Directed Jumping	40	points
Maximum total score	**200**	*points*

Since 1995 the American Kennel Club has issued a Utility Dog Excellent title. Dogs meeting the requirements carry the degree UDX after their names. The main requirement is that the dog shall have earned ten qualifying scores in both Open B and Utility B at ten separate shows.

The American Kennel Club will issue a Tracking Dog certificate (TD) to a dog who has passed a Tracking Test, and a Tracking Dog Excellent certificate (TDX) to a dog who has passed a more difficult Tracking Test. Today there is a new type of Tracking Test that is very difficult and complex. It is called the Variable Surface Tracking Test and the AKC will issue a certificate for a dog that successfully passes it (VST). When a dog has earned all three tracking titles, the prefix CT (Champion Tracker) may be used before its name.

Ch. Kismet's Gold Rush, OFA (a
  winner of four Herding Groups)
Sire: Am. & Can. GV Ch. Proven
  Hill's Banker of Altana, ROM,
  OFA
Dam: Pinebuck's Myra of Kismet,
  OFA
Breeders: Robert and Maryellen Kish
Owners: Karin and Al Wagner

chapter 25

Judging

As I mentioned earlier in our chapter on Dog Shows, it is necessary to get your German Shepherds out and show them in Conformation if you want to see how they compare with the Shepherds other fanciers are raising. You probably noted that when I mentioned how important it was to have your dog evaluated, I suggested you show under judges who have a sound knowledge of the breed. While this is particularly important at Point Shows, where your dog has the chance to win Championship points, this advice also applies to Sanction Matches.

Generally speaking, Sanction Matches should be considered as just an opportunity to get your puppies out and gain ring experience, because you rarely find any knowledgeable judges officiating at them. Novice people who are starting out, breeders with their first litters and established breeders all attend these shows for practice purposes, and it would be beneficial if they could all get a sound evaluation of their puppies as well as give them the actual ring experience they need. Everyone concerned would learn much more if a judge who had a sound knowledge of the breed was there to give them advice, guidance and encouragement.

During my years as president of the Diamond State German Shepherd Dog Club (which I founded), I always invited very knowledgeable German Shepherd breed authorities to judge our Sanction Matches.

In direct contrast, we have noted that most of the All-Breed Clubs that hold Sanction Matches invite people who know practically nothing about German Shepherds to judge them. Beginners who observe or show their dogs do not learn anything at these shows. Most of the German Shepherd Specialty clubs will invite someone to judge their Sanction Matches who has raised Shepherds for a few years. These people need the experience of judging a few of these shows before they apply for a judging license. The exhibitors will find the ring experience beneficial for their dogs and themselves.

We have a sizable number of knowledgeable judges in this country, but included in this group we have about a dozen exceptionally astute German Shepherd authorities who have spent a large portion of their lives studying the breed. A person in this category is never content to sit idly by and wait for the next dog show so that he can observe German Shepherds. He makes it a point to see them constantly, and whether the dogs are playing together in a pen, being exercised on-leash, being shown at a dog show or merely walking across a room, his mind is busy studying them, deciding what structural qualities make the dogs move as they do and noting which good or bad points are evident and for what reason. It is this continual search for answers and the never-ending study of the dog's anatomy that makes these specialists in the German Shepherd field able to analyze a dog's structure so accurately and quickly. It is a labor of love for the breed.

You don't become a knowledgeable judge overnight by reading books or by watching or judging the breed at an occasional dog show. To gain more proficiency and to continue learning about the breed, you must keep seeing quality animals by raising them yourself, visiting friends who have kennels, officiating at Sanction Matches or Point Shows or studying and appraising the breed at every opportunity in real life or in films.

Some German Shepherd dog clubs are far wiser than others in selecting for their Sanction Matches and Point Shows the kind of judges that both the novice and experienced fanciers respect. Shows put on by these clubs are always successful and very well attended. They realize there is a great thirst for knowledge among all German Shepherd owners and know they will travel great distances to observe or show under a judge they respect.

Many clubs will find it profitable and rewarding to engage a knowledgeable judge from the opposite end of the country to officiate at their show. If this judge hasn't done any judging in their area for several years, he will draw a great number of entries. The dog owners and handlers will feel they have an equal chance to win under this judge and are willing to enter several dogs from their kennels to find out. This type of judge, not knowing the local dogs, is apt to be very fair and honest in his judging.

Jim suggests the following procedure for evaluating dogs in the allotted time. He feels that we have many judges who have a good eye for dogs and a good depth of knowledge, but sometimes fail to do a good job of judging because of poor ring procedure. Ring procedure is a prime factor that allows a judge to find the best dogs and correctly evaluate them in the time allowed.

The dogs should be lined up in catalog order and then the handlers should be asked to gait them *at a slow trot* so that they can be observed moving. A slow trot is a handler's fast walk. A judge can evaluate a dog's gait more accurately when the dog is trotting at a pace his eye can follow. Numerous faults can be hidden at a fast gait when a dog is straining at the end of the leash. In fact, the best way for a judge to see a dog's true gait is for him to *insist* that each dog be moved on a loose leash for a specific distance, or until the judge is sure in his own mind that he has seen the dog moving completely on its own.

As the judge is evaluating the dogs and placing them according to his preference, he should place the best side-mover at the front of the line and the next best in second place, and so on to the end of the class. Then the dogs should be stopped to rest. While the dogs and handlers are resting, the judge should examine the dogs individually. If the first dog in line is examined individually and is found to have a good temperament, good dentition, is sound coming and going and has no faults serious enough to warrant a change in placement, it is the best in this class and should be the Class Winner.

If, after examining the second and third dogs, the judge finds that the second dog has a hidden fault, such as a dentition problem, or has a fault coming or going that is serious enough to warrant a change in place, he should move the third dog into second place. If the hidden faults in this dog who is now in third place are serious enough, the judge can continue to place dogs ahead of it until he feels it is in the correct place in line. This procedure will enable the spectators and exhibitors to see and compare the best movers in the class and help them to understand correct German Shepherd gait. When dogs are moved back in this manner, spectators and exhibitors alike understand the judging procedure and quickly realize that those dogs who are falling back in line must have a hidden fault such as temperament, dentition, et cetera, that only the judge can see.

Some judges examine each dog individually before having them gait together. No judge can remember the minor faults of twenty or thirty dogs, such as dentition problems or if certain dogs were faulty coming or going, and he will have to waste a lot of time rechecking them later. If the judge found a hidden fault in the beginning, the spectators would remain unaware of it. If the best-moving dog in the class was not moved to the front of the line, the spectators would think that the judge missed a good one. To avoid this impression, a judge will often go back to a good side-moving dog and ask to see it coming and going. Or he may look at the dog's mouth once or twice to show the ringside there is a hidden fault there. All this time-consuming procedure could be avoided if the judge gaited all the dogs first and placed them according to his preference.

On many occasions a handler who has won Winners Dog at a show will receive the Reserve Winners Bitch award when he rightfully deserves to win Winners Bitch. On numerous occasions different judges have told Jim that they liked the bitch he was handling, but since they had given him Winners Dog, they didn't think he should receive both awards. In other instances, if a top handler doesn't win Winners Dog in his entry, the judge feels obliged to give him Winners Bitch. This is equally wrong. The judges felt that people would say they were dishonest if they gave the same handler both awards. Is this judging dogs or handlers, or is it just trying to appease the spectators? A good handler will show five or six dogs at one show—and they might all have different owners. Each of these dogs should be judged on his own merits and should win or lose on them alone. It is not a contest to divide the spoils among professional handlers or to give points to the most popular owner, breeder or handler. If the judge is not confident of his ability to judge the dogs, he shouldn't be judging.

Due to the judging situation in the United States, showing German Shepherds is fast becoming a contest between professional handlers. This is unfortunate because it is fun to show dogs, and many owners and breeders enjoy handling their own dogs when they feel they have an equal chance to win. One sees fewer and fewer amateurs in the Shepherd rings today because the dogs are gaited too fast, ignored if the handler is unknown, and are refused the points if there are other dogs of the same quality who are professionally handled. There will always be a great need for good professional handlers for many reasons, but the nonprofessional should have an equal opportunity to win if his dog merits the award.

At one National Specialty Show, the judge knocked an exceptionally beautiful-moving Shepherd out of the Select class because her handler was unknown to him. This Shepherd had won her Championship with four majors under Specialty judges. The judge, looking for an excuse to dump the handler, had her move back and forth several times. However, the ruse didn't work since his subsequent Grand Victor was faulty in this respect.

A good handler will know if his dog should win, and if he wins points under a certain judge with a poor dog, he will continue to show poor dogs under that judge because he realizes the judge is not knowledgeable. If a handler realizes that he must show top-quality dogs under a certain judge in order to win, he will show his best dogs under that judge.

Some judges will put a handler at the front of the line and tell him that he wants to see the dogs moved at a slow trot. As soon as another dog in the class starts pulling more vigorously, he is placed at the head of the line. This starts a rat race, for the handlers know that what the judge is really looking for is the dog that will pull the hardest on the leash and that good structure is secondary. After showing once under this judge, a handler will immediately break into a run when the judge tells him to go at a slow trot. It is the only way he has a chance to win. A judge of this caliber is more of a detriment than a credit to the profession. It is entirely the judge's responsibility to have control of his ring. He should see to it that the handlers present their dogs in the manner in which he wants to judge them. A judge who lets handlers, exhibitors and spectators influence him in controlling the speed of the dogs or in making decisions will receive little regard. By contrast, an efficient judge with an orderly judging procedure, who maintains proper ring control, will command respect from both inside and outside the ring.

There are judges who will keep the dog they prefer in the middle of the line until the last few minutes of judging, when they start gaiting the dogs at excessive speeds and then move their preferred dog up one place at a time until he is in first place. This is very confusing to the spectators and it appears that the judge is placing emphasis on the dog's desire to move and willingness to pull and strain on the leash, rather than upon correct structure and gait. This type of judging is very popular with novice and unknowledgeable people and is called grandstand judging. The judge is an exhibitionist who wishes to be the center of attraction, so he plays up to the audience by trying to create a dramatic finish. If, after all the excessive gaiting, this dog starts to tire before he gets to the front of the line, the judge will give the award to an inferior dog. Another owner of a fine Shepherd has wasted his money on a show entry.

Sometimes a Breed judge, who normally has a good eye for a dog and can do a good judging job, will use a different system of judging if a breeder friend is showing a dog. If the dog is inferior, the judge will hide it in fourth place until the last second and then tell the handler he has first place. This is particularly annoying to all the other dog owners in the different classes and is a classic example of political judging. A judge who lets personal friendship alter his decisions in the ring should not be judging.

Some of our Specialty judges act as if they are judging a different breed when they judge German Shepherds at an All-Breed Show. They award Best of Breed to the German Shepherd they feel will have a chance to win the Herding Group, even though they know it is not the best German Shepherd in the show. This leads us to believe that this type of judge is sacrificing our breed to cater to the known preference of the Herding Group judge, hoping that his Best of Breed winner will be placed in the Herding Group. A judge should be firm enough in his convictions to put up the dog of his choice, rather than that of someone else. It would be far better for the breed if the Specialty judge put up the best German Shepherd in the show and hoped that by doing so he would further the education of the Herding Group judge. It does the German Shepherd breed very little good to have mediocre specimens keep winning the Herding Group. The public will see this dog winning show after show and think it is a perfect example of a German Shepherd when, in reality, it is a second-rate animal. The only ones who profit by such poor judgment are the dog's owner and the handler. The former profits by stud fees and the sale of puppies, while the latter gains recognition with other All-Breed judges who tend to favor any other dogs he shows.

Unfortunately, many of the All-Breed judges do not have a thorough understanding of the German Shepherd Dog Standard, and do not realize when a German Shepherd is single-tracking correctly. They are looking for German Shepherds that *parallel track*. It is for this reason that many of our best dogs do not have great All-Breed show careers. The statement in our Standard that causes the most confusion to both specialist and All-Breed judges is: "Viewed from the front, the front legs function from the shoulder joint to the pad in a straight line, viewed from the rear, the hind legs function from the hip joint to the pad in a straight line." *There is nothing in this statement to indicate that legs should move perpendicular to the ground.* A German Shepherd that does not single-track cannot be correct in motion when viewed from the side. For a more detailed analysis of single-tracking, refer to chapter 33, "Structural Analysis of the German Shepherd Dog."

The emphasis on side gait in the American showring is too strong. In an all-too-familiar scenario, a judge will make his initial placements after having seen all the dogs move. In a large Specialty, if it is a big class, he will then spend considerable time examining each dog and placing him where he feels he should be. Later, when he starts moving all the dogs again, he will notice one with a spectacular side gait and will move him to the front. He assumes that he overlooked it. He has not taken notes, and doesn't recall that this dog had three missing teeth, was very bad coming or going or originally displayed very poor temperament. This sort of thing could and does happen when judges get carried away by side gait. Of course, it doesn't help the judge make the right decision when the crowd is screaming with delight. For some reason, many spectators feel impelled to cheer when the dogs start side gaiting, and all other qualities are forgotten.

It would certainly help to educate the breeders, as well as the general public, if more judges had the courage to place the dogs with good side gaits at the end of the line if they showed poor temperaments, soft, weak ears, bad backs, or were so extreme in hindquarter that they were very incorrect coming and going.

There are a number of beautiful German Shepherds in various sections of this country with very good side gaits. Quite a few of these are also true coming and going and they have good temperaments. But they are in the minority. Until the judges start penalizing the dogs with poor temperaments, even though they are good movers, this problem will get worse.

Judging character and temperament in the showring is a very difficult task. Many shy dogs can fool judges if they are well ring trained and are double handled wisely. The ring-trained, mentally unsound dog might permit the judge to examine him, providing the routine and the general atmosphere did not upset him, but if a chair accidentally toppled over next to him, he would panic and might try to run away. This dog is basically afraid of everything unless conditioned through training to appear steady.

Today, various German Shepherd clubs hold Conformation classes and many shy dogs learn to stand and stay when people approach and examine them. Dogs that move are corrected immediately with a sharp slap, or jerk of the collar, and the verbal command "Stay." To avoid this correction, shy dogs will eventually learn to stand still and permit strangers to examine them. Since these clubs have committed themselves to work to improve the breed, they should advise the owners of shy Shepherds that they should *not* be shown in Conformation classes.

In an attempt to test temperaments, a judge may instruct the handlers to stand in the middle of the ring with their dogs on loose leads, and will caution them not to give their dogs any "Stay" commands. Then he will walk among the dogs to see if any of them will shy away from him. This test wouldn't bother an unsound dog who is trained to stay, for his handler could give him a signal that the judge wouldn't notice.

A dog's fear or apprehension is mirrored in his eyes, but a clever handler will hide this by having the dog's owners attract the dog's attention just as the judge approaches him. The dog will be so anxious to watch his owners outside the ring that he will momentarily forget his fears and stand there staring at them.

The shy dog is much easier to spot when he is being examined individually, for he doesn't want to be the center of attention. The judge can also check temperaments when the dogs are being posed in line and he can double back and recheck a dog's expression and attitude if he thinks the dog is unsure of himself.

Occasionally, a judge will find a top-quality dog that would be placed high in its class, except for the fact that it has a temperament problem. When this situation arises the judge, in a vain attempt to show the spectators he hasn't missed anything, will order the handler to bring his dog into the center of the ring. If the dog shies away from the judge, he will follow it around in circles, mocking the dog and embarrassing the handler. Fanciers who tend to be self-conscious if ridiculed in this manner may never show their dogs in Conformation again. If the aforementioned judge used the proper ring procedure, he would have had the dog at the front of the line because he was a good mover, but would have noticed the temperament problem during the individual examinations, and would have placed dogs ahead of him until he was at the end of the line. This method would have shown the spectators the dog had a fault without needlessly embarrassing anyone. Some judges will approach a dog five or six times if the dog seems unsure of himself. A dog that takes up so much of the judge's time should not receive any award.

A judge should use the utmost discretion when judging the temperament and character of puppies. He should be gentle, soft spoken and tolerant when examining them. A puppy's first ring experience is a confusing one, and any unpleasant experience at this time could have an disastrous effect on his future.

Judging the German Shepherd's character and temperament should not be taken lightly because a German Shepherd with a poor temperament and/ or dubious character is a worthless creature and should never become a Champion. If judges give points to these dogs, people will breed to them and perpetuate this fault. Temperament and character are two important factors in the breed and should be rewarded and considered along with equally important features such as good shoulders, strong backs, good gaits, et cetera. Too frequently a dog with an uncertain temperament will be placed over a dog with a minor fault. This is wrong. It is time temperament was recognized as a very desirable characteristic instead of being taken for granted or ignored.

Jim is more aware of the judging situation than most people because he shows dogs practically every weekend. He feels that we have too many unqualified judges who do not understand the German Shepherd Standard. He believes a judge must have the proper emotional and mental attitude and must be firm in his convictions. He must be able to make decisions, be poised and calm at all times and take the emotional strain of judging dogs in a ring. Some people can develop an "eye" for a good dog in a very short time and be able to recognize depth of quality and harmonious structure, while others will be fooled forever by superficial beauty and general appearance. A judge must be able to take criticism as there will always be more losers than winners and they will make up reasons why their dogs did not win.

There are a great number of All-Breed judges who will put up the dog of their choice regardless of the handler. They are honest judges who are looking for the best representative of the breed in the ring on that day. They are looking for a dog that shows great "ring presence," is sound coming and going, and is well-balanced and beautiful to behold. Many amateurs have won under judges when they had good dogs.

Before applying for a judge's license, a person should ask himself if he has enough experience, a sufficient depth of knowledge, a sincere love for the breed and the necessary integrity to make a good judge. When people tell Jim that they are thinking of applying for a judge's license, he asks them if they feel they have the proper qualifications to be an excellent judge. The standard answer he gets is, "I think I could do a better job of judging than so and so," naming a poor judge. Is this the answer? This is probably why we have so many poor judges, because each one thought he was better than an unknowledgeable one. If this book helps people to understand the German Shepherd breed, it is worth the hundreds of hours spent writing it.

In this revision several of our most respected and knowledgeable judges have graciously accepted the invitation to give us their personal observations of today's German Shepherd Dog.

MORTON GOLDFARB, M.D., F.A.C.S.
"Ohne Zucht keine Leistung, ohne Leistung keine Zucht"

I am very pleased to be an American Kennel Club judge and the only judge in North America that is licensed by the SV to judge the German Shepherd in Germany. The above German translates into "Without breed type there is no working ability, without working ability there is no breed type." This basically summarizes it all. Holding dear to this statement, I will backtrack just a bit and let you know the qualifications required to judge the German Shepherd in Germany.

In order to conserve time, suffice it to say that the prospective judge must complete seven apprentice assignments under teacher judges and must write a critique of every animal that has been brought before him or her.

This critique is submitted to the Board of Directors for approval. The German system and basically that of the world union in all countries except the United States requires that each animal is judged from first to last place and critiques be given on each animal.

Breed responsibility is foremost in the minds and hearts of those who have a true love of the German Shepherd. We humans are entrusted with the safekeeping of one of God's creatures. We influence the breed dramatically, and that influence must be positive, not negative. As the founder of the breed so deftly put it in 1899, "Breed to the Standard, not the marketplace."

I could write a lengthy discussion about proper anatomy and its relation to the animal's ability to perform the task that it was bred to do. We all know that form and function are hand in hand and therefore realize that an animal that is properly constructed will function and be able to carry out the tasks that are demanded of it much better than an animal with improper construction.

Conformation judges look for many different things and a knowledgeable judge only requires a short period of time to evaluate an animal in its entirety. What do we look for in a properly constructed animal? The German Shepherd Dog must have specific breed type. The animal must have strong secondary sex characteristics which in the United States is severely lacking. The animal must have proper proportions of height to length and proper proportions of wither, back and croup. We all know that a good German Shepherd, whether it be American-bred, Mexican-bred, German-bred, English-bred or from any other country in the world, will win anywhere in the world if he meets the proper Standard. The United States has great dogs that could win anywhere in the world with proper qualifications, but overall we need continued improvement.

These remarks have been brief, but hopefully you have gathered some insight into what an international judge thinks when viewing the German Shepherd Dog. All dedicated people, whether their primary interest lies in working ability or in conformation, must join together for the betterment of the breed. These factions of conformation and working ability, which sometimes are definitely polarized, must work together to achieve what truly is the greatest purebred dog in the world.

ED BARRITT

After more than thirty-five years of association with the German Shepherd as an exhibitor, breeder and judge, I think we are finally recovering from the era of overangulation and focusing more on balanced structure that fits more correctly into our Standard.

In my opinion the major problem is that many do not take the time to read and study the German Shepherd Standard as we have too many varied interpretations as to what is good, balanced German Shepherd structure. We have many varieties of styles of dogs shown today that are accepted as good specimens but are lacking the concept of the total dog.

Some of the problems that are apparent in the dog of today are: 1) Animals that lack substance, too fine in bone and a bit too high on the leg; 2) High head carriage in motion because of straightness in front and a degree of too much length of stifle; 3) Some softness in character; 4) Heads with muzzles too long, lacking in underjaw development; and 5) And the most obvious problem is the number of dogs that do *not* extend their hocks much past the 90-degree point when in motion.

The best dog in a given class may *not* be a good representative of the total dog concept. I would suggest that *we* put more effort into studying our Standard, focusing more attention on balanced structure and less on performance.

MARYELLEN KISH

We are fortunate to have one of the best breed Standards in purebred dogs. This Standard describes a true trotting dog designed to earn his living tirelessly trotting all day. He must move "powerfully but easily" with no wasted motion, covering the maximum amount of ground with the minimum amount of effort. What the Standard does not describe is an overly extreme dog with static angles that do not function. Unfortunately, overemphasis on outline, extreme topline and rear-quarter angulation have resulted in a preponderance of just such an animal. Dogs have difficulty straightening their hind legs to drive under properly and are totally unable to straighten them to give a smooth follow-through. Indeed, because of the fixed angulation, the hindquarters function in a circular motion neither reaching under, nor extending behind.

The right angle between the upper thigh and lower thigh described in the Standard applies to the dog standing with the pad of his hind foot under the hip joint. It does not mean that the hindquarters should exhibit a right angle when the hind leg is pulled back as the dog is "stacked." And it certainly does not mean the hindquarter should always be a right angle when the dog is moving.

We are breeding for longer bones because this means a longer stride. Unfortunately, a longer stifle and longer hocks poses quite an engineering problem for our dogs to overcome and still be able to trot efficiently. They compensate by throwing their hocks in or out or by actually driving under with their whole hock on the ground and, in many instances, by dragging their toes on the ground; all at the expense of a tremendous amount of muscular energy.

The Standard says the croup is long and gradually sloping. Once again we have gone to extremes by trying to improve on an approximate 30-degree angle of the pelvis by breeding dogs with a 45-degree-or-more angle to the pelvis. The resultant steep croup also makes it impossible for the dog to function properly in the rear.

Our dogs receive substantial help in the showring from the handlers holding up the forequarters with the leash. In the unlikely event that a judge should demand a "loose lead," the dog inevitably tips forward and kicks up badly in the rear. These dogs have no real stamina and are not built to do the work they were intended to do.

This is the most wonderful breed of dog ever developed. A German Shepherd, according to our breed Standard, never lacks confidence. Dogs with pronounced character deficiencies must be excused from the breed ring. A dog that jumps at loud noises and slinks behind its owner on the approach of a stranger is not a German Shepherd. Such animals should be pitied and are an embarrassment to the breed. They should not be promoted, nor should excuses be made for their behavior. Without proper character and temperament, such a dog is a sad imitation of a German Shepherd.

In an era in which it is very difficult to find representatives of this breed with stable temperament, excellent breed type, correct extended side gait and even minimum soundness, it is time to concentrate our efforts where they belong—on our breed Standard. Whether breeding or judging, we need to select dogs with proper character and breed type as described in the German Shepherd Standard. Next, we select for straight legs, good feet and pasterns, medium length of bone; straight, hard backs; true single-tracking, accepting only minor deviations coming and going; and the most fluid, powerful, extended side gait possible without sacrificing the other essential attributes of the German Shepherd Dog.

GEORGE W. AND VIRGINIA COLLINS

We have always felt the Germans' way of thinking and their methods have proven to be the best for the German Shepherd breed. The Germans consider the mental soundness first, then working ability and physical soundness. They feel that with this, one can produce excellence of body structure. This is also our belief. Unfortunately, we have breeders in the United States who are only interested in producing structure and are willing to sacrifice everything else for that alone. The result is not the animal which was intended by the father of the breed, Captain von Stephanitz. In order for the Shepherd to do the work for which he was intended, he should have a balanced structure. Here again, many breeders are willing to sacrifice. They forget that the angulation of the forehand must balance with the angulation of the rear quarter for a Shepherd to move properly with a ground-covering side gait. To deviate from this is to lose balance. An animal will not have the proper side gait when either the front or rear quarter lacks the proper angulation. This can also affect going and coming. We see a great many German Shepherds today who have an extremely long curve of stifle but lack the proper angulation of the shoulder. These animals can only move at an excessive rate of speed. An animal with proper balance, both front and rear, is able to move correctly at slow, medium and fast rates of speed.

As stated earlier, I believe in the German system. I am not in favor of the inbreeding that has become the American way. When one inbreeds, problems can develop that are very difficult to correct. The American-bred German Shepherd males, today, have become too refined or bitchy. They not only lack nobility, but they lack underjaw and strength of head; broadness. One seldom sees a "stallion," which is important in a male German Shepherd Dog.

The majority of German Shepherd Dogs today, both male and female, may not be shy, but they lack guts. Most could not pass the courage test that all German Shepherds used for breeding in Germany must pass. In other words, the American German Shepherd breeder is not breeding to the Standard as intended.

Many American breeders do not like the German method because they feel it is too rigidly controlled. They forget however, that we live in a regulated society. In Germany all animals used for breeding must be *Koered;* approved for breeding. The advantages are that breed weaknesses can be more easily corrected. Through this method, hip dysplasia has been significantly reduced in the breed. Temperament is seldom a problem. One can distinguish sex characteristics from a distance, and overall body structure is more balanced. The working ability of the animals is maintained, as intended.

As a breeder for thirty-five years and a judge for twenty-five years, I find that the German Shepherd Dog has greatly improved, especially in the areas of temperament, motion and missing teeth. Years ago it was not uncommon to see several dogs in a class with unsound temperament plus several missing teeth. Today this is not a problem, especially in the dogs I have been judging, which shows any given area can be improved with desire and concentration.

Today I feel some of our biggest problems are with our judges and their judging. First of all, there are judges who lack enough years of experience in raising litters, studying puppies through their growing stages and keeping these youngsters long enough to know what changes occur and being able to recognize them, so that evaluations can be made in the showring.

Isn't it ironic how most of us after five years in the breed think we know everything, probably giving all kinds of advice to many novice people, not having even bred or finished a champion. Then most of these novices get off to a bad start. Thinking back, we even plead guilty to this. But the most important experience was the five years before we even started breeding, trying to learn all we could about showing, obedience, club functions and every other related matter. However, five years down the road, thanks to "Lance," we had several champions—two in Lance's litter, three in our Mannix litter and three in our Kelly litter. If you have been breeding for five years and not had any success, you would be wise to look at what knowledge you have acquired and what you are doing wrong.

In my observation, too many judges are fault judging, not looking at the total dog, a dog of beauty, overall soundness, and let's not forget that beautiful floating motion that you cannot miss in the ring, and not the dog with the million steps who can run the fastest. You must be able to recognize the dogs' attributes first and foremost—the extremely difficult points to improve in our breed, like follow-through, shoulders and let's not forget intelligence and temperament.

Our judges have to start judging dogs and not who is on the end of the lead or outside the ring. If you have an intimidation problem, you should not be in the ring judging. Today showing dogs is very expensive and it is of the utmost importance that our judges concentrate only on what is inside the ring and on doing the very best job possible, because every judge owes it to our breed and, more importantly, to themselves. Personality conflicts, politics and friendship have no place inside the ring.

Today the most prevalent problems in our breed seem to be locked hocks—poorly placed shoulders that are stilted or pushed far forward—and the scuffing or dragging of the rear toes, possibly caused by the locked hocks. Backs need some improvement also. It appears a lot of the Fancy (breeders) and some judges are unable to see these problems in the ring—especially the locked hocks and lifting of the forehand—or choose to ignore it.

I feel that we have come a long way in the past thirty-five years in improving the serious problems in our breed. Let's continue in that direction and keep breeding better dogs.

ERNEST LOEB

German Shepherd breeders have realized that something must be done to improve the breed. In recent years we have lost very important parts of the structure, such as secondary sex characteristics. One should be able to see from a distance which is a male and which is a female. Other areas that still need improvement are feet and pasterns. Substance needs to be better.

Temperament is another area in which we are lacking. Many sins have been committed through training to cover the lack of sound temperament. Double handling covers poor temperament. Every double-handled dog does not necessarily have poor temperament, but the owners feel they have to double handle in order to be competitive.

An area where the breeders have done a tremendous job is dentition. We have seen great improvement in recent years. Angulation has also been improved. For a time we saw many overangulated dogs. Overangulation with short croups and high tail sets are the cause of insufficient reach and follow-through. Many of our breeders are beginning to see the light.

At one point the parent club had started a Conformation judges' school. This should be continued on a permanent basis, with experienced teachers who have the welfare of the breed at heart. It is important for these teachers to look at the program like-mindedly and conduct it in a uniform fashion. Newcomers to our breed need to be taught by experienced people and not by novices.

I feel that this in general needs to be done.

chapter 26

The Professional Handler

Nowhere in the world do professional handlers exert such a strong influence in dog shows as they do in the United States. This can be observed at any All-Breed Show, including the large ones, where the top professional handlers are exhibiting dogs. If you check the list of top American Kennel Club licensed All-Breed judges, you will find that most of them were handlers at one time. It is only natural that an All-Breed judge who was not very knowledgeable about, say, German Shepherds, would feel safe in giving the points and placings to handlers. He would go on the assumption that the handlers would only have top specimens to show. If he were wrong, the exhibitors with good dogs might refuse to show under him again, but the handlers would continue to give him entries. While it is doubtful whether this judge could draw enough Shepherd entries to make a major, his services would be repeatedly utilized by clubs who wanted him to judge quite a few breeds of dogs.

In the German Shepherd breed, the handler's place is becoming even more prominent. In the other breeds, many breeders and owners are able to exhibit their own dogs, but in the Shepherd ring, because of the prolonged gaiting, large classes, and strong competition, most of the exhibitors employ handlers to show their dogs.

There are numerous occasions when a German Shepherd breeder or owner would prefer to show his own dog if he thought he had an equal chance of winning the points. It is not only far less expensive, it is more fun to participate than to watch from the sidelines. You could say that these people should only exhibit their dogs under judges of integrity and character, but it is unlikely they will gain this information except through trial and error. It takes a very competent judge to give points to a superior dog handled by a stranger when the class is full of handlers with good dogs.

Breeders, or members of their families, should be able to show their dogs in the Bred-by-Exhibitor class without having to compete against professionals. Some breeders are inducing handlers to show in the Bred-by-Exhibitor class by offering them co-ownership of their dogs, and in some cases it is the handler who makes the proposition. It is unlikely the breeders would offer handlers the same inducement to show them in the Open class.

Some exhibitors complain upon seeing the professional handler in the Puppy and Novice classes. Often, due to ill health, business or other reasons, people cannot show their own dogs but want them shown properly. If a person cannot show his own eight-month-old puppy and wants him shown, he should be exhibited in the Puppy class, not in the American-bred or Open classes. The Novice class is a very good place to show a young, green dog who needs ring experience. The Novice class stipulations pertain to the dog, not to the handler.

A newcomer to the sport, who believes he has a beautiful Shepherd, will generally try to handle his dog himself the first few times. Due to his complete lack of knowledge he handles his dog so poorly that he makes it look much worse than it really is. After wasting time and money at several shows he begins to become discouraged and ask other exhibitors what is wrong. The stock reply is, "Oh, you need a handler if you want to win." This negative attitude discourages a great number of would-be fanciers who are then convinced that Conformation showing is strictly political. These are the people who turn to Obedience because they feel they can actively participate in this sport. If these Shepherd owners could attend Conformation classes as easily as they do Obedience classes, they could learn enough about handling their own dogs to present them properly in the Breed ring. There would be far less griping about professional handlers if the average exhibitor realized that it took both knowledge and skill to handle dogs. Some of these newcomers may never have the good fortune it takes to acquire a top-quality dog, or the skill to handle it superbly, but they could enjoy the thrill of showing the dogs they own, and it is a safe bet they would acquire better Shepherds when they learned more about the breed.

Some exhibitors complain that the professional handlers win too often, but if they would evaluate the situation, they would realize that the best handlers generally have the pick of many of the top dogs in the country. Therefore, it is usually possible for the professional to show each judge the type of dog he prefers. The average exhibitor has only one or two dogs that he is showing, and they are repeatedly shown under every judge. It is unlikely one could find a dog that is liked by all the judges even though our breed Standard calls for one correct type.

Many people believe that the top professional handlers are too expensive and overcharge for their services. If a top handler could finish a dog's Championship in ten shows, it is much less expensive than the handler who takes thirty shows to accomplish the same thing. The judge can only evaluate what he sees in the showring, and the top professionals will minimize the faults they are aware of and enhance the virtues of each individual dog they show. The dog that always looks good will "finish" quickly.

The exhibitors complain when the professional's dog, who is not the best in his class, wins. It seems that the blame is being placed on the wrong person; if the judge was honest and knowledgeable, the best dog would win. Unfortunately, some dogs will win only because they are being handled by a big-name handler. But there are also times when a judge will put the best dog down because he is being handled by a big-name handler—this is an effort to prove to the ringside that he has the courage to dump the dog and is not intimidated by the handlers renown. If the judge is competent, he will not let faces or personalities interfere with his placements.

Some handlers are under the mistaken impression that they should not handle a dog that was handled by another handler, while others are so unethical they try to solicit the business of a fancier who already has a handler. A client should certainly be able to employ any handler he chooses, providing his previous handler has been notified and paid for his services. On the other side of the picture, some very worthy dogs are denied their Championships because of the callous, disinterested attitude of some handlers.

Although the professional handler is responsible for much that is wrong with the sport, he is also responsible for much that is good. The top professional handlers, like the top breeders, have a strong influence over the future of the breed. Many of our present and future judges get much of their knowledge of the breed from their handlers. When some exhibitors start showing dogs, they use the services of a professional handler, and if one of these breeders or owners becomes a judge later, much of his handler's teaching and advice will influence his judging.

There are more requirements to being a good handler than having a genuine love for dogs, knowing how to feed and take care of them and being able to present them in the showring. The handler should have clean, safe kennel facilities and consider the health and safety of his dogs at all times. He should conduct himself with integrity and honesty at all times, give his client the best advice he can and not make rash or ill-advised promises just to get clients. He should encourage his clients to be good losers and gracious winners. He should not play politics himself, and should discourage his clients from doing so. He should send his client a marked catalog, along with ribbons and trophies, after every show. The client should be kept informed about the health and condition of his dog. And he should have a clear understanding of the different handling rates involved at different shows, the share of traveling expenses he will be expected to pay and any and all hidden costs. On top of this the handler should have a sound anatomical knowledge of his dogs and understand their breed Standard. Some handlers are sincere and work very hard at being good handlers, but lack that "certain touch" or natural skill that is required to become a top professional handler.

Some people are under the false impression that the only work a handler does is walk a dog into the showring and when the judging is over, collect a large handling fee. This is not necessarily true. Handlers assist their clients in other ways. The top handlers are able to observe many litters of different bloodlines every year, evaluate the prepotency of different sires and offer breeding advice to their clients. Many of the handler's future show dogs will result from his breeding recommendations. The unscrupulous handler will urge everyone who will listen to use his own stud dog, while in the same breath he condemns all others. This unethical behavior is generally practiced by the handler who shows his own dogs for monetary gain rather than the good of the breed.

A good handler should never accept a dog if he doesn't feel the dog has the potential to become a Champion. Many times when Jim has been asked to handle a dog, he has told the owners that their dog was not Championship quality, only to be proven wrong by an unscrupulous handler and unknowledgeable judges. A handler should be honest, for his client will have much more faith in him when he helps him obtain a quality specimen, than with a handler who repeatedly and unsuccessfully shows a poor specimen. It is to the handler's advantage to purchase the best dog possible for his client for it will be shown quite often, and he will not only collect handling fees but will have a satisfied client. Unfortunately, many handlers would rather show a poor specimen several times for the handling fees than tell the truth and take the chance of losing a client. A truthful handler will not only improve the breed, but will enjoy longer and more gratifying relationships with his clients. Jim has found that people who don't want to hear the truth about their dogs are not interested in improving and promoting the breed, but are only interested in personal glory.

In the sport of exhibiting dogs, the handler-client relationship is a very close one. Together, the handler and client will have many ups and downs; today victory, tomorrow defeat. If the client and handler have faith in one another, the victories are sweeter and the defeats much easier to bear. A handler owes it to his client to give, in his opinion, the truthful reason why they were defeated by another dog or dogs. Each dog is an individual and will perform better some days than others, and believe it or not, it is also possible to be defeated by a better dog. Jim would like to ask any handlers who might read this to consider how many times they have returned home from a show and told their clients that their dogs were defeated by better dogs. Instead, most handlers will say that the judge was stupid, incompetent or an out-and-out crook. It is true that judges make mistakes—after all, judges are only human—and some judges are totally incompetent, but the top professional handler should see that his clients do not waste energy and handling fees under judges of this caliber.

Some handlers will discourage a potentially sincere exhibitor by giving them the false impression that the sport of showing dogs is 100 percent political. True, there are some politics in the dog game, and the best dog could be beaten at a given show through politics. But we have far too many honest, knowledgeable judges for a good dog to be kept down forever. A good dog, like a beautiful woman, will always attract favorable attention.

A client has several obligations when he employs a professional handler. He should keep his handler informed of his dog's health and general condition at all times. The top handlers usually have several good dogs to show at the same time. It would be unwise for the handler to show one dog that was out of coat and in poor general condition when the other two might be in good coat and excellent shape. If a client wishes to use the services of a different handler, he should have the courtesy to inform his previous handler in advance. Many handlers plan their shows well in advance and should know which dogs they will be handling. Many handlers do not require an advance payment from their clients and have quite a large amount of their own money invested in their dogs, such as entry fees, traveling expenses and any vet bills if incurred, so they appreciate prompt payment of their bills.

If you plan to hire a handler, I would urge you to be cautious. Before you make a commitment, get all the particulars: his handling fee, exactly what he charges for expenses and the fee if your dog wins points in Best of Breed, the Group or Best in Show. Once your dog becomes a Champion and the handler has received his fee, you are under no obligation to permit him to make money at your dog's expense. If you don't have a written agreement he might bring all of his clients' bitches to your stud dog and expect to get free services for them. A contract will eliminate any misunderstanding.

To be a good handler, amateur or professional, you must have a sound understanding of the dog's anatomy and the Standard of the German Shepherd breed. It is not enough to memorize the Standard; you should know the reasoning behind it.

Handling Tips

Handling a German Shepherd Dog is an art. It is an art that not everyone can master, but in this chapter we will give you the basic things to do, and what not to do, to present your dog properly.

Before taking your dog into the showring he should be groomed to perfection. First of all, he should be vigorously brushed with a slicker brush, both against, and with, the growth of hair, and then rubbed with a damp towel. At this time you could use a grooming aid such as Pro-Groom, or any of the more popular men's grooming creams, but just use a small amount and be careful to rub it all into his coat. Then rub your dog dry with a towel and, last of all, comb his coat evenly and smoothly.

Make sure that your dog's nails are kept trimmed at all times. It is not advisable to trim toenails right before a show as you may cut one too close and cause the dog to limp. Any long or uneven hairs should be trimmed from around the toenails, making the foot as neat in appearance as possible. When combing your dog, make sure that all of the dead hair is combed out of his neck. Many people do a good job of grooming, only to spoil the overall picture by leaving the neck full of dead hair which causes the dog's neck to appear short and bullish.

After a dog is lead trained, and will stand for examination while having his teeth checked, we do not recommend very much more Conformation training. We try to keep as much spirit and animation in the dog as possible. Too much training will sometimes make a dog bored, or "show wise," and he will only show animation when he is getting out of the showring and heading for the car. If a dog is being shown several times per month, he will get all of the training he will need right in the showring.

The first impression a judge gets of your dog is a very important one. When you first go into the ring, make sure your dog looks his best when the judge takes his first look at him. It is very easy to walk a Shepherd into a show pose and if your dog has reasonably good structure, he will look much more natural and harmonious when he is walked into a pose rather than placed in position by hand. Many judges feel that you are trying to cover up faults when you hand pose a dog.

To walk a dog into a show pose you start by standing in front of him, keeping his head slightly down, level with his withers. Hook your fingers through his choke collar under his neck, and start walking backwards slowly as you rub him under the chin. In time he will know that when you rub him under the chin it is a signal for him to start walking. As he moves toward you, watch for his left hock to become perpendicular to the ground, then push his head up and slightly backwards as this will make him stop in a show pose. Use your dog's head as a lever, head down as you scratch him under the chin to move him forward, head up to stop him in a show pose. With a little practice you will be able to walk your dog into a show pose very easily. An important thing to remember at this time is not to force your dog to walk toward you by pulling him with the choke collar. If you try to force him to walk into a pose he will usually end up being bridged, with his front feet too far out in front of his body, instead of perpendicular to the ground.

There will be times when you will have to pose your dog by hand, which is called hand setting. If, for instance, you are in the center of the line, and the person behind you has not left enough room for you to walk your dog into a pose, and you have to set your dog up quickly, you must be able to place all four legs by hand. To start, we set the front legs first as many judges start with the first dog in line and examine each one in succession. The first impression that many judges get of your dog will be a front rather than a side view. It would be foolish to set up your dog's hindquarters first while the judge is watching him stand east-west in front. Stay on the right side of your dog and set the left front leg first as it is closest to the judge. Grasp it at the elbow with your left hand, as you hold the dog's ruff with your right hand, and pull some of his weight over to his right side. This will force him to keep his left foot off the ground while you position his left leg straight in line under his body, with the toes turning neither in nor out. You then push the dog's weight back on to his left side, locking the left leg into place. You repeat the process for the right front leg by grasping his elbow with your right hand, as you shift his weight over to his left side with your left hand as you place his right leg in position. After doing this let his weight fall back to his right side so that the right leg will also remain in position.

Some dogs are so poorly constructed in fore assembly that they stand with their feet turned way out, and it is almost impossible to make them appear correct even when positioned by hand. The only thing one can do when confronted with this type of problem is to set the front legs in position just

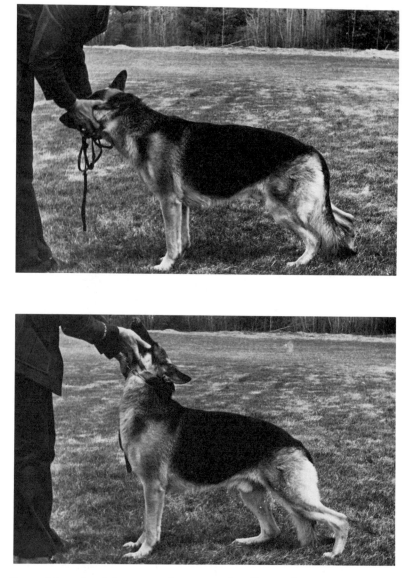

James Moses (top) demonstrating correct handling techniques. Hold dog's head slightly down as you walk slowly backwards. The left hand is hooked in dog's collar, the right is scratching dog under chin. As the dog's left hock (bottom) becomes perpendicular to the ground, push his head up and slightly backwards. This will stop him in show pose.

Hand-setting

Hand-setting

Hand-setting

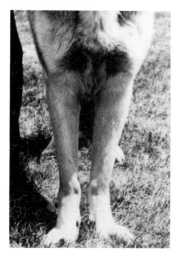

If a dog is east–west—

lift his left leg at elbow.

Position it straight in line with his body.

Lift his right foreleg at the elbow.

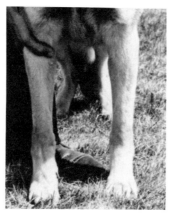

Position it straight in line with his body.

A good front.

If a dog is cow-hocked—

lift his left hock and place it in a straight line with his body.

Then lift his right hock and place it in line with his body.

A good rear.

before the judge approaches the dog, hold the dog's head slightly upward and forward by holding the collar up behind the dog's ears and keep some of the dog's body weight on his fore assembly to help hold his front legs in position. If your dog will bait for liver, or some other tidbit, hold it high and forward, to bring extra weight on his forehand. If you are showing your dog under a knowledgeable judge, this will not help as the judge will ask you to make the dog take a step or two forward to see him stand naturally. If you are showing a dog that stands slightly east-west in front, and you are exhibiting under a judge who wishes to view the dogs standing on loose leads, try to stand your dog facing out of the ring. If you are using a double handler outside the ring, make sure he is aware of the dog's fault and will stand where his dog will be facing him. This will give the judge a good side view of your dog, rather than the unflattering study of his front.

After setting up the front, you should then set the hindquarters, or rear legs, in the proper position. If you are tall enough you should set the dog's rear legs in position while kneeling by his right side. His left rear leg should be placed in position first, and to do this, hold his ruff with your right hand while you grasp his left hock with your left hand and place it perpendicular to the ground. Make sure that the hock is in a straight line with his body and left front leg. Then place the right rear leg under his body until the toes of the right foot are directly under the bend of stifle of the same leg. Make sure at this time that the right rear leg is in line with the right front, and that the hocks are not turning in or out. If you are not tall enough to place your dog's hindquarters while kneeling by his side, you can stand on his left side to place the rear legs. Hold him by his collar with your left hand and use your right hand to place his legs. This should be done quickly as you will be in the judge's line of vision if he wishes to view your dog while you are setting him up. A common fault many handlers make is to overstretch their dogs' hindquarters in an attempt to improve their toplines.

If you feel that the dog you are handling does not have a sloping enough topline, there are several ways that you can improve it without overstretching his hindquarters. You can place his left rear foot about one inch farther back than the point where it would be perpendicular to the ground, taking care that you do not pull it so far back that the stifle becomes straight and the dog appears to be off balance. After placing the left leg slightly back, take the right rear leg and pull it slightly forward and outward, spreading the rear legs. By spreading the rear legs you will lower the dog's croup and give him a more sloping topline without making him look exaggerated or unbalanced. If you have your dog posed this way, make sure that you place the legs back in their proper position when the judge views your dog from the rear, but spread them out again when the judge views the dog from the side. If you have a dog who will bait for liver or some other tidbit, there is a good way to improve his topline and hindquarter angulation. If you hold the tidbit a little high and slightly back it will force the dog's head up and back and cause him to lower his hindquarter, thus making him appear to have more rear angulation and a more sloping topline than he actually does.

Showing a dog's teeth and bite properly is very important. It is very annoying to the judge to have to spend extra time with a dog that is unruly, or with a handler who will not keep his hands and head out of the judge's vision when he is trying to examine the dog's teeth and bite. When showing the judge your dog's mouth, start by grasping the dog's choke collar with your right hand under his chin, which prevents the dog from pulling his head back. While holding it thus, pull the dog's lower lip down, and with your left hand pull the upper lip up, showing the judge your dog's bite. This is always shown first. Next, show one side of the dog's mouth and then the other. Do not open the dog's mouth too wide as this is very painful and irritating to him.

There are some mouth faults that can be covered up by a clever handler, although it is almost impossible to fool a knowledgeable judge. If you have a dog that is slightly overshot you can cover this to some degree by showing the bite in the following manner. Insert one finger in the side of the dog's mouth far enough so that when the dog's jaws are closed on your finger, the upper front teeth just meet the lower front teeth. By practicing this at home you will know exactly how far you will have to insert your finger to make the teeth appear to meet in a scissors bite. With a certain amount of practice at home, you can go into the showring and make it appear quite natural. When showing the bite this way, make sure that you hold the dog's mouth directly up, facing the judge, as this will help to create the illusion of a correct bite. When showing the rest of the dog's teeth, take care to keep his mouth open

Unattractive stance.

Baiting improves the topline.

This dog is overstretched.

This dog is bridged; his fore-legs should be directly under his body.

The same dog posed correctly.

Walking and guiding the dog into the correct stance.

Jim handling Wynthea's Camelot. The most impressive way to pose a dog is to walk him into it. The dog must be structurally correct in order to do this.

during the examination so that the judge will not catch a glimpse of the dog's bite when his jaws are closed. If the judge cannot see the lower teeth when he is examining the bite, he will suspect the dog is overshot.

When showing a dog with a missing premolar, you will have the advantage of hiding it from the judge if he examines the dog's mouth himself and does not ask you to show it to him. In this case teach your dog to catch a ball or stick, which you take into the ring with you. When the judge bends over to examine your dog's mouth, show your dog the toy over the judge's shoulder. This will make him quite excited and he will resent the judge for blocking his view of the toy. The dog will shake his head and become generally unruly as he tries to keep his eyes on his toy. Most judges will not fight with a dog to get a complete look as long as they have seen the bite, and usually do not think to ask the handler to show them the mouth once they have tried to look at it themselves. Many handlers make the mistake of showing the judge's their dog's mouth when it has a missing tooth and try to keep their finger in the hole. Most judges will get very suspicious if you keep your fingers in the way while you are showing the side view of the mouth. They will then insist upon a good look at all of the dog's teeth. Once you are caught trying to hide a missing tooth it seems to make the judge more aware of it and the dog is penalized more severely. It inspires confidence if the judge looks at the teeth himself.

The German Shepherd is a working dog and it is of the utmost importance that he move correctly. The more knowledgeable judges are cognizant of this fact and choose their top placings after seeing the dogs in motion. At most of our German Shepherd Specialties and large All-Breed Shows there is enough depth of quality for the judges to base their ultimate decision on the excellence of the dogs in motion. It is only right that in the final analysis the deciding factor should be the working dogs' ability to move properly.

To show teeth, first hook your fingers into the dog's collar.

First the scissors bite is shown to the judge.

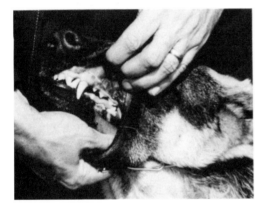

The correct way to show side dentition.

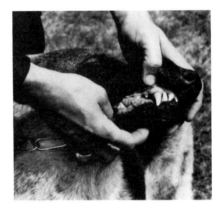

The other side.

The biggest fault the amateur and professional handlers make is to move German Shepherds incorrectly. When moving the average dog there are many things one can do to assist and improve his appearance. There are also many ways to impair the movement of an excellent moving dog. Learning to move the German Shepherd correctly so that he is shown at his best should be the aim of every handler, amateur or professional. Here is where the top professional handler, who has a wealth of experience, has the edge. The judge can only evaluate the dog while he is being shown, and if he is shown properly it may mean the difference between First and Fourth place.

A dog in the showring will appear to have an alert attitude if the person he loves is at the same show. The dog will be watching for him and will move with more spirit and animation. Double handling is against American Kennel Club rules and regulations so we must caution you not to call, whistle or make any noises that might distract the other dogs in the ring.

Dogs who are dissimilar in structure should be gaited differently to compensate for their faults. The most common fault handlers make is to gait their dogs too fast. A dog will become discouraged and lose his desire to move if his handler runs off ahead of him and jerks and pulls on his collar to force him to move at an excessive speed. A dog who is excellent in structure will look far less attractive if he loses his desire to move. A good-moving dog, who starts out at the head of a line, may end up out of the ribbons because his handler continually harasses him to move at excessive speeds until the dog becomes discouraged and stops moving altogether.

The correct way to move a dog is to start out very slowly and let the dog trot out ahead of you. If the judge wants you to move faster, you can gradually increase your speed. One rarely ever hears judges ask handlers to move their dogs at the ridiculously fast speeds that many handlers do. We would all like to see the dogs moving easily and effortlessly in front of the handlers, but this cannot be accomplished by the handler who moves ahead of his dog. If a dog is interested in looking for someone he loves who is on the show grounds it is very easy to follow along behind him. The dog may have to be guided around the corners, but it is best if the handler doesn't attract the dog's attention at this time.

It is very difficult to make some dogs take a corner smoothly. You should never hit or slap a dog on the side of his head or muzzle to make him turn, as this might make him hand-shy. If you do, he will spend more time watching your hands than he will moving. The best way to approach a corner is to slide your hands down the lead to shorten it, so that you can guide him around the corner, then, after turning it, increase the length of the lead by playing it out, as this will permit the dog to move out in front of you.

During the individual examination most judges will ask the handler to move his dog around the ring. It is important to move the dog at the speed he looks his best. Don't be afraid to move your dog at a fast walk if he does this most easily and effortlessly. Don't be afraid that the judge will think your dog is incapable of moving at a faster speed, on the contrary, the knowledgeable judge will prefer to see him moving at a moderate speed. It is very unusual when a German Shepherd looks better moving at a fast speed, and the few that do are generally incorrect in structure. if you have one of those exceptionally good Shepherds who looks equally good on a tight or loose lead, make every attempt to show him to the judge on a loose lead.

Be sure to move your dog properly when the judge wishes to view your dog going away and coming toward him. A dog's minor faults that can be observed when he is coming or going will be less noticeable with good handling. It is also important to handle a sound-moving dog correctly when he is coming and going, as poor handling could make him look faulty. Many handlers feel that if their dogs are faulty coming and going they should let the dogs wander from side to side in an attempt to cover up the dogs' true action. This is the wrong thing to do because a dog's gait will look even worse as he wanders from side to side, and the judge Will suspect that the handler is trying to hide something, and ask him to move his dog again. If you show the judge that you are trying to hide a certain fault, it will magnify itself in the judge's mind, and he will probably penalize the dog more severely. A knowledgeable judge will know if your dog has a serious fault coming or going when he views your dog's side gait. If it is serious enough so that it affects his side gait you will not be able to hide it from most judges.

When you have a dog with moderate rear angulation who moves too close when viewed going away, you should get him to pull on the lead which will make him spread his rear feet and he will appear to be more correct in motion. If a dog has extreme rear angulation and moves too close when going away, he should be moved on a completely loose lead. The harder this dog pulls on lead the closer his hind legs will get. A dog with loose hocks will also look much better if moved in a straight line on a loose lead. Tension on the lead will cause this dog to twist his hocks much more than he normally would. A handler who keeps looking over his shoulder at his dog's hindquarters is simply drawing the attention of the judge, and the ringside, to his dog's fault. A good handler should be able to feel if his dog is moving properly just by holding the lead.

If you have a dog that is loose in elbows it will help if he is moved toward the judge on a tight lead. This will keep his elbows under his body. Many times the judge will ask the handler to let the dog stand on his own after he has moved him going and coming. If the dog is loose in elbows or stands with his front feet east-west, never let him stand facing the judge. Show the dog's profile. If your dog will bait for liver, you can use it to make the dog position his front feet under his body by making him shift his weight from side to side.

You shouldn't get unduly upset, as many handlers, including some "Old Pro's" do, if the person following you lets his dog get too close to yours while you are gaiting. As long as the dog behind you does not disturb your dog or hide him from the judge's view, you have nothing to worry about. Generally, when this happens the handler in front moves faster to increase the distance between the two dogs, but this merely encourages the next handler to increase his speed to catch up and it becomes a "rat race," a speed contest to see who can go the fastest. The dog who is following will look the best because he is doing the chasing. If a handler behind you repeatedly urges his dog to run up on yours and hide yours from the judge's view, politely ask him to stop. In most cases the guilty person will stop. However, if he doesn't, you should ask the judge to make him stop. Never degrade yourself by becoming involved in a shouting match with another handler.

The use of the choke chain or collar is important when showing your dog. There are many different types of collars that you can use, depending on the age and size of your dog. We personally prefer a wider collar as opposed to a narrow one. If the collar is too narrow or too thin, it tends to dig into the dog's neck and hurt him. Snap the lead to the dead ring on the collar so that if your dog does pull you it will not choke him. Keep the collar down low on the base of the dog's neck, just above his shoulders. Many handlers insist on putting the collar up behind their dogs' ears. A dog will not want to move with vigor if the choke collar is ready to cut off his wind at the slightest pressure, or if the collar hurts his neck in any way. If your dog gaits with his head lower than his withers, don't put his collar up behind his ears to keep his head up. It is better to train him at home not to do this, because if you force him to hold his head up he will strain to lower it and will not gait in a natural manner. The dog who dips his head in this manner is said to have a "goose neck" which is most unattractive.

The two most common faults made by handlers are underhandling and overhandling. The handler who underhandles his dog rarely ever watches the judge. He permits his dog to stand in an unattractive pose when the judge is watching, lets the dog pace, break his stride, or jump around when he should be gaiting smoothly, and never seems to be aware of what is going on around him. Generally speaking, these handlers show dogs who object to having their teeth or testicles examined and the ensuing struggle wastes the judge's valuable time.

The handler who overhandles his dog poses and fusses over him every minute by hand-setting each leg even when the judge is busy examining other dogs. He never relaxes in the ring and makes his dog nervous because he is continually moving him in circles to reset him. In the German Shepherd ring, where the entries are quite large, there will be many occasions when the handlers will have to wait their turn to have their dogs examined. Instead of tiring the dog by continually posing and handling it, the handler should let his dog relax until it is his turn to be individually examined. The handler should keep his eye on the judge and be ready to move or pose his dog at the exact moment the judge wants to see it. By being alert in the showring the handler can present his dog to the judge in the most advantageous way.

chapter 28

Register of Merit Sires and Dams

The Register of Merit Point System for German Shepherd Dogs was introduced in the early 1950s by Burr Robbins, who was then president of the German Shepherd Dog Club of America, and was patterned after the highly successful Register of Merit System formulated by the American Hereford Association. The ROM System was offered to breeders so that they could use it as a guide in establishing their breeding programs. It also served as an excellent means of giving well-deserved recognition to those sires and dams who distinguished themselves through their progeny. If you study the Register of Merit list, you will discover which lines have been instrumental in preserving and improving the quality of the German Shepherds.

The first ROM points could only be acquired at specified shows, but as time went by, these rules were modified and today all major shows are included in the program. At one time a dog or bitch could pick up points by winning the Working Group or Best in Show. As a result of this, a few dogs ran up a large number of ROM points. In some cases the win was justified, however in many instances the all-rounder merely acknowledged the popularity of the handler, not the excellence of the dog. Some of our greatest German Shepherd Champions and producers would never win Groups or Best in Show awards if an unknown handler were showing them. This ruling was changed and now neither of these wins is included, as it is felt that the points should only come from the German Shepherd classes. This is certainly a more realistic outlook.

Today you will notice that credit is given to the sires and dams whose progeny have earned Obedience titles, providing they have earned at least a Reserve in Conformation at a major Point Show. A German Shepherd Dog's character, intelligence and utility are an integral part of this breed. The sires and dams who preserve these qualities in their progeny, who are also worthy of earning a Major Reserve, fully deserve the ROM points awarded them.

On the following pages, we will explain the manner in which the Register of Merit points are acquired. We will also honor the famous ROM dogs and bitches of the past and their winning progeny, and salute the ROM dogs and bitches of today and their progeny.

REGISTER OF MERIT POINT SYSTEM
FOR GERMAN SHEPHERD DOGS

1. In order for a sire to become eligible for the ROM designation, the following requirements must be met:

   a. His point total must be 100 points or more.
   b. The points must be earned by ten or more progeny.
   c. Five of these progeny must achieve the American Kennel Club title of Champion.

2. In order for a bitch to become eligible for the ROM designation, the following requirements must be met:

   a. Her point total must be 40 points or more.
   b. The points must be earned by four or more progeny.
   c. Two of these progeny must achieve the American Kennel Club title of Champion.

3. Conformation Competition

	SHOWS		
	3 Pts.	*4 Pts.*	*5 Pts.*
Best of Breed from Specials	6	8	10
Best Opposite from Specials	6	8	10
Best of Breed from Classes	3	4	5
Best Opposite from Classes a tab	3	4	5
Winners Dog and Winners Bitch	3	4	5
Reserve Winners	1	2	3
Dog (either sex) making Championship			10 points
Select ratings at National Specialty			10 points
Grand Victor or Grand Victrix			15 points
ROM progeny of ROM Sires and ROM Dams contribute 15 points to their Sires and Dams.			
Best in National Futurity and Maturity			3 points
Best Opposite in National Futurity and Maturity			3 points

SHOWS

AOE (Award of Excellence)	10 points

Alaska, Hawaii and Puerto Rico shows are
included in the ROM point system.

4. Working Competition
Awarded only to dogs that have won at least a Major Reserve in conformation.

Companion Dog title (CD)	5 points
Companion Dog Excellent title (CDX)	1 point
Utility Dog title (UD)	15 points
Utility Dog Excellent (UDX)	15 points
Obedience Trial Champion (OTCH)	10 points
Obedience Victor/Victrix (OV)	15 points
Temperament Certification (TC)	5 points
Herding Tested (HT)	3 points
Pre-Trial Tested (PT)	4 points
Herding Started (HS)	5 points
Herding Intermediate (HI)	1 point
Herding Excellent (HX)	15 points
Herding Champion (H.CH)	10 points

The following lists of ROM sires and dams are divided into two groups for each sex—Active and Inactive. (When a sire's points remain unchanged for three years, he is transferred to the inactive list. Even though a sire may be deceased, his name will remain on the active list until his point total has become stable.)

ACTIVE REGISTER OF MERIT SIRES FOR 1996

Total points	Sire	Champions
4,516	Ch. Stuttgart's Sundance Kid	78
1,910	Ch. Proven Hill's Up 'N Adam	20
1,881	Ch. Covy's Mazarati of Tucker Hill	53
1,871	Ch. Nike-Clayfield Andretti	40
1,863	Ch. Brentaryl's Gunner	39
1,854	Ch. Hoheneichen's Flag	37
1,639	Cobert's Sirocco of Windigail	22
1,578	Ch. Prime Time of Billo	33
1,357	GV Ch. Cobert's Trollstigen	34
1,039	Ch. Lairolyn's Fantasy Island, CD	8
1,006	Ch. Earth Wind & Fire of Edan, CD	14
1,006	Ch. Heart Breaker of Bob-Lyn	19
975	Ch. Langenau's Beau of Jeanden	17
957	Ch. Lothario of Heinerburg, CD	26
950	Ch. Hoheneichen's Magnum	19
925	Ch. Woodacre's Dakota	17
910	GV Ch. Woodside Nestle's Quik v. Merwestyn	22
894	GV Ch. Baobab's Chaz	15
887	Ch. Hoheneichen Conan Survival	22
853	Ch. Amber's Stockbroker	15

INACTIVE REGISTER OF MERIT SIRES FOR 1996

Points	Sire
3,256	Ch. Lance of Fan-Jo
2,366	Ch. Cobert's Reno of Lakeside
2,306	Ch. Doppelt-Tay's Hawkeye
2,222	Ch. Ulk Wikingerblut
2,133	GV Ch. Lakeside's Harrigan
2,035	GV Ch.Troll v. Richterbach
1,827	Ch. Eko-Lan's Paladen
1,783	Ch. Kubistraum's Kane
1,375	Ch. Bernd v. Kallengarten
1,228	Ch. Doppelt-Tay's Hammer

INACTIVE REGISTER OF MERIT DAMS FOR 1996

Points	Dam	Champions
1,249	Ch. Covy's Altana of Tucker Hill	3
574	Diamond Jade of Bramblewood	4
512	Ch. Awful Good of Edan, CD, TC	3
467	DuChien's Jane of Langenau	7
442	Covy-Tucker Hill's Sinderella	8
425	Ch. Clayfield Allways a Lady	6
376	Ch. Covy-Tucker Hill's Windswept	5
344	Ch. Echolane's Jo-San's Eve	5
341	Hoheneichen Cassandra Survival	6
331	Marlin's Mandy of Brandy	3

Points	Dam	Champions
324	GV Ch. Amber's Rosie of Bracewood	3
315	Heart's Desire of Bob-Lyn	8
306	Ch. Love At First Bite of Edan	4
287	Si-Don's Tennile of Bethesda	5
281	Ch. Campaigner's Gatewood Haganah	3
259	Ch. Eva-Heim's My My	5
258	T-Ho's Randida of Woodside, CD	4
247	Werttemberg's Remington Steel	6
245	Mordor's Cologne, TC	6
242	Ch. Jecoda's Double Trouble, CD	6

INACTIVE REGISTER OF MERIT DAMS FOR 1996

Points	Dam
1,021	Ch. Lynrik's Shanon of Winchester
960	GV Ch. Covy's Rosemary of Tucker Hill
735	Cobert's Melissa
594	Ch. Covy's Rosita of Tucker Hill
551	Frohlich's Elsa v. Grunestahl
550	Ch. Amber's Flair
518	Covy-Tucker Hill's Carmelita
512	Sacha Wikingerblut
511	Frigga of Silver Lane
495	Clayfield Smithfield Jordan

VA–Axel von der Deininghauserheide, SchH3, DFH, FH
Sire: Immo vom Hasenfang, SchH3
Dam: Helma vom Hildergardsheim, SchH3

Generation after generation, the immortal Axel continues to dominate German Shepherd bloodlines through the excellence of his progeny. Listed here are but a few of the great German Shepherds who are descendants of this famous producer.

U.S. GV and Int. Ch. Troll v. Richterbach, SchH3, FH, ROM
Sieger Alf von Nordfelsen, SchH3
Watzer von Bad Melle, SchH3
Ch. Wotan von Richterbach, ROM
VA Lido von der Wienerau, SchH3
Ch. Fels of Arbywood, ROM
Ch. Fortune of Arbywood, ROM
Ch. Field Marshall of Arbywood, ROM
GV Ch. Lance of Fran-Jo, ROM
Ch. Eko-Lan's Morgan, ROM
Ch. Eko-Lan's Paladen, ROM
Ch. Bernd v. Kallengarten, SchH3, ROM
GV Ch. Yoncalla's Mike, ROM
Ch. Llano Estacado's Gengis, ROM
Ch. Eko-Lan's Aragon, CDX
Ch. Cobert's Ernestine, CD, ROM
Ch. Ulk Wikingerblut. SchH3, ROM
Ch. Lakeside's Gilligan's Island, ROM
GV Ch. Lakeside's Harrigan
VA Mutz von der Pelztierfarm, SchH3
VA Quanto von der Wienerau, SchH3
Sieger Marko von Cellerland, SchH3
Sieger Dick von Adeloga, SchH2
Ch. Doppelt-Tay's Jesse James, ROM
GV Ch. Mannix of Fran-Jo
GV Ch. Hollamor's Judd, ROM

1957 U.S. GV, Holland
Sieger and Int. Ch. Troll
vom Richterbach, SchH3,
FH, ROM, owned by
Irvin R. Apelbaum
Sire: Axel v. d. Deining-
hauserheide, SchH3
Dam: Lende v. Richter-
bach, SchH3

Troll sired a great number of magnificent Champions
who, in turn, became famous producers.

TWO DISTINGUISHED TROLL SONS

Ch. Field Marshall of Arbywood, ROM
Owner: Lucy Woodard

Ch. Fortune of Arbywood, ROM
Owner: Lucy Woodard

1962 Can. GV, U.S. and Can. Ch. Ulk Wikingerblut, ROM, SchH3, AD, CACIB

Owners: Ralph and Mary Roberts

Ulk was imported from Germany when he was three and one-half years old. Handled by his co-owner, Mary Roberts, he won 128 Best of Breeds, 50 Group Firsts, and 28 Bests in Show. He produced forty-eight Champions, including one Grand Victrix.

```
                                  Nestor vom Wiegerfelsen, SchH3
                       Immo vom Hasenfang, SchH3
                                  Dorte v. Hasenfang, SchH1
          VA Axel von der Deininghauserheide, SchH3, DFH, FH
                                  Gnom v. Kalsmunttor, SchH3
                       Helma vom Hildergardsheim, SchH3
                                  Tita von der Starrenburg, SchH2
GV Ch. Troll vom Richterbach, SchH3, FH
                                  Claudius vom Hain, SchH2
                       Fels vom Vogtlandshof, SchH3
                                  Barbel vom Haus Trippe, SchH1
          Lende vom Richterbach, SchH2
                                  Lex Preussenblut, SchH3
                       Rosel vom Osnabruckerland, SchH1
                                  Maja vom Osnabruckerland, SchH3


                                  Rolf vom Osnabruckerland, SchH3
                       Drusus zu den Sieben Faulen, SchH3
                                  Wally zu den Sieben Faulen, SchH3
          Ch. Amor vom Haus Hoheide, SchH3
                                  Pitzo vom Fliederschlob, SchH3
                       Christel vom Fredeholz, SchH2
                                  Amsel von Menkenmoor, SchH3
Natja Wikingerblut, SchH2
                                  Lex Preussenblut, SchH3
                       Rolf vom Osnabruckerland, SchH3, FH
                                  Maja vom Osnabruckerland, SchH3
          Moni vom Stuveschacht, SchH1
                                  Liebo von Stuveschacht, SchH3
                       Quote vom Stuveschacht, SchH1
                                  Ute Preussenblut, SchH1
```

THREE ULK PROGENY

Am. & Can. Ch. Fant Wikingerblut,
  SchH3
Owner: Marion Darling

Ch. Raymor's Fleetoway, ROM
Owner: Audrey Ortega

Ch. Sregor's Grand Slam
Owner: Mr. & Mrs. S. Yoshioka

1967 Am. & Can. GV Ch. Lance of Fran-Jo, ROM
Owners: Joan and Francis Ford, Sr.

Lance, a Troll grandson, did more in his lifetime to raise the quality of German Shepherds in this country than any other dog. He passed on his elegant structure, nobility, sound temperament and excellent gait to hundreds of his offspring. His impact on the breed was felt for many years. He sired sixty Champions, including two Grand Victors, two Canadian Grand Victors, one Grand Victrix and twelve ROM progeny.

<pre>
                                Immo vom Hasenfang
                     Axel von der Deininghauserheide
                                Helma vom Hildegardsheim
          GV Int. Ch. Troll von Richterbach, SchH3, ROM
                                Fels vom Vogtlandshof
                     Lende vom Richterbac
                                Rosel v. Osnabruckerland
     Ch. Fortune of Arbywood, ROM
                                Ajax vom Stieg-Anger
                     Ch. Cito von der Hermannschleuse
                                Hanna von Equord
          Frigga of Silver Lane, ROM
                                Ch. Dex of Parrylin, UD
                     Ch. Jewel of Judex
                                Judith of Blossmoor
                                Hein v. Richterbach, ROM
                     GV Ch. Bill vom Kleistweg, ROM
                                Adda vom Reiffeck
          Ch. Rikter von Liebestraum
                                Ch. Dolvic von Liebestraum
                     Sigga vom Liebestraum
                                Jade vom Liebestraum
     Frohlich's Elsa v. Grunestahl, ROM
                                Hein v. Richterbach, ROM
                     Harold von Schlenhenbusche
                                Aggi vom Nibelungengold
          Burgunda von Lindendorf
                                Dolf vom Volkerbrunnen
                     Ch. Ylerta von Liebestraum
                                Ch. Vania von Liebestraum
</pre>

THREE LANCE PROGENY

1971 U.S. GV Ch. Mannix of
   Fran-Jo
Owners: Joan and Francis Ford, Sr.

Ch. Gailand's Magic of Fran-Jo
Owners: Joe Horst and Robert Slay

Ch. Alator's Folero
Owners: Ronald Nunnally and Alan
   Sandell

Ch. Bernd V. Kallengarten, SchH3, ROM
Owner: Ernest Loeb

This German import has produced many Champions, including Grand Victrix Ch. Valtara's Image. Bernd's grandchildren have done equally well in the showring and when bred to the Lance line have produced beautiful fluid movers.

```
                                              Nestor vom Wiegerfelsen
                                 Immo vom Hasenfang
                                              Dorte vom Hasenfang
                   Axel v. d. Deininghauserheide, SchH3
                                              Gnom vom Kalsmunttor
                                 Helma v. Hildegardsheim
                                              Tita von der Starrenburg
        Watzer von Bad Melle, SchH3
                                              Lex Preussenblut
                                 Rolf v. Osnabruckerland
                                              Maja v. Osnabruckerland
                   Imme v. Bad Melle
                                              Claudius vom Hain
                                 Betty v. Haus Herberhold
                                              Biene v. d. Rosenhecke
                                              Volker v. d. Zeitzer Schweiz
                                 Iran v. d. Buchenhohe
                                              Tuta z. d. Sieben Faulen
                   Kuno v. Jungfernsprung
                                              Drusus v. d. Loberschlucht
                                 Bella v. Haus Weinberg
                                              Delia Nordische Treue
        Carin v. d. Rassweilermuhle
                                              Rolf v. Osnabruckerland
                                 Lesko aus Kattenstroth
                                              Hadda aus Kattenstroth
                   Cora v. d. Silberweide
                                              Marko v. d. Wotansburg
                                 Bioka v. d. Silberweide
                                              Xyla vom Walburgitor
```

THREE BERND PROGENY

Ch. Falco of Thunder Rock
Owner: Antonio Maurizio

Ch. Cobert's Ernestine, CD
Owners: Connie and Ted Beckhardt

Ch. Omar un Dargo of Bihari Wonder
Owner: Joseph Bihari

Ch. Dot-Wall's Vance, CD, ROM
Owners: Dorothea and Ann Graham

			Bar von Haus Carbo
		Mix vom Lochem	
			Kuna v. Colonial Agrippina
	Ch. Treu von Wolfsstock		
			Ex Ard Der Gerhardtstrasse
		Lilly vom Gipsbergwerk	
			Karin v. Kipsbergwerk
Cobert's Jet Ace			
			Watzer von Bad Melle
		Ch. Bernd v. Kallengarten, SchH2, ROM	
			Carin v. d. Rassweilermuhle
	Ch. Cobert's Ernestine, CD		
			Ch. Marko v. Gurkenland
		Ch. Cobert's Amber	
			Hobby House Katja of the Hills

- Cobert's Jet Ace
  - Ch. Treu von Wolfsstock
    - Mix vom Lochem
      - Bar von Haus Carbo
      - Kuna v. Colonial Agrippina
    - Lilly vom Gipsbergwerk
      - Ex Ard Der Gerhardtstrasse
      - Karin v. Kipsbergwerk
  - Ch. Cobert's Ernestine, CD
    - Ch. Bernd v. Kallengarten, SchH2, ROM
      - Watzer von Bad Melle
      - Carin v. d. Rassweilermuhle
    - Ch. Cobert's Amber
      - Ch. Marko v. Gurkenland
      - Hobby House Katja of the Hills

- Dot-Wall's Valda
  - Baron Burybone of Tru D Lew, CD
    - Ch. Giralda's Deacon
      - Giralda's Gary
      - Ch. Giralda's Anne
    - Zelia of San Miguel, CD
      - Ch. Squire of San Miguel
      - Holden of San Miguel
  - Dot-Wall's Katwin, CDX
    - Cobert's San Juan
      - Ch. Aro zur Geigerklause
      - Hobby House Katja of the Hills
    - Dot-Wall's April, CDX
      - Harras of Veralda, CD
      - Tanya of Armar, UD

THREE VANCE PROGENY

Ch. Wynthea's Julie, CDX
Owner: Winifred Gibson Strickland

Ch. Wynthea's Jasmin
Owners: Nelson and Sheila Hildreth

Can. Grand Victrix and Am. Ch.
Wynthea's Tillie, UDT, Can. UDT
Owners: Mr. and Mrs. Freeman
Spencer, Jr.

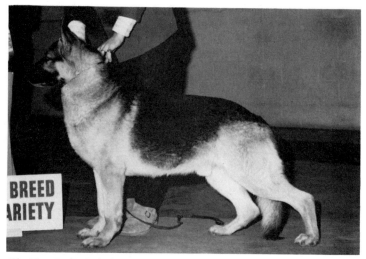

Ch. Eko-Lan's Paladen, ROM
Owner: Frederick Migliore

                                        GV Ch. Troll von Richterbach, ROM
                            Ch. Fortune of Arbywood, ROM
                                        Frigga of Silver Lane, ROM
                GV Ch. Lance of Fran-Jo, ROM
                                        Am. & Can. Ch. Rikter v. Liebestraum
                            Frohlich's Elsa v. Grunestahl, ROM
                                        Burgunda v. Lindendorf
    Ch. Eko-Lan's Morgan, ROM
                                        Ch. Llano Estacado's Gengis
                            Ch. Elwillo's Ursus
                                        Elwillo's Francine
                Eko-Lan's Gemini
                                        Ch. Eko-Lan's Aragon, CDX
                            Eko-Lan's Ebb Tide
                                        Eko-Lan's Anna Karinina

                                        GV Ch. Axel v. Poldihaus, ROM
                            Ch. Llano Estacado's Gengis
                                        Ch. Llano Estacado's Cece
                Ch. Elwillo's Ursus
                                        Ch. Llano Estacado's Gengis
                            Elwillo's Francine
                                        Llano Estacado's Miss Millie
    Eko-Lan's Glory
                                        GV Ch. Troll v. Richterbach, ROM
                            Ch. Eko-Lan's Aragon, CDX
                                        Copper Lady of Kanawaki
                Eko-Lan's Ebb-Tide
                                        Am. & Can. Ch. Harry v. Donaukai, ROM
                            Eko-Lan's Anna Karinina
                                        Lady Anne of Pinehurst

THREE PALADEN PROGENY

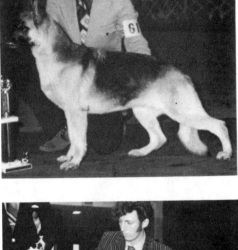

Ch. Eisenberg's Erika of Fran-Jo
Owners: George and Ursula Zim-
merman

Ch. Waldeslust's Lumpazius
Owners: William and Erna McCoy

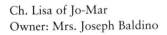

Ch. Lisa of Jo-Mar
Owner: Mrs. Joseph Baldino

1966 and 1968 GV Ch. Yoncalla's Mike, ROM
Owners: Bob and Linda Freeny

```
                                              Axel v. d. Deininghauserheide
                                    Watzer von Bad Melle, SchH3
                                              Imme von Bad Melle
                        Ch. Bernd vom Kallengarten, ROM
                                              Kuno vom Jungfernsprung
                                    Carin v. d. Rassweilermuhle
                                              Cora v. d. Silberweide
        Yoncalla's Mr. America
                                              Ch. Nordraak of Matterhorn, ROM
                                    Ch. Fritz of Maryden
                                              Blanka v. Celler Schloss
                        Yoncalla's Jola
                                              Baldur von Edelhaus
                                    Yoncalla's Adona v. Edelhaus
                                              Ada vom Huerther Waldchen

                                              GV Ch. Jory of Edgetowne, CD, ROM
                                    Ch. Nordraak of Matterhorn, CD, ROM
                                              Charm of Dornwaid
                        Ch. Fritz of Maryden
                                              Enoch of Rocky Reach
                                    Bianka v. Celler Schloss
                                              Afra v. Celler Schloss
        Yoncalla's Colette
                                              Ch. Arno of Bervic
                                    Von Schrief's Feudist
                                              Belgard's Roguetta
                        DeLoma's Priscilla
                                              Ch. Arno of Bervic
                                    Von Schrief's Quadra
                                              Von Schrief's Effie
```

THREE MIKE PROGENY

Ch. Kovaya's Jill, CD
Owners: G. W. Head and G. Birch

Ch. Marjon's Kane, CD
Owner: Mel E. McKee

Am. & Can. GV Ch. Hollamor's
   Judd, ROM
Owners: Robert and Sandra Card

Select Ch. Cobert's Reno of Lakeside, ROM
Owners: Connie Beckhardt and Vito Moreno

Reno has produced fifty-three American and thirty Canadian Champions. These include
GV Ch. Jo-San's Charisma and Canadian GV Ch. Bero's Just Lovely, five Select Winners,
and numerous ROM title holders. He possessed a great personality, masculinity, total soundness and was able to pass his good points along to his progeny.

                           Axel v. Deininghauserheide
             GV Ch. Troll vom Richterbach, ROM
                         Lende v. Richterbach
      Ch. Fortune of Arbywood, ROM
                         Ch. Cito v. Hermannschleuse
          Frigga of Silver Lane, ROM
                         Ch. Jewel of Judex
GV Ch. Lance of Fran-Jo, ROM
                         GV Ch. Bill v. Kleistweg, ROM
         Ch. Rikter v. Liebestraum
                         Sigga v. Liebestraum
     Frohlich's Elsa v. Grunestahl, ROM
                         Harold v. Schlenhenbusch
        Burgunda v. Lindendorf
                         Ch. Ylerta v. Liebestraum

                         Watzer von Bad Melle
         Ch. Bernd vom Kallengarten, ROM
                         Carin v. d. Rassweilermuhle
      Ch. Falk of Bihari Wonder, CD
                         Ch. Wotan vom Richterbach, CDX
         Agnes Gold of Biharl Wonder
                         Kobeil's Jetta
Cobert's Melissa, ROM
                         Watzer von Bad Melle
         Ch. Bernd vom Kallengarten, ROM
                         Carin v. d. Rassweilermuhle
      Ch. Cobert's Ernestine, CD
                         Ch. Marko vom Gurkenland
        Ch. Cobert's Amber
                         Hobby House Katja of the Hills

THREE RENO PROGENY

Ch. Cobert's Zephyr of Windigail,
  ROM
Owners: Connie and Ted Beckhardt

Ch. Peddacres Regal Ruler
Owners: Claude and Peggy Douglas

Select Ch. Mayloch's Adria v.
  Engelman
Owner: Carol Engelman

Covy's Oregano of Tucker Hill, ROM

"Reggie" is the sire of three ROM sons, GV Ch. Schokrest on Parade, ROM, one Maturity Victor, one Futurity Victor, five Selects and ten Champions.

```
                                        U.S. GV Ch. Troll v. Richterbach, ROM
                          Ch. Fortune of Arbywood, ROM
                                        Frigga of Silver Lane, ROM
              U.S. GV Ch. Lance of Fran-Jo, ROM
                                        Ch. Rikter v. Liebestraum
                          Frohlich's Elsa v. Grunestahl, ROM
                                        Burgunda v. Lindendorf
  U.S. GV Ch. Lakeside's Harrigan, ROM
                                        Ch. Bernd vom Kallengarten, ROM
                          Ch. Falk of Bihari Wonder, CD
                                        Agnes Gold of Bihari Wonder
              Cobert's Melissa, ROM
                                        Ch. Bernd vom Kallengarten, ROM
                          Ch. Cobert's Ernestine, CD
                                        Ch. Cobert's Amber

                                        Arno vom Haus Gersie, SchH3
                          Valet vom Busecker Schloss, SchH3
                                        Daja vom Bernstein-Strand, SchH2
              Gauss vom Stauderpark, SchH3
                                        Elite vom Mainsieg, SchH3
                          Itti vom Stober Hay, SchH3
                                        Gitta vom Schloss Grimberg, SchH3
  7x Select, Ch. Tucker Hill's Angelique, CD, ROM
                                        Mix von Lochem, SchH2
                          Ch. Treu vom Wolfsstock, ROM
                                        Lilly vom Gipsbergwerk, SchH2
              Jodi of Tucker Hill
                                        Ch. Arko vom Gasthaus Rose
                          Golden Gwen of Tucker Hill, CD
                                        Amber N Gold of Tucker Hill, CD
```

THREE OREGANO PROGENY

Select Ch. Covy-Tucker Hill's Durango, ROM
Owners: R. and B. Schafer, Cappy Pottle and Gloria Birch

GV Ch. Schokrest on Parade, ROM
Breeder-Owner: Lorraine Schowalter

Best in Show winner Ch. Covy-Tucker Hill's Finnegan, ROM
Owners: Ralph and Mary Roberts

GV Ch. Scorpio of Shiloh Gardens, ROM
Owners: Thomas and Carol McPheron

Although Scorpio died while in his prime, he left a legacy of great dogs to follow him. He sired GV Ch. Langenau's Watson, ROM; GV Ch. Charo of Shiloh Gardens; five Select winners; twenty-some Champions and many ROM title holders.

```
                                        GV Ch. Troll v. Richterbach, ROM
                              Ch. Fortune of Arbywood, ROM
                                        Frigga of Silver Lane, ROM
                    GV Ch. Lance of Fran-Jo, ROM
                                        Ch. Rikter v. Liebestraum
                              Frohlich's Elsa v. Grunestahl, ROM
                                        Burgunda v. Lindendorf
      GV Ch. Mannix of Fran-Jo, ROM
                                        Watzer v. Bad Melle
                              Ch. Bernd v. Kallengarten, ROM
                                        Carin v. d. Rassweilermuhle
                    Hillgrove's Erie, ROM
                                        Ch. Alf v. Loherfeld
                              Ch. Toni of Fieldstone
                                        Freia v. d. Wiekau

                                        GV Ch. Troll v. Richterbach, ROM
                              Ch. Fortune of Arbywood, ROM
                                        Frigga of Silver Lane, ROM
                    GV Ch. Lance of Fran-Jo, ROM
                                        Ch. Rikter v. Liebestraum
                              Frohlich's Elsa v. Grunestahl, ROM
                                        Burgunda v. Lindendorf
      Waldesruh's Pud of Shiloh Gardens
                                        GV Ch. Brix v. d. Grafenkrone
                              Ch. Korporal von Waldesruh
                                        Del-Dena of Waldesruh, ROM
                    Lil' Lulu of Waldesruh
                                        Ch. Biff of Ken-Rose
                              Del-Dena of Waldesruh, ROM
                                        Ch. Cassy of Waldesruh, CD, ROM
```

THREE SCORPIO PROGENY

GV Ch. Charo of Shiloh
  Gardens
Breeders-Owners: Thomas
  and Carol McPheron

Ch. Proven Hills Sunshine
Owner: Judy Teidel

Ch. Tara of Shiloh Gar-
  dens
Owners: Carol McPheron
  and Jon White

Zeus of Fran-Jo, ROM
Owners: Lucille and James Moses

Zeus has produced twenty Champions, including GV Ch. Padechma's Persuasion, ROM; GV Ch. Anton's Jesse; GV Ch. Lacey Britches of Billo; GV Ch. Anton's Jenne; Select Winners and ROM title holders. He sired a great number of elegant bitches.

```
                                              Axel v. d. Deininghauserheide
                              GV Ch. Troll v. Richterbach, ROM
                                              Lende v. Richterbach
              Ch. Fortune of Arbywood, ROM
                                              Ch. Cito v. d. Hermannschleuse
                              Frigga of Silver Lane, ROM
                                              Ch. Jewel of Judex
    GV Ch. Lance of Fran-Jo, ROM
                                              GV Ch. Bill v. Kleistweg, ROM
                              Ch. Rikter v. Liebestraum
                                              Sigga v. Liebestraum
              Frohlich's Elsa v. Grunestahl, ROM
                                              Harold v. Schlenhenbusche
                              Burgunda v. Lindendorf
                                              Ch. Ylerta v. Liebestraum


                                              GV Ch. Troll v. Richterbach, ROM
                              Ch. Fortune of Arbywood, ROM
                                              Frigga of Silver Lane, ROM
              GV Ch. Lance of Fran-Jo, ROM
                                              Ch. Rikter v. Liebestraum
                              Frohlich's Elsa v. Grunestahl, ROM
                                              Burgunda v. Lindendorf
    Ch. Mirheim's Abbey, ROM
                                              Ch. Bernd v. Kallengarten, ROM
                              Ch. Falco of Thunder Rock
                                              Ch. Cobert's Amber
              Ch. Kingsdown's Amber
                                              Ch. Rocket of Cara-Mia
                              Haus-Chloes Heather
                                              Haus-Chloes Fly-Kink
```

THREE ZEUS PROGENY

GV Ch. Padechma's Per-
suasion, ROM
Owner: Margeretha Cun-
ningham

GV Ch. Anton's Jesse
Owner: Joseph Bihari

Ch. Amber's Flair, ROM
Owner: Rosalind and Frank-
lyn Schaefer

Ch. Doppelt-Tay's Hammer, ROM
Owners: Jesse and Larraine Clifford

Hammer is the sire of twenty-five Champions, including GV
Ch. Baobab's Chaz, ROM; three Select Champions; ROM
champions and others who brought great distinction to themselves, their breeding and the breed.

        Ch. Fortune of Arbywood
      1967 GV Ch. Lance of Fran-Jo, ROM
        Frohlich's Elsa v. Grunestahl, ROM
    1969 Select Ch. Eko-Lan's Morgan, ROM
        Ch. Elwillo's Ursus
      Eko-Lan's Gemini
        Eko-Lan's Ebb-Tide
Ch. Eko-Lan's Paladen, ROM

        Ch. Llano Estacado's Genghis, ROM
      Ch. Elwillo's Ursus
        Elwillo's Francine
    Eko-Lan's Glory, ROM
        Ch. Eko-Lan's Aragon, CDX
      Eko-Lan's Ebb-Tide
        Eko-Lan's Anna Karinina

        GV Ch. Troll v. Richterbach, ROM
      Ch. Fortune of Arbywood, ROM
        Frigga of Silver Lane, ROM
    1967 GV Ch. Lance of Fran-Jo, ROM
        Ch. Riker v. Liebestraum
      Frohlich's Elsa v. Grunestahl, ROM
        Burgunda v. Lindendorf
Doppelt-Tay's Jessette

        Ch. Fortune of Arbywood, ROM
      Ch. Doppelt-Tay's Jesse James, ROM
        Ch. Nether-Lair's Gayiety, ROM
    Laurlloy's Admira, ROM
        Aero v. Liebestraum
      Classica v. Ceages
        Ch. Tami v. Liebestraum

THREE HAMMER PROGENY

Ch. Merkel's Quaestor, CD
Owner: Dyan Merkel

Ch. Barren's Oscar
Owner: Peggy J. Sinnett

Select Ch. Lorien's Marnie
   of Pinebeach, UD
Owners: Darlene Ghigleri
   and Twyla Miner Clif-
   ford

Select Ch. Doppelt-Tay's Hawkeye, ROM
Owners: Jesse and Larraine Clifford

Hawkeye has repeatedly proven his ability to produce great moving Champions with overall soundness and excellent temperaments. These include GV Ch. Von Ivo's Blithe Spirit, forty champions, several Select Winners and numerous ROM title holders. His impact on the breed will be felt through many generations of exceptionally beautiful German Shepherds.

<pre>
                                              Ch. Fortune of Arbywood
                                1967 GV Ch. Lance of Fran-Jo, ROM
                                              Frohlich's Elsa v. Grunestahl, ROM
                    1969 Select Ch. Eko-Lan's Morgan, ROM
                                              Ch. Elwillo's Ursus
                                Eko-Lan's Gemini
                                              Eko-Lan's Ebb-Tide
    Ch. Eko-Lan's Paladen, ROM
                                              Ch. Llano Estacado's Genghis, ROM
                                Ch. Elwillo's Ursus
                                              Elwillo's Francine
                    Eko-Lan's Glory, ROM
                                              Ch. Eko-Lan's Aragon, CDX
                                Eko-Lan's Ebb-Tide
                                              Eko-Lan's Anna Karinina

                                              GV Ch. Troll v. Richterbach, ROM
                                Ch. Fortune of Arbywood, ROM
                                              Frigga of Silver Lane, ROM
                    GV Ch. Lance of Fran-Jo, ROM
                                              Ch. Riker v. Liebestraum
                                Frohlich's Elsa v. Grunestahl, ROM
                                              Burgunda v. Lindendorf
    Doppelt-Tay's Jessette
                                              Ch. Fortune of Arbywood, ROM
                                Ch. Doppelt-Tay's Jesse James, ROM
                                              Ch. Nether-Lair's Gayiety, ROM
                    Lauriloy's Admira, ROM
                                              Aero v. Liebestraum
                                Classica v. Ceages
                                              Ch. Tami v. Liebestraum
</pre>

THREE HAWKEYE PROGENY

Select Ch. Wellspring's
  Ironsides, ROM
Owner: Mary Flounders

Select Ch. Wellspring's
  Howard Johnson, ROM
Owners: Frank and Rosa-
  lind Schaefer

GV Ch. Von Ivo's Blithe
  Spirit
Owner: Addie Speziale

Four years, Select Ch. Stuttgart's Sundance Kid, ROM, ROMC, OFA
Owner: Inge Vyprachticky

"Bear" has produced seventy-eight Champions, including Grand Victors, Select Champions, ROM Champions and Canadian Champions. He passed on his fluid gait, his physical soundness, masculinity and beautiful appearance to his progeny. A great number of his progeny became top producers.

                                    Ch. Eko-Lan's Paladen, ROM
              Select Ch. Doppelt-Tay's Hawkeye, ROM
                                    Doppelt-Tay's Jessette, ROM
Select Ch. Lochwood Sundance v. Stuttgart
                                    Select Ch. Tom vom Estahaus
              Ch. Lochwood's Zaja
                                    Chenango's Little Tammy

                                    Ch. Eko-Lan's Paladen, ROM
              Select Ch. Doppelt-Tay's Hawkeye, ROM
                                    Doppelt-Tay's Jessette, ROM
Ch. Caprice Kitty Hawk
                                    Lang of Waldesruh
              Galewynd's TNT of Gan Edan
                                    Galewynd's Symphony

THREE SUNDANCE KID PROGENY

Ch. Rohan's Reaction
Owner: Roberta Kindy

Ch. Rio Valle's Nestle's
   Crunch
Owners: Dr. Hugh and
   Frances Williamson

Ch. Roje's Horseshoe of
   Kovaya
Owners: Joan Fox, Sally
   Holcombe, J. Gossett
   and P. Kurz

Ch. Covy-Tucker Hill's Manhattan
Owners: Shirlee Braunstein and Jane Firestone
Expertly handled by James A. Moses

"Hatter" won 201 all-breed Bests in Show and 332 Herding Group Firsts. He was the Top Winning German Shepherd male of all time and the first German Shepherd to win Best in Show at the Westminster Kennel Club (1987). He was named Show Dog of the Year at the Tournament of Champions. He won BIS at the AKC Centennial, Chicago International, Santa Barbara KC, Houston KC, Westchester KC and the Canadian Show of Shows.

```
                                        Ch. Fortune of Arbywood, ROM
                        GV Ch. Lance of Fran-Jo, ROM
                                        Frohlich's Elsa v. Grunestahl, ROM
            Ch. Lakeside's Gilligan's Island
                                        Ch. Falk of Bihari Wonder, CD
                        Cobert's Melissa
                                        Ch. Cobert's Ernestine, CD
Covy's Flanigan of Tucker Hill
                                        Enoch of Rocky Reach
                        Obernauf's Daemon
                                        Ray-Mor's Heller, CD
            Ch. Kovaya's Contessa, CD
                                        Ch. Bernd vom Kallengarten, ROM
                        Chickwood's Gillie
                                        Ch. Chickwood's Feather

                                        Ch. Fortune of Arbywood, ROM
                        GV Ch. Lance of Fran-Jo, ROM
                                        Frohlich's Elsa v. Grunestahl, ROM
            GV Ch. Lakeside's Harrigan, ROM
                                        Ch. Falk of Bihari Wonder, CD
                        Cobert's Melissa, ROM
                                        Ch. Cobert's Ernestine, CD
Ch. Covy's Rosemary of Tucker Hill
                                        Valet von Busecker Schloss, SchH3
                        Gauss vom Stauderpark, SchH3
                                        Itti vom Stober Hay, SchH2
            Sel. Ch. Tucker Hill's Angelique, CD, ROM
                                        Ch. Treu vom Wolfsstock, ROM
                        Jodi of Tucker Hill
                                        Ch. Golden Gwen of Tucker Hill, CD
```

THREE MANHATTAN PROGENY

Ch. Woodlee's Chelsea of Landmark
Owner: Jane Firestone

Ch. Woodlee's Malibu
Owner: Shirlee G. Braunstein

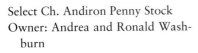

Select Ch. Andiron Penny Stock
Owner: Andrea and Ronald Wash-
  burn

GV Ch. Ossipee Caesar v. Clover Acres, CD
Owner: Diane Piagentini

Caesar was a good producer, with champions from his first seven litters.

			Ch. Doppelt-Tay's Hawkeye, ROM
		Ch. Tamirack's Eli v. Hansen	
			Von Nassau's Fire 'N Ice
	Ch. Clover Acres' X-Citation		
			Dolmar's Iros
		Clover Acres' Touch of Class	
			Clover Acres' Fancy Free
			GV Ch. Lakeside's Harrigan, ROM
		Von Nassau's Bo Jack	
			Von Nassau's Mirage
	Spirit of Clover Acres		
			Ch. Quasar of Clover Acres, CD
		Cameo of Clover Acres	
			Glucklick's Sunshine, CD

THREE CAESAR PROGENY

Ch. Deb-Mar's Alexis v. Forte
Breeders-Owners: Diane Piagentini
  and Pat Forte

Ch. Cobert's Empire
Owners: Ted and Connie Beckhardt

Deb-Mar's Dakota
Owner: Diane Piagentini

Am. & Can. Ch., Sel. Woodhaven's In Search Of, TC, ROM, OFA
Owners: Joe and Maria Bihari

Sel. Ch. Frack v. Rosshous, ROM
Ch. Kolbrook's Ol' Waylen, OFA
Ch. Kolbrook's Glad to Be

Woodhaven's Ashley

GV Kismet's Impulse Von Bismark, ROM, OFA
Pine Buck's Chill Chaser
Kolbrook's Orio v. Warrick

Am. & Can. Sel., Ch. Woodhaven's In Search Of, ROM, TC

Ryder of Fran-Jo
Kolbrook's Smoke of Mali Bar
Mali Bar's Delhi of Lorien

Kolbrook's Leah of Woodhaven

GV Ch. Kismet's Von Bismark, ROM, OFA
Kolbrook's Subaru
Kolbrook's Odesa

THREE IN SEARCH OF PROGENY

Ch. Bihari's Droll
Owner: George Werner

Ch. Amber's Lady in Red of Jo-El's
Owner: Barbara Amidon

Sel. Ch. Bertalon's Miss Sassafras,
   TC
Owner: James Mezey

Sel. Ch. Hoheneichen's Flag, ROM, ROMC
Owners: Thomas and Katherine Sherman

Sel., Ch. Doppelt-Tay's Hawkeye, ROM
Proven Hill's A Sun Hawk
Sel., Ch. Proven Hill's Sunshine
Ch. Proven Hill's Jock Hoheneichen
Ch. Eko-Lan's Morgan, ROM
Jazmin v. Hoheneichen
Burga v. Hoheneichen
Twice Sel., Am. & Can. Sel. Ch. Hoheneichen's Magnum, ROM, ROMC
Ch. Eko-Lan's Paladen, ROM
Ch. Doppelt-Tay's Hammer, ROM
Doppelt-Tay's Jessette
Ch. Carmil's Koko Chanel
Zeus of Fran-Jo
Carmil's Ebony v. Hoheneichen
Jazmin v. Hoheneichen

GV Ch. Baobab's Chaz, ROM
Ch. Alpine's Bullet of Pinebeach
Pinebeach's G. Dark Shadow, ROM
Pinebeach's Cerpico
Ch. Eko-Lan's Paladen, ROM
Pinebeach's O'My of Glisando
Pinebeach's Balihoo
Jeral's Eutin
Ch. Abraxas Gable of Langenau, ROM
Ch. Stonekroft's JR
Ch. Winaki's Libra of Sonderhaus, ROM
Ch. Stonekroft's Magic of Brasban
Ch. Kubistraum's Kane, ROM
Stonekroft's Hannah
Ch. Winaki's Libra of Sonderhaus

TWO FLAG PROGENY

Am. Ch., Can. GV Ch.
Hoheneichen Sar Mar
Lexus, OFA
Owners: Christi Fritsch &
Judy James

Sel. Ch. Plainbrownpaper
v. Jada-Edan
Owners: Penny Kroh and
Charlene Marchand

Ch. Ticketman of Fran-Jo, ROM, OFA
Owners: Fran and Joan Ford

Sel. Ch. Jettland's Rambler
    Sel. Ch. Charisma's Stonewall Jackson
        GV Ch. Aspen of Fran-Jo, ROM
        Sel. Ch. Dolmar's Noel of Spring Rock
    Ch. Jettland's Latin Lace
        Ch. Kubistraum's Kane, ROM
        Jettland's Jewel Twist

Edie of Fran-Jo II
    Ch. Proven Hill's Jock Hoheneichen, ROM
        Proven Hill's A Sun Hawk
        Jazmin von Hoheneichen
    Ch. A Phoebe of Fran-Jo
        GV Ch. Aspen of Fran-Jo, ROM
        Ch. Lorlocke's Tatta of Fran-Jo, ROM

THREE TICKETMAN PROGENY

Ch. Ken-Delaine's Taylor Made
Breeders-Owners: Ken and Delaine
   Thompson

Ch. Del-Mar's Dirty Harry
Breeder-Owner: Diane Piagentini

Ch. Ken-Delaine's Mastercharge, ROM
Breeders-Owners: Ken & Delaine
   Thompson

Ch. Pete of Fran-Jo, OFA, TC, ROM
Owners: Fran and Joan Ford

```
                                                GV Ch. Aspen of Fran-Jo, ROM
                                    Sel. Ch. Charisma's Stonewall Jackson
                                                Sel. Ch. Dolmar's Noel of Spring Rock
                        Sel. Ch. Jetland's Rambler
                                                Ch. Kubistraum's Kane, ROM
                                    Ch. Jettland's Latin Lace
                                                Jettland's Jewel Twist
        Ch. Ticketman of Fran-Jo, ROM
                                                Proven Hill's A Sun Hawk
                                    Ch. Proven Hill's Jock Hoheneichen, ROM
                                                Jazmin von Hoheneichen
                        Edie of Fran-Jo II
                                                GV Ch. Aspen of Fran-Jo, ROM
                                    Ch. A Phoebe of Fran-Jo
                                                Ch. Lorlocke's Tatta of Fran-Jo, ROM

                                                Cobert's Sirroco of Windigail
                                    Proven Hill's Grand Marshall
                                                Proven Hill's Locket v. Phioldore
                        Ch. Jeba's Mitchum
                                                Proven Hill's Free Will
                                    Jeba's My Kind of Love
                                                Linlocke's Iodine
Cimi of Fran-Jo
                                                Ch. Doppelt-Tay's Hammer, ROM
                                    Sel. Ch. Pappillon of Fran-Jo
                                                Arcadia's C-J of Fran-Jo, ROM
                        Keily of Fran-Jo
                                                GV Ch. Aspen of Fran-Jo, ROM
                                    Ch. Joansie of Fran-Jo
                                                Ch. Tatta Too Lorlocke Fran-Jo
```

TWO PETE PROGENY

Ch. Ken-Lyn's Illu-
  minator v. Fran-
  Jo, OFA
Owners: Joan Ford
  and Lynette Boyles

Ch. Ponca Hill's Jes-
  sie, II, OFA
Owners: Jack Budd
  and Joan Ford

Ch. Pinebeach's Stars 'N Stripes, ROM, OFA
Owners: Joan Ortigara and Donna Tressler

		GV Ch. Baobab's Chaz, ROM
	Ch. Alpine's Bullet of Pinebeach	
		Pinebeach's G Dark Shadow
	Ch. Pinebeach's Casanova	
		Ch. Eko-Lan's Paladen, ROM
	Pinebeach's O'My of Glisando	
		Pinebeach's Ballihoo
MV Ch. Bachchen's Spendabuck		
		GV Ch. Baobab's Chaz, ROM
	Valmy's Coaltown, ROM	
		Valmy's Uncola, ROM
	Sel. Ch. Bachchen's Jori	
		Sel. Ch. Cobert's Reno of Lakeside, ROM
	Bachchen's Echo of Pinebeach	
		Pinebeach's Forget Me Not
		Proven Hill's A Sunhawk
	Ch. Proven Hill's Jock Hoheneichen, ROM	
		Jazmin von Hoheneichen
	Ch. Kolbrook's Sudden Decision, ROM	
		Ch. Kolbrook's Ol' Waylon
	Kolbrook's Rainy Lake, ROM	
		Kolbrook's Gingham
Sel. Ch. Kolbrook's Allez France		
		Ch. Frack v. Rosshaus, ROM
	Ch. Kolbrook's Ol' Waylon	
		Ch. Kolbrook's Glad To Be
	Kolbrook's Zenina	
		GV Ch. Kismet's Impulse v. Bismark, ROM
	Kolbrook's Subaru	
		Kolbrook's Odessa

TWO STARS 'N STRIPES PROGENY

Sel. Ch. Skyline's Honduras
Breeders-Owners: James & Lynn Herrick

Ch. Georjan's Steel Magnolia
Owners: Mr. and Mrs. Gabor Fuchs

1990 GV Ch. Proven Hill's Banker of Altana, TC, ROM, ROMC, OFA
Owners: Dr. Robert and Maryellen Kish

<pre>
                                    Proven Hill's A Sunhawk
                        Ch. Proven Hill's Jock Hoheneichen, ROM
                                    Jazmin von Hoheneichen
            Sel. Ch. Hoheneichen's Magnum, ROM
                                    Ch. Doppelt-Tay's Hammer
                        Ch. Carmil's Koko Chanel
                                    Carmil's Ebony von Hoheneichen
    Proven Hill's Obi Wan
                                    Sel. Ch. Doppelt-Tay's Hawkeye, ROM
                        Proven Hill's A Sunhawk
                                    Sel. Ch. Proven Hill's Sunshine
            Proven Hill's Jillian
                                    GV Ch. Scorpio of Shiloh Gardens, ROM
                        Sel. Ch. Proven Hill's Sunshine
                                    Proven Hill's Randy
                                    Sel. Ch. Doppelt-Tay's Hawkeye, ROM
                        Proven Hill's A Sunhawk
                                    Sel. Ch. Proven Hill's Sunshine
            Ch. Proven Hill's Jock Hoheneichen, ROM
                                    Sel. Ch. Eko-Lan's Morgan, ROM
                        Jazmin von Hoheneichen
                                    Burga von Hoheneichen
    Kolbrook's Favorite Decision
                                    Sel. Ch. Frack von Rosshaus, ROM
                        Ch. Kolbrook's Ol' Waylon
                                    Ch. Kolbrook's Glad To Be
            Kolbrook's Rainy Lake, ROM
                                    Sel. Ch. Cobert's Reno of Lakeside, ROM
                        Kolbrook's Gingham
                                    Kolbrook's Cymric
</pre>

THREE BANKER PROGENY

Sel. Ch. Jo-San's Ebony Gold
Owners: Maryellen Kish and Joe and
Sandy Abbruzzese

Sel. Ch. Trafalgar's Heat of the
Night, OFA
Owners: Dr. Robert Kish and
Michael Cheeks

Ch. Kismet's Portfolio
Owners: Dr. Robert Kish and Rose
O'Connell

Sel. Ch. Ken-Delaine's Mastercharge, OFA, ROM
Owners: Ken and Delaine Thompson

```
                                    GV Ch. Aspen of Fran-Jo, ROM
                         Sel. Ch. Charisma's StonewallJackson
                                    Sel. Ch. Dolmar's Noel of Spring Rock
             Sel. Ch. Jettland's Rambler
                                    Ch. Kubistraum's Kane, ROM
                         Ch. Jettland's Latin Lace
                                    Jettland's Jewel Twist
Ch. Ticketman of Fran-Jo, ROM
                                    Proven Hill's A Sun Hawk
                         Ch. Proven Hill's Jock Hoheneichen, ROM
                                    Jazmin von Hoheneichen
             Edie of Fran-Jo II
                                    GV Ch. Aspen of Fran-Jo, ROM
                         Ch. A Phoebe of Fran-Jo
                                    Ch. Lorlocke's Tatta of Fran-Jo, ROM
                                    Sel. Ch. Lockwood's Sundance v. Stuttgart
                         Am. & Can. Sel. Ch. Stuttgart's Sundance Kid, ROM
                                    Am. & Can. Ch. Caprice Kitty Hawk, ROM
             Ch. Nike-Clayfield Andretti, ROM
                                    Sel. Ch. Covy's Mazarati of Tucker Hill, ROM
                         Sel. Ch. Clayfield Allways A Lady, ROM
                                    Clayfield Smithfield Jordan, ROM
                                    Sel. Ch. Doppelt-Tay's Hawkeye, ROM
Sel. Ch. Ken-Delaine's Avia, ROM
                                    GV Ch. Cobert's Trollstigen, ROM
                         Ch. Cobert's Zephyr of Windygail, ROM
             Ch. Janry's Givenchy, ROM
                                    Ch. Doppelt-Tay's Hawkeye, ROM
                         Wellspring's Kathleen, ROM
                                    Ch. Amber's Flair, ROM
```

THREE MASTERCHARGE PROGENY

Sel. Ch. Skylark's Lady Jane
Owners: John and Leslye Treglown

Sel. Ch. Ken-Delaine's Clarice, OFA
Owners: Karen Harrison and Ken
    and Delaine Thompson

Sel. Ch. Tournaline Kena Ken-
    Delaine, OFA
Owners: Ken and Delaine Thompson

Am. & Can. Sel. Ch. Nike Clayfield Andretti, ROM, ROMC
Owners: Robert Scholes and Earl A. Stegner

                                    Sel. Ch. Doppelt-Tay's Hawkeye, ROM
               Sel. Ch. Lockwood's Sundance v. Stuttgart
                                    Ch. Lockwood's Zaja
      Sel. Ch. Stuttgart's Sundance Kid, ROM
                                    Sel. Ch. Doppelt-Tay's Hawkeye
             Ch. Caprice Kitty Hawk
                                    Gaylewynd's TNT of Gan Edan
                                    Cobert's Sirocco of Windigail, ROM
               Sel. Ch. Covy's Mazarati of Tucker Hill, ROM
                                    GV Ch. Covy's Rosemary of Tucker Hill, ROM
      Sel. Ch. Clayfield's Allways A Lady
                                    Sel. Ch. Karagin's Crusader, ROM
             Clayfield Smithfield Jordan, ROM
                                  Clayfield Devon v. Hausmekon, ROM

THREE ANDRETTI PROGENY

2x Sel. Ch. Ken Delaine's Avia,
  ROM, OFA
Owners: Ken and Delaine Thompson

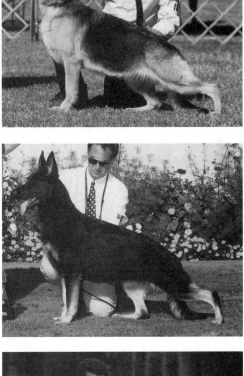

Ch. Obsession of Nordlicht
Breeder-Owner: Robert Scholes

Ch. Final Fantasy of Nordlicht
Breeder-Owner: Robert Scholes

Ch. Leiter's Excalibur, OFA, ROM
Owner: Robin M. Leiter

Proven Hill's A Sunhawk
Ch. Proven Hill's Jock Hoheneichen
Jazmin von Hoheneichen
Sel. Ch. Proven Hill's Up 'N Adam, ROM, ROMC
Sel. Ch. Doppelt-Tay's Hawkeye, ROM
Proven Hill's Keepsake v. Sandon
Proven Hill's Tequila Sunup
Proven Hill's Justin
Sel. Ch. Doppelt-Tay's Hawkeye, ROM
Proven Hill's A Sunhawk
Sel. Ch. Proven Hill's Sunshine
Proven Hill's Jillian
GV Ch. Scorpio of Shiloh Gardens, ROM
Sel. Ch. Proven Hill's Sunshine
Proven Hill's Randy

Ch. Eko-Lan's Paladen, ROM
Sel. Ch. Doppelt-Tay's Hawkeye, ROM
Doppelt-Tay's Jessette
Witmer's Executive
Sel. Ch. Doppelt-Tay's Hawkeye, ROM
Witmer's Little Angel
Quig's Town-Haus Nova
Weicho's Casino
Cobert's Sirocco of Windigail, ROM
Covy's Bentley of Tucker Hill
GV Ch. Covy's Rosemary of Tucker Hill, ROM
Weidor's Isotta
Zeus of Fran-Jo
Dolmar's Kirsten
Dolmar's Cameo of Spring Rock

THREE EXCALIBUR PROGENY

Ch. Leiter's Run For The Money
Owner: Robin Leiter

Ch. Leiter's Abracadabra
Owner: Robin Leiter

Ch. Rivendell's George Michael,
    OFA
Owners: Paul and Jennifer Root

1992, 1994 GV Ch. Campaigner's-Gatewood Uzi, OFA, ROM
Owners: Joan and Murray Fox

                        Am. & Can. Sel., Can. GV Ch. Prime Time of Billo, ROM, ROMC
            Carmil's Prime Rate
                        Carmil's Halo
    Ch. Carmil's Stetson
                        Sel. Ch. Doppelt-Tay's Hawkeye, ROM
            Carmil's Martini
                        Yoncalla's Von Nassau, Yulla
                        Sel. Ch. Lockwood's Sundance v. Stuttgart
            Am. & Can. Sel. Ch. Stuttgart's Sundance Kid, ROM, ROMC
                        Ch. Caprice Kitty Hawk, ROM
    Sel. Ch. Campaigner's-Gatewood Haganah
                        Ch. Merkel's Quastor, CD
            GV Ch. Merkel's Vendetta, ROM
                        Merivern's MS Fortune v. Sierra

THREE UZI PROGENY

Ch. Campaigner's Percussion
Owner: Joan Fox

Ch. Campaigner's Gatewood Had-
    assah, OFA
Owners: Val Free and Joan Fox

Ch. Campaigner's Aim To Please
Owners: Joan Fox and Linda Bank-
    head

Ch. Hylock's Prosecutor, CD, ROM, OFA
Owners: Frances and Jerry Rood, Linda and David Tofel

```
                                        Sel. Ch. Doppelt-Tay's Hawkeye, ROM
                              Proven Hill's A Sunhawk
                                        Ch. Proven Hill's Sunshine
                    Ch. Proven Hill's Jock Hoheneichen, ROM
                                        Sel. Ch. Eko-Lan's Morgan, ROM
                              Jazmin von Hoheneichen
                                        Burga von Hoheneichen
        Sel. Ch. Hoheneichen's Magnum, ROM
                                        Ch. Eko-Lan's Paladen
                              Ch. Doppelt-Tay's Hammer, ROM
                                        Doppelt-Tay's Jessette
                    Ch. Carmil's Koko Chanel
                                        Zeus of Fran-Jo
                              Carmil's Ebony von Hoheneichen
                              Jazmin von Hoheneichen
                                        Dal-Be's Ambler of Anthmar
                              Anthmar's Dean
                                        Anthmar's Belle
                    Ch. Sonsan's R.C. Dillon of Hylock
                                        Ch. Shurwin's Domino
                              Sonsan's Interlude
                                        Sonsan's East of Eden
        Ch. Hylock's Crackerjack, CD
                                        Ch. Sonsan's Ajax
                              I-Ken-El's Khemosabi
                                        Sonsan's Kay-Dee
                    I-Ken-El's Chanel of Hylock
                                        Ch. Wyndean's Ivano
                              I-Ken-El's Elan of Hylock
                                        I-Ken-El's Georgy Girl
```

THREE PROSECUTOR PROGENY

Ch. Palamor's Chance of Hylock
Owners: Jerry and Frances Rood,
   Jerry and Pat Turrise

Am. & Can. Sel. Ch. Ardric's Strom-
   berg, OFA
Owners: Sam and Shirley Raymond

Am. & Can. Ch. Don Chris's Lucille
   Ball, CD
Owner: Donna Christiansen

Nike Clayfield Chateau, CD, ROM
Owners: Bob Ghigleri, Angela Stegner and Sharon Earl

                                              Sel. Ch. Covy-Tucker Hill's Durango
                              Ch. Karagin's Crusader, ROM
                                                Caralon's Illa v. d. Lockenheim
                  Ch. Woodacre's Dakota, ROM
                                              Tanglefoot of Katzenjamer
                              Asgard's Dale of Katzenjamer
                                              Katzenjamer's Sugarfoot
         Ch. Heartbreaker of Bob-Lyn
                                              Covy-Tucker Hill's Zinfandel
                              Dapamo's Laser
                                                Sel. Ch. Tanglewood's Janel of Dapamo
                  Ch. Ginger Ale of Bob-Lyn, ROM
                                            Ch. Eko-Lan's Paladen
                              Pinebeach's October v. Glisando, ROM
                                              Pinebeach's Ballihoo
                                            Sel. Ch. Cobert's Reno of Lakeside, ROM
                              Cobert's Sirocco of Windigail, ROM
                                              Ch. Cobert's Windsong, ROM
                  Ch. Covy's Mazarati of Tucker Hill, ROM
                                          GV Ch. Lakeside's Harrigan, ROM
                              GV Ch. Covy's Rosemary of Tucker Hill, ROM
                                                Sel. Ch. Tucker Hill's Angelique
        Sel. Ch. Clayfield Allway's A Lady
                                            Sel. Ch. Covy-Tucker Hill's Durango, ROM
                              Ch. Karagins Crusader, ROM
                                              Caralon's Illa v. d. Lockenheim
                  Clayfield Smithfield Jordan, ROM
                                            Clayfield Brennan
                              Clayfield Devon v. Hausmekon, ROM
                                            Smithfield Harvi v. Hausmekon

THREE CHATEAU PROGENY

Ch. Windwalker's Jolly Roger
Owner: Jamie Walker

Ch. Coastline Circus v. Asgard, CD
Owners: Bob and Darlene Ghigleri

Ch. Nike Clayfield Ilsa v. Lorien
Owners: Twyla Miner, Angela Stegner
and Sharon Earl

Sel. Ch. Brentaryl's Gunner, ROM
Owners: Ken and Carolyn Rose

Ch. Eko-Lan's Paladen, ROM

Select Ch. Doppelt-Tay's Hawkeye, ROM

Doppelt-Tay's Jessette, ROM

Select Ch. Lochwood Sundance v. Stuttgart

Select Ch. Tom vom Estahaus

Ch. Lochwood's Zaja

Chenango's Little Tammy

Am. & Can. Sel. Ch. Stuttgart's Sundance Kid, ROM

Ch. Eko-Lan's Paladen, ROM

Select Ch. Doppelt-Tay's Hawkeye, ROM

Doppelt-Tay's Jessette, ROM

Ch. Caprice Kitty Hawk

Lang of Waldesruh

Galewynd's TNT of Gan Edan

Galewynd's Symphony

GV Ch. Scorpio of Shiloh Gardens, ROM

GV Ch. Langenau's Watson, ROM

Langenau's Quessa, ROM

Ch. Abraxas Gable of Langenau

Sel. Ch. Donovan of Pinebeach

Mardean's Abraxas

Shar-Mac's Princess Jill

Ch. Stonekroft's Josie, ROM

Ch. Eko-Lan's Paladen, ROM

Waldeslust's Nageeb Mosay

Waldeslust's Xora

Ch. Winaki's Libra of Sonderhaus, ROM

Ch. Lavaland's Sam of Kovaya

Ch. Winaki's Sasha

Winaki's Charra

TWO GUNNER PROGENY

Ch. Brentaryl's Unforgettable Fire
Owners: Ken and Carolyn Rose

Am. & Can. Sel. Ch. Landaleigh's High Tech
Owners: Hank and Gail Cobleigh, Bill and Clara Hope

1988 GV Ch. Piper-Hill's Polo, ROM, ROMC, OFA
Owners: Frank and Barbara W. Lopez

```
                                      Ch. Doppelt-Tay's Hawkeye, ROM
                          Sel. Ch. Lockwood Sundance v. Stuttgart
                                      Ch. Lockwood's Zaja
            Sel. Ch. Stuttgart's Sundance Kid, ROM
                                      Ch. Doppelt-Tay's Hawkeye, ROM
                          Ch. Caprice Kitty Hawk
                                      Gaylewynd's TNT of Gan Edan
GV Ch. Rio Valle's Nestle's Crunch, ROM
                                      GV Ch. Lance of Fran-Jo
                          Ch. Cobert's Reno of Lakeside, ROM
                                      Cobert's Melissa, ROM
            Dolmar's Megan of Spring Rock
                                      Ch. Eko-Lan's Paladen, ROM
                          Eko-Lan's Rhyme, ROM
                                      Eko-Lan's Quella

                                      Ch. Doppelt-Tay's Hawkeye, ROM
                          Amber's Strider of Zar-Zal, ROM
                                      Ch. Amber's Lolita of Zar-Zal
            Ch. Piper Hill's Polaris
                                      Ch. Irrenhaus Kosher Cowboy
                          Sachem Hill's Almond Joy
                                      Nanhall's Fantasia
Piper Hill's Kodachrome, ROM
                                      Ch. Doppelt-Tay's Hawkeye, ROM
                          Sel. Ch. Wellspring's Howard Johnson, ROM
                                      Ch. Amber's Flair
            Cobert's Radcliffe
                                      Sel. Ch. Cobert's Reno of Lakeside, ROM
                          Ch. Cobert's Zephyr of Windigail, ROM
                                      Ch. Cobert's Windsong
```

THREE POLO PROGENY

Sel. Ch. Totana's Bronze of Piper Hill
Owners: Drs. Jose Nova and Abner
   Mercado

Ch. Totana Piper Hill's Nightcruise
Owners: Frank and Barbara Lopez

Ch. Totana's Bullet of Piper Hill
Owners: Frank and Barbara Lopez

Ch. Amber's Stockbroker, ROM
Owner: Barbara Amidon

	Ch. Proven Hill's Hoheneichen
Sel. Ch. Hoheneichen's Magnum	
	Ch. Carmil's Koko Chanel
Sel. Ch. Langenau's Beau of Jeanden	
	Ch. Doppelt-Tay's Hammer
GV Ch. Jeanden's L'Erin of Langenau	
	Langenau's Minx Renaissance
	Sel. Ch. Doppelt-Tay's Hawkeye
Amber's Strider of Zar-Zal, ROM	
	Ch. Amer's Lolita of Zar-Zal
Ch. Alpha Angelina of Issa	
	Sel. Ch. Frack v. Rosshaus
Ch. Amber's Rita of Zar-Zal	
	Ch. Amber's Valiant Robin, ROM

THREE STOCKBROKER PROGENY

Ch. Amber's Design
Owner: Barbara Amidon

Sel. Ch. Olympus Simply
    Irresistable
Owners: Tony and Rose Olympus

Ch. Marlin's Place Your Bet
Owners: Lynn and Chris Beale

chapter 29

Breeding German Shepherds

THE BROOD BITCH

If you intend to breed German Shepherd Dogs, your first consideration should be your bitch. The first step is to decide whether she is worthy of producing a litter. If she has a poor temperament, is shy, highly nervous or too aggressive, she should not be bred. Even though you may love her dearly, despite her temperament, you should not perpetuate this fault in her puppies. If you have a pet bitch and want to breed her just for the sake of letting her raise a litter, we feel we must advise you not to do so. Bitches do not need to have a litter to fulfill their destiny in life. On the contrary, a pet bitch should never be bred because the puppies they bring into the world will do nothing to further the German Shepherd breed. If you want to do something constructive for your pet, my advice would be to train her. She will be much happier with the attention you give her when she is being trained than she would with a litter of puppies that would be very difficult to sell. Unwanted puppies are sold for practically nothing or given to pet shops by disappointed, frustrated owners.

Many people with pet bitches breed them for the sole purpose of educating their children. When the bitch is ready to whelp her puppies, they issue an "open house" invitation to all the children and adults in the neighborhood to sit around and watch the proceedings. I thoroughly deplore this sort of circus. My feelings and compassion at this time are all for the bitch, who should have peace and quiet. Giving birth to six or eight puppies is very traumatic and tiring, and could be difficult and painful. She should have the quiet assurance of one or two understanding people who will stand by ready to help her and reassure her by their very presence. A roomful of giggling, noisy children or adults is not conducive to breeding sound, even-tempered puppies. It can only be compared to a woman being forced to give birth to a child in Macy's store window, with anyone and everyone invited to watch.

We have suggested in an earlier chapter that the foundation of your kennel should be a typey bitch who is from proven producing lines and who carries excellent bloodlines. Whether you have one like this, an average bitch with fairly good bloodlines or just a pet whom you insist upon breeding, we will give you our ideas on breeding them.

THE STUD DOG

Before you select a stud dog, there are many things to be taken into consideration. You have the bitch, so your choice of a stud dog should revolve around her. You should have a thorough knowledge of the breed and be able to recognize desirable or undesirable features in a dog when you see him. When selecting a stud dog, choose one not only because he is the same type as your bitch, but because he has the characteristics you want to incorporate in your breeding program. You should be familiar with the type of progeny the stud dog produces so that you can judge the quality of his get by different bitches. This will show you if he is a prepotent sire who is able to pass on his good characteristics when bred to bitches of different types or bloodlines. If he is being used for the first time, it will be more of a gamble, but you could note if he is the prototype of his breeding. You could check into his background and determine the quality of his brothers and sisters and their progeny, if they have been bred.

If you are fortunate enough to own a bitch of good type and structure with excellent bloodlines, you will want to find a stud dog of a similar type. He doesn't need to carry the same bloodlines, but he should possess the same genes so that together they will produce the desired characteristics. Most of the qualities that you admire in certain stud dogs are probably in their genetic makeup and will be passed on to their progeny.

The stud dog should have a perfect temperament and be of good character because these characteristics are important not only to their progeny but are equally important to future generations. Bad temperament is very difficult to eradicate in a strain and will crop up for many generations. The structurally correct stud dog is not worth a second glance if he has a poor temperament or bad character. Even if you breed a sound bitch to him, the bad temperament will show up in the puppies sooner or later.

Consider the health of the stud dog you choose, for you want to breed puppies that live long, healthy lives. This point is often overlooked when selecting both a bitch and a stud. Some dogs are so healthy that they go through their whole lives without any illnesses. We have had scores of dogs who never had a sick day in their lives and produced equally strong, healthy puppies. Although we gave them excellent care, which included well-balanced diets and plenty of exercise, the important factor was that they came from a line that produced sound, strong, healthy bodies.

Some brood bitches have all kinds of weird medical problems and yet the people who own them continue to breed them, and the puppies that survive inherit the same weaknesses. Even though these bitches whelp nine or ten puppies, they lose most of them, and those that live are never physically sound despite their seemingly normal outward appearance. Other bitches produce one or two puppies in a litter which, when mature, also whelp very small litters. Dogs from such litters will pass on various deficiencies. How much better for everyone concerned if such bitches and dogs were never bred. Make inquiries to be sure the stud dog you choose is healthy and comes from strong, vigorous, long-lived ancestors.

If you have a beautiful bitch that comes from a mediocre litter and an undistinguished line that hasn't produced quality, you will have to be careful in your selection of a stud dog. Try to choose one from a proven producing line, preferably a dog that has been linebred so that the type is stabilized. If his type is the same as that of your bitch, even though the breeding is an outcross, you should get a better-than-average litter. Even though there may be no individuals in this litter that could finish their Championships, you will now have valuable bloodlines, and next time you can breed back to another dog who is closely related to their sire. You should establish a type before you consider another outcross. It is wise to consider the third and fourth breeding that lies ahead, rather than concentrating your efforts solely upon the first breeding. If you have a realistic, long-range plan, you are more likely to succeed in your breeding program.

If you have a pet bitch you insist upon breeding and wish to use her as your foundation bitch, study her pedigree and breed her back to the best available dog in her pedigree. If none of these is any better than your bitch, you would be better off breeding her to a Champion that you like, providing he has a good temperament, normal hips and is known to produce his own type. Choose the bitch puppy that most closely resembles her sire and breed her back to her grandsire. When a puppy from this second generation is old enough to be bred, choose a son of the original sire that most resembles him in type. This litter should give you some show-quality puppies. You have to be patient when you start a kennel with pet stock. If you don't breed wisely, you might always have a kennel full of mediocre German Shepherds. Once you start to improve your stock, you should never go back to the original pet bitch or her first-generation daughters—just use the bitches in the succeeding generations for breeding stock.

If you have a pet bitch who has excellent bloodlines behind her but none of these ancestors are available to use at stud (as in the case of a German bitch whose ancestors are all in Germany), look for a stud dog who closely resembles her sire in type. By breeding for type, you can, in two generations, start producing show-quality puppies. The right selection of a stud dog will be the key to success, so consider the genes your bitch needs to produce the quality evident in her background.

The specific type and characteristics of the parents are a better guide to what you can expect in the progeny than the pedigree alone. A pedigree is an extremely important document if you know the dogs in it as individuals and not just as names on a piece of paper. You can trace the dogs through each generation to determine which individuals were outstanding producers in their own right, who possessed the ability to produce uniformity in their litters and who gave the best of themselves most frequently. If the stud dog and his ancestors are uniform in type, it is reasonable to assume that his progeny by your bitch will be uniform in type also.

In this country it is not very difficult to obtain information about the individual American dogs listed in the first three generations of a pedigree. If they have distinguished themselves, you could see these dogs at dog shows, the German Shepherd National Specialty or at the homes of their owners. You might obtain information about them from their owners, handlers or judges. Many of them will be pictured in the *German Shepherd Review*, where you might also see pictures of their progeny.

If you wish to breed your bitch to an imported dog, it will be more difficult for you to obtain information about his ancestors. If his owner will show you his dog's German pedigree, and translate the description of his immediate ancestors for you, it will give you some idea what they are like. It is still not as satisfactory as seeing the individual dogs in person so that you can draw your own conclusions. In Germany, Koer reports on German dogs are available to German breeders and they make very good use of them as is shown by their success in breeding German Shepherds. If the imported dog you choose to use for a stud has a German show record he will have a Koer report. You might inquire about it as it will give you a very lengthy description of the dog, plus breed warnings if there are any. Your best bet with an American-bred or a German import is to find one whose genes are similar to those of your bitch.

In breeding we want to build up a foundation of good, dominant genes, so we breed bitches to dogs that carry the same genes or characteristics. A prepotent dog is able to pass along his good characteristics, but his litter brother may not possess this power of transmission even though he is a fairly good representative of the breed. Therefore, it helps if you can see the progeny of the stud dog to determine what characteristics he does transmit.

If you linebreed on certain bloodlines, you will establish a type and be able to keep the characteristics you want in your dogs. However, by the same token, by breeding back to the same bloodlines, you are also perpetuating the same faults which are bound to crop up in each generation. You will have to cull your litters quite ruthlessly to keep the faults down to a minimum. Some breeders cull when the puppies are very young, others wait many months until they are sure how they will mature. In the latter case it will take time, patience and money. Culling should be done with the head as it is very easy to be influenced by your heart.

Remember when you linebreed, breed back to a first cousin, uncle, grandsire, et cetera. You should choose one with the same desirable genes as your bitch or you will pick up more undesirable traits. If you linebreed, the dam and sire will have a common ancestor in the first five generations. The long-range objective of linebreeding is to perpetuate the genes of one animal through successive breedings, so the animal, or a close relative, to whom you are linebreeding should appear one or more times in four generations. By carefully selecting top-quality breeding animals, you will end up with dominant stock.

Characteristics of a German Shepherd Dog are not transmitted through the blood. Each male and each female has thirty-nine pairs of chromosomes, or combined, a total of seventy-eight in each of their reproductive gene cells. The chromosomes are always found in identically shaped pairs, each pair slightly different from each other, except in the sex chromosomes where an identically shaped pair (XX) is found in the female and an unequal pair (XY) in the male. Each chromosome contains many, many thousands of genes. Each of these genes has a special effect upon the function or appearance of a dog and this is generally accomplished by controlling specific biochemical reactions. Here, then, are the genetic factors that determine the characteristics of the progeny. One chromosome from the male unites with one chromosome from the female, which gives the new puppy seventy-eight chromosomes, exactly half from each parent. The genetic combinations that a puppy could receive run into the thousands and stagger one's imagination.

Within each pair of chromosomes, the genes that are located in the same place will affect the same characteristic. These genes are said to be allelic to each other; if the dog has two alleles of a series alike, it is homozygous for that characteristic and will breed true to it. If they are not alike, the dog will be heterozygous and may breed untrue for that characteristic.

A dominant gene is one that suppresses all others and does not skip generations. Certain characteristics that you admire in a strain are dominant, and any dog or bitch who is able to transmit these qualities on to most of their progeny is called prepotent. It is quite likely that these excellent qualities that are being transmitted are inherited by two or more ancestors who are related. One direct way to produce prepotency is to breed brother and sister, or sire to daughter, et cetera, providing there is great depth of quality in the individuals, and the breeder is very familiar with the ancestors involved. Since you are inbreeding to produce highly uniform stock, the puppies that do not meet this high standard must be culled.

At this point I must mention that I, personally, do *not* believe in this kind of breeding. Even though you succeed, and many breeders have, in producing a few puppies in the litter that closely resemble their parents in conformation and gait, you will lose something much more precious: temperament and character. With each generation of puppies, you will have to work harder on their temperaments to make them socially acceptable. With each generation the shyness will be more pronounced and harder to hide. It is different with character: A dog is either born with good sound character or not. It can't be changed by training. What is character? Any functional trait in a dog resulting from the interaction of genes and regarded as hereditary in origin. A dog with a completely sound character will be friendly, fearless and courageous. He will have had at least four generations of sound dogs in back of him. Something to be considered when one is looking for a stud dog.

Let me just mention one fact. The German breeders who are renowned for breeding German Shepherds with sound characters and temperaments do not inbreed. They simply do not do so since it is against the sound breeding practices established by the SV.

A recessive gene is one whose influence is hidden or concealed when it comes in contact with a dominant gene, and it may skip one or more generations and come through both sides. It is acknowledged that a recessive trait will show up more frequently in males, so this should be considered when linebreeding. A recessive fault could be either major or minor and, if inherited from one parent, will remain hidden unless a similar recessive gene is inherited from the other parent. By studying the ancestors selectively, the recessives can be kept hidden.

The total genetic makeup of the dog, which includes both dominant and recessive alleles, is called the genotype. The number of male puppies in a litter is solely determined by the male. The number of puppies in a litter is controlled by the bitch.

The reproductive glands (gonads) are located in the ovaries of the bitch and contain her eggs. All the undeveloped eggs the newborn bitch puppy will ever have are in her ovaries. When these eggs ripen, they are flushed into the fallopian tubes that extend from the ovaries, and into the two horns of her uterus.

The gonads of the male are located in his testicles and contain spermatozoa. During one copulation millions of spermatozoa are released, and since the dog has no seminal vesicles to store sperm, a tie is necessary for copulation. Prolonged copulation is needed for semen to be pumped from the testicles of the dog into the vagina of the bitch. During this time the dog has three distinct emissions; the first is while he is probing, pushing and trying to find his way in, and this is a lubricating fluid; the second, when he has penetrated as far as he can and emits the seminal fluid in which the sperm is carried; and the third stage is when he is tied to the bitch and is again emitting a clear fluid which carries the seminal fluid to the ova. Even if there has been no actual tie, conception should result providing the dog has been in the right place for the second phase of copulation. However, if it is possible, I believe it is wise to repeat the breeding later to be sure they have a proper tie.

The number of puppies that are born are generally from those eggs that are expelled by the bitch during one heat period and which remain in the fallopian tubes. The dog's spermatozoa, with little propelling tails, have to make their way from the vagina through the cervix, the horns of the uterus and up into the fallopian tubes where the eggs are waiting to be fertilized. As each sperm unites with an egg, it buries itself and a zygote is formed. When all the eggs have been fertilized, the rest of the spermatozoa dissipate, and the zygotes descend into the uterus. They attach themselves to the safety of the uterine walls where their development is assured with warmth and nourishment. The mother's nervous system is not connected to the embryos nor does her blood flow through them. At the time the sperm and the egg unite, all inherited characteristics are sealed in.

BREEDING THE BITCH

Whether you plan to breed your bitch to one of your own stud dogs or take her to someone else's stud, you should take her to your vet to have her examined. She should get a brucellosis test. Brucellosis is a bacterial disease that is sexually transmitted, so if she is bred, she should have this test. The vet will draw a blood sample and either check it in his office, or send it to some lab to determine if it is negative. Your female should be tested two or three weeks before she comes in season. Stud dogs should be checked for brucellosis twice a year.

Before the breeding takes place, the bitch should be checked to be sure she is free of worms and, if necessary, she should be wormed. A normal bitch is in season for twenty-one days, and the first day that she shows a colored discharge should be considered her first day. She should conceive when bred on her twelfth day. There are bitches who remain in season for four or five weeks and these can be bred successfully during their third week. However, there are exceptions—one bitch we had wouldn't conceive unless she was bred on her ninth day, another had a litter when she was bred on her twentieth day. Experience is the best teacher in determining the right breeding day for a bitch.

However, if you are sending your bitch to a distant stud and she has in her past had an abnormal cycle, this calls for a different approach. When she is in the tenth day of her season, have your vet do a progesterone test to find out when she will be ready to be bred. This is more accurate than a smear, but you may need more than one test to pinpoint it within a three-day period. Some stud fees are very high, the owner of the stud may not be cooperative and only give one service or the stud might have been bred to another bitch earlier in the day. This sort of thing has happened, so be forewarned. Under the circumstances if you have the results of a progesterone test, you can feel more certain that the breeding will be successful.

Some friends of mine used to have their veterinarian check their bitch by means of a smear test to determine her best ovulation time. However, experience showed that this test was only correct 33 percent of the time. They eventually found that if their bitch flagged her tail and the stud dog was interested, that was the best time to breed her. The stud dog was experienced, and when he wanted to breed to their bitch, she always had puppies. As is often the case, the simple, direct method is the best.

The first time a bitch is bred it is wise to breed her on her twelfth and fourteenth days. A bitch will show signs of being ready for breeding by flirting with the male, wanting to play with him, flagging her tail to the side as he approaches and standing while the male mounts her back.

The new owner will have to watch his bitch carefully if he plans to breed her, as she might otherwise be in season for several days before he notices that she is "in." In breeding dogs there are more "misses" from trying to breed a bitch too late than for any other reason. If the owner is not certain when his bitch came in season, he should be ready to breed her when her vulva is soft and swollen, when her discharge has turned from bright red to pale pink and when the bitch gets excited when she sees a dog. This period lasts about five days with most bitches.

You should always keep your bitch confined while she is in season and never let her out in your yard alone. Later, if she has been bred successfully, you should still take every precaution to see that no other dog comes near her. If neglected, she could conceivably breed to another dog and have puppies by both of them. In this case you would not be able to register them as you would never be certain who sired the individual puppies.

Many novices have asked me what adverse effect it will have on their purebred bitch if she is accidentally bred to a mongrel. Other than the unnecessary experience of carrying and whelping a litter of mixed breeds, it will have no harmful effect on her ability to produce purebred dogs in the future. The unwanted puppies should be put to sleep immediately, and the dam can serve as a foster mother for another bitch who had a large litter of purebred puppies. The foster mother will be happy to take care of a litter of four or five puppies even though they aren't her own.

If your bitch is accidentally bred to a dog of her choice and not yours, or if she was bred to a fine Champion one day and the neighborhood mutt the next, you should have the litter aborted by taking her to your veterinarian immediately. By doing this the sire's owner would probably give you a repeat breeding the next time she came in season, whereas the alternative would be a litter of unregistered puppies.

A maiden bitch should be bred to an experienced stud dog who has been used before, and a young dog should be bred to an older brood bitch the first time he is used. This arrangement makes it much easier for all concerned, and the experienced dog has a calming influence on the other.

An older bitch should be bred sooner than usual in order to conceive. If she is in excellent health and spirits and has been bred each of her last few seasons, she could be bred in her eighth year. I believe that a young bitch should be bred every other season as this gives her one season to rest. A strong, healthy bitch can be bred two seasons in succession and then, when given a season to rest, will suffer no ill effects whatsoever. Captain von Stephanitz advised breeders to breed their bitches every six months, but he also instructed them to cull their litters and leave no more than five puppies with the dam. One could see where this advice was sound since this number of puppies would not tax the mother's strength. Von Stephanitz also thought that if a heat was neglected, the bitch would gain nothing but fat, which would reduce her fertility and suitability for breeding. It is interesting to note that even today German breeders are not permitted to leave more than six puppies with the dam. They must find a foster mother for the extra puppies or destroy them. German bitches must have a SchH1 title before they can be bred. The SchH1 title encompasses all the basic Obedience work such as Heeling, Coming, Staying, Retrieving and Jumping. This is required because von Stephanitz directed that, "The proof of the education of the dog for work should be *a sine qua non* for admission for breeding and not exhibition honors which constitute a very misleading description of a dog's value for breeding. The chief consideration is that the latent talents in the dog should be brought out, invigorated, and thereby be made transmittable."

There are different opinions about the age a young male should be the first time he is used. I believe he should be about twenty months of age and should have watched a quiet, older dog be bred a couple of times. By watching an experienced stud dog, he will learn by observation and be eager to try it himself. He should receive a little assistance when it is his turn so that his first breeding will be a successful one. A dog who fails to tie may become so discouraged that he will get a mental block about breeding and fumble around so long that he will repeatedly fail to copulate. If you wish to use this dog at stud, you should again use an older brood bitch who will be patient with him while you assist him in effecting a tie. Once he has had a tie, his next breedings should be successful; however, he should be used very sparingly until he is two years old.

It is customary for the owner to take his bitch to the stud dog for breeding purposes. Most bitch owners have no idea what will occur when they breed their bitch. They expect they may have to leave their bitch at the stud dog owner's kennel and think the two Shepherds will be let loose together until they are eventually bred. Breeding two purebred dogs requires a little more preparation than this. The bitch's owner should examine her vagina to be sure it is large enough for the male to enter and to be certain there is no ring of flesh obstructing the passage. If it seems abnormal, her veterinarian could rectify this condition. The bitch should be groomed and be free of fleas before she meets the stud dog. She will probably be shedding at this time and a good brushing will help her feel and look better. If you have to ship your bitch by air, let her get used to being in a crate at least a week beforehand so that this new experience will be less traumatic. If at all possible, I recommend that you take your bitch to the stud dog, even though you have to fly her there, to guarantee her safety.

If you are the owner of the stud dog, there are several things to check when a bitch comes in for breeding. Examine her to see if her vulva is swollen, and if the discharge is light in color. If the owner has not examined her, you should do so. Wear a sterile surgical glove and place a little Johnson & Johnson KY Jelly™ on your index finger and insert it in her vagina to determine whether the opening is large enough and unobstructed.

Some bitches have a very small opening and it is impossible for a dog to penetrate this ring of flesh. You could try to push your finger through this ring and enlarge the opening. Somebody should hold the bitch's head firmly so that she doesn't bite you while you are examining her.

If you took her to a veterinarian, he might stretch the opening by inserting an instrument in her vagina or tear the ring of flesh with his fingers to make the opening larger. Either method will give the bitch a moment of discomfort. Before introducing your stud dog to the bitch, spray him from tail to head with a bug repellent, as she might have fleas. This should prevent your dog from becoming infested with them.

The bitch should be muzzled before the male is brought to her. Some bitches are very placid and will stand very quietly, encouraging the male to try harder by being very coy, playful and pleasant to him. Other maiden bitches are so difficult that it takes four people to hold them. The bitch's owner should hold both sides of her ruff firmly in his hands, another person should hold the bitch over his knee to hold her up and to steady her and a third person should assist the male by gently guiding him into position. If the bitch has been bred before, one or two people can breed her quite easily.

The owner should encourage the young stud dog to mount the bitch by patting her hindquarter and saying "Up" to the dog. If he doesn't understand, just lift his front legs over her back so that he is straddling her. Some bitches cry out when the male's penis touches the lining or opening of the vagina, and a young or sensitive male will dismount. The owner should encourage the stud dog to ignore such cries and keep trying. Even bitches who are ready to be bred will often do this, or be most uncooperative, and the male must learn to persist.

Someone should hold the bitch still while the stud probes and thrusts, feeling for the opening. It is wise to give him a little help at this time by moving her vulva up with your left hand while you guide his penis into it with your right. Some dogs may appear not to want help, but when they become interested in the bitch you can help them without them being aware of it. It is always best to help the stud dog consummate the breeding as quickly as possible so that he will retain the right mental attitude about it. When he consummates a tie, the bitch's attitude will change completely. She will become very docile and wag her tail happily. At this time her muzzle should be removed.

It is always reassuring to both parties to have a "tie," but it is not absolutely necessary to have one for conception.

Occasionally the stud dog will enter correctly, but due to some irregularity, the dog will not be able to get far enough into the vagina to remain locked, or tied, for the normal period. In this case the male should be held in place on the bitch's back for about five minutes. You will note after a few minutes that the large bulbs on his penis are swollen on the outside instead of being locked inside the muscular ring of her vagina. If he is held there quietly he will emit enough of the sperm contained in the seminal fluid to provide conception.

A male who has not had a proper "tie" might not want to try again until the next day, and in this case it is wise to let him rest. However, we have found that most males are very eager to try again if you give them a fifteen-minute rest, and they can effect a normal "tie" at this time.

When the dogs are tied, the stud dog may want to stand by the bitch's side for the remaining time, which varies from seven minutes to one hour and forty-five minutes, or he may wish to lift his hind leg over her back and stand tail to tail in opposite directions. The bitch's owner should continue to hold her so that she won't sit or lie down and injure herself or the male. They should both be made to stand quietly until the stud dog's penis shrinks to a size where he can remove it. When this happens the male should be taken away, given a drink of water, and placed in an outdoor run. The bitch should also be given a drink of water and placed somewhere where she can be quiet. She should not be permitted to jump around.

The bitch should whelp her litter any time from fifty-nine to sixty-three days after she is bred. I have found that the time varies with the individual bitches, so it is wise to have the whelping box ready by the fiftieth day.

THE WHELPING BOX

Many pregnant bitches become uneasy if they do not have a secluded corner of their own. Some actually plan ahead and try to get a nest ready for their puppies. If left alone in a yard, they will investigate all the quiet little places where they could have their puppies unobserved. You might find your bitch digging a hole under the porch, under a wide-spreading spruce tree or in a hidden nook under some vines. It will always be a spot that is within sight of the house but hidden from passersby. Let her see that her whelping box is readily accessible to her as it will give her a sense of security and a feeling of preparedness.

Some new mothers may not show any desire to stay in the whelping box until they are actually in labor, but if you remain with them, they will be content to be with you. Once they have had a puppy in the whelping box, they will want to remain there. Just be sure the box is placed where they will have some privacy.

The whelping box should be four feet square. The bottom of the box should be raised up off the floor two inches, on two- by three-inch legs. The bottom and the two-foot-high sides should be made of a good quality exterior plywood that is finished on one side. There should be a four-inch ledge around the inside of the box, four inches from the bottom, so that the mother will not inadvertently crush a puppy behind her when she is in labor, or later, when the puppies are nursing. The puppy would instead be pushed safely under the ledge where he will cry for attention and his mother, or you, upon hearing him cry, will attend to him. The front side of the box is four feet wide. There will be sixteen inches of plywood on either side. The sixteen-inch middle section is open and will have grooves on both sides so that one four-inch and two eight-inch boards can be added as needed. In the beginning use just a four-inch board so that the mother can step in and out at will. Later, as the puppies get bigger, it will be necessary to add the other boards to keep them contained.

As the time draws nearer for the bitch to have her puppies, it is a good idea to keep your eye on her. Do not let her go outdoors unattended or she may wander off to look for a nesting place. As soon as she is out of sight, she will find a secluded corner and start digging a hole. If she must be left alone for some reason, leave her in a room with her whelping box. If she should suddenly have labor pains, she will want to be in her box. In your absence she will probably dig up the papers or towels you have neatly placed in her box; this is a normal reaction so don't be alarmed about it.

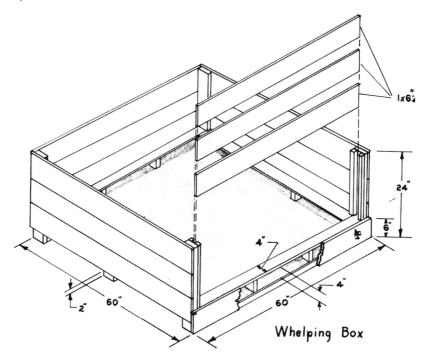

Whelping Box

A well-constructed whelping box, showing appropriate dimensions for a German Shepherd bitch and her litter.

There are different materials that you can use to line the whelping box. Some of these are: rags; corrugated paper; newspapers, whole or shredded; cedar chips; or burlap bags. We line the bottom of the whelping box with newspapers, then fold a mattress pad over them, and cover this with two or three beach towels. During the period when the bitch is whelping her puppies, we repeatedly change the beach towels so that she is always lying on dry towels. The soiled towels can be quickly cleaned in the washer and dryer. It is very important to keep the mother and her puppies warm and dry.

The temperature in the whelping box should be about 76 degrees. You could place an electric heater on a stand in one corner of the box that would automatically shut off when the temperature has been reached. You can purchase electric heaters that will turn off if they are tipped over. It just takes a small heater to keep the temperature steady.

We have runs in our puppy nursery about five- by fifteen-feet long and each one has its own whelping box at one end. The heat in these runs is thermostatically controlled so that the mother and her puppies are warm and free from drafts. The nursery is completely segregated from all our other dogs.

PRENATAL CARE

I believe it is important that a bitch be kept calm, happy and free of worry during her pregnancy. She shouldn't be forced to endure moments of stress such as being confined with another dog who is aggressive or unpleasant, being teased by children, abused by adults or having to worry for any reason. You should take precautions to see that she has a happy pregnancy so that her puppies will be mentally sound. A bitch who is under pressure for some reason will transmit this anxiety to her puppies and they will suffer for it. Be kind and considerate to her, don't be rough or harsh. She will have to go out more often when she is carrying her puppies, and although she shouldn't be permitted to jump or play roughly, she should have a normal amount of exercise. Remember that she will feel awkward and uncomfortable.

She should be rechecked for worms during her third week and if some are present, she should be wormed with a drug that does not have an adverse effect on the puppies.

About the second week, most of our bitches give us a sign that they are pregnant by refusing their morning meal. They just feel full and are quite willing to eat it later. We put our bitches on two meals per day when they are bred, and they go on a high-protein diet. The diet consists of freshly ground beef, a top-quality kibbled biscuit, milk, Prenatal Theralin, a hard-boiled egg daily and fresh vegetables. The eggshell is crushed and mixed in with one of the meals. Cod-liver oil or halibut-liver oil with Viosterol could be added to the morning meal.

The bitch will show signs of being pregnant about her fifth week. At this time she should be on three meals per day. She will have little space for a large meal, but will readily accept three small ones.

WHELPING

German Shepherd bitches make very good mothers and can generally take care of their puppies without any outside help. Nevertheless, it is wise to stay with the bitch the entire time she is whelping her litter in case she needs any assistance. A young bitch with her first litter may not understand what to do when the first puppy is born, particularly if the litter is early. Have a clean pair of scissors, a pan full of hot water, a large, soft face cloth and several soft Turkish towels handy.

When the bitch's abdomen drops and she carries her puppies low, she will whelp within the week. Most of our bitches refuse to eat the day that they whelp. Another way to tell that the puppies will arrive that day is by a drop of 1 degree in their normal body temperature of 101.4 degrees. Lubricate a rectal thermometer with Vaseline, insert three-quarters of it in the bitch's rectum and wait two minutes before you remove it. Wipe the excess Vaseline off with a tissue and you will be able to read it easily. The bitch won't enjoy having her temperature taken, so don't upset her at this time by checking it repeatedly. We don't take the temperatures of our bitches as we prefer to tend to them when they seem uneasy. We go about our usual tasks and this puts them at ease.

The first sign the bitch will give you that the puppies are coming is when she starts trying to dig up her bedding and pile it into a corner. You will have to keep straightening it out so that she will have a neat bed when the first puppy arrives. It is just a matter of waiting. Do not confine her to a small box, but let her walk around the room and get some exercise. This will help her to deliver her first puppy.

Then, suddenly, the bitch will turn around several times in a circle, have a muscular spasm just as if she were in labor, and shortly a puppy will come into her vagina encased in a sac.

After a couple of more turns, another muscular spasm or two and several grunts, the puppy slips down to the floor as the mother sits down and turns to take care of him. The puppy is enveloped in a sac made of membranous material which the mother will immediately tear open; she will then chew off the umbilical cord, swallow all this material, plus the afterbirth if it came with the puppy, and start licking the puppy to clean it off. The puppy's nose and mouth will be covered with mucous so she will take particular care to lick these clean. Most bitches will lick their puppies quite vigorously, pushing them around as they are doing so. Don't be alarmed. This is good for the puppy and will make him cry out a little. This in turn will help him to clear his nose and throat. His instincts will immediately tell him to search for food. The brightest puppies will immediately look for their mother and nuzzle her in search of milk. They can't see at this time, but their instincts plus their senses of smell and taste and ability to feel their mother's body heat guides them to her. Not all litters will do this and with some you have to actually start the milk flowing in a nipple, place it in the puppy's mouth and hold the puppy in position there until he starts nursing. Puppies from certain bloodlines are much slower than others at being aware of simple little basic things like this.

A bitch may be uncertain what she should do when her first puppy is born. This is particularly true when a dam has her puppies early. It almost seems as if her instinct is out of step with the physical aspect of her being. Later, and it might be one or two days later, she will assume her motherly duties as if she had been tending to them for years. One bitch that I bought was completely unnerved when she had her first litter of five puppies. As each succeeding puppy arrived, she would look at it with horror and try to run from the room. She thought it was all a dreadful mistake and didn't understand what was happening. She had to be held forcibly in order for her puppies to nurse, and although she wouldn't attend to them when they were born, she could be persuaded to lick them. The next day, which was her sixtieth day, her natural instincts returned and she suddenly understood how she should take care of her puppies and became a very conscientious mother.

A friend of mine called me one day, almost in hysterics, and said her bitch was in labor, ready to whelp any minute, and she didn't know what to do. It was impossible for me to leave, so I invited her to bring her bitch over to my

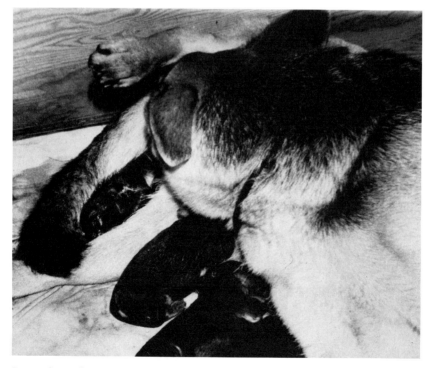

Puppy being born.

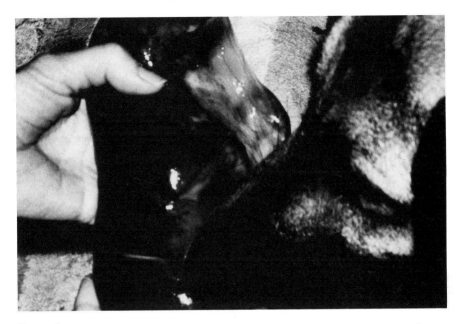

Puppy in sac.

house. While she was driving over, I got a whelping box ready for her. Joan arrived ready to panic, so I told her to leave us and relax while I took care of her bitch. The dam was so upset by Joan's apparent distress that she was beside herself. I had the bitch lie down in her whelping box and spoke to her and handled her in a very calm, matter-of-fact sort of way, and shortly she stopped trembling and panting so hard. Half an hour later a puppy arrived and I toweled it dry and held it while she licked it. She lay down calmly with her puppy beside her, content that everything was under control. I called Joan to see her, but wouldn't let her pet her or stay too long. A nervous person should not be around when a bitch is delivering her puppies as she is a very bad influence. They need someone around who will reassure them that everything is all right, be calm enough to help them if they need it, and praise them quietly so that they can attend to their business with confidence.

I believe it is advisable to have a pan of comfortably hot water, a soft Turkish face cloth and a soft Turkish towel handy to wipe the puppies clean and rub them dry. Let the mother watch you, and let her nuzzle the puppy while you hold him, so that she won't become upset. If the afterbirth comes with the puppy, let the mother eat it if she wants to do so. However, if she has more than four puppies, you should discard half of the afterbirths after that. Try to do so without disturbing her. You should work quickly when helping the mother and not cause her any anxiety by your slowness or uncertainty.

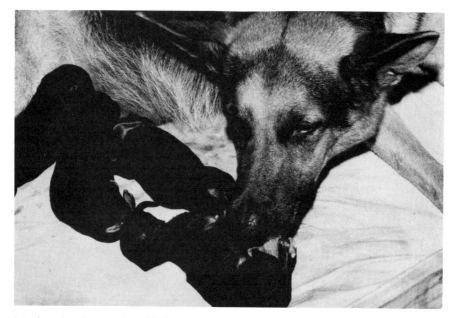

Mother chewing cord and licking puppy clean.

If you find it necessary to open the sac yourself, remove it from the puppy's head first so that you can immediately wipe the mucous off the puppy's nose and mouth. Once you have done this, cut the cord in a jagged way (with the scissors you have sterilized in boiling water), about three inches from the body. Don't cut it straight across, the mother always chews it and leaves an uneven break which quickly stops it from bleeding. It will dry up and drop off within the next two or three days. Let the mother lick her puppy as much as she wants. Once the puppy is out of the sac and the cord is cut, wash the puppy gently by holding him in one hand as you clean him with the face cloth which was dipped in very warm water. Don't scald it. Next, hold the puppy on a small Turkish towel in your hand as you vigorously rub him dry with another. If you tap him lightly, he will cry, and this will clear the puppy's lungs and nose. When the puppy cries, the mother will want to lick him, so let her do so. When the puppy is clean, put him near the mother's breast and help him start nursing. If necessary, open the puppy's mouth, place the nipple in it and hold the puppy's head there for a few minutes or until he begins to nurse.

The temperature in the whelping box at this time should be 76 degrees. The mother will be panting hard, but don't lower the temperature the first week. Offer her frequent drinks of water, beef broth or milk.

If you help the mother, notice whether an afterbirth, or placenta, accompanies every puppy. The placenta is attached to the newborn puppy via the cord and, if you pull it gently, many times it will slip out; then you can dispose of it. If the afterbirth is missing, it will probably be expelled as

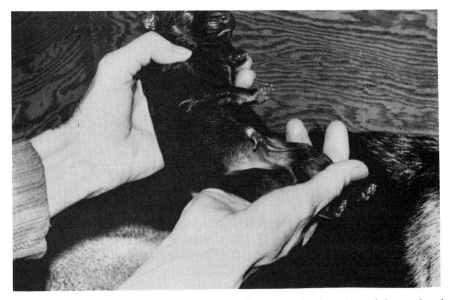

Newborn puppy photographed immediately after its mother has chewed the cord and licked the puppy clean.

the next puppy is being born. There should be an afterbirth for every puppy, so count them to be sure the mother eventually expels all of them. Not every puppy is enclosed in a sac, but he will still need to have his umbilical cord cut and the puppy will need cleaning.

Puppies are born headfirst or buttocks first. If a puppy is born buttocks first (which is called a breech birth) and the mother has trouble expelling him because he has a large head, you should help by pulling the puppy gently as the mother strains. Wrap a face cloth around the puppy so that you won't injure it. Sometimes a puppy with a large head that is being born headfirst will get stuck, the sac will break, you will notice a dark, greenish discharge and the puppy dies while being born. The puppy's legs are not tucked up under his chin, but are in an awkward position, and the puppy suffocates while the mother stands up and turns in circles trying to free him. This exercise, plus several muscular spasms, helps to free the puppy so he can be born. If the head itself is expelled, you can grasp it very gently in a soft face cloth and pull very carefully while the mother is having a contraction. The wrong move will break the puppy's neck. This is a very painful birth and some bitches may try to bite the hand that is helping them. If in doubt, let the mother handle the situation, but be ready to try to save the puppy by cleaning it immediately. If the puppy has a heartbeat, you can get it going faster by administering mouth-to-mouth resuscitation.

If she looks as if she will have a large litter of eight or more puppies and four have already been born, I would suggest that you give her one-half cubic centimeter of Oxytocin, which you can get from your vet. When you place the needle of the syringe in her hind leg, be careful to withdraw the needle a fraction before administering the Oxytocin to be sure you haven't hit a vein. If not, continue. This will get her started contracting again so that the delivery period will not be too long and tiring. Later, when you think she has finished delivering her puppies, you should give her one cubic centimeter of Oxytocin. This will cause a contraction of the uterus and clean out any afterbirths that are present, or if one more puppy is waiting, this will get it out right away. A long, drawn-out delivery can be very exhausting to both the bitch and her owners. *Do not* give the bitch Oxytocin *before* she has had a puppy.

If your bitch goes two or three hours without having a puppy, yet you see she is having contractions, she may have a puppy lying across the passage. Wash your hands with medicated soap, then spread some KY Jelly over your hand to make them slippery, insert your thumb and first two fingers into her vagina and see if you can turn the puppy so that he can enter the passage. Someone should be holding the bitch's head as this may be painful for her. Be very cautious, do not pull the puppy out, but try to slip him into another position so that the mother can deliver him during one of her contractions.

German Shepherds are very good-natured and tolerant mothers and rarely need help when whelping a litter of puppies. However, this doesn't mean you

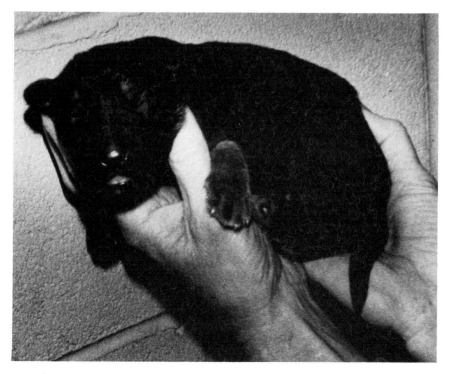

Two-day-old puppy.

shouldn't stand by to assist her if the time should arise when she needs you. If she goes beyond her sixtieth day, take her for a walk at least twice daily, but stay close to home as walking may induce labor. If your bitch goes three days beyond the sixty-third day, or has been in prolonged labor without delivery, you should have your veterinarian examine her to determine whether she should have a Cesarean section. A bitch having her first litter late in life, an overweight bitch, one bred her first season who is immature or an extra large puppy, could all mean trouble. If the bitch labors too long, she may become exhausted and give up. The uterine muscle may lose its powers of contraction and flexibility and uterine inertia may occur. Call your veterinarian before it is too late. The newborn puppies from a Cesarean section operation must be tube-fed every three hours around the clock. Four days after the operation, the mother should be able to nurse and take care of her puppies. If you stay with her while the puppies are nursing, you can prevent them from being too rough.

Halfway through a normal whelping, and later when she has finished, take your bitch outdoors to relieve herself. She may not want to leave her puppies, so put her on-leash and insist that she at least urinates while outdoors. Most mothers will not leave their box to have a drink of water, so hold her dish for her. Give her some nourishing broth from time to time.

If there are any abnormal puppies, white, brown, blue, or very small puppies, they should be put to sleep. The litter should be culled after the third day if there are more than eight puppies in it, unless you supplement the feeding. Often, one or two puppies are born dead and these should be removed immediately while the mother's attention is diverted to a live puppy. A very conscientious mother will want to follow you, leaving all her healthy puppies behind, to see what you were doing with her dead puppy. She will feel very protective and concerned about each and every one of them. This is a healthy attitude and I prefer bitches like this as they make the best mothers.

When the mother has finished whelping her puppies, she should be washed with a medicated shampoo, as her panties (the long fur on her hindquarters) and legs will be stained with blackish-green fluid. This is the time to remove it before it becomes a permanent stain. Rinse her off thoroughly, towel her dry and be sure she has plenty of water to drink. Give her something nourishing to drink like beef broth, vanilla yogurt or ice cream if she likes it. She will have a discharge for the next two weeks that will gradually lessen. Give her a clean, dry bed, then leave her alone for several hours so that she can nurse her puppies and get a well-deserved rest.

The dewclaws on a German Shepherd's forelegs should not be removed. However, you should check all the puppies to see whether they have dewclaws on their hind legs. It is very unlikely that they will have any, but if they do, every bit of the dewclaw should be cleanly snipped off with a pair of sharp scissors. This should be done on the second day when the mother is absent from her box. Upon her return she will stop the bleeding by licking the wound.

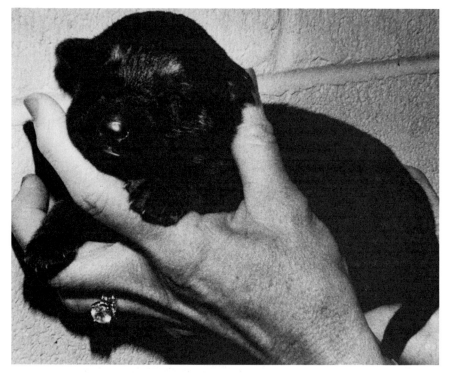

Four-day-old puppy.

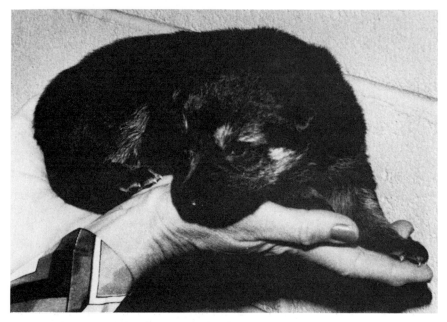

Ten-day-old puppy.

The most critical period of a puppy's life is the first three days after he is born. A puppy may appear to be perfectly healthy and normal when he is born, but he may have internal problems that will show up after he has digested his first meal. You may go out to the whelping box sometime and find a puppy off by himself. He will be lying there very still and limp, and his skin will seem cold. If you place your finger in his mouth he will try to push it out, or turn his head to the side. A healthy puppy will try to suck on your finger, and when asleep will be jerking and twitching as he sprawls over his littermates. This is called activated sleep and a newborn puppy develops because of this exercise. If you pick up the sick puppy he will cry pitifully as though hungry, but he will be unable to nurse, even though you support his head on his mother's breast. During the first week of a puppy's life his temperature is about 94 to 97 degrees and he maintains this partly because of his mother's 100 to 102-degree body temperature, and partly because of the temperature of his box. If the temperature in his box should drop and his mother should push him aside, he will die from the cold. If he is alive when you find him, don't try to warm him up too quickly by putting him in a box on a radiator as you will only be warming his skin or exterior. His heart deep within him is still operating at about 74 to 78 degrees. In other words, his warm exterior will be demanding large amounts of oxygen, but his cold heart will prevent his body from supplying it and his metabolism will not be maintained. If you come across a cold puppy, put it in your inside shirt pocket and let it get warm gradually as it absorbs your body heat. When it is warm it will become more active and then you can try to feed it. Never try to feed a puppy when it is cold or you will lose it.

The cold puppy has a low body temperature and would not be able to digest his food because his digestive tract is paralyzed. His reserve supply of blood sugar is very low and the puppy will become hypoglycemic very quickly and die if not given food or sugar within three hours. Mix a teaspoonful of sugar to an ounce of water and tube-feed it to the puppy every half-hour. Unlike formula, this sugar-water is absorbed directly through the stomach where it will do the most good. It is said that a newborn puppy's body weight is 82 percent water, as compared to 68 percent in the adult dog, therefore it is important that he get water. The factors to remember in trying to save a sick puppy's life are: slow warming, tube-feeding sugar-water and providing fluids to offset dehydration.

If your bitch has milk fever (*eclampsia*), it is because she needs more calcium and phosphorus in her diet. She should be on a high-protein diet: beef, top-quality biscuit, milk, liver, hard-boiled eggs, cottage cheese and vitamin supplements. Symptoms of calcium deficiency are partial paralysis, shortness of breath, staggering gait and convulsions. The veterinarian should be called immediately to give her an injection of calcium into the bloodstream. She should recover in a few hours, but the puppies should be tube-fed from then on.

A loving mother.

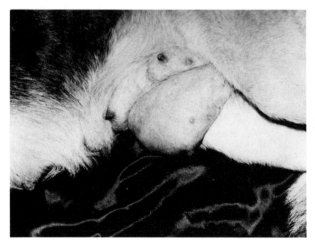

Mastitis—swollen breast.

After your bitch has whelped her litter, her breasts and hindquarters should be washed each day, and the bedding should be changed at least twice a day. If the mother and her bedding are not kept clean, she might develop *Mastitis,* which is an infection of the breasts. One or more of her breasts may become very swollen and painful. She should be given antibiotics and her breasts should be milked by hand morning and evening until the swelling goes down. The puppies should not nurse an infected breast or they will become sick and die, either from the infection or from hunger. They should be tube-fed at this time, or given to a foster mother. Try to find a foster mother who is large enough to feed them. Some milk from the foster mother should be lightly rubbed into the coats of the puppies so that they will carry her scent. Someone should stay with her until she nurses and cleans them, signs that she will accept them.

The same condition may also arise if the litter is small and the puppies are selective about feeding from the breasts. Those not milked will become caked and the milk when forced out by hand will be thick. Warm towels should be applied to the breast while it is being milked.

TUBE-FEEDING

Occasionally in a litter you will find one or two puppies who are not able to suck very well. They must get an adequate supply of milk from the mother to keep them alive, but unless you hand hold them in position on the breasts, they will fall off. Even if they try to hold on to a nipple, another stronger puppy will come along and knock them out of position before they get enough to eat. Tube-feeding these puppies might save their lives. Then, when they are three weeks old, they will be able to lap their milk from a dish.

To supplement the feeding of a large, valuable litter of eight or more puppies, when it is impossible to find a foster mother, we suggest tube-feeding. Buy a size #8 French infant-feeding tube and a thirty-five cubic centimeter plastic hypodermic syringe at a hospital supply store. Place the tube against the puppy, as illustrated, so that you can determine the length of tube to be inserted. Mark the feeding tube with a dot of red nail polish at a point three-quarters of the distance from the puppy's last rib to his nose. Each time you feed a puppy, this dot will assure you that the tube is inserted the correct length and the formula will go directly into his stomach. A tube that is not inserted properly could carry formula to the puppy's lungs and drown him.

I recommend a formula of one cup of whole milk mixed with one teaspoonful of Karo syrup. Another formula you could use is made up of two ounces of evaporated milk, two ounces of regular milk and one teaspoonful of honey. Since honey has been predigested by the bees, it supplies quick energy without upsetting the digestion. Mix it together very well and warm it so that it is lukewarm.

The amount of formula you should give the puppy depends upon his size. Generally speaking, the right amount at first is fifteen cubic centimeters, but within a few days this should be gradually increased to sixty cubic centimeters. For a litter of seven or eight puppies, two feedings a day is enough. For larger litters, we recommend one tube-feeding every eight hours, and one feeding by the mother every eight hours. The puppies will thus be fed every four hours with alternating breast- and tube-feeding.

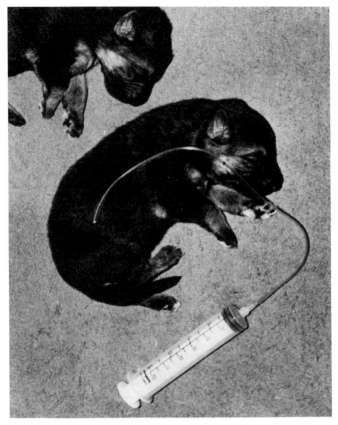

Place tube against puppy to determine how far it should be inserted. Mark with a dot.

Attach the feeding tube to the syringe and draw about fifteen cubic centimeters of formula into it. Hold the puppy in one hand. The puppy should cooperate by trying to swallow the tube as it is being inserted. If he doesn't try to swallow the tube, reinsert it and gently press his tongue down. Stop when you reach the red dot and slowly let the formula in the syringe pass through the tube into the puppy's stomach. Then carefully withdraw the tube from the puppy, refill the syringe with formula, and feed the next puppy. For the first few days, check the puppy's tummy after he has had six cubic centimeters to see if it is nicely rounded. The formula should be substantially increased as the puppy's weight increases. It is best to feed all the puppies in the litter at one time.

If you are feeding puppies that do not have a mother or foster mother to take care of them, it is imperative that you give them the care they would receive from their mother. She licks each puppy from head to tail as she pushes him around and rolls him over. This licking stimulates the flow of urine and feces and if she didn't do this, the puppy would be unable to eliminate and would die. You should copy the mother in caring for her puppies. Moisten a soft face cloth in warm water and gently wipe each puppy with it from head

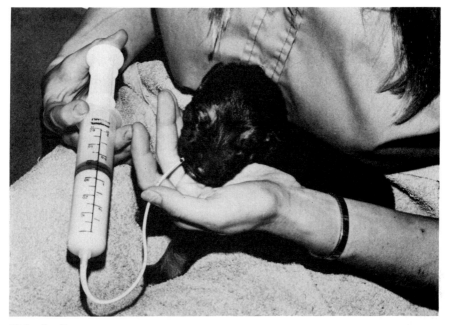

Tube-feeding a puppy.

to tail, including the eyes, which will be closed at this age, start the flow of urine and feces and wipe the puppy clean as you do so.

Tube-feeding is very simple, there is little chance for error in feeding puppies, and it is a great time-saver. The puppies should be weighed every day or two to be sure there is an adequate weight gain.

Culling a litter is an unpleasant but necessary duty at times. The most humane and painless way to put the unwanted puppies to sleep is to drown them in a bucket of water. It is no problem culling a litter when it is not uniform in quality, but this is not the case when all the puppies are uniform in size, quality and appearance. In this case you would be hard-pressed to know which puppies to destroy. If a foster mother is not available, you could save the whole litter by supplementing tube-feeding every eight hours. Then, if you start the puppies on meat at two and one-half weeks of age, gradually add more meals to their diet, and start weaning them at four and one-half weeks, the nursing will not be injurious to the mother's health. She should continue to get a high-protein diet that includes meat, eggs, liver and milk until she is back in condition.

Keep an eye on the puppy's toenails, as they become very sharp in just a few days. If the nails are neglected, the puppies will be scratching their mother so badly that she will not want to stay with them. It is very simple to cut the sharp tips with a pair of pet nail-scissors.

The puppies are born with their eyes and ears closed. The eyes will gradually open and appear to be blue in color. They won't be able to focus at first, but after two weeks will start to see shapes. From this point they will soon be able to see specific things. However, it will be several weeks before they can follow a fast moving object like a ball being rolled on a rug. When the litter is two and one-half weeks old, start them on lean, raw, ground beef. Some of the puppies in the litter may seem reluctant to eat the meat, but by the time they are three weeks of age they will be very eager to get it. As soon as possible, give them three meat meals per day. Introduce milk to them at four weeks of age by pouring it over the meat. This makes the transition to drinking milk very simple and palatable. When the puppies are drinking milk out of a dish, you can add a milk meal at noon and another late in the evening. You can introduce a puppy to kibbled biscuit the same way, but at first it should be soaked in hot water to soften it. Gradually get them on a diet of two-thirds kibbled biscuit and milk and one-third meat. The mother should just feed them during the night.

The average litter should be weaned when the puppies are five weeks old. The mother should be kept away all day, feed her puppies that night, then

Ch. Stormin' Norman v Schwartzkopf
Breeders-Owners: Stephen and Linda Burchett

twelve, twenty-four, thirty-six and forty-eight hours later. She should not let them nurse her again for five days. After that time she can play with them and be allowed to check them over two or three times a day. By this time they will be big and rough and she will be glad to get away from them.

The puppies should be inoculated with the measles distemper vaccine when they are between three and four weeks of age. It is wise to keep everyone away from your puppies until they have been inoculated.

We suggest that the puppies be wormed around four weeks of age if a stool check shows that they have some. However, if the puppies look thin, go ahead and worm them for roundworms. Keep the mother away for a few hours until they have had bowel movements. If you notice worms in their stools, worm them again in ten days.

Many breeders find that they can best pick a "flyer" (top-quality puppy) when it is eight weeks of age, then again at four months of age. It is at these times that you can most readily determine how the puppy will look when it is mature.

Puppies should receive an inoculation of a canine-origin modified live parvovirus vaccine when they are six weeks of age and every three weeks thereafter until they are sixteen weeks of age. Parvovirus is a deadly disease that acts quickly and can wipe out a litter in a few days or less. It is easily transmitted by people or dogs, so kennel facilities should be kept clean and disinfected daily with Clorox. Today the parvovirus vaccine is combined with the other vaccines: distemper, parainfluenza, adenovirus 11 and leptospirosis. This combination is given to older dogs once a year in the form of a booster shot.

Ch. Landaleigh's Instant Replay, BIM, HIC, OFA
Sire: Sel. Ch. Brentaryl's Gunner, ROM
Dam: Landaleigh's Fontana, ROM, HIC, OFA
Breeders-Owners: Hank and Gail Cobleigh

chapter 30

The Genetic Factor

The German Shepherd today is the product of very careful inbreeding and linebreeding. Captain von Stephanitz had made a very thorough study of dog-breeding practices in England and tried them out before he found his ideal Shepherd, Horand. By combining this knowledge with his own genius and foresight, he was able to shape the breed the way he wanted it. Today, German Shepherd breeders in Germany continue to use his sound breeding ideas to carry on his life's work.

Everyone has his own idea of the perfect German Shepherd and would like to perfect a strain within the breed that, through heredity, would keep reproducing its own excellence. To succeed in this endeavor, the breeder must have a profound knowledge of breeding laws, a generous endowment of common sense and a thorough knowledge of all the hereditary factors in the dogs he plans to use. This doesn't mean that one must be a geneticist in order to breed dogs. The number of geneticists in the United States who are successful German Shepherd breeders is negligible, whereas the number of knowledgeable fanciers who have become highly successful German Shepherd breeders is quite large.

Breeding laws and theories are useless unless one can recognize the correct German Shepherd structure, gait and temperament. Practical knowledge and experience are the most valuable attributes one can possess when breeding dogs, and the study of genetics will be applied at this time.

The science of genetics is very complex and, despite the amount of time people spend studying it, it is unlikely it will ever become an exact science. In the art of breeding dogs, for instance, there is, after all the planning and studying, an element of chance that one can't control. Success is more constant when knowledge is blessed with a little luck.

When we speak of genetics, we mean the regrouping of the chromosomes into pairs which are made up of so many genes that differ with each new generation and are the real carriers of hereditary characteristics. To be able to control these genes, we must be very familiar with the hereditary tendencies of each individual on a pedigree and realize these tendencies may be either dominant or recessive. If both a dominant and a recessive factor are present, the dominant will conceal the recessive factor. We must acknowledge each dog's faults and virtues and try to perpetuate the good points and eradicate the faults.

Therefore, with this in mind, if one is to establish a true breeding strain, one must breed back along the ancestral lines to the dog one considers both physically and genetically ideal. The newborn puppy receives an equal number of genes from his sire and from his dam. One often sees a sire who is so prepotent that his progeny greatly resemble him. However, even in this case, the progeny have received 50 percent of their genes from their dam. Occasionally, the progeny will closely resemble a grandparent, or in rare cases, a great-grandparent, who was very prepotent.

If one wants to preserve the good characteristics of the ideal ancestor, his blood should appear in each generation. It could be through one of his prepotent sons, daughters, grandsons, et cetera, but it should be there in order to preserve his type. Von Stephanitz has said that "the best results are obtained by linebreeding with descendants of the fourth generation from a common ancestor." But each generation should preserve the type of the ideal common ancestor. An ideal ancestor back in the fourth or fifth generation might seem too far removed to have any influence on a litter, but the type he has passed on will exert some good through his progeny.

If the ancestor's physical and genetic qualities that one is trying to intensify are close to the ideal, it is relatively safe to inbreed or linebreed. Breeding father to daughter, dam to her son, brother to sister and half brother to half sister is called inbreeding and produces a preponderance of one individual's blood. Breeding a daughter to her sire will give you bloodlines that are three-quarters the sire's. Breeding a son to his dam will give you three-quarters the blood of the dam. One can, if knowledgeable, produce animals that are true to type by careful inbreeding and linebreeding. However, by consolidating the good traits, one takes the risk of intensifying the dormant faults. Here, then, is where one should be cognizant of the faults, and have the courage to cull at birth, or any time later when it is wise to do so. Old-timers have a favorite breeding theory, "Let the sire of the sire be the grandsire of the dam, on the dam's side."

It is called an open pedigree when none of the animals in the first five generations are related. Generally speaking, litters with this type of pedigree are unpredictable. In breeding back to an animal in the fourth or fifth generation that carried all the external characteristics that you wanted, you would be forced to use the bloodlines of the other less desirable ancestors. The ideal phenotype (external characteristics) might carry recessive genes in his pattern, and a breeder, in order to be successful, must be realistic and consider the genotype (internal reproducing factors) at all times. The ideal animal is a genotype capable of reproducing his best characteristics as well as being a most attractive animal himself.

In dealing with an open pedigree, the breeder must be capable of breeding out the recessives while retaining the dominant genes that gave the phenotype his excellence. The outward appearance of a dog does not guarantee that he can reproduce his type. He may possess dominant factors but transmit recessive ones, and when bred his partner may have the same recessives. The object should be to keep the recessives hidden. Many beautiful dogs who are Champions are poor producers. Others with less eye-appeal who are, nevertheless, structurally sound are able to produce excellent progeny by any bitch. The finest example of an open pedigree was the immortal Axel von der Deininghauserheide, SchH3, who produced some of the greatest dogs of all time. He was an excellent example of the correct phenotype and genotype. This was a rare stroke of good genes and good fortune. Normally, the best results are experienced by inbreeding and linebreeding to preserve type.

It follows that a dog who is close to the ideal will possess polygenic characteristics that are dominant and, to establish these traits, one should breed him to a bitch with similar traits who has already proven her ability to reproduce them. The best producers will nearly always be physically and mentally sound. If you breed dogs of poor quality, you will get puppies of poor quality.

If you have established a strain within the breed by linebreeding, you may find it necessary to outcross to introduce a desirable chracteristic into your stock. If, for instance, your strain of purebred stock lacks good ear carriage, you could make a single outcross to an animal of similar type who carries the genes for good ears, then inbreed one of these puppies back into your line. This breeding should produce the results you desire. This is possible if the feature you are trying to produce is not a combination of genetic factors. If it is, the problem is much more complex.

In the early years of the breed in Germany, some long coated dogs were bred into certain bloodlines because of the scarcity of top-quality German Shepherds and because the emphasis was always placed on the dog's working ability. Today this condition is difficult to eradicate because it is carried as a recessive in nearly all the bloodlines, and the long coats are sold and used in breeding programs. There are so many excellent German Shepherds being raised that it is unnecessary to breed long coated dogs who will perpetuate this fault. It is economically unsound, too, for a breeder to continue to produce long coated puppies that should either be sold as pets or culled.

It is said that if a certain mating pair produce progeny that are lighter in color than themselves, they both carry genes for paling. The mate who throws puppies paler than himself is the one who transmits the paling genes. One should not use a line that has produced whites.

If a dog and a bitch carry recessive genes for the maldevelopment of the male gonads, the progeny will be faulty in this regard. Both sexes can carry and transmit this recessive, and it is wise to remember that these genes also control the production of sex hormones in general. If a genetically sound bitch is bred to a monorchid male, the progeny will be sound but half the puppies will carry the genes for monorchidism.

Recessive genes can skip one or more generations, but if a parent carries a single recessive factor, 50 percent of the progeny will carry them. This will not be noticed externally unless each of the partners contributed similar recessive genes. It has been acknowledged that there is no bloodline that is free of the recessive genes for monorchidism or cryptorchidism, but by careful selection one can keep it suppressed.

In the matter of dentition, certain bloodlines carry recessive genes for teeth problems, and if one knows the dogs who transmit them, one can avoid the problems. The key is always "proper selection of the breeding animals."

Extreme shyness is a dominant characteristic and will crop up for many generations unless one selects the breeding animals with care. The genes for temperament are very complex and there are different degrees of shyness. Dogs who are extremely shy should never be bred. Dogs with a small degree of shyness can produce mentally sound puppies when bred to a line that has been mentally sound for three or more generations. The ideal phenotype could transmit recessives for mental instability, so knowledge of the individuals in his pedigree is all-important. A highly respected German breeder once warned me not to buy any German Shepherds unless the temperaments and characters of the dogs had been sound for five generations; an excellent piece of advice I have always remembered.

Sometimes appearances will fool you. A dog with poor bone but otherwse ideal, may be this way because of improper feeding, even though he actually carries the genes for good bone. A dog who has been gifted with excellent genes may never reach his full potential because of his environment, but a dog living in a perfect environment can never exceed his genetic limit.

Although each parent contributes 50 percent of the genes, one parent may give undesirable genes, so both are not equally responsible for good or bad characteristics. For example, a dog with good shoulders may be able to transmit this good quality and, if bred to a bitch with poor shoulders, would produce progeny with better-than-average shoulders. This would happen despite the bitch, for it is likely that if she were bred to a dog with poor shoulders like her own, the resulting progeny would have shoulders like hers or worse. If you were trying to establish good shoulders in your litters you would have to be sure to find a stud dog whose ancestors also had good shoulders. In trying to secure a certain good characteristic, one must always be very selective and consider those animals in back of the sire and dam who gave them their excellent characteristics.

Animals with light eyes are said to be untrustworthy and aggressive but this is not true. I have known a countless number of very highly intelligent, trustworthy dogs with light eyes. This type of eye seems to glare at you from

Sel. Ch. Omega's American
Express, HT, OFA
Breeders-Owners: Joseph,
Frank and Clary Douwes

a dark face and is not particularly attractive but blends and harmonizes with a light-colored head. The dark eye is definitely preferred for esthetic reasons. Today one sees more dark-eyed German Shepherds than heretofore as the breeders of top-quality dogs have bred them into their strains. Regardless of the dog's coloring, the dark eyes are very beautiful and expressive and actually enhance the dog's overall appearance. It is a dominant factor and not too difficult to establish in your line.

The right diet and exercise will have a tremendous influence on feet, but the best care will not improve a genetic fault. Poor feet will remain so despite the best of care. If you want good feet in your strain, breed to a dog that consistently produces progeny with good feet.

Features of major importance, such as temperament, character, body length, shoulders and rear angulation, are controlled by a good number of genes being dominant, partially dominant or recessive, and the number of possible combinations is too great to foretell the outcome. Knowing the background of each dog you breed is the safest and surest road to success.

I have written this chapter on the basis of what I have learned and experienced in raising dogs. In passing this information along, I have tried to express myself in terms that would be easily understood. The breeder who wishes to read a more detailed and intensive study of genetics should avail himself of the many excellent books that have been published on this subject.

Nike Clayfield First Love, Best Puppy, RWB, at her first show.
Sire: Am. & Can. Sel. Ch. Jericho's Gatineau, TC, HT, OFA
Dam: Sel. Ch. Nike Clayfield Lady Love, TC, OFA
Breeders-Owners: Angela Stegner and Sharlonna McGaha

chapter 31

The Color Factor in German Shepherds

In a breeding program, one should not place too much emphasis on color. We feel it is enough to breed dogs with good pigment, and in our breed black-and-tans, black-and-silver, sable, gray and black are all good colors. The faded-out grays, sables and whites are undesirable.

In 1960 Maureen Yentzen of Maur-ray Kennels, who specialized in breeding solid-black German Shepherds, made the following observations on color inheritance.

She bred thirty-three litters in which the factor for solid blacks figured in at least one parent, and her clients who owned black bitches or black-and-tan bitches out of black bitches, bred an additional nineteen litters. From these breedings it was concluded that solid black is transmitted as a self-color only when both parents carry the gene for black, and black is in all cases recessive as a self-color to agouti (brindles, sables, mottled grays), and to the pattern (black-and-tan or black-and-silver).

A black-and-tan dog with a black dam will always produce some blacks when bred to a black bitch or one who carries the black factor as a recessive. No dog, whether sable or black-and-tan, will produce blacks unless he carries the black recessive and is bred to a bitch who also carries it. A homozygous black-and-tan bitch with no black recessive will not produce black puppies when bred to a black dog, but the puppies will inherit their black sire's black gene as a recessive.

Black in German Shepherds is always recessive, both to the pattern and to the agouti. Mrs. Yentzen's six-generation black strain started with two black-and-tan animals. The bitch was the daughter of an all-black sire, and the dog came down through an all-black bitch. No matter how often a solid black was bred to a dog who did not carry a recessive gene for black (and black bitches or bitches carrying the black factor were bred to fifteen studs who were homozygous for the pattern, or were agoutis), no all-blacks were produced from such a breeding.

When two blacks were bred together, each with one black-and-tan parent, all the puppies were solid blacks. If black-and-tan were recessive to black, there should have been 25 percent black-and-tan puppies. Furthermore, the genetic averages hold true over the whole picture (though not in each individual litter), and breeding black-and-tan to black-and-tan (each having a black parent) results in an average of 25 percent blacks. In breeding black to any other color, all the puppies will inherit the black recessive from the black parent, even though they themselves are not black; and if the sire carries the black recessive factor also, there will be a 50 percent average of black puppies from a black dam. When breeding two black-and-tans together, each of whom carry the black recessive, though only an average of 25 percent of the progeny are blacks, 50 percent of the litter may be expected to carry the black recessive, while the remaining 25 percent are homozygous black-and-tans.

The breeding of blacks together will not produce whites. Only if blacks are not true blacks but carry in their genetic inheritance a white factor which is recessive, even to black, will there be any white offspring. (The same would hold true if the gene for dilution were carried by both black parents; however, in this case, the puppies would not be white, but dilute blacks or self-colored blues.) The breeding of a black to a black who are both genetically true blacks will, on the other hand, intensify pigment so that even a blacker black will result. Blacks with a five-generation pedigree in which every one of the sixty-two ancestors are all-black have no scattered tan or gray hairs anywhere on them, but are really a blacker black than one generally sees. Anyone who has seriously studied skin tones, gums, pads of feet and nails on the black will attest to its great difference in pigment from the white. The black puppy is born with solid black pads resembling shiny patent leather and black nails, while the white puppy has pink pads and light nails that will remain light. There is no mystic nor esoteric connection between black and white.

A black who carries a white recessive would most likely show this by white toes and nails, or a large white blaze on his chest, or both. White toes with their accompanying white nails are certainly undesirable in a black, or in any other color, and any serious breeder who wishes to be sure of maintaining pigment, whether in agouti, pattern or self-color, will discard these puppies. The fact that the white toes disappear by later turning silver does not alter the fact that the puppy was born with white toes, and it does not alter the fact that the white toes are a fairly reliable indication of the existence of a gene for paling, for dilution or even for a white factor. The light nails will remain light even though the white toes turn silver or cream.

Solid white should be recessive to all colors, even to solid black and the other self-colors, yet we have a curious instance in our files of a white bitch bred to a black stud who produced ten black-and-silver puppies. We have no pedigrees, unfortunately, but we do have snapshots of black sire, white dam and ten black-and-silver offspring. This seems to be an example of dilution, but it actually is completely contrary to what we've already proved—that the solid color is recessive to the bicolor or pattern. All geneticists agree that white is a recessive, and it would seem to us that a black bred to a white would completely dominate the white, as black should be dominant over any other self-color, even though recessive to the agouti and the pattern. Each puppy in the curious breeding of black to white should be a black which carries the white factor, evidenced most likely by white feet and nails, which are the most frequently seen tip-offs of a white recessive. However, as these puppies are black-and-silvers, we wonder if perhaps the dam is not a cream rather than white, for a cream could conceivably have the black-and-tan genetic pattern with a gene for paling in addition. If the dam falls into the pattern series, of course, her puppies would all be black-and-silvers, as black-and-silver is a pale form of black-and-tan, in which the contrasting markings have been diluted rather than the black saddle.

Another pedigree shows a litter of seven in which solid black, solid white and patterned pups derive from a black-and-tan sire and a black dam. The black-and-tan sire and the black dam both carried the white recessive, and where the sire's white gene united with the dam's white gene, the one white pup in the litter resulted. The sire's black-and-tan dominating over both the black color of the bitch and her white recessive accounted for four black-and-tan pups, while the black dam's black gene dominating over the sire's white recessive accounted for the two black puppies. Both black puppies will carry the white factor from their sire, the lone white puppy inherits his white color from both parents, while the four black-and-tans will have to be bred in order to determine whether they carry the black recessive from their dam or her white recessive.

White German Shepherds have always existed in the breed, as they are mentioned in its earliest histories. They are not to be confused with albinos, as the true albino has pink eyes and nose, while many white German Shepherd Dogs have dark eyes and black noses. Nevertheless, the whites have never been considered desirable and certainly no serious breeders have ever sought deliberately to breed this color.

The so-called whites are disqualified under the German Shepherd Dog Standard. Degeneration is indicated by the lack of color and most all the so-called whites have a bit of tan or buff color on them. They are of no use to the armed services, police forces, guide-dog schools for the blind or sheepherders because white is obviously the wrong color for this work. Also, white dog hairs are too noticeable on uniforms or business suits. They can only be used as pets, and any breeder who is unfortunate enough to find a white puppy in his litter should either dispose of him or sell him without registration papers.

"Dilutes" are more prevalent in the breed than is realized and far more prevalent than either browns or whites. A simple single recessive gene for dilution transmitted through each parent will result in a dilute puppy, commonly called "blue." Any of the three basic color forms can be diluted—the agouti takes on a bluish haze and the strong sable color is diluted to a bluish gray with gray nose, very light eyes which may actually appear blue for the first few months of a puppy's life, gray pads and the overall color of a Weimaraner.

The pattern, when diluted, can vary as much as the pattern undiluted, but the black saddle is diluted to a gray blue, and the markings are usually faded out while again the color of nose and pads are not black but gray.

The most unusual of all the "dilutes" is the self-color blue, which is the dilute of the solid black. As the self-color black is the result of two recessive genes, and the dilution is the result of two other recessive genes, one immediately understands that it is quite rare to meet up with a true self-color blue. We had heard of them from time to time but had never encountered one. Then a Midwest breeder sent us a pedigree and color snapshots of a self-color blue puppy, typical in every respect but color. The eyes, nose and pads of the feet were gray. His pedigree was most interesting. He was out of two black-and-tan animals and, though these animals were not closely related, they had the same sort of color inheritance. Both their sires are well-known Champions who carry the black recessive and who have sired many solid blacks when mated to bitches with the black factor. Both their dams came through bloodlines to which a great many dilutes have been traced and which figure predominantly in dilute pedigrees. We, therefore, must conclude that each parent of the solid-blue puppy inherited the black recessive gene from its sire and the recessive gene for dilution from its dam. Result: a diluted black or self-color blue puppy. The puppy showed big bone, a healthy, alert appearance and, according to his breeders, was the largest of the litter.

There does not seem to be any disagreement among geneticists as to the recessive nature of the gene for dilution in general, and a study of pedigrees that have produced dilutes in abundance bears out all the accepted conclusions as applying to the German Shepherd breed also.

"Brown" is not supposed to exist in German Shepherd Dogs but it does. Whether it is a mutation or not in our breed, we do not know. Perhaps it has always existed, but is linked with a lethal gene and therefore very few have been seen. At any rate, the browns seem to be few in number and have a high mortality rate when they do appear. They are characterized by a brown nose and brown pads and eye rims. Brown or liver is recessive to black, and the brown nose and pads are recessive to the black nose and pads, just as the gray nose and pads of the "blues" are recessive to the blacks. The "browns" have only been observed in the pattern form, but as there are so very few of them, one cannot assume that the brown could not appear both in the agouti and the self-color, given the right conditions. Certainly, if the brown is linked with a lethal gene, no one would want to experiment with the color in order to perpetuate it, even if he could. The only pedigrees which we have seen in which browns or livers have appeared are substantially the same pedigrees that produce blues.

There is little doubt in our minds that it would be possible to breed almost any color in German Shepherd Dogs if anyone wished to set about it in a scientific manner. But it would accomplish nothing constructive for our breed, in which color must always be subordinated to type, structure, gait and character. And it might be a very destructive force, allowing many highly undesirable characteristics to infiltrate the breed, besides the obvious loss of pigment with probable accompanying loss of vigor and stamina.

In the interest of truth, it is only reasonable to add that the great majority of normal-colored dogs that figure in dilute pedigrees are not black and rich tans, but black-and-silvers and black-and-creams. These varieties of the pattern are so very popular in some quarters that they have been bred too extensively, with little attention to gradual loss of pigment in their descendants. There is a great deal of evidence to prove that they are responsible for much of the dilution and carry a recessive gene for dilution which, when coupled with the same recessive from a dog of similar coloring, produces the "blue" version of the black-and-tan.

Washed-out grays are probably carrying a dilute gene also, or a gene for paling, which will manifest itself when bred to similarly colored animals of similar genetic inheritance, as dilute or "blue" grays. Even animals of strong pigment can carry a gene for dilution, though I don't believe nearly as many sables, brindles or black-and-strong-tans carry it as do the washed-out grays, the black-and-silvers and the black-and-creams.

Von Stephanitz felt that loss of pigment was associated with loss of vigor, stamina and resistance to disease. The serious breeder must take into account the great dangers of introducing any factor into his breeding program that would tend to weaken and degenerate his strain.

We believe that many have wondered why the German Shepherd Standard explicitly demands a black nose. As the blues have gray noses and the few surviving livers have brown noses, we think the reason is clear. It is the one means to bar off-colors in the showring. If they are not allowed to be shown, they will not be bred to by serious breeders. There is no more reason to allow a German Shepherd Dog with a gray or brown nose in the ring than to allow a white German Shepherd Dog with a black nose. The off-colors are due to recessive genes and they could become so strongly entrenched in the various bloodlines that an average of 25 percent of every litter could be off-color.

Not as much research has been done to prove that the sable is dominant over all other colors including the black-and-tan. However, we strongly suspect that the sable is dominant over all other colors. One has only to observe the color results from a popular dominant sable to recognize the high degree of dominance of the sable color. Ch. Cito v. d. Hermann Schleuse was an agouti who produced a vast majority of sables, grays and bridles when bred to black-and-tan bitches.

As all three categories of color, agouti, pattern and self-color blacks are acceptable in the showring, you may wonder what difference it all makes. Knowledge of color inheritance, like all other knowledge, can be a tool in the hands of the astute breeder. Color is very often allied to certain structural traits. Many great dogs seem to pass on their finest qualities to those of their progeny who have also inherited their color.

One has only to recall the strong genetic influence of the great gray, Ch. Odin vom Busecker Schloss, on his gray progeny. His iron back and excellent depth of middle piece seem especially to have been transmitted to those progeny who also inherited his color.

MacDowell Lyon once said he had bred a black-and-tan bitch to a certain gray dog several times hoping to put some of the dog's structural excellencies, including good feet, on this attractively colored bitch's puppies. However, her black-and-tan progeny continued to inherit her poor feet while her gray puppies had good feet, and even three generations of breeding from this pair did not alter the basic facts—the black-and-tans had poor feet and the grays had good feet. The wise breeder recognizes certain "signposts" and observes them, and if his best-structured animals come up in any allowed color, although that color is not as attractive to him as other flashier colors, he leaves well enough alone. If it is not in the genetic makeup of the flashy one, it will do the breeder little good to attempt to combine both structure and flash.

Sel. Ch. Palamor's Sara Lee
Sire: Ch. Hylock's Prosecutor, CD, ROM, OFA
Owner: Linda Tofel

The German Shepherd Dog Breed Standard

GENERAL APPEARANCE

The first impression of a good German Shepherd dog is that of a strong, agile, well-muscled animal, alert and full of life. It is well balanced, with harmonious development of the forequarter and hindquarter. The dog is longer than tall, deep-bodied and presents an outline of smooth curves rather than angles. It looks substantial and not spindly, giving the impression, both at rest and in motion, of muscular fitness and nimbleness without any look of clumsiness or soft living. The ideal dog is stamped with a look of quality and nobility, difficult to define, but unmistakable when present. Secondary sex characteristics are strongly marked, and every animal gives a definite impression of masculinity or femininity, according to its sex.

Author's comments: Here "nobility" is the key, for, without it, the German Shepherd would look common. To a knowledgeable German Shepherd fancier the word "nobility" is synonymous with a German Shepherd of incorruptible character, physical beauty and prowess, the highest intelligence, glowing health, an extremely attractive male or female that unquestionably denotes its sex characteristics and presents itself in the ring with all the confidence and self assurance of a "star."

CHARACTER

The breed has a distinct personality marked by direct and fearless, but not hostile, expression, self-confidence and a certain aloofness that does not lend itself to immediate and indiscriminate friendships. The dog must be approachable, quietly standing its ground and showing confidence and willingness to meet overtures without itself making them. It is poised, but when occasion demands, eager and alert; both fit and willing to serve in its capacity as companion, watchdog, blind leader, herding dog or guardian, whichever the circumstances may demand. The dog must not be timid, shrinking behind its

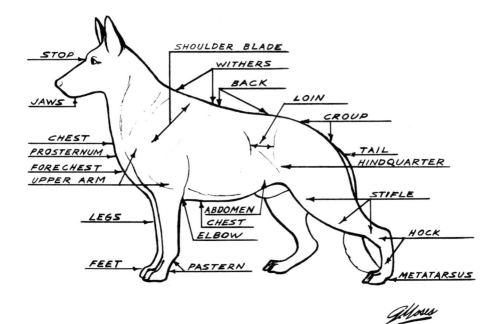

External features of the German Shepherd.

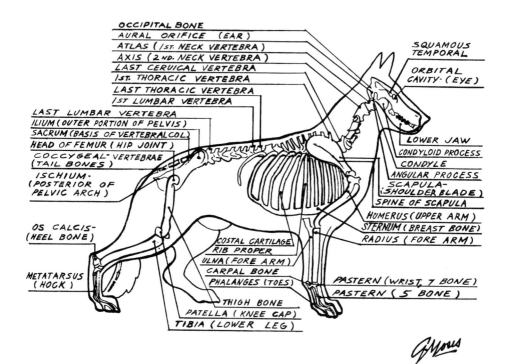

The German Shepherd skeleton.

master or handler; it should not be nervous, looking about or upward with anxious expression or showing nervous reactions, such as tucking of tail, to strange sounds or sights. Lack of confidence under any surroundings is not typical of good character. Any of the above deficiencies in character which indicate shyness must be penalized as very serious faults. It must be possible for the judge to observe the teeth and to determine that both testicles are descended. Any dog that attempts to bite the judge must be disqualified. The ideal dog is a working animal with an incorruptible character combined with body and gait suitable for the arduous work that constitutes its primary purpose.

Author's comments: Good character and sound temperament are just as important to the overall dog as is a strong back, good shoulder, good gait or some other feature. Unsound temperament, a very serious fault, is a dominant trait that keeps reappearing in each succeeding generation, making it very difficult to fully eradicate. The Standard is ignored altogether too often when judges are testing temperaments. A dog with one or two missing teeth is often heavily penalized, while the dog that shrinks behind its handler is placed in the ribbons or given the points. A German Shepherd can serve humanity in spite of his missing teeth, but he is worthless if he has a bad character or unsound temperament.

HEAD

The head is noble, cleanly chiseled, strong without coarseness, but above all not fine, and in proportion to the body. The head of the male is distinctively

Nobility personified in this beautiful masculine head.

Beautiful feminine head, alert expression, dark, almond-shaped eyes, good ear set.

masculine, and that of the bitch distinctly feminine. The muzzle is long and strong with the lips firmly fitted, and its topline is parallel to the topline of the skull. Seen from the front, the forehead is only moderately arched, and the skull slopes into the long, wedge-shaped muzzle without abrupt stop. Jaws are strongly developed.

Author's comments: It is very desirable for the dog to have an alert, fearless expression. The dog should not be Roman-nosed; dish faced (a face too wide); apple-headed (the skull too round); have a big skull with a snipey muzzle; or have heavy, hanging flews (as the lips tend to become infected).

EARS

Ears are moderately pointed, in proportion to the skull, open toward the front, and carried erect when at attention, the ideal carriage being one in which the center lines of the ears, viewed from the front, are parallel to each other and perpendicular to the ground. A dog with cropped or hanging ears must be disqualified.

Author's comments: Ears that are too short or too tall, or that are not set on the head correctly, detract from the dog's general appearance and are most unattractive. Dogs with weak, floppy ears are tolerated too often.

EYES

Of medium size, almond shaped, set a little obliquely and not protruding. The color is as dark as possible. The expression keen, intelligent and composed.

Round eyes, poor ear set.

Author's comments: Dark eyes are more expressive and attractive and enhance any dog's appearance, regardless of his coat color. The round eye is unattractive even when dark-colored. A shy dog will show his fear in his eyes. Much can be learned about a dog's character, intelligence and personality by looking into his eyes. When training dogs I find myself reading the dog's thoughts, which are mirrored in his eyes, and this enables me to apply the right psychology.

TEETH

Forty-two in number—20 upper and 22 lower—are strongly developed and meet in a scissors bite in which part of the inner surface of the upper incisors meet and engage part of the outer surface of the lower incisors. An overshot jaw or a level bite is undesirable. An undershot jaw is a disqualifying fault. Complete dentition is to be preferred. Any missing teeth other than first premolars is a serious fault.

Author's comments: A dog's bite contributes to the shape of his head, so one should consider this when evaluating him. A level bite wears down the front teeth, while the dog who is undershot has trouble eating anything but soft foods. When premolars are missing, it is indicative of hereditary faults, yet the dog who has one large tooth missing is seldom seen and the fault is rarely ever transmitted. It makes us wonder why this condition should be faulted more than a premolar, and why some judges consider it more serious than an unsound temperament or gaiting fault, when the latter two faults are considered very serious faults in the Standard.

NECK

The neck is strong and muscular, clean-cut and relatively long, proportionate in size to the head and without loose folds of skin. When the dog is at attention or excited, the head is raised and the neck carried high; otherwise, typical carriage of the head is forward rather than up and only a little higher than the top of the shoulders, particularly in motion.

Author's comments: A short neck on a German Shepherd is very unattractive. The long neck is both more attractive and also more efficient as the long neck muscles aid the dog in activating the forelegs, while the short neck is indicative of poor shoulder placement.

FOREQUARTERS

The shoulder blades are long and obliquely angled, laid on flat and not placed forward. The upper arm joins the shoulder blade at about a right angle. Both the upper arm and the shoulder blade are well muscled. The forelegs, viewed from all sides, are straight and the bone oval rather than round. The pasterns are strong and springy and angulated at approximately a 25 degree angle from the vertical.

Author's comments: See chapter 33 for an analysis of the forequarters.

FEET

The feet are short, compact, with toes well-arched, pads thick and firm, nails short and dark. The dewclaws, if any, should be removed from the hind legs. Dewclaws on the forelegs may be removed, but are normally left on.

Author's comments: The feet should be judged on more than their aesthetic appeal. The compact feet with the thick pads are not only beautiful, they are correct. A Working Dog needs good, strong, compact feet that will complement and be in harmony with an energetic body. Splay feet should be faulted, for they are a sign of weakness.

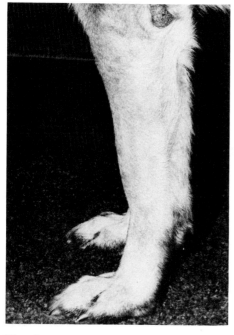

Hare foot.

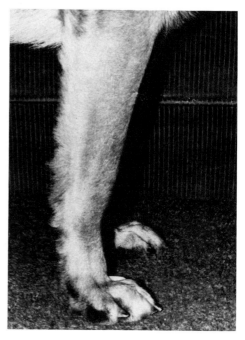

Good feet, thick pads.

PROPORTION

The German Shepherd dog is longer than tall, with the most desirable proportion as 10 to 8½. The desired height for males at the top of the highest point of the shoulder blade is 24 to 26 inches; and for bitches, 22 to 24 inches. The length is measured from the point of the prosternum or breast bone to the rear edge of the pelvis, the ischial tuberosity.

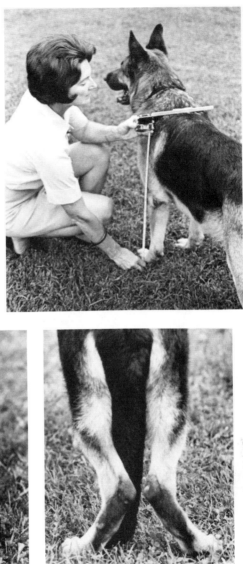

Every dog owner should know his dog's height at the withers.

Poor front, east-west. Elbows pinched in.   Poor rear, cow-hocked.

BODY

The whole structure of the body gives an impression of depth and solidity without bulkiness. *Chest:* Commencing at the prosternum, it is well filled and carried well down between the legs. It is deep and capacious, never shallow, with ample room for lungs and heart, carried well forward, with the prosternum showing ahead of the shoulder in profile. *Ribs:* Well sprung and long, neither barrel-shaped nor too flat and carried down to a sternum which reaches to the elbows. Correct ribbing allows the elbows to move back freely when the dog is at a trot. Too round, causes interference and throws the elbows out; too flat or short, causes pinched elbows. Ribbing is carried well back so that the loin is relatively short. *Abdomen:* Firmly held and not paunchy. The bottom line is only moderately tucked up in loin.

Author's comments: See chapter 33 for analysis of the body.

TOPLINE

Withers: The withers are higher than and sloping into the level back. *Back:* The back is straight, very strongly developed without sag or roach, and relatively short. The desirable long proportion is not derived from a long back, but from overall length of withers and hindquarters, viewed from the side. *Loin:* Viewed from the top, broad and strong. Undue length between the last rib and the thigh, when viewed from the side, is undesirable. *Croup:* Long and gradually sloping. *Tail:* Bushy, with the last vertebra extended at least to the hock joint. It is set smoothly into the croup and, low rather than high. At rest, the tail hangs in a slight curve like a saber. A slight hook—sometimes carried to one side—is faulty only to the extent that it mars general appearance. When the dog is excited or in motion, the curve is accentuated and the tail raised, but it should never be curled forward beyond a vertical line. Tails too short, or with clumpy ends due to ankylosis, are serious faults. A dog with a docked tail must be disqualified.

Harmonious structure: Excellent forequarter and hindquarter. Good topline, strong back. Ch. Wynthea's Bruce, II, UD.

A poorly proportioned dog: Soft back, flat crop, insufficient rear angulation, pastern too steep.

HINDQUARTERS

The whole assembly of the thigh, viewed from the side, is broad, with both upper and lower thigh well muscled, forming as nearly as possible a right angle. The upper thigh bone parallels the shoulder blade while the lower thigh bone parallels the upper arm. The metatarsus (the unit between the hock joint and the foot) is short, strong and tightly articulated.

Author's comments: See Chapter 33 for an analysis of the hindquarters.

GAIT

A German Shepherd dog is a trotting dog, and its structure has been developed to meet the requirements of its work. *General Impression*—The gait is outreaching, elastic, seemingly without effort, smooth and rhythmic, covering the maximum amount of ground with the minimum number of steps. At a walk it covers a great deal of ground, with long stride of both hind legs and forelegs. At a trot the dog covers still more ground with even longer stride, and moves powerfully but easily, with coordination and balance so that the gait appears to be the steady motion of a well-lubricated machine. The feet travel close to the ground on both forward reach and backward push. In order to achieve ideal movement of this kind, there must be good muscular development and ligamentation. The hindquarters deliver, through the back, a powerful forward thrust which slightly lifts the whole animal and drives the body forward. Reaching far under, and passing the imprint left by the front foot, the hind foot takes hold of the ground; then hock, stifle and upper thigh come into play and sweep back, the stroke of the hind leg finishing with the foot still close to the ground in a smooth follow-through. The overreach of the hindquarter usually necessitates one hind foot passing outside and the other hind foot passing inside the track of the forefeet, and such action is not faulty unless the locomotion is crabwise with the dog's body sideways out of the normal straight line.

TRANSMISSION

The typical smooth, flowing gait is maintained with great strength and firmness of back. The whole effort of the hindquarter is transmitted to the forequarter through the loin, back and withers. At full trot, the back must remain firm and level without sway, roll, whip or roach. Unlevel topline with withers lower than the hip is a fault. To compensate for the forward motion imparted by the hindquarters, the shoulder should open to its full extent. The forelegs should reach out close to the ground in a long stride in harmony with that of the hindquarters. The dog does not track on widely separated parallel lines, but brings the feet inward toward the middle line of the body when trotting in order to maintain balance. The feet track closely but do not strike or cross over. Viewed from the front, the front legs function from the shoulder joint to the pad in a straight line. Viewed from the rear, the hind legs function from the hip joint to the pad in a straight line. Faults of gait, whether from front, rear, or side, are to be considered very serious faults.

Author's comments: We prefer a dog with exceptionally good rear angulation as it gives him that strong forward propulsion and powerful drive he needs to maintain a smooth, effortless gait. This type of hindquarter, besides being esthetically pleasing to the eye, is also enduring, for well-angulated dogs keep their feet low to the ground, eliminating wasted motion.

Some people erroneously criticize a dog with good rear angulation, blaming this feature for any gaiting faults. In all probability the faulty dog has a poor shoulder and is not a balanced animal. If the dog had a good shoulder to accompany the good rear angulation, he would be able to out-move any others. It is possible to breed dogs with this type of angulation that are also true behind and one should always be cognizant of this fact. In an attempt to breed dogs with very good rear angulation, many breeders have been producing dogs that are very extreme in this feature. This is just as bad or worse than dogs with poor angulation. It is also unrealistic. At least the dogs with poor angulation could be used as working dogs. There is no way extremely overangulated dogs could do a day's work.

A dog with exceptionally good rear angulation, who has a tremendous amount of power and drive, moves very fluidly and easily off-leash as well as on. This dog is not to be confused, although he often is, with the dog who is pulling so hard on-lead that he is actually scrambling and digging in with his hind feet. Take this latter type of dog off-leash and his whole appearance and topline will change completely. He will probably drop at the withers and raise his hindquarter; the very least we want of a dog in motion is a level topline.

The dog with poor rear angulation who has a poor shoulder may move with a certain degree of balance. However, this dog is far from perfect since he will have very little drive, or follow-through, and will be forced to take very short steps instead of the desired, long, ground-covering strides. If one were to use a dog of this type in a breeding program, it would take many generations to produce a long-striding animal because the dog is incorrect at both ends. There are too many factors involved to waste years trying to improve his progeny.

The dog with the good shoulder and poor rear angulation will be forced to lift his hind feet high in the follow-through, or he may compensate by using his shoulder incorrectly and take a shorter reach. The lack of hindquarter drive will force the dog to kick up his hind feet and take choppy steps which will make his back bounce up and down. Dogs with this fault normally lose their topline when in motion.

The dog with good rear angulation who has a long upper arm and a well laid-on scapula will travel with the long stride and smooth follow-through that is beautiful to watch. Although this dog does not have the correct 90-degree shoulder angulation, he is able to compensate for this and gait very well at proper working speeds, whether on- or off-leash. When a dog has a minor shoulder fault but a good back and hindquarter, he can, whether on- or off-lead, still maintain a very pleasing outline in motion.

When evaluating the correct shoulder in motion, most people keep their eyes on the dog's feet. They should watch the opening between the scapula and the upper arm. When in motion the dog with the correct shoulder will show no visible signs of stress, but will move with a fluidity that is beautiful to behold; it is literally poetry in motion.

A dog that has a poorly laid-on scapula, which is too far forward on his neck, will reach from his elbows, and this results in short steps. Also, the dog with an incorrect shoulder can be seen to pad or pound from the side if you are watching his scapula and upper arm. When dogs with an incorrect shoulder lose their desire to move, they lose their extension and start taking short steps.

Too many people at ringside, whether novices or more experienced fanciers, mistake a dog's attitude for excellence in motion. The fast-moving, quick, high-stepping dog catches the eye of the crowd, who become excited by the dog's behavior. If the judge puts up a dog with this gait, which the Standard lists as a serious fault, the novices will try to get one for themselves, and more mediocre Shepherds will be shown.

COLOR

The German Shepherd dog varies in color, and most colors are permissible. Strong rich colors are preferred. Nose black. Pale, washed-out colors and blues or livers are serious faults. A white dog or a dog with a nose that is not predominantly black must be disqualified.

Author's comments: See chapter 31 on the color factor in German Shepherds.

COAT

The ideal dog has a double coat of medium length. The outer coat should be as dense as possible, hair straight, harsh, and lying close to the body. A slightly wavy outer coat, often of wiry texture, is permissible. The head, including the inner ear and foreface, and the legs and paws are covered with short hair, and the neck with longer and thicker hair. The rear of the forelegs and hind legs has somewhat longer hair extending to the pastern and hock, respectively. Faults in coat include soft, silky, too-long outer coat, woolly, curly and open coat.

DISQUALIFICATIONS

Cropped or hanging ears

Undershot jaw

Docked tail

White dogs

Dogs with noses not predominantly black

Any dog that attempts to bite the judge

Structural Analysis of the German Shepherd Dog

ANALYSIS OF THE IDEAL FOREQUARTER

The forequarter, as shown in Figure 1, is defined to consist of: (a) the shoulder blade or *scapula;* (b) the upper arm or *humerus;* (c) the forearm or *radius and ulna;* (d) the *pisiform* and the seven bones of the pastern joint; (e) the pastern or five *metacarpals;* and (f) the toes or *phalanges.* This whole assembly is attached to the body solely by muscles and tendons. There is no skeletal connection as there is with the hindquarter. The ideal construction and configuration of these bones is described in the Standard under the heading "Forequarters." Before much meaning can be attached to the written description, however, it is essential that the function of the forequarter when the dog is in motion be understood.

Figure 2 shows five positions assumed by the dog when trotting. Only the trot is considered here; however, during the walk and gallop the forequarter performs essentially the same functions as described below.

The German Shepherd Dog, as well known by the Fancy, is one of the few animals that moves with a suspended gait (i.e., there are repeated times during the trot when all four feet are completely off the ground).

Figure 2 (a) depicts the position of the dog just at the completion of the period of suspension. The hind foot is shown contacting the ground and absorbing some impact from the landing. The front leg is reaching forward with pastern muscles taut in preparation for the concussion it will receive in arresting the downward and forward motion of the body. In Figure 2 (b) the front pad has struck the ground and the concussion has passed through the leg to the muscles of the upper arm and shoulder blade. Thus, one function of the foreassembly is to absorb concussion.

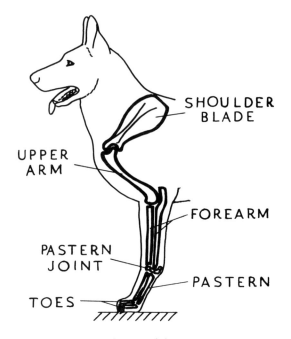

SHOULDER
BLADE

UPPER
ARM

FOREARM

PASTERN
JOINT

PASTERN

TOES

Figure 1   Nomenclature of the Forequarter.

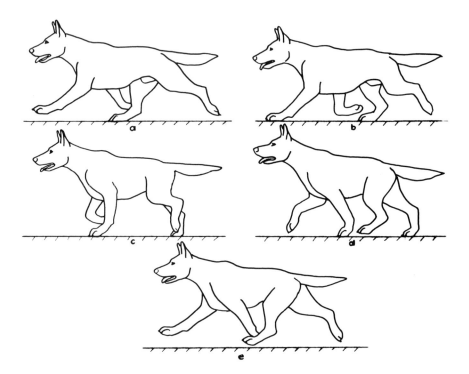

Figure 2   Typical positions assumed while trotting.

In Figure 2 (c) the back leg, which has contracted and passed under the center of the pelvis, is applying push or drive, causing the body, in effect, to pole-vault over the front leg. At this moment practically the entire weight of the dog is supported by the forequarters, which are performing their second function, that of supporting weight.

In Figure 2 (d) the front leg has straightened and hence is performing a third function, that of lifting and applying forward thrust to the body. The ratio of the contracted length of the forequarter in 2 (c) to the straightened length in 2 (d) is a direct measure of the lifting and thrusting power generated by the front assembly. This comment will be discussed in detail subsequently.

Finally, as shown in 2 (e), the drive from the rear quarter, and the lift and thrust from the front quarter, have propelled the dog forward and into the period of suspension. The action described above is then repeated with the opposing two legs.

Two additional functions performed by the foreassembly, not evident while viewing the side gait, are propelling on turns and combatting lateral displacement. For a definition of the latter term, attention is directed to Figure 3.

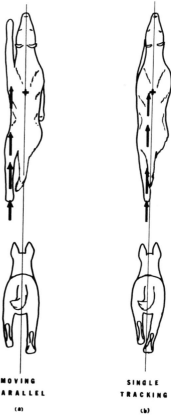

Figure 3   Off-center force from rear-quarter drive produces lateral displacement.

MOVING
PARALLEL
(a)

SINGLE
TRACKING
(b)

If a dog viewed from behind moves with his rear legs perpendicular to the ground and parallel to one another, as illustrated in Figure 3 (a), the force produced by each step acts along the direction of the arrows shown. The resulting effect, in addition to thrusting the dog forward, tends to rotate the body around the point marked with a + sign and away from the direction of travel. This alternate displacement of the body from left to right with successive steps is called lateral displacement. To maintain forward motion in a straight line, the forequarter must apply a side thrust to overcome the lateral displacement.

Fortunately, the problem is not as severe as it appears, since a correctly moving German Shepherd Dog single-tracks, which means he places his feet beneath the center of his body as shown in Figure 3 (b). This minimizes the rotating action by directing the rear thrust more closely along the line of travel. Although reduced, the lateral displacement is never completely eliminated, however, and the forequarter must continually function to combat it.

With the action of the forequarter understood, we are now in a position to ask what structural conformation is best suited to carry out this action with the minimum expenditure of muscular energy. It is necessary to suffix the phrase "with the minimum expenditure of muscular energy," for this is an important criterion that must be kept in mind when interpreting the Standard. We do not seek just an adequate conformation, we seek the most efficient conformation in accordance with the requirement of an effortless gait demanded of animals bred for herding or service work.

Examining now the written description of the forequarter, we find the Standard calls for shoulder blades which are long and obliquely angled. The need for long blades is related to the length of muscle which they can support. The mobility and strength of a muscle is proportional to its length and cross-sectional area, respectively. A longer blade, which is generally accompanied by greater width, permits the attachment of longer and thicker shoulder muscles.

Inspection of the dog's anatomy indicates that space on the body for attachment of the shoulder blade is limited to a square area having sides approximately half a body depth in length. The square envisioned is illustrated in Figure 4. It is apparent that the longest possible blade must be positioned at a 45-degree angle. Any lesser angle, such as 60 degrees, results in a shorter blade with less muscle and, as will be demonstrated subsequently, less lifting power. It seems evident that one can conclude the word oblique used in the Standard implies an angle approaching 45 degrees.

Further evidence confirming the foregoing conclusion is that a 45-degree blade set permits the greatest reach of the forequarter. High-speed motion pictures reveal that a dog on a given stride will not step beyond the intersection of the ground with a line drawn through the shoulder blade while the blade is in a stationary position. This statement is illustrated by Figure 5 from which the improved reach associated with the 45-degree blade is readily

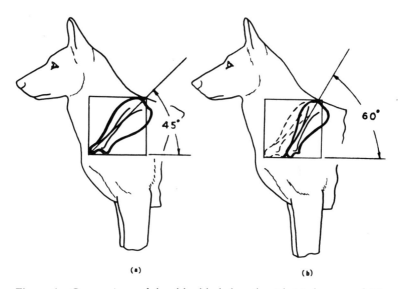

Figure 4   Comparison of shoulder blade length with 45-degree and 60-degree angles.

apparent. Functionally, the amount of reach in the forequarter is directly coupled with the rear-quarter angulation which provides the push to the dog's movement. A dog with ideal rear angulation will require a stride equivalent to that depicted in Figure 5 (a) in order to place his front pad on the ground at the moment the thrust from the hindquarter is completed. If he does not achieve this and steps short in the front, the forequarter must absorb over and above the momentum of the body weight (see Figure 2b), additional momentum imparted by the unexhausted rear drive. Severe concussion is thus transferred in this manner to the muscles of the shoulder and the upper arm, and it is only absorbed through the expenditure of a large amount of muscular energy. Hence the muscles tire quickly and the efficiency of the gait is markedly reduced.

The foregoing discussion emphasizes the importance of maintaining a balance between forequarter and hindquarter angulation. Without balance (with a straight front and excellent or correct rear-quarter angulation) a dog must move faultily to overcome his lack of reach produced by the deficiency in shoulder blade layback or angulation. In general, he will move with either of the three faulty motions shown in Figure 6 (a), (b), and (c).

Figure 6 (a) illustrates what is called pounding. During this type of movement the dog steps short with the front leg, absorbing a large percent of the rear drive with the muscles of his shoulder and upper arm as described above. One can readily detect a dog that is pounding by having the dog moved at a moderately fast trot and by carefully observing the foreassembly, which will literally appear to pound or drive in the ground.

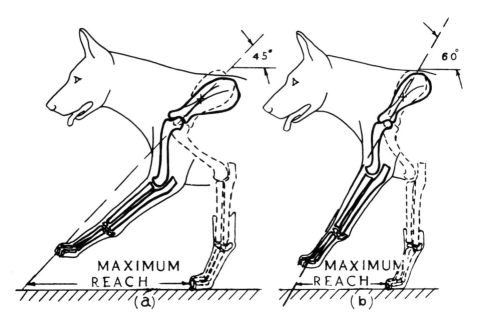

Figure 5 Comparison of reach achieved with 45-degree and 60-degree shoulder-blade angles.

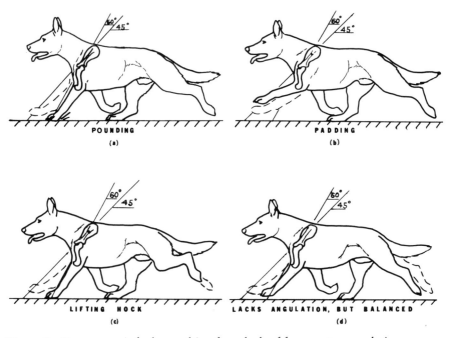

Figure 6 Common gait faults resulting from lack of forequarter angulation.

Frequently, however, when one attempts to accelerate the gait of a straight-shouldered dog, the dog begins to pad. Padding refers to lifting the forearm at the elbow and breaking the tautness of the pattern (Figure 6 [b]). Such motion appears flashy to the inexperienced and is sometimes mistaken for the ideal gait. However, it is far from ideal, inasmuch as it requires considerably more muscular effort, causing the dog to tire and often to stumble.

Finally, the dog may counteract his deficiency in shoulder angulation by reducing his rear-quarter drive. At a moderately fast pace, this movement is readily detected by viewing the dog's hocks which, instead of straightening, will be raised high in a pumping action as illustrated by Figure 6 (c). This disrupts the action of the hindquarter and reduces the efficiency of the gait, despite the fact that the hindquarter itself may have the correct structural conformation.

The point to be learned from the preceding discussion is that a dog which is unbalanced with respect to front and rear angulation will invariably move faultily. In this regard it is instructive to compare the motion depicted by Figures 6 (a), (b) and (c) with that of Figure 6 (d).

Figure 6 (d) illustrates the gait of a dog which is balanced but straight in both front and rear angulation. Such a dog must be penalized because he requires a greater number of steps to cover the same amount of ground as required by a dog with ideal angulation. However, with respect to case of movement, it can be argued that this balanced dog that is not quite perfect on both ends has a lesser fault than the dog that is perfect on only one end. The novice who is often heard to rave about the beautiful well-bent stifle on his favorite Shepherd will do well to bear this in mind.

Thus far, although we have made reference to angulation, we have only described the optimum angle of the shoulder blade without regard for the remaining bones of the forequarter. It is hoped that the preceding illustrations have provided the reader with an intuitive concept of angulation to follow the foregoing comments. However, a more detailed description of the angular relationship between the bones of the forequarter is now needed and we turn our attention to the upper arm; why does the Standard request the upper arm to meet the shoulder blade at a right angle (90 degrees)? The answer is that this configuration gives the maximum ratio of contracted length to extended length, which, as previously stated, is directly proportional to the lifting and thrusting power of the forequarter. Although this point may be verified by the laws of mechanics, Figure 7 and the following discussion will be sufficient verification for our purpose.

Figure 7 compares the maximum contracted length to the maximum extended length of three differently constructed forequarters. The maximum contracted length (dashed outline) occurs when the forequarter is supporting most of the body weight. This position will result both during motion (Figure 2b) and while the dog is standing at rest; the latter position being referred to as the static position. The maximum extended length (solid out-line) occurs when the front leg is completely straightened just prior to leav-ing the ground for the forward swing.

The most useful comparison to make between the three configurations shown in Figure 7 is the length A–B. This length is a measure of the distance through which the action of the forequarter provides lift and thrust during a given stride. The length of A–B is the greatest in Figure 7 (a), which portrays the correct conformation of the front assembly. That is, a 45-degree shoul-der blade lay-back, which meets an equally long upper arm at 90 degrees. Although the Standard does not specifically call for the upper arm to be equal in length to the shoulder blade, as stated in the preceding sentence, inspec-tion of Figure 7 (b) indicates that this is necessary and preferred.

Figure 7 (b) depicts a foreassembly with the correct shoulder placement, but with the upper arm shorter than the shoulder blade. One notes that un-der these conditions the angle between the blade and upper arm must be greater than the required 90 degrees if the dog is to maintain the same height at the withers. Hence, to achieve the called-for right angle, it is necessary for the length of the upper arm and the shoulder blade to be equal. Moreover it is to be preferred, since the length A–B in Figure 7 (b) is less than that of Fig-ure 7 (a), indicating less lift and thrust from the conformation having the shorter upper arm.

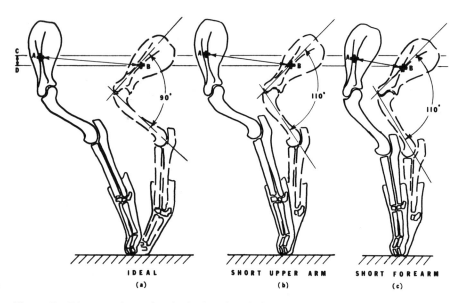

Figure 7   Distance through which the ideal forequarter thrusts and supports body, compared with that of faulty forequarter.

Drawing (c) of Figure 7 has been included to illustrate the result of holding the length of the upper arm and the shoulder blade equal, but not maintaining the called for 90-degree angle between them. For a dog of equal height, this requires shortening the forearm and dropping the elbow below the brisket. The drastic reduction of the length A–B apparent in Figure 7 (c) is sufficient evidence to brand this conformation as undesirable.

The preceding may be summarized as follows. A right angle between the upper arm and shoulder blade is specified in the Standard because this angle, supplemented with equal length of shoulder blade and upper arm, establishes the conformation which provides the longest length A–B; and hence, the greatest distance through which the front assembly supports and propels the body forward during a given stride.

As a matter of interest, the distance C–D indicated on Figure 7 represents the distance the body will fall, due to the action of gravity, when it is unsupported during the period of suspension. Calculations show this to be on the order of one-half inch. It is the responsibility of the forequarter to overcome the fall experienced by the dog during the suspended period and lift the body back to the level C with each step.

We now turn our attention to the angulation of the pastern which, in accordance with the Standard, should form an approximate 25-degree angle with the vertical. The object here is that it enables the dog with correct placement of the shoulder blade and upper arm to place his foot pad directly under the center of his shoulder blade.

Referring to Figure 8 (a), the center of the shoulder blade (marked with a + sign) is essentially the point or axis around which the shoulder blade rotates. With the foot pad positioned directly below the indicated axis of rotation (Figure 8a), the force supporting the body acts through the center point as illustrated by the arrows. Thus, there is no tendency for the blade to rotate when the forequarter is in the weight-supporting or static position, and no need for the dog to expend muscular energy to counteract such rotation.

This is not the case, however, in Figure 8 (b), where the foot pad is placed behind a vertical line through the center of the blade and the supporting force tends to rotate the blade counterclockwise. Just standing, a dog with this forequarter conformation must exert muscular effort to keep from knuckling over. Moreover, the muscles applying this effort are weak muscles, designed by nature solely to swing the unloaded pastern forward. Consequently, due to the additional forces acting when the pasterns are straight, their muscles become overloaded and are frequently injured.

The opposite shoulder rotation, accompanied with equally undesirable muscular effort, is experienced by a dog who places his pads in front of the indicated vertical line. Rather than muscles, in this case, the bones of the pastern joint are subjected to overloading forces and consequently are vulnerable to injury.

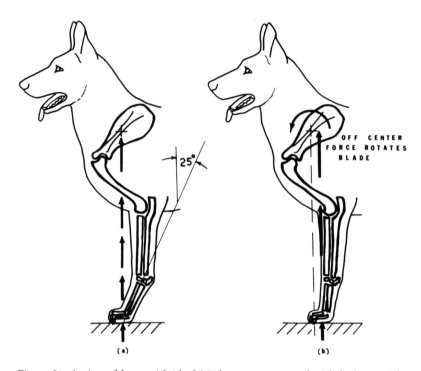

Figure 8   Action of force with ideal 25-degree pastern and with faulty straight pastern.

Thus it is apparent why the Standard asks for the pasterns to form an approximate 25-degree angle with the vertical. For having met the requirements of a long and sloping shoulder blade which joins the upper arm at a right angle, only a 25-degree slope to the pastern will place the foot pad beneath the center of the shoulder blade and provide the necessary balance to the forequarter.

Having discussed the pastern, we could logically continue our analysis by investigating the structural purpose inherent in the ideally conformed feet, which in fact, are an integral part of the forequarter. However, as the Standard assigns feet to a separate subheading, we will not pursue their design, but turn for our concluding remarks to the front view of the dog and interpret the wording "laid on flat" as applied to the shoulder blade.

Again, if we were to apply the laws of mechanics, we would find that the strongest support is given by a straight column of bones with the center of support (the foot pad) directly under the center of the shoulder blade. Figure 9 (a) shows how this is achieved by laying the shoulder blade on flat. If the shoulder blade was pushed out from the rib cage by heavy muscles beneath the blade, the bone structure would take the form shown in Figure 9 (b). This is called "loaded shoulders" and has the effect of breaking the straight column of bone, forcing the joint between the shoulder blade and upper arm

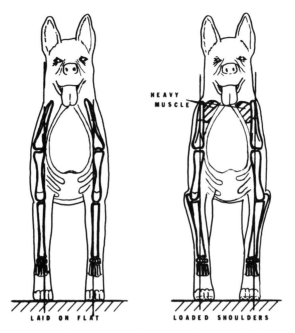

Figure 9   Comparison of structural balance obtained with shoulder blades laid on flat and with loaded shoulders.

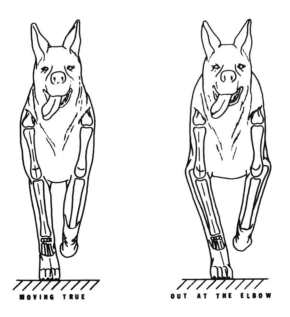

Figure 10   Comparison of gait with shoulder blades laid on flat and with loaded shoulders.

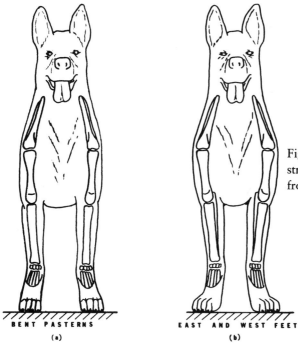

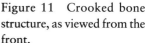

Figure 11 Crooked bone structure, as viewed from the front.

inward and the elbows out. Additionally, the supporting center pad of the foot is shifted somewhat from below the center of the blade, and the dog must exert muscular energy to counteract the resulting unbalanced forces. Of course, their comments assume that the dog has the correct well-sprung but not barrel-shaped rib structure. Barrel-shaped ribs cause the blades to rotate inward, over the top of the body, producing the same deleterious effects as when loaded shoulders rotate them outward. This is a structural fault of the ribs, however, and not the forequarter. In either event, regardless of how the shoulder blades are pushed out of a flat position, their displacement causes the dog even more discomfort when in motion. We have described how a dog must single-track to minimize lateral displacement. In the forequarter this is correctly achieved by rotating the leg inward from the shoulder joint, as shown in Figure 10 (a). It is important to note that the column of bone from the shoulder joint down remains straight and thus retains its structural strength.

In Figure 10 (b) the effects of loaded shoulders on motion viewed from the front are illustrated. The forced-in shoulder joint does not allow the upper arm to move inward, hence the dog must place his feet under the center of his body by rotating his elbow joint. This throws his elbows out, making him "out at the elbow." Again, faulty rib structure can cause this same imperfection in movement.

Finally, the Standard calls for straight bone. We now understand this request in view of our comments regarding the preferred straight column of bone for structural strength. Some dogs deviate from the straight front by bending at the pastern as shown in Figure 11 (a). This differs from the "Frenchy" or east-west front shown in Figure 11 (b). Whereas the former structure is always a fault, the latter is only a fault if the dog moves with his toes turned out.

ANALYSIS OF THE IDEAL BODY

The body as discussed here will be defined to consist of the parts illustrated in Figure 12 (a), from an *external* view as the prosternum or breastbone; the forechest; the bottom line; the abdomen and the chest: and in Figure 12 (b), from an *internal* view as the sternum, of which the forward part is called the prosternum and the rearward part, the metasternum; the thirteen pairs of ribs; the thoracic or chest cavity; the diaphragm; and the abdominal cavity.

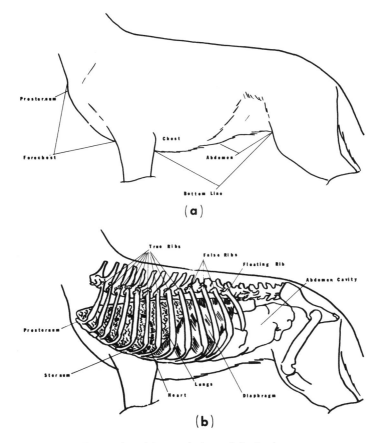

Figure 12   External and internal view of the body.

The first nine pairs of ribs are attached individually to the sternum through costal cartilage and are called true ribs. The following three pair of ribs unite with the cartilage of the preceding ribs and are called false ribs. The last pair of ribs end freely in the musculature and are called floating ribs.

The thoracic cavity, which contains the lungs and heart, is the space enclosed between the backbone, the ribs, the sternum and the diaphragm. The diaphragm is a major muscle required for respiration or breathing. It is a large, sheetlike muscle which curves convexly inward against the thoracic cavity and separates it from the abdominal cavity. The abdominal cavity contains the stomach, liver and intestines.

The body of the dog is similar to the engine of an automobile. It generates energy to activate the muscles by which the dog moves. Endurance and health depend upon the ability of the body to provide this energy. In the previous articles on the forequarter and on the hindquarter, we have discussed the physical structure which minimizes the muscular energy required for locomotion, or alternately stated, the structure of the limbs which permits the dog to gait the greatest distance on a given supply of energy. Increasing this given supply of energy by optimizing the body conformation further increases endurance. We are interested, therefore, in breeding animals which combine the ideal forequarter and hindquarter conformation with a body structure which provides maximum energy output over prolonged periods of time.

Generating energy, however, is not the only function of the body structure. Recalling that the forequarter is attached to the body solely by muscles, the body must provide the foundation to which many of these muscles are attached and the supporting base upon which the shoulder blade and upper arm slide backward and forward during motion. The body conformation best suited for serving this purpose, and also for generating energy, is described in the German Shepherd Dog Standard under the section entitled "Body." To interpret this written description, however, we must first analyze and outline the factors which control the energy output of the body and then rationalize how these may best be incorporated into a structure which will support the forequarter and permit it to operate correctly.

As noted earlier, the body or trunk is divided into two parts; the chest or the thoracic cavity and the abdominal cavity. The abdominal cavity contains the stomach, liver and intestines, which are the organs that convert food into substances that react with oxygen in the muscles to produce energy. The oxygen is provided by the lungs and circulated to the muscles through the heart and blood vessels. The cavities which house these various organs must be of sufficient size to permit them to operate efficiently.

A brief description of the process of breathing is beneficial to an understanding of the ideal chest conformation. Breathing is the process by which the body obtains oxygen. Air is drawn into the lungs by an expansion of the thoracic cavity and the oxygen is passed through the lungs into the blood stream. At the same time, carbon dioxide (the waste gas of the energy conversion process) flows from the bloodstream back through the lungs into the

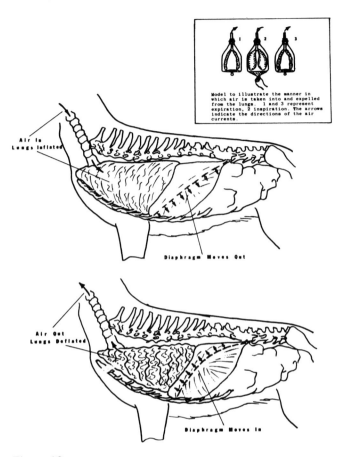

Figure 13

residual air remaining in the lungs, and the air is expelled from the lungs by a contraction of the thoracic cavity. Expansion of the chest cavity is achieved through a tightening of the diaphragm and a rotation of the ribs outward, and expelled by a relaxation of the rib muscles and diaphragm back to the normal position. Since the more oxygen a dog can take in, the greater is his capability to produce energy, it is important that the action of the diaphragm and ribs produce an appreciable difference between the volume of the expanded and contracted chest cavity.

Figure 13 illustrates how chest-cavity expansion is achieved by diaphragm action. The insert in Figure 13 shows a familiar demonstration of how one can draw air into and expel it from a bell jar which has a rubber membrane stretched across the open bottom. When the membrane is pulled down, air rushes in, and when the membrane is pushed up, air is forced out. The diaphragm acts in the same manner to inhale and exhale air into and from the lungs as illustrated (with artistic license) in Figure 13. The diaphragm originates on the loin vertebrae and runs diagonally down the rib walls to attach to the sternum just behind the seventh rib. Viewed from the rear the diaphragm

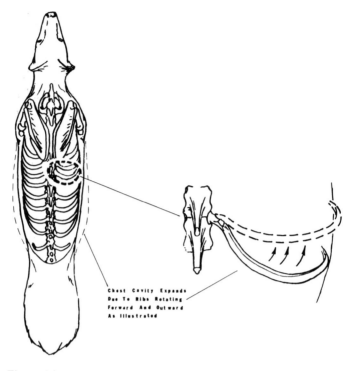

Chest Cavity Expands
Due To Ribs Rotating
Forward And Outward
As Illustrated

Figure 14

is concave, fitting against the lungs when relaxed and the air is expelled, and flattening into a plane surface when the muscles are taut and air is inhaled.

Under normal resting conditions, a dog breathes solely by diaphragm action. However, under conditions of strenuous exercise where a large supply of oxygen is required, additional expansion of the chest cavity is achieved by a rotation of the ribs forward and outward. Figure 14 illustrates this rib action. Notice that the ribs do not expand straight out from the dog's body but rather, due to their curved shape, pivot forward and outward on the ball-and-socket joint at the vertebrae and on the lower cartilage joint at the sternum. Muscular action rotates the ribs forward and air is inhaled. Muscular tension is then released and the ribs return elastically to their original position, which is at a backward incline to the body, and air is exhaled.

The difference in volume between the expanded chest and the contracted chest (which is equivalent to the maximum volume of air that can be exchanged in one respiratory cycle) is known as the vital capacity. In humans it is scientifically demonstrated that a large vital capacity is directly related to the ability of an individual to do useful work. This relationship undoubtedly holds true for the dog.

Finally, we should note that large lungs greatly enhance the breathing of an animal. This is true because the greater surface area associated with large lungs is an important factor in the diffusion of the oxygen from the inhaled air to the blood stream. Thus, with regard to supplying the oxygen vital to the dog in generating muscular energy, the chest cavity should be as big as possible with a large vital capacity (i.e., a substantial difference in volume between the expanded and contracted chest cavity).

We could easily envision a large, barrel-shaped chest satisfying the aforementioned requirements. However, the specification of the body conformation which gives maximum lung capacity is, as mentioned earlier, not completely arbitrary. The forequarter is attached by muscle to the sides of the chest and many of the muscles which control the movement of the front limbs are connected to the ribs and sternum. Bearing in mind that long and broad muscles are required for mobility and strength, the body conformation must provide depth and length for muscle attachment. Moreover, in view of the need for the shoulder blade and upper arm to slide back and forth on the sides of the rib cage, preferably parallel to the direction of motion, lateral displacement becomes an important factor. Recall from the preceding material that lateral displacement is the tendency for the front of the dog's body to be rotated out of the direction of travel, due to the drive of the back leg not being perfectly directed through the center of the body. This is illustrated in Figure 3. The dog combats lateral displacement by single-tracking, however, and if the chest is unduly broad the ability to single-track will be greatly hindered.

Summarizing: The chest cavity should be voluminous to provide ample room for the lungs and the heart without the volume being achieved through excessive breadth, since this would hinder the ability to single-track; it should have the capability to expand and contract; and it should have relatively flat sides to provide surface area for muscular attachment and movement of the forequarter. It is clear that the Standard has these requirements in mind in its description of the body.

Beginning with the chest, the Standard requires the chest commencing at the prosternum to be well filled and carried well down between the legs. It also requires that the prosternum should show ahead of the shoulder in profile.

Figure 15 aids in illustrating the reason for the prosternum to show ahead of the shoulder in profile. In addition to providing extra space for the lungs, the muscles (indicated by the shaded area) which pull the upper arm forward are attached to the prosternum. If the prosternum is well ahead of the shoulder, these muscles act in a forward direction and thus efficiently open or extend the upper arm. If the prosternum is not forward, but between the shoulder, the muscles pull inward rather than forward and much of their effect is wasted. Moreover, since the rib cage curves in to the prosternum at the front of the dog, the shoulder blade and upper-arm assembly angle inward with the curvature when the prosternum is not carried well forward. The top view of the chest cavity in Figure 15 illustrates this effect.

In the ideal conformation, Figure 15 (a), the shoulder blade is situated on the flattened portion of the rib cage and consequently moves back and forth along line A–B in a direction almost parallel to the direction of travel. In Figure 15 (b) the prosternum is short, causing the rib cage to curve in abruptly and the shoulder blade and upper-arm assembly to act at an exaggerated angle to the direction of travel. Thus the elbows are thrown out and the forearms are rotated inward when the dog endeavors to place his foot under the center line of his body while single-tracking. Muscular energy expended in doing this is wasted and the efficiency of the animal is reduced. A dog with his shoulders placed forward will have the same appearance of lacking forechest and will also exhibit the same faults of forequarter action as the dog whose prosternum is not well extended.

The request by the Standard for the forechest to be well filled is simply asking for the aforementioned muscles, which attach to the prosternum and pull the upper arm forward, to be broad or thick. Breadth of muscles is related to strength, and a well-filled chest indicates these muscles are strong.

It is interesting to note that the *Fortunate Field's* study, conducted by Elliott Humphrey and Lucien Warner, indicated a correlation between good chest development and general health of the animal. Their statement of good chest development was that forechest and depth of chest considered together are the best index of chest capacity. Thus, an animal with good chest development may be expected to have general good health; an obvious asset to a working animal.

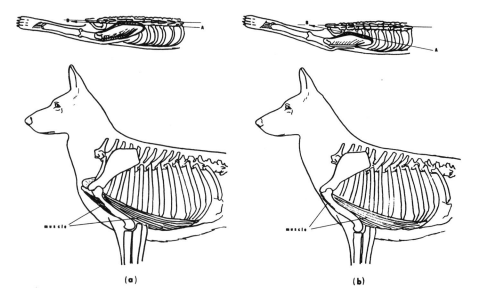

(a)   (b)

Figure 15   Comparison of ideal and faulty prosternum conformation.

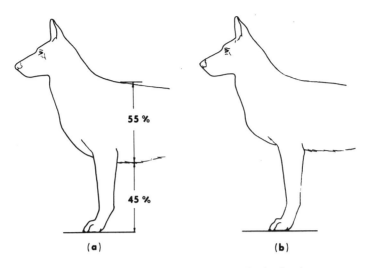

Figure 16   Comparison of ideal and shallow body depth.

The depth of chest is described by two statements in the section of the Standard on body: "It should be carried well down," as already mentioned, and "the ribs should be carried down to a sternum which reaches to the elbow." The actual bottom line of the dog, however, should appear to be somewhat lower than the elbow, due to the thickness of the muscles on the underside of the body. We feel that the silhouette of the dog through the shoulder should show 55 percent body and 45 percent daylight as illustrated in Figure 16 (a). Figure 16 (b) illustrates a shallow-bodied dog who obviously lacks both lung capacity and supporting structure for broad muscle attachment.

As already noted, it is the length of ribs which dictates the depth of chest, which in addition to being carried down to a sternum that reaches to the elbow, should be long and well sprung and neither barrel-shaped nor too flat.

The upper part of Figure 17 (a) illustrates a cross-sectional view taken behind the withers of a dog with well-sprung ribs. Well sprung means that the ribs bow outward rather sharply from the backbone and inward sharply at the sternum, but remain relatively flat in the center portion. Obviously, such a geometry gives ample room for the lungs and heart, yet provides a level surface for the shoulder blade and upper arm to move back and forth during motion.

The barrel-shaped ribs, shown in Figure 17 (b), probably give equal room for lungs and heart, but do not provide the flattened surface for movement of the forequarter. Due to the roundness of the ribs, the shoulder blade must lie on top of the curvature, forcing the upper arm and the elbow out. This breaks the straight column of bone which gives the best weight-supporting structure, and shifts the center of the foot pad from beneath the balance point

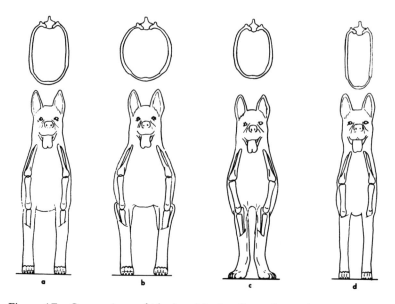

Figure 17   Comparison of ideal and faulty rib conformation.

of the shoulder blade, creating an unbalanced force which must be counter-acted by the expenditure of muscular energy.

Figure 17 (c) illustrates ribs which are too short, resulting in a sternum that does not reach to the elbow. This not only greatly reduces lung capacity, but results in the upper arms being pulled inward under the body, giving the dog pinched elbows. Again, the preferred straight supporting column of bone is broken and the dog stands with his front feet in a position called "Frenchy" or "east-west."

Ribs too flat or not well sprung are illustrated in Figure 17 (d). Obvi-ously lung room is drastically reduced in animals with this rib cage geometry and such animals are frequently spindly and unhealthy. The term "slap sided" is commonly used to describe these dogs.

The effect on gait of the various rib-cage conformations described in the preceding paragraph is readily apparent when the dog is viewed gaiting to-ward you. Figure 18 (a) illustrates the gait of an animal with the ideal body conformation. Recall that in the German Shepherd Standard, under the head-ing of "Gait," the legs when viewed from the front are required to converge toward the center line on the ground with a straight line from the shoulder-blade joint to the foot. The relatively narrow body, with however ample volume, and the relatively flat sides associated with well-sprung ribs, permit the dog to single-track efficiently in the manner described by the Standard.

When the ribs are too round or barrel-shaped, the upper arm cannot move back parallel to the direction of travel and must be rotated outward to avoid the ribs throwing the elbows out, Figure 18 (b). Also, the great breadth of chest associated with barrel-shaped ribs shifts the shoulder blade high up on the body, making it difficult for the dog to place its feet under the center line of the body and effectively combat lateral displacement by single-tracking. The dog, in its effort to overcome this defect, when viewed from the front moves with a rolling, bulldog effect which is very inefficient.

Equally or perhaps even more inefficient is the gait associated with the shallow rib cage. Here the elbows act inward under the body and the legs move close together, tending to interfere with each other. Moreover, the feet are placed on the ground at an angle to the direction of travel, and much of the pull of the muscles is sideward and hence wasted. Viewed from the front, the legs appear to weave in and out with the pasterns and feet, having the appearance of flopping outward. Not only does this inefficient gait require an excessive expenditure of muscular energy which in itself is exhausting, but the lack of lung capacity inherent with the shallow body inhibits energy production and the dog's endurance is drastically limited (see Figure 18 [c]).

Finally, Figure 18 (d) illustrates the appearance of the gait viewed from the front when the prosternum does not extend ahead of the forequarter in profile. The blades and upper arms act at an angle to the direction of travel as previously discussed. The dog tends to be out at the elbows and has a rolling action directly under the neck in front of the forechest. Once again, since the action of the forequarter is not directly forward, but at an angle, its effort is not fully utilized and a dog with this fault works harder to cover the same distance than a dog with ideal conformation.

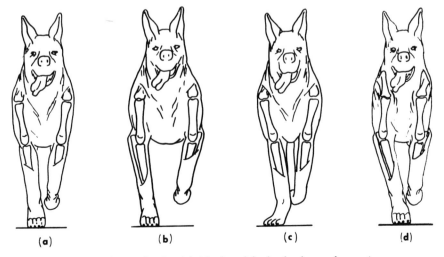

(a)   (b)   (c)   (d)

Figure 18   Comparison of gait with ideal and faulty body conformation.

The Standard goes on to require the ribbing to be carried well back so that the loin is relatively short. Directing attention to Figure 19, the purpose of the ribs being carried well back is related in part to the indicated muscles which originate on the sternum and costal cartilage beginning with the twelfth rib and ending on the upper arm. These muscles draw the upper arm back. When the ribbing is carried well back, as illustrated in Figure 19 (a), these muscles are long and broad giving mobility and strength.

Figure 19 (a) illustrates that the bottom line of the dog remains level with the ground (to approximately the eighth rib) before sloping upward to the abdomen. This upward slope of the bottom line is called tuck-up, which according to the Standard should only be moderate in the German Shepherd dog. Extreme tuck-up, as illustrated in Figure 19 (b), is caused by the ribbing drawing up rapidly well before the eighth rib. This pushes the heart upward into the lungs and reduces the volume of the chest cavity. In turn, the size of the diaphragm is decreased, as is noted from a comparison of the length A-B indicated on the ideal and the tucked-up body conformations shown in Figure 19. The smaller diaphragm has associated with it a smaller vital capacity which is detrimental to the efficiency of the respiratory cycle.

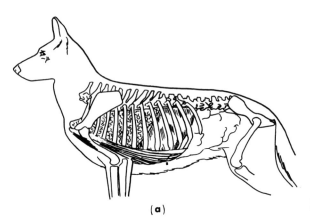

(a)

Figure 19 Comparison of moderate and excessive tuck-up.

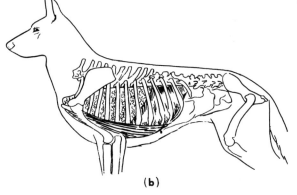

(b)

Another unfavorable effect of too much tuck-up occurs in the action of the aforementioned muscles which draw the upper arm back. These muscles now pull the arm upward more than backward and consequently reduce the driving and lifting power imparted to the gait by the forequarter. The efficiency of the dog's movement is thus lessened, as described in the first part of this chapter, "Analysis of the Ideal Forequarter."

Finally, the Standard requests the abdomen to be firmly held and not paunchy. The paunchy abdomen illustrated in Figure 20 (b) is compared with the ideal, firmly held abdomen illustrated in Figure 20 (a). A paunchy abdomen is often associated with weak muscles, called *rectus abdominis,* which are attached to the underside of the pelvis and extend forward and attach to the base of the ribs and along the sternum and the prosternum. These muscles draw the ribs backward, compress the intestines, and are also the principal muscles which bring the pelvis forward and bend the spine. Any slackness in these muscles, such as indicated by a paunchy belly, means that the muscles will not have the desired action necessary for good back flexion.

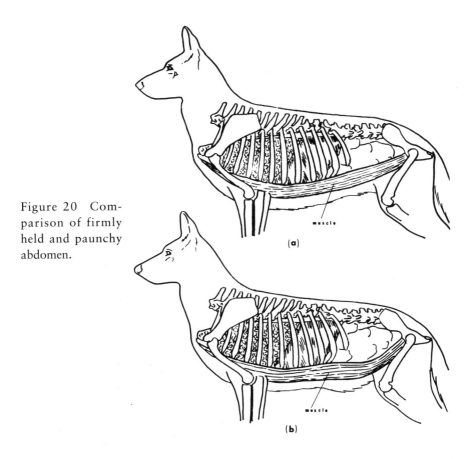

Figure 20 Comparison of firmly held and paunchy abdomen.

Moreover, when these muscles contract, as they do when the dog is gallop-ing or jumping, their effect on a pot belly is to push the abdomen up into the diaphragm which interferes with the dog's breathing, and hence the dog is easily winded.

ANALYSIS OF THE IDEAL HINDQUARTER

A hindquarter is defined to consist of those parts of the body shown in Fig-ure 21. The pelvis forms the foundation of the hindquarters. Its position and the relative position of the tail bones *(coccygeal* bones) shape the croup.

Connected to the pelvis by a ball-and-socket type joint is the *upper thigh* bone or the femur. The upper thigh bone joins at the *stifle joint* to two bones called the *tibia and fibula.* These are collectively referred to either as the *lower thigh bone* or the stifle bone.

The hock is formed from five metatarsal bones, four of which are active. The connection between the hock and the lower thigh bone is technically called the *tarsus,* but for simplicity it will be referred to as the hock joint in the present writing. The hock joint is a complicated arrangement of seven bones, the most significant being a relatively large bone having the name *os calcis.* Frequently, the tip of the os calcis is called the point of the hock. The toes or phalanges complete the hindquarter.

The task of the hindquarter is to provide the power or thrust which pro-pels the dog forward while gaiting. Consequently, unlike the forequarter, the hindquarter is rigidly attached to the other skeletal parts of the body through an essentially immobile joint called the sacroiliac joint (Figure 22). This positive union of the pelvis with the spinal column assures that the drive generated by the hind legs is converted without mechanical loss to forward locomotion of the dog.

In beginning to analyze the hindquarters, we must first inquire how the hindquarter functions in propelling the dog forward. Figure 23 illustrates a sequence of positions assumed by the dog while trotting. Only the trot will be considered here since the Shepherd is basically a trotting animal. As pointed out earlier in this chapter, the Shepherd trots with a suspended gait which means there are repeated times during motion when all four feet are simulta-neously off the ground. Figure 23 (a) shows the position assumed by the dog immediately upon landing from the period of suspension.

The hind leg has extended forward and the heel pad is shown striking the ground. The muscles of the leg at this point are taut to absorb the con-cussion of the landing and to dissipate any shock before it reaches the spine. The degree to which the leg reaches forward is dependent on the speed of the gait; however, in all cases, it should extend far enough forward so that con-tact with the ground does not occur until the momentum from the drive of the opposite hind leg is exhausted.

The foot pad now grips the ground as the momentum of the body carries the dog forward over the leg. The muscles of the hock, stifle and upper thigh

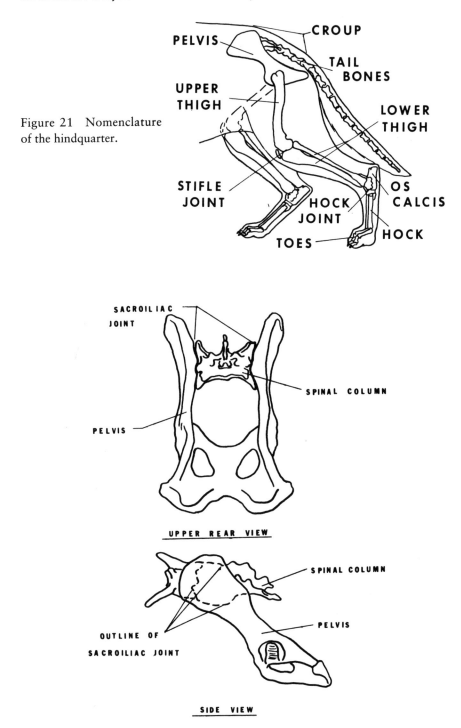

Figure 21 Nomenclature of the hindquarter.

Figure 22 Positive union of the pelvis and spinal column through sacroiliac joint.

contract, pressing the foot more solidly against the ground and causing the entire dog to be slightly lifted. As the body moves forward, the leg bends at the hock, stifle and pelvic joint until it reaches a state of maximum contraction at the point where the foot pad is directly under the hip socket, as shown in Figure 23 (b). Thus the main function of the hindquarter during the motion from the position depicted by Figure 23 (a) to that depicted by Figure 23 (b) is contracting and lifting. The lift is produced through the action of powerful rearing muscles which operate between the pelvis, the upper and lower thigh bones and the hock.

Upon reaching the point of maximum contraction, the leg then begins to straighten rapidly and powerfully, generating a thrust that is maintained until the leg is completely extended (Figure 23 [c]), and the toes leave the ground in a smooth follow-through (Figure 23 [d]). The whole propelling force of the rear quarter is dependent upon the ability of the back leg to straighten from the state of maximum contraction into the state of complete extension as forcibly and as rapidly as possible. This requires powerful and well-developed thigh muscles which can thrust the dog forward and into the period of suspension.

The importance of a smooth follow-through (Figure 23 [d]) on the perfection of the gait should not be overlooked; for the laws of mechanics tell us that if the backward leg motion is immediately checked upon leaving the ground, momentum is dissipated, and much of the force of the drive is lost. This is the same principle involved in the follow-through of a golf club or a baseball bat which is known to be of utmost importance in producing a good drive.

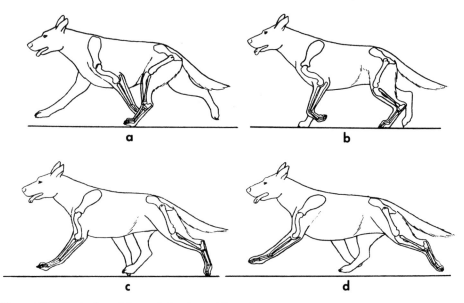

Figure 23   Typical positions of the dog while gaiting.

In summary, the functions of the hindquarter are: absorbing concussion, providing lift through powerful rearing muscles and generating forward thrust by extending powerfully and rapidly.

The most efficient conformation for performance of the above-mentioned functions is specified in the Standard. However, the written description is often so concise that we must delve deeper to obtain a satisfactory understanding of the functional principles involved.

It is strongly emphasized that the most efficient conformation is sought; for there are any number of structures which will function as required for locomotion. In fact, some will perform certain functions better than the ideal structure for short intervals of time. However, this better performance either requires a large expenditure of muscular energy or disrupts the balance of the dog, resulting in other parts of the body being overworked. In both cases the dog soon tires and consequently cannot gait continuously for extended periods of time as the Service or Working Dog must.

Considering, now, the section of the Standard entitled "Hindquarters," one notes that no mention is made of the pelvis or croup. However, since the pelvis is the foundation for any analysis of the hindquarter, we must consider it first. We begin, therefore, by directing attention to the section in the Standard entitled "Topline," where it is stated that the croup shall be long and gradually sloping. The question that immediately arises is: What is long, and what is gradually sloping?

It has been established in the field that the length of the pelvis should approximately equal the length of the scapula or shoulder blade of the forequarter; and that the pelvis should slope from the level back at an angle approaching 30 degrees for optimum efficiency of motion. This set of the pelvis and the resulting outline of the croup is compared with other possible settings in Figure 24.

In the normal dog, the tail bones meet the pelvis at an approximate angle of 15 degrees. Thus the ideal croup gradually slopes from the level back at an angle on the order of 15 degrees (Figure 24 [a]). Assuming a fixed relationship of 15 degrees between the tail bones and the pelvis, the topline of a dog with a pelvis set at 45 degrees and one with a pelvis set at 20 degrees would appear as shown in Figures 24 (b) and 24 (c), respectively. The former is called a steep croup and the latter a flat croup.

Frequently, the angle between the tail bones and the pelvis departs from the normal value of 15 degrees, and although the pelvis is set at the preferred angle of 30 degrees, the tail may be set high, disrupting the lines of the croup. A dog with his tail so placed is said to have a high tail set and the outline of his croup appears as depicted in Figure 24 (d).

We have asserted that a pelvis set at 30 degrees to the horizontal back is optimum for efficient motion. We shall now attempt to verify this with the aid of Figure 25.

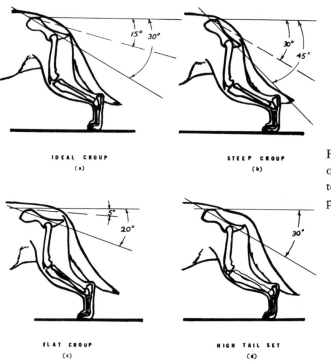

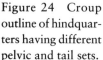

IDEAL CROUP
(a)

STEEP CROUP
(b)

FLAT CROUP
(c)

HIGH TAIL SET
(d)

Figure 24   Croup outline of hindquarters having different pelvic and tail sets.

Figure 25 shows the forward reach and backward extension of the hind leg of a dog with a steep croup, with an ideal croup and with a flat croup. When the croup is steep, as shown in the upper figure, the extension of the leg tends to push the back upward rather than forward.

An engineering explanation of the acting force is that the force from the extension of the back leg acts along the line a–b. However, the components of force which contributes to forward motion of the dog acts along a–c. The ratio of the length a–c to a–b is the percentage of the force from the hind leg, which is effectively converted to forward thrust. This ratio being small for the steep croup indicates that a large percentage of the hindquarter drive is directed upward rather than forward. Consequently, the dog is prone to run with his rear end high and with a bobbing up and down action to his back. It is also apparent from the figure that the steep croup restricts the backward stroke of the hind limb and, as a consequence, the really snappy follow-through necessary for a strong gait and a good period of suspension is absent.

Also, a steep croup augments the forward reach, and hence places the hind foot further under the body than does a less steep croup. A comparison of this augmented reach with that of the flat and ideal croup is illustrated pictorially by the placement of the foot relative to the vertical dashed line in

Figure 25. The foot is placed beyond the line with the steep croup, to the line with the ideal croup and behind the line with the flat croup.

Placing the foot well forward beneath the body, as is possible with a steep croup, gives greater lifting capability to the rear quarter and thus is beneficial to a dog with poor forequarter angulation (i.e., the hindquarter can compensate for the failings of the forequarter). However, coupled with a good front, the additional reach of hind limb results in the action of the back feet interfering with the motion of the front feet. Moving off-lead, the dog generally combats this interference by crabbing (to be described later), or pacing (moving both legs on the same side of the body forward and backward simultaneously). On the other hand, if forced on-leash to move true, the dog will avoid interference between the front and back feet by taking short, high steps with the rear legs. This motion results in a cyclic pumping action which wastes muscular energy and is not a good movement.

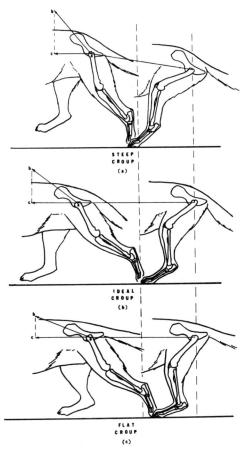

Figure 25   Comparison of croups.

The middle figure shows the motion of the hind leg with the pelvis set at 30 degrees. Here, when the leg is extended, the thrust in the forward direction is considerably greater than that obtained with the steep croup, as evidenced by the longer length of a–c. Moreover, on the forward step, the leg reaches sufficiently well forward to balance but not to interfere with the action of the forequarter.

Finally, from Figure 25 (c), it is readily apparent that greater length of a–c, and hence stronger forward thrust, is achieved by setting the croup flat. However, this improvement in thrust is counteracted by a restricted forward reach which reduces the lifting power of the hindquarter. Consequently, although the drive may be strong, an excessive lifting load is placed on the forequarter and the dog soon tires up front. Regardless of the stronger drive achieved, therefore, a flat croup is a fault because endurance is inhibited.

From the foregoing arguments, one is led to believe that the expression "gradually sloping," as employed by the Standard, implies an approximately 15-degree croup resulting from a pelvis set at 30 degrees with the normal 15-degree relationship between the pelvis and tail bones.

Returning now to the section in the Standard entitled "Hindquarters," we find stated there that, "The whole assembly of the thigh viewed from the side is broad, with both upper and lower thighs well muscled, forming as nearly as possible a right angle."

Little explanation of the first part of this statement is required, for as noted previously, the strength of a muscle is proportional to its cross-sectional area. Hence the well-muscled thigh must be very broad if it is to be strong. Figure 26 shows typical musculature of the hindquarter with lines a–b and c–d indicating breadth of muscle. However, the fact that the Standard calls for the upper and lower thigh to form as nearly as possible a right angle, and then goes on to specify that, "The upper thigh bone parallels the shoulder blade while the lower thigh bone parallels the upper arm," needs some explanation.

In interpreting the ideal relationship between the bones of the hind leg, as described by the Standard, confusion often arises because there are any number of positions which the hindquarter will assume when the dog is standing at ease. Figure 27 shows two possible positions. The stance depicted by Figure 27 (a) is defined as standing naturally. In this stance most authoritative texts describe the ideal conformation as one for which the upper thigh meets both the pelvis and the lower thigh at a right angle as shown. Under these conditions, a line dropped perpendicularly from the tip of the pelvis, with the hock perpendicular to the ground, will pass just through the front of the toes.

In order for this geometrical relationship to be achieved, the stifle bone must be slightly longer than the upper thigh bone, which to fix relative magnitudes, is about one-fifth longer than the upper arm or humerus in the forequarter.

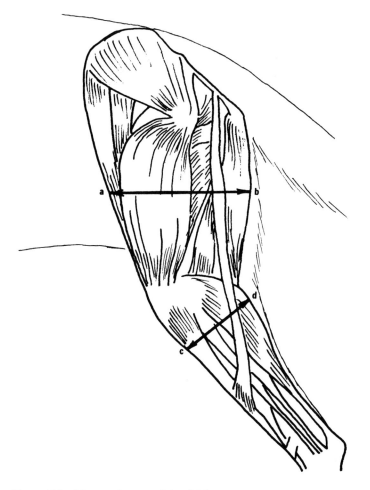

Figure 26   Nomenclature of the thigh.

On first thought, the conformation associated with standing naturally would appear to be in variance with that described in the Standard; however, such is not the case. For if the foot pad is placed directly beneath the socket joint of the pelvis, as shown in Figure 27 (b), the upper thigh bone will take on a 45-degree slope and thus parallel the shoulder blade. The lower thigh bone then parallels the upper arm while maintaining the required 90-degree relationship to the upper thigh. Thus, although not specifically stated, the description of rear-quarter angulation given in the Standard is to be assessed with the dog standing foursquare and with the foot pad directly beneath the socket joint of the pelvis.

Variations in length of either the lower or upper thigh bone, or both, from the relative magnitudes depicted in Figure 27, result in a number of commonly

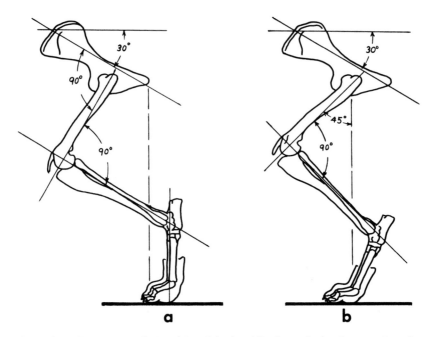

Figure 27   Geometric relationship of the hind limbs with the dog: (a) Standing naturally, and (b) standing with foot pad directly under the hip socket.

encountered faults of the hindquarter. Figure 28 compares some of those most frequently observed with the preferred or ideal rear-quarter angulation. Parts a, b and c of each figure respectively show: the angulation of the dog as viewed with the leg drawn back in a show pose; the same angulation as viewed with the dog standing foursquare, as dictated by the Standard; and the forward reach and backward extension associated with the given angulation when the dog is in motion.

Insufficient angulation is a result of both the upper and lower thigh bones being shorter than the ideal. The dog then stands with very little bend of stifle joint—compare Figure 28 (Ia) and Figure 28 (IIa)—and cannot possibly be posed so that the upper thigh parallels the shoulder blade and the lower thigh parallels the humerus. Furthermore, the ratio of extended length of leg to contracted length of leg is small, and hence the dog drives with limited power, covering little ground with each step.

A dog with a long lower thigh bone will stand as shown in Figure 28 (III). To many people the long thigh bone has esthetic value, but to the engineer it is structurally weak. Evidence of this is the wobbly hocks generally observed when the dog is viewed moving away. The reason for this shakiness in hock is that the dog cannot effectively control the direction of his body weight when it is supported on such a long cantilever. Moreover, it

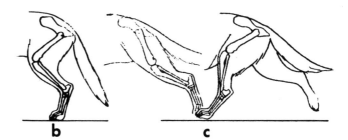

IDEAL ANGULATION
(i)

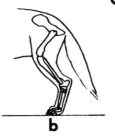
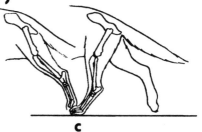

INSUFFICIENT ANGULATION
(ii)

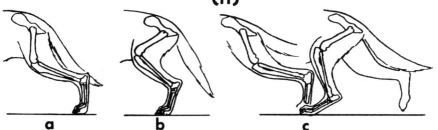

LONG LOWER THIGH
(iii)

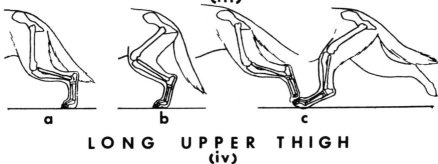

LONG UPPER THIGH
(iv)

Figure 28   Comparison of commonly observed faults of rear angulation with the ideal rear angulation: (a) in show pose, (b) with foot pad under socket joint, and (c) in motion.

is uncommon for a dog with a long stifle bone to adequately straighten his hock and thus to achieve a strong drive with good suspension. This constant bend to the hock joint is readily apparent when the dog is viewed moving from the side. The motion is reminiscent of the sweep of a sickle and the name "sickle hock" has become synonymous with a long stifle.

It is intuitive that, should the hock have the ability to open, the ratio of extended to contracted length of leg, which is a measure of power, would be considerably greater than that of the ideal. However, if this were the case, which it generally is not, the rear-quarter drive would then be unbalanced with respect to the reach of the forequarter, causing the latter to soon become overtaxed. Thus, irrespective of the sleek, low-slung appearance given to the hindquarter by a long stifle, it is of little value to an efficient gait.

A long upper thigh bone appears with the dog standing as shown in Figure 28 (IV). It is impossible to pose a dog having this fault with the upper and lower thigh bones paralleling the respective forequarter bones as requested by the Standard. This immediately implies that the front- and rear-quarter assemblies are out of balance.

In motion, a dog with a long upper thigh has a large ratio of extended-to-contracted leg length and theoretically moves with great strength of drive. In practice, however, the excessive forward reach permitted by the extra length of upper thigh bone results in interference between the front and hind feet. Thus faults of motion similar to those encountered due to the overreach of a steep croup are observed in the dog with a long upper thigh. With the exception, however, that the dog has a strong, smooth follow-through and normally moves quite strongly until the unbalanced forequarter gives out.

One might conclude from the preceding discussion that the hindquarter angulation called for in the Standard, although not giving the absolute maximum thrust, does give the maximum thrust possible while still maintaining balance between the front and rear quarters, and consequently results in the most effortless gait.

Returning to the Standard, the last statement regarding the hindquarter is that "the metatarsus [hock, in our terminology] is short and tightly articulated." The need for a short hock is purely a matter of efficiency. The hock is in essence a lever of the second kind. This simply means that the load moved by the lever is applied between the point where the force acts and the fulcrum (see Figure 29). The closer the load is to the fulcrum, the less effort is required to move the load (this is a law of mechanics), but in turn, the shorter the distance the load moves.

Figure 29 illustrates how the principle of the lever applies to the hock. The pads of the toes act as the fulcrum of the lever. The force is applied at the os calcis by the powerful thigh muscles and the load is carried by the hock joint (see heavy-lined arrows). The distance the hock joint moves during a stride is thus the distance the dog moves forward with each step. With this in mind, it is apparent from Figure 29, where the action of a short hock is superimposed on the action of a longer hock, that a dog with a long hock

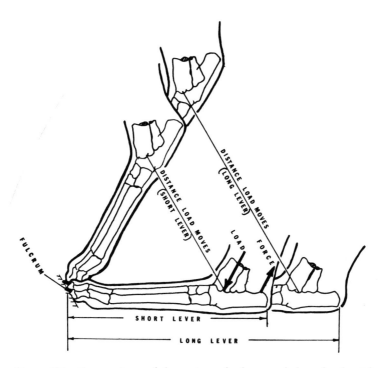

Figure 29   Comparison of the action of a long and short hock with the principle of a second-class lever.

moves farther with each stride than does a dog with a short hock. Further, assuming that the stride of a long hock is completed in the same period of time as that of a short hock, it is obvious that the long hock imparts greater speed to the forward motion. Thus, where speed is desired, a long hock is an advantage (as an example, compare the hock length of the greyhound with that of the average Working Dog), but where endurance is important it becomes a disadvantage. On the other hand, if the hock becomes exceptionally short, minimum muscular effort is required per step, but very little forward motion or speed is achieved. Consequently, a compromise between shortness of hock and action of hock must be made. Figure 30 attempts to illustrate pictorially a comparison of a good hock length with a high hock. One observes greater distance of stride with the long hock, but must remember this is achieved at a high cost of muscular energy and is not desirable.

Up to this point, having considered the hindquarter only from the side view, it is now instructive to move behind and view it from the rear. Although not specifically stated in the Standard, a straight column of bone gives the strongest support and the legs viewed from behind should appear straight as shown in Figure 31 (a). All drawings in Figure 31 are made with the dog standing foursquare, as opposed to the normal show pose of one leg ahead and

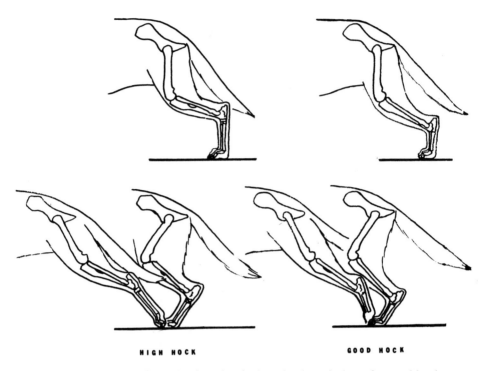

HIGH HOCK   GOOD HOCK

Figure 30 Comparison of length of stride of a long hock with that of a good hock.

one leg back. This stance provides for easier illustration of the faults to be discussed.

Figures 31 (b) and 31 (c) show hindquarter structures where the supporting column of bones is not straight. There is a tendency for these hindquarters to buckle either inward or outward when the dog is standing; and hence, to prevent this, muscular energy is expended even in the absence of motion.

The structure shown in Figure 31 (b) represents what is called a cow-hocked hindquarter. Dogs built steep in croup or short in loin, with long thigh bones, will lack clearance for the stifle to move and frequently stand and move cow-hocked. Also, a faulty pelvis which is wide at the sacral joint and narrow through the pin bones will cause a cow-hocked stance and movement. Finally, a dog with poor temperament will often stand cow-hocked, although he will not move that way in general.

Figure 31 (c) shows a toed-in stance. Slack in loin or defective pelvis structure (i.e., narrow on top and wide at the base) will cause toeing-in. A spreading of the outer toe is often indicative of a toed-in hindquarter, whereas a spreading of the inner toe denotes a cow-hocked hindquarter.

When in motion, the hindquarters viewed from the rear should appear as shown in Figure 32 (a). This is clearly described in the Standard under the heading "Gait," where it states, "Viewed from the rear, the hind legs

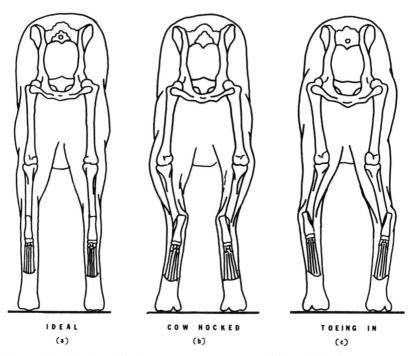

Figure 31   Ideal and faulty rear quarters as viewed from behind.

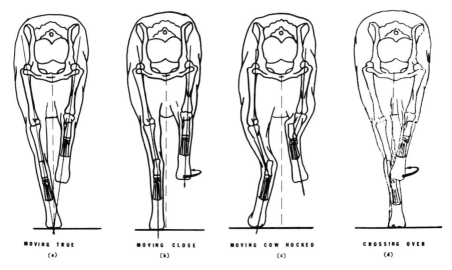

Figure 32   Typical appearance of ideal and faulty rear-quarter movement viewed from behind.

function from the hip joint to the pad in a straight line." Prior to that the Standard reads, "The dog does not track on widely separated parallel lines, but brings the feet inward toward the middle line of the body when trotting in order to maintain balance." The converging of the legs toward the center line is called single-tracking and the dog moves this way to combat lateral displacement (which was explained in detail in our earlier discussion of the forequarters). Note in Figure 32 (a) how the forward-moving leg of the single-tracking dog is raised to pass the weight-bearing leg without interference, but yet with the straight line from hip socket to foot pad maintained.

Clearly, the Standard specifies the back legs should form a straight column of bone which moves back and forth in a plane, passing through the pelvic joint and converging at the ground to a center line through the body. They should neither swing in nor out, nor should the hocks show in or out.

Figure 32 (b) shows a dog moving close. This is sometimes confused with single-tracking, but is quite different in that the point of hock often converges in toward the center line as much as the foot pad. The desired straight column of bone is thus broken. Furthermore, the converged-in hock interferes with the forward motion of the opposite leg, causing it to swing wide as indicated by the arrow.

In the cow-hocked dog (Figure 32 [c]), the action of the leg is not in the direction of travel, and the straight column of bone is completely disrupted. Obviously such motion is inefficient. A similar impression, but with hocks out and stifles in, would be observed in the motion of a toed-in hindquarter.

The final illustration, Figure 32 (d), depicts the movement referred to as crossing over. Here the dog actually converges his feet past the center line of the body. Looseness of muscle or faulty pelvic formation can cause this motion. In any event, despite the fact that the leg forms a straight column of bone when viewed from behind, this gait is undesirable because the opposite leg must waste muscular energy in swinging outward past the leg supporting the weight. Moreover, the direction of the drive overcompensates for lateral displacement, and hence, upsets the motion of the forequarter.

The concluding illustration, Figure 33, is intended to illustrate the meaning of the sentence regarding gait in the Standard which reads: "The overreach of the hindquarter usually necessitates one hind foot passing outside and the other hind foot passing inside the track of the forefeet, and such action is not faulty unless the locomotion is crabwise with the dog's body sideways out of the normal straight line." Figure 33 (a) illustrates true movement where the line of the back is straight forward in the direction of motion. The front foot is seen passing outside the back foot. This is contrasted with "crabbing," shown in Figure 33 (b), where both front feet are outside the track of both back feet and the line of the back is sideways to the forward motion.

A number of factors will cause a dog to crab. Notable among these are a steep croup, a long upper thigh or a short body. Also, even a structurally correct dog will crab if incorrectly handled on the leash.

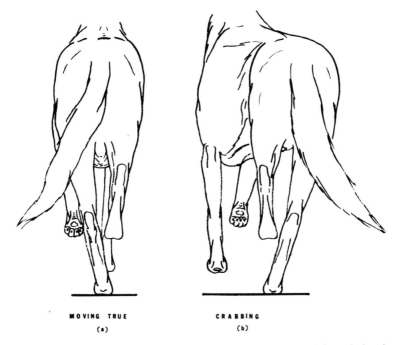

MOVING TRUE   CRABBING
(a)   (b)

Figure 33   Illustration of hindquarter overreach viewed from behind, as contrasted to crabbing.

In compiling the material for this chapter, the authors, Walter Frost, Ph.D., and George W. Frost, wish to acknowledge the following references: M. E. Miler et al., *The Anatomy of the Dog*; R. H. Smythe, *The Conformation of the Dog*; D. Gardiner, *R. O. C. Deviations*; McDowell Lyon, *The Dog in Action*; J. Schwabacher, *The Popular Alsatian*; Max v. Stephanitz, *The German Shepherd Dog*; J. F. Fulton, M.D., *Textbook of Physiology*; C. H. Hest and N. B. Taylor, *The Human Body its Anatomy and Physiology*; W. Goldbecker and E. Hart, *This is the German Shepherd*; P. T. Marshall and G. M. Hughes, *The Physiology of Mammals and other Vertebrates*.

chapter 34

Diseases

We offer this chapter on diseases to acquaint you with some of the illnesses that afflict dogs. You will be better able to care for your dog if you know what you are up against. However, you should become acquainted with the most knowledgeable veterinarian in your area, so that you will know where to take your dog if he becomes sick.

You should have observed your dog often enough to notice when he doesn't feel well. Signs of illness could be: lack of appetite, listlessness, abnormal thirst, runny eyes, diarrhea, vomiting, constipation, restlessness, et cetera. You should isolate the sick dog from any others you may have, keep his food and water dishes separate from all others, keep him quiet and take his temperature.

However, there is an exception to the above. I have had highly trained dogs who were so well mannered and responsive to commands that I couldn't detect the fact that they weren't feeling well until they were forced by their illness to give some definite sign, such as throwing up.

Many years ago, my first Topper used his head to handle a situation that came up. He had had a stubborn case of car sickness that lasted for six months, but finally, after hundreds of rides, had reached a point where he could ride in a car without getting sick. A few months later we had taken a twenty-mile ride to an outdoor Obedience Trial, and twenty minutes after our arrival it was our turn to compete in the Open class. He was working beautifully, and when I threw the dumbbell over the jump and sent him after it, he jumped easily, raced toward the dumbbell, but went right past it to the corner of the ring. He threw up quietly next to the corner post, trotted back quickly to the dumbbell, picked it up, jumped, returned and sat perfectly in front of me. The judge, who realized this diversion was beyond the dog's control, didn't penalize him for it. He won Highest Score in Show that day with 199 points, despite the fact that his stomach was queasy from being carsick.

I can recall similar incidents with other dogs I have trained who were also able to conceal their feelings until forced to show them. I mention this incident because some dogs are so wonderful they don't want to be any trouble if they can help it. So, if you are training a responsive dog some day and he suddenly becomes a little less precise, try to notice if he is sick. A dog who works consistently well doesn't give in to his aches and pains at first.

When you own a dog, it is as important to have a medicine cabinet for him as it is to have one for yourself. You should have such items as scissors, cotton, Q-tips, alcohol, Kaopectate, tweezers, a rectal thermometer and Vaseline. I would also suggest getting your supplies as you need them so that they will always be fresh.

To take a dog's temperature, you should use a rectal thermometer that has a loop on one end to which you can attach a string. If you are not adept at using a thermometer, you might lose it in the dog's rectum, but there is no possibility of doing this if there is a ten-inch string attached to it. Before you use it, shake it to get the temperature down, dip the end in Vaseline so it will slide into the rectum easily and leave it there for two minutes. When you remove it, wipe it off with a clean tissue to facilitate reading. Later, wash it off with alcohol. A puppy's normal temperature is 101.5 degrees, and that of an adult dog is 101 degrees. A dog's temperature will be higher if he is excited.

To administer pills or tablets, place your left hand over the dog's muzzle, insert your thumb behind one upper canine and your index finger behind the other canine. With your right hand, push the tablet down to the base of the dog's tongue, quickly remove your hands, close his mouth and stroke his throat gently. The dog will swallow and let the tablet go down.

To give the dog medicine, use a deep spoon, or a small plastic cup like a jigger, pull the dog's lip out to the side and pour the medicine in it. If you keep the dog's head tilted up and his mouth slightly closed, he will swallow the medicine as you pour it into his lip.

To give a dog an enema, buy the type used for adult humans and administer it outdoors so that the dog can relieve himself immediately.

When your dog is sick, be sympathetic. He will probably be very quiet and you should talk calmly and reassuringly to him. He will appreciate your tender loving care at this time.

BEE STINGS

If your dog gets stung by a bee and he shows signs of being allergic to the sting, he should be given an antihistamine. This can be obtained from your druggist.

BITES, CUTS

Carefully wash the bite or cut with peroxide or Phisohex and, if small, leave it unbandaged. If it is a good size, it should be washed very thoroughly, then some medication, such as an antibiotic ointment, should be administered. Next, it should be bandaged so that the wound is drawn together. Large gaping cuts or bites should be stitched by your veterinarian so that they won't leave a scar. Be sure to cleanse them first, apply a pressure bandage and a regular bandage, then get the dog to the veterinarian as quickly as possible.

ACCIDENTS

In case of an accident where the dog has been hit by a car, or the dog is in a state of shock, place him on two blankets that have been folded in half to make a stretcher, and cover him with another blanket to keep him warm. Talk soothingly and calmly to him so that he will relax, and get him to your veterinarian at once. Try to get him to lie very quietly in case he has any broken bones.

CYSTS

At some time in his life, a dog may get one or more cysts. A cyst is small lump, hard or soft, that could appear anywhere on his body. They are quite harmless and frequently disappear by themselves. Sometimes they break open and emit a hard white pus. If they do, they should be squeezed each day for about three days and then washed with a disinfectant. If the dog should have a large cyst that is irritating him, it can easily be removed by your veterinarian.

DIARRHEA

Diarrhea is a loose, watery stool and is generally a symptom of some other condition. If it is just a change of water, diet, environment or stress, it can be treated by giving cooked meat and rice, hard-boiled eggs and dry foods such as kibbled biscuits. One should determine the cause in order to treat it correctly. Sulpha drugs and Kaopectate are effective, or ask your veterinarian to supply you with his choice of medication so that you may keep it on hand in your dog's medicine cabinet.

EAR FUNGUS

This is fairly common and easily cured if treated immediately. If you notice the inside of your dog's ear is red, swollen and looks dirty, he probably has fungus in his ear. Cleanse the ear with cotton that has been moistened in alcohol, and use Q-tips to reach the difficult places, then apply some Panolog, which is a Squibb's product, twice a day. The ear should be cleaned out this way each day until the condition has cleared up.

EYES

Your dog's eyes should be checked each day to be sure they are all right. Early in the morning you may notice a little sleep in his eyes, which should be removed. If the dog has a slight discharge or a little matter in his eyes, it should be wiped out very gently and carefully with a clean tissue or a piece of water-soaked cotton. The dog can't do this for himself and it is just one small act of kindness you can do for him. If he should get a slight cold in his eyes from lying in front of the air conditioner, or for some other reason, he will probably need some ophthalmic ointment put in his eyes every evening. Just pull out his lower lid gently, and place about one-half inch of the ointment in it. He will blink and the ointment will spread over his eye.

POISONOUS SNAKE BITE

The treatment is the same as for humans. Cut a deep X over the bite, give the recommended antidote and keep the dog quiet.

POISONS

Try to determine what kind of poison the dog ate, and get him to your veterinarian immediately. If necessary, if you do not know the antidote, call any hospital emergency room and ask them for the number of the poison center. They will have a master file on poisons and can give you the antidote for any of them.

HEAT STROKE

During the hot weather, your dog can get heat stroke easily if he is left in the sun or in a car with very little ventilation. One often hears of someone leaving a dog in their closed car at a dog show and it gets heat stroke. This can be fatal if not discovered and treated in time. Be prepared if you take your dog in your car with you on a hot day. Take an insulated chest with you that is packed with ice and ice packs. If you find your dog is too hot, place an ice pack on his head and this will give him immediate relief.

One hot spring day, I let one of our bitches out to play just before we sat down to lunch, and while we ate we watched her playing with her ball. Suddenly she lay down in the shade and was very still. I ran outdoors and discovered she was having a heat stroke. We carried her indoors quickly, placed her in the bathtub, filled it full of cold water and kept her head above water while I swirled the water around her. In about thirty minutes, she was her normal lively self. Evidently, the unusually hot spring day, when she was just starting to shed her heavy winter undercoat, had been too much for her.

TICKS

Ticks are especially numerous and troublesome in the spring. The Brown Dog Tick variety is carried into the home by dogs or humans. They are to be found in the long grass so it is wise the keep all the grass short where your dog is apt to play. These and Wood Ticks are also found in wooded areas and drop off the trees and bushes onto the dogs. In areas that are heavily infested with them, it is wise to spray or dip your dog with one of the well-known flea and tick remedies, which will keep your dog free of them for about two weeks. Generally, where you find a tick on a dog you will find the male hiding under the female. The female gorges herself on the dog's blood, swelling to a size comparable to your fingernail, at which time she drops off. She then deposits about two thousand eggs at one time. The little newly hatched seed ticks are six-legged and they feed on the dog before they molt into eight-legged ticks. These drop off the dog and change into adults. You can use ether or nail-polish remover to remove the ticks, as either will make the tick loosen its hold. You can control ticks by spraying baseboards, cracks, crevices and your pet's favorite resting places.

Deer Ticks

These ticks can now be found most everywhere in the country. They have been spread by deer, mice and other creatures. They are the size of a small pin head, so tiny that they can go unnoticed. While not all Lyme ticks carry the Lyme disease, the majority of them do. At one time there was an inoculation for Lyme disease, but the veterinarians have found that the side effects were worse than the disease, so they do not recommend it any more. If you find that your dog is acting listless, doesn't want to eat and is lame and in some cases refuses to get up, he probably has Lyme disease. Have your vet give him Doxycycline for four days. If the dog recovers in that time you can be fairly certain that it was Lyme disease.

Hundreds of people get Lyme disease every year. If you notice you have a red spot, like a bull's eye, that gradually turns purplish, be suspicious of the origin. If you take antibiotics for ten days, you probably will not get Lyme disease. Many people get bitten and never realize it until they have all kinds of horrendous side effects, such as arthritis, swollen joints, flulike symptoms, etc. By then it is too late and they can suffer from the disease for many months. If you are aware of this fact, you can take the necessary precautions.

Now there are several products on the market that can protect your dogs from tick, flea or Lyme tick bites and they can be purchased from your veterinarian. Advantage and Frontline are two of these. Discuss this problem with your vet, for you can keep your dog free of ticks and fleas today.

BLOAT

If you have ever seen an animal with bloat you will never forget it, for it is a horrible sight. It is relatively common in cattle and horses, but the consequences are not so severe, as they have more room for expansion, and this gives the owner more time to get medical assistance. The mortality rate is very high for large dogs, running around 60 percent. Time is the critical factor and to save a dog's life, he must receive immediate help.

The stomach may twist or rotate on its long axis and become blocked at both ends. The bacteria that are normally in the stomach continue their work of digestion, and the gases they produce also continue to form. Drainage is blocked from the stomach and spleen. Gas and ingesta are trapped in the stomach, which distends and exerts pressure on circulatory and respiratory organs. This, combined with venous congestion of the stomach walls and spleen, leads to shock, then coma. The gas is produced very rapidly and the bloating will develop rapidly also. If the obstruction is not released within a very short time, the dog will die.

To prevent bloat, dogs should not be fed large quantities of food at one time; they should not be exercised after they have eaten; older dogs should receive two or three meals a day instead of one and dogs should be fed in the morning so that you can notice whether they are in distress and be ready to help them. Dogs fed at night might develop a problem during the night when no one is around to help them. Doctors advise using phosphate-free drugs and products, and dogs should be given well-balanced diets, particularly in calcium-phosphorous content. Conditions should be avoided that make dogs pant and drool heavily, and if this occurs, they should receive milk instead of water.

The etiology is not known most of the time, but it is thought that bloat is often caused by a dog swallowing a foreign object such as a piece of rug, towel, stone, stick, etc. Overeating will trigger an attack in puppies or older dogs. Kennel dogs or older dogs who receive little exercise are subject to bloat. You would notice that there were very few new stools in their kennel runs. However, in most cases, the cause of bloat is unknown.

Some doctors feel that large, deep-chested dogs are more prone to it. Large dogs with good bone and a lot of skin (such as Bloodhounds) are apt to get it, whereas small dogs with tight skins do not have this problem. My OT Ch. Bar vom Weissen Zwinger, UD, was a dog with a big chest and deep body. He had fourteen points including two majors when he got cancer of the spleen. He recovered from the operation very nicely and two weeks later he died from a twisted stomach. He was staying with friends in Maine at the time and although he was rushed to an animal hospital some thirty miles away, it was too late to save his life.

Ch. Santana's Man of War, ROM, was near death from this condition, but swift action and excellent care saved his life. Not all dogs are so fortunate and many other fine German Shepherds have succumbed to this illness. It is very important for dog owners to be aware of this condition and be ready to act swiftly should it occur.

The following signs are symptoms of this condition: Your dog might be very, very restless, he might try to vomit repeatedly and unsuccessfully (dry heaves), start whining, moaning or breathing hard, his stomach may become increasingly distended, he may froth at the mouth and he may stretch his forelegs in a praying-mantis position or lie on his side. When you see the latter two signs, the condition is in an acute stage. And occasionally the condition may be present and will go undetected until the last phase, when it is too late to save the dog. Bloat calls for immediate action. You must rush your dog to an animal hospital and have emergency surgery performed to save your dog's life.

Since this condition might very likely recur, you could suggest to your doctor when he operates on your dog that he try to suture the stomach to the peritoneum to prevent recurrence. This will form an adhesion and hold the stomach from future rotation. This is done after the stomach is deflated, untwisted and all other repairs are made. On a large dog, the incision will split open, so a good strong suture material, such as wire, should be used. Medications after surgery will probably include antibiotics, injectable fluids, vitamins and even corticosteroids. The convalescence is stormy, but once he has survived the first forty-eight hours, the prognosis is better. Your dog will need careful wound care, a good diet and lots of tender loving care after surgery.

CANCER

Cancer is not one disease, but a variety of diseases that are limited only by the number of organs and structures in the body; in other words, every living cell in the body has the potential to develop or be transformed to cancer.

The causes of cancer are, with few exceptions, unknown. There are documented situations where cancer is caused by viruses, chemicals, radiation and other similar phenomena, but the majority of cancers arise from unidentifiable causes. Cancer is identified most easily when it occurs on the outside of the body, on the skin and adjacent organs. It is far more difficult to find when it grows inside the body. This is true because the cancer must become large enough to be seen, felt or make the dog sick. When this happens, many times the cancer is out of control or beyond treatment.

This brings up an important point. The size of a growth has little bearing on its seriousness. A tumor less than one-half inch in diameter can contain 100 million cells and yet be hard even to find. The fact that the "lump" does not grow is *not* a good sign. The cancer may be shedding millions of cells into the body and destroying the dog, although it appears to stay the same size.

An illustration comes to mind of a Shepherd bitch who had to be operated on for a cancer in the mammary gland. The lump was present for only five days and all the breasts were removed on the affected side. The pathologist reported all the glands removed were filled with small tumors that could only be seen under a microscope. The bitch died in four months with cancer throughout her body. In contrast, a male Shepherd with a "basketball-sized tumor" in his belly lived five years after his surgery and died of old age.

Once an animal has had a cancer removed from its body, the possibility of similar tumors occurring is greater than before, and the owner should be doubly conscious of the danger.

Cancer can be treated if the disease has not spread throughout the entire body. The methods of treatment are surgery, X ray, drugs or a combination of the above. The surgery serves to remove as much of the tumor as possible and to establish the type of cancer. The X ray and drugs can also reduce the tumor size and effect cancer control by killing tumor cells not removed during surgery.

It is mandatory to know the kind of cancer with which you are dealing in order to institute effective treatment. Without the knowledge of cancer type, attempts at treatment will be futile. It would be of little value to catalog all tumor types. Some of the more common kinds are cancer of the skin, breast, gums and spleen.

In summary, lumps on dogs should not be ignored or just monitored for growth. The earlier a cancer is identified and treated, the greater the opportunity for control of the disease.

SKIN DISEASES

If these are treated immediately they can be cured easily. If the dog has an itch, for any reason, he may break the skin when he scratches and cause an infection. His hair will fall out and he will soon have a bare patch, which can spread rapidly. Keep a good medication handy, which your veterinarian can prescribe, so that you can attack the problem as soon as it appears. As a precaution, keep your dog free of fleas, ticks and dead hair by grooming him every day. If he has a skin problem and you must bathe him, use a good medicinal shampoo.

INTESTINAL PARASITES

Puppies generally have worms and most adult dogs need to be wormed occasionally. Worms are nothing to worry about if they are treated properly, but if they are neglected, or if the dog is dosed incorrectly, they can become a serious problem. The same week that you purchase a new puppy or an adult dog, you should have his stool checked for worms by your veterinarian. This is of the utmost importance because worms can rob a dog of all the nourishment that you are giving him and can sap his strength and vitality within a short time. A dog who appears to be in excellent health when you get him may still harbor worms, and this dog can go downhill fast if he has worms because of the change of environment, diet and water. It normally takes two wormings to rid a dog of intestinal parasites, but his stool should be checked twice a year with the flotation method to make certain he hasn't picked them up.

It is so easy for a dog to pick up worms that a new dog owner will find it hard to believe that the dog could get them in his own backyard, or by walking down the street. Dogs can pick up worms through no fault of their own or yours, as they can get them from the ground or places where other dogs, small wild animals or rodents have passed. They can also get them from mosquitoes, fleas and ticks. Puppies may become infested when they nurse by swallowing the larvae or worm eggs stuck to the dam's skin or fur. Dogs who pick up worm eggs or larvae on their feet lick them off and send them into their digestive tracts. The stomach juices dissolve the egg's protective enclosed shell and permit it to continue its life cycle in the dog's intestines.

If you have the slightest suspicion that your dog has worms because of poor coat, skin problems, finicky appetite, often a ravenous appetite, loose stool, pale gums or a stubborn contrariness that is hard to define, have his stool checked immediately by your veterinarian. There are several ways to determine whether a dog's stool has worms, but the most reliable method is by means of a flotation test in which the worm eggs in the stool float to the surface and are then examined under a microscope. Your veterinarian can advise you what kind of worms are present. There are other ways of examining stools but they are not as reliable. A dog can be checked and found negative when in actuality he has one or two types of worms. If your dog has worm symptoms, but his stool checks out negative, have a veterinarian check another early morning stool with the flotation method that employs centrifuge.

Roundworms (*Toxocara canis*) are quite common but, fortunately, it is easy to get rid of them. The adult worms are round, white, about three or four inches long and may be curled up. The worms feed on the best food factors in the dog's intestines, leaving him little nutrition and injuring his digestive system. Roundworms travel along the digestive tract and some may be vomited if they enter the stomach. They can often be found in the dog's feces. A pregnant bitch can be checked and found negative, but her puppies will develop roundworms when they are three weeks old. Researchers have found that the mother has roundworm larvae encysted in her muscles, and hormones activate the larvae about her fortieth day of pregnancy. When the puppies are born, they already have roundworms because they were infected *in utero*. We worm new litters for roundworms when they are three and five weeks of age without testing them. Be sure to keep the puppies on paper the day that you worm them so that you can clean the stools up *before* the mother does, and before the puppies step in them. 6Keep her away from her puppies that day except at feeding time. Puppies starting at six weeks and older dogs can be treated with strongid with excellent results.

Hookworms (*Ancylostoma caninum*) are fairly common, cause more problems and are difficult to eradicate. A hookworm has several hooks in its mouth that enable it to attach itself to the mucous membrane of the intestine. It produces a severe anemia and general debility by drawing blood from the intestinal wall; and since the worms secrete an anticoagulant, when they move to another site, the old site continues to bleed and blood is in the stool.

Hookworms live on the blood of the intestinal walls and, if you see any of the following signs, you can suspect that your dog has them: spots of blood in the stool, loss of appetite and weight, diarrhea, occasionally a ravenous appetite and loss of weight and anemia. The dog will appear to be in very poor condition, seem nervous and be very dehydrated. Bitches should be checked for hookworms before they are bred so that they won't transmit them to their puppies. Hookworm infections can wipe out whole litters and one has to be on guard against this possibility. It is said that one hookworm can cause the loss of one-tenth of a cubic centimeter of blood per day. Since the puppies become infested with hookworms very rapidly, it doesn't take many hookworms to make a puppy anemic. If it is possible to wait until they are three weeks of age, it is better to do so. If there is any doubt in your mind, have your veterinarian check them. This is one problem you can't ignore or you will lose the whole litter.

Whipworms (*trichuriasis*) are not as common as others, but are considered a serious parasite. They have a small, whiplike body about one-and-one-half to two-and-one-half inches long, about as thick as a needle. They inhabit the colon and cecum (a blind pouch located between the large and small intestines and somewhat comparable to the appendix in humans). In very stubborn cases, some veterinarians suggest the cecum be removed surgically. Dizan is very effective in the treatment of whipworms and threadworms (*Strongyloides stercoralis*), and partly effective in the treatment of hookworms. Whipworms are difficult to get rid of because they live in both the intestines and the cecum. They can be killed in the intestines, but rarely in the cecum, so the dog's stool should be checked every few months even when it has been diagnosed as negative. Dogs with these worms are likely to have dull coats, diarrhea, loss of appetite, a weight loss and become stubborn and unruly. Dizan has an intense blue color and is a polymethine dye. It is supplied in specially coated tablets to minimize gastric irritations and to provide for slow release of the drug in the intestines. The drug is administered over a five- to seven-day period, 600 milligrams daily in two or three doses to dogs weighing over sixty pounds. The dogs will either have diarrhea or a very soft stool and cleaning up after them becomes a major chore. House dogs should be watched carefully as one accident on a floor or rug at this time would ruin either. Administering the drug with meals, or after meals, reduces the side effects. This drug will also eliminate roundworms at the same time if the dog has them.

Panacur™(Fenbendazole), a relatively new product, will eradicate round-worms, hookworms and whipworms. It is available from your veterinarian. It is easy to administer and has proven very effective.

Coccidia is not uncommon and the oocysts can be detected by microscopic examination of the feces. Coccidiosis is considered one of the most trouble-some of intestinal parasitic diseases in puppies and young dogs. The coccidia usually inhabit the mucous membrane lining of the small intestine as well as the colon. Acute cases may present symptoms that closely resemble distem-per. Coccidiosis generally develops under conditions that are crowded and unsanitary.

Some litters of puppies become infested with coccidia from the mother. Her stool may be negative until the puppies are three or four weeks old, then you will find it loaded with coccidiosis oocysts. The puppies then get coc-cidia and spread it themselves. The mother can be cured temporarily, but if she is bred again, she will encounter the same problem in her next litter. To rid a kennel of this parasite, everything must be scrupulously clean and bitches who foster it should not be bred.

A puppy that has coccidia can seem perfectly healthy in a kennel because it is well adjusted to its environment and diet, but as soon as it goes to a new home, with a new diet, the coccidia becomes troublesome. It is quite easy to get rid of them in a puppy by administering Sodium Sulpha Cetamide or Neomycin. Older dogs rarely get coccidia but the same drugs should be equally effective for them.

The **tapeworm** requires an intermediate host to complete its life cycle, the most common being the flea. Tapeworms are long, flat and ribbonlike, sometimes measuring several feet in length, and are made up of segments that look like flat grains of rice. Each of the segments is complete in itself and is capable of reproducing. Even when a large number of segments have passed in the form of a string, it is important that the heads of the individual worms are also removed as they will grow new bodies, and it is also possible for reinfection to occur.

It is up to the owner to detect the tapeworm segments as they are not always evident in a stool sample and, therefore, may not always show up under the microscope. The owner could find them wiggling around in a fresh stool sample, in the dog's bed or possibly at the base of the dog's tail. Fleas are the hosts and the larvae are carried by them. Besides worming the dog to get rid of the tapeworms, you should spray the whole kennel area and everywhere the dog sleeps with a flea killer. There is nothing much worse than having fleas in a kennel for they spread from one dog to the next. If you spray the kennels regularly, spray the dogs when they go to shows or Obedience classes, spray visiting bitches and have outdoor dogs wear flea collars at intervals, you will keep your place free of these pests. Frontline is the answer to fleas and ticks.

Dogs with tapeworms can be noticed biting their rear ends, dragging their hindquarters on the ground and licking themselves around the tail area.

ANAL GLANDS

There are two saclike glands on either side of the anus and the contents of these are normally emptied into the dog's rectum ring. The hard-to-normal stools a dog passes press against the glands and empty their contents. This is another reason why you should keep a daily check on your dog's stools to be sure he is in good health. A dog that has normal stools should never have his anal glands squeezed, for you will create a problem that doesn't exist. Nature will take care of this function if you do not interfere.

However, there may be the one exception when the glands become packed with a pastelike fluid that has an extremely bad odor, and the dog is helpless to remedy the situation. They should be squeezed to remove this matter and you should have your veterinarian do it. If blood or pus is seen, this means that they are infected. When the anal glands become impacted, the dog will run a short distance, then sit down quickly, or repeatedly bite and lick that area to rid himself of the fluid.

If the glands become chronically infected, it is wise to have them removed surgically. If they are not treated, the area adjacent to the glands may become infected and this will be much more difficult to cure. Although it is unusual, it is possible that a dog who licks his anal glands continually will develop a throat or intestinal infection.

Dogs that are frightened suddenly are quite apt to release the anal-sac fluid, and if you ever smell this strong odor you can expect that something happened to upset your dog. My Joll never sleeps in the car because he is too busy watching the other drivers. He notices all the drivers who cut in on us, pass us and approach too close for comfort. He looks around to see why the brakes are being applied, or why the turn signals are being used, nudges me if a car is about to sideswipe us, and is as close to being a back-seat driver as a dog can be. He is quiet and well-mannered, but he gets his message across very clearly.

One day when I had left him in the car while visiting the dentist, he was frightened suddenly and discharged a pungent odor. When I opened the car door upon my return I realized something had happened because of the odor and his obvious excitement as if he were trying to tell me something. I noticed a note on my window that a witness had left to inform me that a hit-and-run driver had backed into my car. Sure enough, on examination, I found that a car had hit the other side of my car broadside by backing into it. Joll, being the sole witness in the car, had relieved his feelings the only way he could besides barking.

Authorities on wild animals say that they use these anal glands to demarcate the territorial boundaries in their domains. However, our domestic animals have no such need for them. The odor of the anal glands changes when bitches come in season and makes them more attractive to the males. It is quite possible that each dog has a slightly different scent, which they catalog in their minds and remember at a later date when they meet again.

PANOSTEITIS

This disease is also called *enostosis and eosinophilic panosteitis.* It causes lameness in young dogs between five and thirteen months of age, and may affect one or more legs intermittently over a period of several weeks. The lameness is usually not associated with any injury and the youngster may suffer a loss of appetite and be inclined to be less active during this period.

By applying firm pressure on the long bones of the legs, you can locate the affected area. Radiography is the most reliable means of differentiating lameness caused by panosteitis, and, in the middle phase of the disease, characteristic radio-dense, patchy areas appear in the medullary canal of the long bones such as the humerus, femur, tibia, radius and ulna.

Although panosteitis is a disease of unknown origin, the lameness caused by it is self-limiting and symptoms usually abate with time. Some doctors prescribe aspirin, Bufferin or costeroids to help relieve the pain, while others suggest that the dog be kept off drugs, but confined, for several weeks. They feel that a dog will be less likely to injure himself exercising if he is aware of the pain.

RABIES

Rabies is a very infectious disease that can be 100 percent fatal to all warm-blooded animals, including man. It infects the central nervous system, which leads to a most painful and horrible death.

It can only be contacted from an animal with the disease, and to develop, the saliva of the rabid animal must get into the bloodstream of the one bitten through an opening in the skin like a bite or a cut. It is not uncommon to hear about a rabid fox, rabbit or bat being discovered in some area. This is one more reason why you shouldn't permit your dog to leave your property and run free.

If a dog or a person is bitten by a rabid animal, they should seek out professional help immediately. A person should receive the Pasteur treatment, which is a series of fourteen injections. One inoculation is given each day and they are not as painful as they are rumored to be. An animal should receive a similar treatment. When one is bitten by a rabid animal there is no choice— a person who wants to survive must take the treatment.

The dog that has rabies may first show symptoms of this disease by a complete change in personality and behavior. The outgoing dog becomes shy, keeps to himself and becomes vicious. This dog feels impelled to roam and bites at anything that gets in his path. As the disease progresses, he goes completely mad and is extremely dangerous.

Another symptom of rabies is the "dumb" form where the dog's lower jaw becomes paralyzed and he cannot drink, although he is extremely thirsty. His voice mechanism becomes paralyzed and he makes a very weird noise. Eventually, his whole body becomes paralyzed and he dies.

Although young puppies cannot be immunized against rabies, they are susceptible to it. One family who had a six-week-old puppy with a behavior problem was shocked to find out the puppy actually had rabies. Twenty people who had been playfully bitten or scratched by the puppy had to take the antirabies vaccine.

There is some controversy about the length of time the vaccines provide immunity. At this time only the CEO-LEP Flury vaccines provided immunity for three years, and not all authorities agree on this. To be certain our dogs are immunized, we give them this vaccination every two years.

PERMEAL DEGENERATION

There is a condition called permeal degeneration that seems to occur most often in German Shepherd Dogs and can affect either sex. There is progressive cellular degeneration of the skin, connective tissue and muscle fibers in the areas adjacent to the anus. Usually the process is deepest in the areas bilateral to the anus. It is not usually associated with inflammation or infection of the anal glands.

Dr. Marsh of the Marsh Hospital for Animals has found gram negative rod bacterial infections on culturing the lesions. While most people feel that these can be controlled with appropriate antibiotics, as directed by antibiotic sensitivity tests, Dr. Marsh, having tried this and met with no success, feels the organisms are in most instances only invaders.

His treatment is radical surgical debridgement, with selected antibiotic coverage. The surgery is quite often difficult due to the pudendal and caudal rectal arteries and nerves tracking through the area. Some cases have been complicated with degeneration of the sphincter ani externus and internus muscles. This leaves a relaxed anus from which the stool is free to drop, especially during excitement or barking.

The sooner the dog receives the proper kind of medical treatment, the better chance he has for full recovery. The majority of these operations have been very successful.

DISTEMPER—HEPATITIS—LEPTOSPIROSIS

I have included these three dreadful diseases in one section because any one of them can be fatal to your dog if it is not treated in time, but he can be vaccinated with DHL vaccine to protect him against all three. To safeguard our puppies, we isolate them when they are born and, for the first three weeks, they receive distemper immunity from the colostrum in the mother's milk. Then, at three weeks, we inoculate the puppies with Measles Distemper vaccine to protect them until they get the permanent DHL vaccinations when they are about three months old. Thereafter, each of our dogs receives an annual DHL booster vaccination. This program will protect the average dog against distemper, hepatitis and leptospirosis.

These three diseases are similar in that they are all deadly, very infectious, and many wild and domestic animals are affected by them who can spread them among themselves. Immediate professional help should be sought, and along with good medical treatment, you should be ready to nurse your dog back to health with constant loving care, nourishing food and warm, dry, sanitary quarters.

Distemper is considered one of the oldest known canine diseases and it affects dogs of all ages. It is an acute infectious disease caused by a virus. Although it is an airborne disease, it can also be spread on contact, such as dogs sniffing each other, or by licking a contaminated food dish, bone, toy, et cetera. The virus affects the respiratory, urinary, digestive and nervous systems of the dog.

The symptoms of distemper appear in about five days and cover a wide range. The temperature averages 103 to 104 degrees. The eyes have a clear, watery discharge and are very sensitive to light. The discharge becomes thicker, more whitish or yellowish, and there is more of it as the disease progresses. The dog develops a runny nose that eventually becomes bloody. The dog loses his appetite and must be force-fed nourishing foods and vitamins to keep up his strength. The dog becomes very thirsty and often vomits the water he drinks. He has diarrhea and the stools, which are very watery, become bloody if his condition worsens. He gets a bad cough. Distemper sores develop on his stomach. There are no drugs that will kill the virus, but globulin, the immunizing serum, is helpful, and antibiotics and Bufferin can be used to combat secondary infections. Intravenous feeding can be given when it is no longer possible to feed him.

In the acute stages of **hepatitis,** the virus is passed in the saliva, urine and other excretions of the dogs, and even the dogs that recover will continue to spread the disease for a long time. The symptoms are a higher fever than that of distemper, 104 to 105 degrees, severe tonsillitis, loss of appetite, inflammation of the eyes, vomiting and diarrhea.

Leptospirosis is another infectious disease and is caused by bacteria, known as spirochetes, which localize in the kidneys of the dogs and make the urine very infectious. The color of the urine is deep yellow or orange and has a very strong odor, and the dog has a fever accompanied by chills. These symptoms are very significant of this disease. In combating this disease, you should also rid your grounds of any rodents. Rodents are found to be infected although they show no outward signs of it, and they urinate in areas inhabited by dogs and infect them in this way.

It has been said many times that these diseases are much easier to prevent than to cure. Every dog deserves the protection that DHL can give him.

TONSILLITIS

There are two small glands in the back of a dog's throat. When he is well, they are hardly noticeable because they are encased in hammocks. If your dog is not interested in finishing his dinner, whines a little when you stroke his neck or coughs, check his tonsils to see if they are out of the little hammocks. If they are, they will be red and enlarged. With your left hand under the dog's jaw, grasp it firmly by placing your thumb and middle finger behind his lower canine teeth, and press the back of his tongue down with the middle and forefingers of your right hand. Do this firmly but quickly before your dog has a chance to shake his head. If you hold him firmly, securely but gently, he will not object if you look at his tonsils.

Tonsillitis is very infectious, so the dog that has it should be immediately separated from any others you may have and kept in seclusion until he recovers. Be sure the food and water dishes given to the sick dog are not used by any other dog.

Many doctors advise a tonsillectomy if the dog has repeated attacks. Don't decide to do this on your own as tonsils should not be removed unless it is absolutely necessary. Give your doctor your dog's history so that he can decide whether the condition is chronic.

Dogs, and especially puppies, get tonsillitis for many reasons, a sudden change in temperature, a bath on a cold day, drafts, lying near air-conditioning ducts or getting germs from another dog. Tonsillitis will generally last about two weeks and I have found the best remedy, and one that affords relief, is to swab the dog's throat with Sulmet (a Sulpha drug).

HEARTWORM (DIROFILARIA IMMITIS)

Heartworm is a parasitic infection of increasing concern to dog owners. It produces symptoms by mechanical interference with the right heart and circulation in the pulmonary vascular system. This produces congestive heart failure. Symptoms are coughing—sometimes producing blood—shortness of breath, easy fatigability, malaise, weight loss and fainting.

It is apparent from the above diagram that the promulgation of this parasite is dependent upon the distribution and population of its mosquito vector. Unfortunately, both have been greatly increased by the removal from the market of some of the most effective mosquito control products due to their ecological effect.

Graphic Illustration of Life Cycle

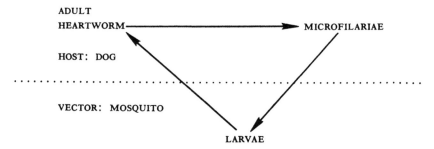

The portion of the cycle above the dotted line occurs in the host dog; the portion of the cycle below the dotted line occurs in the vector: the mosquito (at least thirty varieties). A complete life cycle requires six to ten months.

Initially, heartworm was confined to the warmer and subtropical areas, but now cases have been reported throughout the temperate zone and even into the northern climes.

Once a dog is infected with heartworms, only one course of treatment is generally available. This is by the administration of arsenicals intravenously to kill the adult heartworms. It is imperative after this treatment that the dog be kept closely confined, calm and quiet while his body decomposes and absorbs the dead worms. Six weeks after the completion of the arsenical therapy, a drug must be given to kill the microfilariae. As with most diseases, the earlier the diagnosis is made, the safer the treatment.

The treatment of heartworms as outlined above carries a considerable risk, not only due to the inherent toxicity of the drugs, but also due to the fact that the dead parasites can act as pulmonary emboli—an extremely serious condition.

The surgical removal of adult heartworms by pulmonary arterotomy (essentially, open-heart surgery) is used only as a last resort in dogs so heavily parasitized that they could not possibly tolerate arsenical therapy. The highly specialized surgical and anesthetic techniques are available in only a few veterinary medical centers.

By far the safest and most effective method of protecting the dog from heartworm is by prevention. After your veterinarian has found your dog free of heartworm by the microscopic examination of a blood smear, the dog is given Caricide in his daily ration during the mosquito season and for months thereafter. The dosage is based on the weight. Your veterinarian can advise you of the dates of the mosquito season in your area. A word of caution— if during the winter you take your dog to a subtropical area, have the dog's blood checked and place him on Caricide for the trip and two months thereafter.

If you prefer, you may administer Styrid Caricide, which will not only prevent heartworm but also controls roundworm (*Toxocara canis*) and hookworm (*Ancylostoma caninum*). To make the medicine more palatable in daily ration, you may find it helpful to mix the drug with an equal volume of molasses.

Note: Styrid and Caricide are registered trademarks of the American Cyanamid Company.

OBJECT LODGED IN THROAT

Puppies are notoriously bad about swallowing anything that appears in their paths. Some are like little vacuum cleaners. The safest way to avoid this problem is to keep the puppy where he is less apt to swallow something that would be harmful to him. If he is in the house, keep one eye on him and give him large bones and toys that will keep him amused. When outdoors in a yard, be certain there is nothing accessible to him that would be harmful if he swallowed it. I have heard of puppies swallowing razor blades, pocket knives, diamond rings, stockings, spoons and other weird objects. If your puppy swallows something that is not edible, give him several slices of fresh bread to help him pass it through his system.

At one time I lived next to a golf course and an occasional golf ball would land in my flower garden. Joll found one of these and was chewing it when I noticed him from an upstairs window. I rushed outdoors to take it away from him and in those few seconds found that he had slipped it way back on his tongue and that it was stuck in his throat. The ball was slimy from his saliva and he was beginning to panic because he couldn't breathe. After a few futile attempts, I was able to grasp the ball in my fingertips and nails by keeping close to both sides of his throat. At that point it was none too soon. Joll was so relieved to be rid of it that he ran happily around the yard wagging his tail like mad. Thereafter, whenever he picked up a ball or object that was too small I would just tell him firmly, "Drop it, it's too small." He would look at me knowingly and seriously and drop the ball.

Whenever you have to go in your dog's throat after an object be sure to wipe your fingers dry before each attempt. Keep to the outside of his throat and be careful not to push the object down farther; it must be pried out and quickly. Don't be afraid your dog will bite you. Dogs seem to understand instinctively when you are trying to help them. Talk quietly and calmly to them so they will relax a little.

One morning I noticed my Arry licking his lips and swallowing frequently, which led me to believe that he had swallowed something that had got stuck in his throat. I put my fingers down his throat and felt around, but didn't find anything. He had eaten his breakfast, and later in the morning had no problem drinking water. However, in the afternoon I noticed he was again swallowing hard and his lips were getting foamy. I knew then that something was lodged in his throat even though after several attempts I was still unable to find it.

I could talk to Arry as I could to a person. He was an extremely intelligent dog and had earned his UDT in approximately five months. I told him

I was going to have to go way down his throat and his eyes told me he understood. I pushed two fingers way down his throat and at the base of his tongue I was horrified to feel a needle. One end was stuck into the base of his tongue while the other was lodged in the back of his throat.

I made several unsuccessful attempts to remove the slippery needle, and was beginning to feel rather helpless when my common sense prevailed and I realized I had to remove it, period. I wiped my hand dry for the nth time and told Arry confidently, "I'll get it." Arry, all this time, had been letting me open his mouth and stick my whole hand far down his throat, without applying any pressure whatsoever on my hand with his teeth. I tried once more and this time I discovered that there was about one third of an inch of thread coming from the eye of the needle that was embedded in the base of his tongue. I quickly grasped it, pushed the pointed end of the needle farther into the back of his throat to free one end, and swiftly pulled the needle out.

Arry, relieved of the pain and the pressure of allowing me to probe around in his throat, expressed his joy by jumping on and off the furniture, turning in circles, and racing around the room happily. I stood there watching and smiling, a bit weak from the experience, but full of admiration for the German Shepherd breed.

HIP DYSPLASIA

Almost forty years have passed since Gerry B. Schnelle, D.V.M., described the occurrence of hip dysplasia in dogs. This condition has and is causing great concern as to its etiology, diagnosis and prevention among serious breeders and fanciers of German Shepherds and other large breeds of dogs.

Hip dysplasia is a disease of the coxofemoral (hip) joint. The coxofemoral is a ball-and-socket joint comprised of the femoral head and the acetabulum. H.D. results from a loss of proper contour of the femoral head and loss of depth of the acetabulum. In its ultimate form, subluxation (dislocation) of the joint occurs. This causes crippling and severe pain in the affected animal. Fortunately, this occurs in only a small fraction of dysplastic dogs.

Hip dysplasia is primarily a hereditary disease. It is transmitted by a dominant group of genes with irregular manifestations, responsible for hip development. There are other factors which affect development of H.D. Overweight, "butterball" puppies should be avoided by feeding a well-balanced diet, with vitamins but limited caloric content. It is desirable to breed for puppies with good muscle mass—this can be achieved by selecting breeding partners with this characteristic.

Today many people believe that German Shepherds grow too fast. To slow this growth, they recommend giving them less protein than the dog-food manufacturer's advise. In other words, a dry food with about 17 percent protein instead of 25 percent or more. Mix this with a little lean beef. Give them raw vegetables every day. Start them on vitamins C and E every day. Environment is also a factor. Puppies need plenty of exercise and there is nothing better than long walks where the puppy must trot. Swimming is excellent for youngsters. In other words if you can slow a puppy's growth, it will give the ligaments, muscles and cartilage a chance to catch up with the bone growth, thus preventing hip dysplasia. It is a theory worth trying.

Historically, both the German Shepherd Dog Club of America and the German SV, when first apprised of the extent and seriousness of H.D., refused to discuss the disease in their publications. To their credit, when convinced of the wisdom of informing their members, they reversed this position and lent their efforts to disseminating information on and finding the means to control H.D.

Detection of hip dysplasia is primarily by X ray. Radiography of the dog under general anesthesia in the prescribed position will reveal shallowness of the acetabular cup, recontouring of the femoral head or subluxation of the coxofemoral joint in the dysplastic dog.

In the years after Doctor Schnelle described H.D., and Dr. Otto Schales advanced the theory as to the genetic factor involved, it became apparent that uniform criteria for the interpretation of X rays should be established. In addition, an agency was needed to act as a central registry for the results. Thus in 1966, at the urging of Wayne Riser, D.V.M., the Orthopedic Foundation for Animals was established. The OFA has a staff of veterinary radiologists who give a consensus opinion of X rays submitted to them for evaluation. Should the radiograph be considered normal, the dog is OFA certified and assigned a registration number. The letter(s) prefix indicates the breed of the dog. Should the dog be considered dysplastic, this information is held in confidence between OFA, the veterinarian and the owner and is not published. Dogs are considered for certification after two years of age.

Approximately ten years after Dr. Otto Schales first published his theory of the dominant gene transmission of hip dysplasia, Dr. F. Sachs, a member of the SV Breeding Committee, was permitted to publish a comprehensive study of hip dysplasia in the *SV Zeitung*. Over that period Dr. Sachs had encountered much resistance within the SV, some of whose directors felt hip dysplasia was an American disease. The SV announced shortly afterward that German breeders who voluntarily had radiographic evidence of normal hips would have the "a" stamp upon the dog's registration papers. In 1966 the SV announced that, effective with the 1968 National Sieger Show, only dogs with the "a" stamp would be considered for the Excellent Select (VA) classification.

The certification of dogs for the "a" stamp is very strict in Germany. Films may be taken at a veterinary teaching institute or by a private veterinarian accredited by the SV after examination. Every dog is tattooed, presently in the right ear, at the time of the X ray. All films must be submitted. None are permitted to be withheld or discarded. If severe hip dysplasia is discovered, the name of the animal is published in the *SV Zeitung* with a notice that his progeny will not be registered.

The figure of 20,000 OFA certified German Shepherds in the United States does not mean that all other Shepherds are dysplastic. I personally sell many

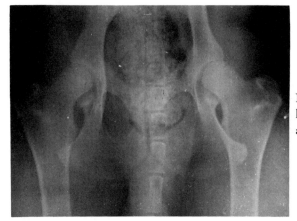

Normal hips. Both femoral heads fit well into their acetabula.

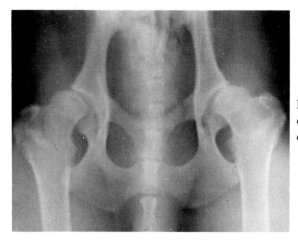

Hip dysplasia. Ill-fitting femoral heads with osteoarthritic changes taking place.

dogs who have been x-rayed normal at one year of age by my veterinarian, and the new owner is satisfied with the doctor's report and the X ray and is not interested in going to the expense of having the dog OFA certified. We have also made it a firm practice to use bitches in our breeding program who were x-rayed normal, and since 1973 we have had our young stock OFA certified for advertising purposes.

I am sure many other German Shepherd kennels that are run by people of integrity have followed a similar course. If this is the case, I am sure the United States figure for normal hips would be greatly increased. One must keep in mind that the German X-ray program is mandatory so it is bound to be successful. In this country we also appreciate the wisdom of selective breeding, but we wish to do it voluntarily.

The Germans certify their dogs at one year of age, and they have three ratings: normal, almost normal and still permissable. It is questionable whether the OFA in this country would give their OFA certification to those German Shepherd Dogs who were rated in the second or third categories. The OFA does not certify a German Shepherd until it is two years of age.

The years have gone by and no one has come up with the answers to hip dysplasia. Dogs in this country and Germany still get it. The only advice the experts give breeders is to breed their OFA dogs to OFA bitches. Some dogs who are extremely overangulated in the rear and look crippled going away have been OFA certified. Some dogs who have herded sheep most of their lives have hip dysplasia, but never have a day's discomfort, because they have built up the muscles in their hindquarters. Dogs who have been rated "near normal" can work all their lives without any health problems. Stud dogs who have been rated "near normal" produce a great number of progeny with normal hips. Then there are those dogs who are OFA certified who produce both good and bad hips.

Today the new puppy owner is advised to keep his or her puppy lean, give vitamins C and E daily, feed an all-natural diet, not give any supplements, let him develop slowly, not let him jump off porches or catch Frisbees or balls in midair and let him swim and hike daily to build up the muscles in his hind legs. If you follow this advice and your puppy turns into a big, strong, healthy youngster, he will probably live to be fifteen years old.

chapter 35

North American German Shepherd Bloodlines

The old American lines were primarily built around Pfeffer von Bern, Odin von Busecker Schloss, Chlodulf von Peltzerhof and Arras aus der Stadt-Velbert, with the emphasis being on Pfeffer. These were combined with the lines available at that time, mostly descendants of Utz von Haus Schutting and his sire, Klodo von Boxberg.

In the eastern United States in the 1940s, it was all Pfeffer with his son, Nox of Ruthland, Grand Victor of the United States one year, then Nox's brother, Noble, winning it the next year, then Nox again the year after. It appears that this tremendous concentration of Pfeffer bred itself into oblivion, because today it is practically impossible to find in the pedigrees of dogs currently used for breeding.

On the West Coast the kennels of San Miguel and Rocky Reach, who worked hand-in-hand with Marie Leary on the East Coast, were doing some fancy inbreeding on Chlodulf through concentrating the blood of his son, Arno of San Miguel, and later his sons and daughter, Illo, Imp and Iva of Rocky Reach. They brought the Odin blood into their lines, which was a good combination, producing many quality animals. San Miguel's Illo of Rocky Reach was the sire of San Miguel's Baron of Afbor, who was the producer of "pillars" of the breed.

In the Midwest, Nyx of Long-Worth, who was a combination of Pfeffer and Odin bloodlines, further concentrated the Pfeffer blood when bred to the Pfeffer son, Marlo von Hoheluft. This produced the Long-Worth "D" litter, which formed the basis for many years of Long-Worth domination of the German Shepherd dog world in America. The main breeding power of the "D" litter came from the males, Derry, Dennis and Drum. Derry, when bred to the Pfeffer daughter, Ophelia of Greenfair, further concentrated not only the Pfeffer blood, but that of his sire and the brother of his sire (who was the sire of Ophelia's mother). From this came Vol of Long-Worth, who was a mass concentration of the Pfeffer blood, and certainly prepotent. Dennis was notably the sire of Winnettee, who was the dam of Mercurio of Long-Worth, a notable producer, whose sire-lines carried strong Odin, some Chlodulf and Arras, as well as other-than-Pfeffer blood.

As the American kennels maintained their breeding program of the late forties and early fifties, a few German imports were introduced, but generally with incompatible results. The incestuous lines of the day combined with the cold blood of the import just didn't go well. Quell v. Fredeholz, one of the exceptions, imported around 1948, startled the United States by being shown twenty times and went Best of Breed twenty times. He was not a great producer, but paved the way for an introduction of more German blood. Many of his offspring gave a refreshing influence, particularly in temperament, to American bloodlines.

Now the battle had begun. Lloyd Brackett of Long-Worth took up the anti-import cause, although even he used the odd one he felt could benefit his kennels, such as Cito v. Tippersruh and Cuno v. d. Teufelslache, with varying results, but the pure American strain cohorts were forced to breed their lines together to preserve type, as they put it. This was a good thing, as now Vol of Long-Worth came into play by combining with the San Miguel blood to produce such dogs as Chimney Sweep of Long-Worth, who has considerable influence on American pedigrees. Previous to Chimney Sweep, Jory of Edgetowne, an earlier Vol son, out of a Derry of Long-Worth daughter, had set the American Fancy on its ear by winning show after show and being finally made U. S. Grand Victor in 1951. However, he died at four years and was lost to the cause except through his excellent prepotent son, Nordraak of Matterhorn, and a few bitches from the Llano Estacado kennels. His brothers, Jolly, Arno and Jaunty, particularly the former, and Jory's son, Nordraak, became "pillars" on the West Coast and were very prominent in the background of the quality there.

From the combination of Midwest and Western bloodlines also came GV Alert of Mi-Noah and Kirk of San Miguel, who were both by Baron of Afbor. Alert's mother was of Long-Worth lines and with a strong Odin influence. Alert produced well when bred to the Quell v. Fredeholz offspring, and in combination with it, is often seen in pedigrees, notably from Hessian and Hart-Wald kennels.

Many of the German imports they tried to introduce into American breeding had one line back to Odin v. Busecker Schloss, apparently imported with the intent of doubling up on him. Such dogs were usually heavy with Sigbert Heidegrund and his sire, Odin Stolzenfels, who were abundant in rear angulation, which was evident in the dogs imported. Examples of this were Heiko v. Menkenmoor, Cuno v. d. Teufelslache and Lord v. Zenntal. They produced their share of champions, but matters were not really improving too much except perhaps in temperament.

Mercurio of Long-Worth was a much underrated dog as a producer, but his own appearance didn't really help his image. He was wiry, strong, well balanced, sound (structurally and temperamentally), and an excellent producer—particularly of bitches. Possibly, his male sons weren't quite bulky enough for the Fancy. He can still be found behind the foundation bitches of many kennels, including Hart-Wald. Mercurio is the sire of Renown of Long-Worth, who produced Flint and Sabre (Renown's mother was Katja, a full sister to Vol). Mercurio was also the sire of Facsimile who, when bred to the import Arry v. Burghalderring, produced Uncus of Long-Worth, one of the great movers.

Around 1950, a lady from Pennsylvania became extremely interested in German Shepherd Dogs and spent several months in Germany looking for dogs. She bought a couple of bitches, but was so taken with a young male that she decided to bring him along too. Before he had been shown to finish his Championship, he went Grand Victor, and the bitch brought over with him was the Grand Victrix. The lady was Mrs. Fischer of Waldenmark Kennels. The male was Ingo v. Wünschelrute, and the bitch, Afra v. Heilholtkamp. Ingo's handler was Jack McMahon. The other bitch she brought over was the Rolf v. Osnabruckerland daughter, Levade Preussenblut. Together these dogs formed a new line within the breed, and bolstered many of the old ones.

Mrs. Fischer bred as close, particularly on Ingo, as any kennel has ever done. She did a lot of winning with the offspring after Ingo finished his show career, but most of the informed would probably agree that she never produced anything as outstanding as Ingo. She brought over his father, Arry v. Burghalderring, and produced many worthwhile dogs by him, among them, the previously mentioned Uncus.

The imports having the biggest demand in the United States and Canada had the extreme rear and type, while in Germany they were building the breed around Rolf v. Osnabruckerland. The Rolf type—wonderful shoulders, but straight behind, heavy head, big in bone and body, and sound in temperament—just didn't go in North America, and his sons that were brought over were virtually ignored as stud dogs. They were later found in the pedigrees of dogs imported to the United States. Such dogs as Lesko aus Kattenstroth by Rolf—grandfather of Sieger Arno v. Haus Gersie, who is now more and more prominent in German pedigrees. Lesko is also the great-grandfather of Ch. Bernd v. Kallengarten. He was also the grandfather, on the mother's side, of Ulk Wikingerblut, who later came to the United States and swept it as a showman and producer. Werro zu den Sieben Faulen also could be said to have been too little utilized, but he lives on in the bloodlines of Sarego kennels, in combination with GV Alice v. d. Guten Fee and GV Brando v. Aichtal. The other Rolf offspring in North America received a similar rejection.

A small gray dog, a Youth Sieger, was imported in the early fifties, primarily the small, extremely angulated, beautifully coordinated type. He not only had the rear but the front to go with it. His mother was closely inbred on Odin v. Stolzenfels, his father was an outcross, old-line breeding. Cito v. d. Hermannschleuse, imported by Gustave Schindler, was to play an important part in American bloodlines, especially in a supportive role.

Around 1955 one of the most prepotent of Hein's sons arrived in the United States. This was Bill v. Kleistweg, who was a type different from the previous Hein sons, more to the American preference, which was more concerned with spectacular side gait than with soundness coming and going. Bill was imported and owned by Grant Mann of Detroit who had bred excellent dogs for years from his kennels and had produced several Grand Victors and Grand Victrixes.

Mr. Mann imported dogs from Germany, which he worked into his breedings, but because he did not concentrate on any one dog or group of dogs, the Liebestraum dogs were generally of open breeding, and they contributed to the quality of bloodlines as individuals rather than as a line. He imported such dogs as Liebo v. Stuveschacht and Leu v. Kahlgrund. Bill was probably the greatest of his imports, not only as a show dog (for he was 1956 U.S. Grand Victor), but as a top producer, although only used with a limited number of bitches. Bill was in the States for only a short time, but produced a couple of Grand Victrixes and many Champions. Probably his most prepotent son was used relatively little. Rikter von Liebestraum can be found a few generations back in many of the top show dogs in America today. In looking back on Rikter, he seemed to produce a large number of outstanding movers, and his litters were noticeably free of bad bites, long coats, floppy ears and the like, which do not appear at dog shows, but which are nevertheless a burden and a disappointment to the serious breeder. He was used quite close with the Hein lines and on a couple of known occasions produced well in conjunction with Wotan v. Richterbach blood. Of course, the true test of a dog's value is whether he can be bred close on without serious problems. Rikter passed this test and seemed to produce dogs better than himself.

Other prominent Hein sons came to the United States and had an impact on American bloodlines, notably Harald v. Haus Tigges, and probably the last great Hein son, Greif v. Elfenhain. Caesar v. d. Malmannscheide was a Hein son who never came to North America, but he exerted a great influence through his progeny.

In the same era, around 1955, Axel v. d. Deininghauserheide was coming into prominence as the great producer in Germany. A natural result was the importation of many of the Axel offspring. A few of his sons had tremendous influences in North America along with many of his grandsons. Axel was a product of completely unrelated breeding, which seems to refute the theory which says an animal has to be from inbreeding to be prepotent. His ancestry was completely different from that of the then overabundant R-litter blood, and fortunately combined beautifully with it, as well as with other lines. He seemed to give the rear angulation so much desired, a real working and exuberant temperament, and hard, dry animals. On the debit side, they started to run into oversize and ranginess.

Ch. Hyline's Duran v. Woodside, TC, OFA
Owners: Margaret and Ronald Nunnally and Joan Hunt Smith

Kolbrook's Crooked Halo (dam of GV Spencer)
Breeder-Owner: Ann Brogden

Ch. Schneiderhof's OJ of Madiera, ROM/C
Owners: Nancy and Tom Schneider, Blackie and Mary Witzel

Ero v. Awallenburg was one of the first sons over and, as mentioned previously, his mother's side went back-doubling on Odin Stolzenfels descendants. He tied in beautifully with resident bloodlines—mostly Long-Worth stock—and he produced the angulation.

Sel. Ch. Schneiderhof's Urban
  Cowboy, CD, AOE
Owner: Don Smith

AM. & Can. Ch. Toskey's Willow V.
  Schneiderhof
Owner: Cheryl Albert

Ch. Wynthea's Min-
  Aqua Mädchen, UD
Owner: Virginia Ross
Handler: Ron Gates
Judge: Ernest Loeb

Woker and Wotan v. Richterbach arrived in the United States. They went back on the mother's side to Rosel through their mother Hexe, Hein's sister. From all the evidence, Wotan was a big plus and, although apparently used sparingly, he is in the background of too many quality animals for it to be a matter of chance. His offspring went well in combination with Bill v. Kleistweg and Amor v. Haus Hoheide offspring, as well as many pure American lines. Another Axel son to go particularly well with American lines was Axel v. Poldihaus, who became U.S. Grand Victor.

Eventually, the greatest of the Axel sons to be imported to America as a producer arrived, and he was so popular and so prepotent that, for a time after his emergence as a producer, it looked as if the danger would be that no lines could be free of Troll von Richterbach. For once, breeders seemed to recognize a value early, and consequently many of his American sons were as good and as prepotent as the Troll sons later brought in from Germany. He was often used in North America just the way the Germans would use such a dog. The F-litter Arbywood combined Cito and Pfeffer blood with the Axel R-litter to produce the prepotent Field Marshall, Fels and Fortune, all fantastic producers in themselves, and the result of open breeding. They have clicked with a variety of combinations. One example is Kurt v. Bid-Scono, one of the first North American Troll sons, and a host of others. Troll was U.S. Grand Victor.

Competing for the honor of being Troll's greatest son, we have to look at the tremendous record of the import Ulk Wikingerblut who was bred in Germany and whose mother was a daughter of the neglected Amor v. Haus Hoheide. Ulk was shown and used all over the United States and Canada and produced excellent quality throughout, including a Grand Victrix.

Nearly all popular studs seemed to go back to Axel, usually through Troll. Of course, the German breed builders had not introduced Axel for this purpose and they, at least, were aware of the pitfalls. They had intended him rather as a quality broadening of the roots, which a study of their system reveals they do from time to time. Other dogs that were used as much, and whose bloodlines are now strong here, were Harry v. Donaukai and his son Volker v. Zollgrenschutzhaus and Klodo aus der Eremitenklause. In Germany Volker was twice Sieger and because of his quality was often used at stud. His quality was not often realized in the first generation, but his many excellent grandchildren proved the wisdom of his introduction. The benefits from Klodo were reaped sooner.

By the early sixties, things were changing again and many of the dogs brought over were either free of Axel or had him in small doses. This created the opportunity for lovely combinations of bloodlines. However, the then top producer in Germany, Alf v. Nordfelsen, being an Axel son, just didn't find a place for his boys over here. Alf v. Loherfeld, an Alf son, found some limited success. More R-litter descendants were coming over but in a disguised form. The greatest of these, although he was a grandson of Axel through Watzer v. Badmalle, was Bernd v. Kallengarten, owned and imported by

Ken–Delaine's Puma, ROM
Sire: Sel. Ch. Tournaline's Kena Ken-Delaine
Dam: Ch. Tournaline's Kelsy
Owner: Cheryl F. Olson

Dondar's Gunsmoke, UD, TC, HI
Owner: Connie Cabanela

Ernest Loeb. What he didn't produce in the first generation invariably came out in the next.

The Lierberg dogs, probably the most successful embodiment of the great German pillar, Vello zu den Sieben Faulen, contained lines to the R-litter through Hein, Rolf and Ina, who was a full sister, but also with

Wynthea's Bear, CPL
  (Companion, protector,
  loyal friend)
Owner: Dr. Michael Kistler

valuable outcross lines. The 1967 Sieger, Bodo v. Lierberg, was a superior specimen with an ideal temperament. Raps v. Piastendamm and his get go back to Racker rather than Rolf, and make good combinations with present bloodlines.

One fine producer from Germany who was brought to the United States was Greif v. Elfenhain, a son of Hein. His mother was from the A-litter Elfenhain of which we find considerable representation: There was Atlas v. Elfenhain, a foundation dog of Hessian kennels; Naka v. Elfenhain, used with Alf v. Nordfelsen to produce Caret v. Elfenhain, used for a pillar for the Sixberg kennels in Germany; and Amsel, Greif's mother. They are a product of taking a Racker daughter to Rolf to produce Lexa. Lexa was then out-crossed to Grimm v. d. Fahrmühle who goes back to Arry v. d. Gassenquelle, who was previously blamed for coat problems. Amsel, then bred to Hein, goes back to concentrate the R-litter blood in Greif.

A STUDY OF THE 1971 AND 1972 SIEGER SHOWS

The main lines of a few years ago have now largely blended together, and the daughters and granddaughters of these greats bred to other greats have formed new foundations. These are based on a new sense of values and mirror to a large degree the convictions of the new leader, Dr. Christoph Rummel. In turn, his decisions bring out the ideas impressed upon him by a very knowl-edgeable breeding fraternity. Fortunately for the breed, Germany also has a number of breeders with their own ideas. These breeders constantly work with the establishment's blessing to produce animals equal or better in quality than the main lines. Some examples of these breeders' efforts will be used later. The cry is always to get back to the Working Dog. The German breeders as a whole want criteria that they can grasp, such as the Courage Test and the "a" stamp. With these requirements, they know the top dogs are going to have the very basic essentials, plus some additional ingredients, that bring them to their positions of excellence in the show.

By the 1971 show, Dr. Rummel was working on this third Sieger Show. Many of his ideas and the new course for the breed were starting to take shape. In his first two years, he had put up the same dog, Sieger Heiko v. Oranian Nassau. Obviously, this was his image of the breed and perhaps he had it in mind to establish Heiko as a new direction. Why not? He was by Select Alf v. Convent, who went back to herding stock, and his Select mother, by Klodo a. d. Eremitenklause, gave the outbreeding line utilized by so many German breeders. There was no Axel blood near the surface and it would appear this could very well be the standard of the new direction.

Whatever does happen, it would appear Heiko will never be that great pillar, and at a glance one might tend to underrate Dr. Rummel. After deep study of the 1971 and 1972 results, I don't think he should be underrated. Patterns are developing which show a well-defined new course. I would say this direction is not only universally accepted, but the consistency comes through in all classes much more clearly than it used to under the late Dr. Funk.

As we go back on the modern German pedigree, we find the tendency to minimize the influence of Axel v. d. Deininghauserheide, with a couple of exceptions. Very desirable is the blood of the Axel son, Sieger Alf v. Nordfelsen, and the great breeders will even take lesser dogs to bring this to the surface. The Vello influence is still largely viewed with suspicion, especially for oversize and fading pigment, and although the SV stud tree in the *Zeitung* shows it as the main line, particularly through Jalk Fohlenbrunnen, I don't believe that this is the chosen direction. Dr. Funk's main line—from Rolf through Donar v. Firnskuppe then primarily to Zibu v. Haus Schutting and, to a lesser degree, Pascha v. Gelnauser Schlossen—without his encouragement, are gradually fading out to supporting lines. Dr. Rummel, however, is too knowledgeable to discount their value entirely and more than a few dogs are coming from this line.

The quest for Rolf v. Osnabruckerland blood, which apparently is very desirable in any form, is through the late Select Dog, Alf v. Waldorf Ernst, usually through his sons, Marko v. Boxhochsburg and Junker v. Summerland, the latter leading up to Heiko. The 1971 Sieger, Arras v. Haus Helma, gets to Rolf through Brando v. Tappenport and to Arras's sire, Tom v. Haus Solms, who was probably very much the Rolf type, as is Arras, who looks every inch the male stud. He has gradually moved up the Select List until in 1971 he was Number One.

Efforts are still made to keep the supporting lines active, and perhaps Dr. Rummel encourages this breeding in his apparent refusal to put what actually have become the main-line pillars right on top. The influence of such dogs as Klodo a. d. Eremitenklause; the Raps v. Piastendamm influence which goes back to Racker not Rolf; the continuing efforts of Alfred Hahn to keep Busecker Schloss a self-maintained line; and the efforts of Dr. Simon of Piastendamm and Josef Wasserman of Zollgrenzschutzhaus are welcomed in the official breed-broadening process.

Whether by plan or by constant stress on the best, the new pillars and secondary lines are developing. The importance of the kennels around these pillars should be elaborated upon.

Quanto v. d. Wienerau, who in 1970 was Select VA5 and by 1971 was up to VA2, is as likely as any to stamp himself as a pillar. He is the gratifying result of many years of line building for quality, according to his own plan, by the amazing Walter Martin. The final result is this great dog and Mr. Martin is further rewarded by seeing two of Quanto's young sons that he also owns go First and Fifth; two bitches, Fourth in their respective young classes; and another Quanto daughter of the Wienerau breeding, Select Two in the adult bitch class, this one owned by Herman Martin. In 1971 he sold Quanto to Italy, obviously sure he could produce more of the same quality, and by 1972 Wienerau is again in the Select.

Let's examine his plan. In the fifties, he bought an excellent daughter of the first proclaimed German Sieger since World War II, Alf von Nordfelsen, out of an excellent bitch. He bred this bitch to the then Select Dog, Amo v. Haus Schwingel. This produced Dixie v. d. Wienerau, who not only had the two greats right behind her, but was 3-3 on the great Axel v. d. Deininghauserheide. Such close breeding was not recommended in better circles, but is sometimes very successfully pulled off. This fairly close breeding pattern, often followed by Martin, provided him with intensive knowledge of his own resources and he used them well. Dixie was always bred out, as far as I could find, and blended superbly with select Jalk v. Fohlenbrunnen to produce the L-litter Wienerau. From this breeding there was a Siegerin and V1 Lido, a great dog in his own right. Lido was eventually bred to his half-sister, Dixie being the common mother, which produced Yoga v. d. Wienerau, Quanto's mother. Then, in Martin style, he went out to quality to get what he wanted. He bred Yoga to Select Condor v. Zollgrenzschutzhaus. As a result there was Quanto and his forgotten brother, Quinn. Perhaps he was overshadowed by some of his young sons or the V1 dog, Canto v. d. Wienerau, who is out of Lido's sister by Hein Königsbrush finding his way back to Alf v. Waldorf Ernst. Canto was owned by Walter Martin at show time 1971. Wienerau also owned the Select 7 bitch, Celly v. d. Wienerau, the sister of Canto, at this time and he also won the Kennel Group in 1971.

Let's step to Lido's great son, Nick v. Dreimarkenstein. He was not at the show, but his influence was very strongly felt. His mother lines go back to Selects Gero v. Katherinentor (Caesar) and Marko v. Boxhockburg, along with Siegerin Assie v. Hexankolk, the latter anything but mainline breeding. Nick, when bred to Hexe v. Rheinbese (who was Select and goes back to Klodo and Greif von Elfenhain), produced the 1971 Siegerin. Only one adult son of Nick was there. He was Siggo v. Elizabethenklause and was rated V43. This dog is from Italy as are so many of Nick's progeny. An interesting fact about Nick is that in the last "a" report on studs from the SV, Nick was Number Two in the production of "a" certified stock. Eventually, more of his stock will be kept back for breeding and he can be looked for as a strong influence on the breed.

Lido is obviously the main line from Vello, but the Vello grandsons look like an umbrella on the SV family tree. So many of his good sons have themselves turned out to be producers. Besides the line stemming from Jalk, which includes Lido, we have the lines through the Lierbergs, through Alf Wertheranerland. There was Aro Woeringer Reitweg, and what seemed to be Veto's last producing son, Quedo v. Felstertal.

At one time Dr. Rummel owned a dog, Mutz v. d. Pelztierfarm, for whom he had the highest regard. The dog was sold to Italy. He was a grandson of Alf v. Nordfelsen on his father's side and his mother was by Gero v. Haus Eikeman out of a Hein daughter. He had the "a" stamp, was rated 10 (tops) in attack work, and V in spirit. He also passed these outstanding qualities on to his progeny. In 1970 he was shown under Dr. Rummel and in the mature German way of judging, he was placed Select Two with no complaints. One wonders if under different circumstances he might not have gone Sieger. It is evident that this dog has something special to give. Six of his male adult sons were in the 1971 Sieger Show, all rating Excellent, one bitch was Excellent, a brother and sister were both Second in their respective classes and everything else was rated Very Good, except for one Good. Most of these dogs were not shown in 1972, but a new crop of offspring did extremely well. He had the highest number of winners with two Selects, seven Vs, twenty SGs, and four Gs out of the thirty-three shown.

Mutz carries much of the style and type of the late Sieger Alf von Nordfelsen and perhaps could have something to do with the resurgence of the Alf influence. The new stress on physical and mental soundness might also have brought out the value of Alf, and consequently Mutz.

Nico v. Haus Beck, an Alf grandson, is by Sieger Veus v. Starrenberg. His mother is a sister to Select Rita v. Wellstein who carries no R-blood near the surface, making this practically an R-litter-free line. Such a quality line without the R-litter makes its value immense. He is the sire of Olden v. Asterplatz who had developed into a stud on his own by 1971. He produced the First-, Third- and Seventh-placed dogs in one class. The 1972 Siegerin was Select Number Two in 1971. Nico was sire of Fedor and Fanta v. Grunen Luckener among other V dogs. The F-litter Grunen Luchener is out of one of the famous E-litter Haus Pari bitches, Espe, whom I will talk about later. Here again, we have the result of taking the close-royally-bred Espe out to another quality line, adding more Siegers to the line. Fedor was a dog to watch and although it appears he himself wasn't destined for the top, his progeny could have been. This dog is also on the twelve top "a" producing lists, which is significant. A breeding concerning this dog was a Wienerau bitch that placed Fifth in her youth class 1971. She was by Fedor and her mother was a Raps daughter, probably by Lido. When Wienerau used him with such results, he proved a dog to watch.

One other dog with Alf background is the Select Two Dog of 1967, who is interesting because he goes back to Alf through Veus ex Nidda v. Beck, a litter sister to Nico v. Beck. Quax rated Select Two the year they ran the Courage Test and although many of the Zibu v. Haus Schutting sons surprised the show with their performances, Quax, who was then just over two years old, stayed with the two great Working Dogs, Bodo and Bernd v. Lierberg. He was three years younger, but he placed between the two of them even though their fighting spirit was universally acclaimed. Quax almost seemed to disappear after that, but now with more emphasis on soundness, may be used more often. Mutz v. Blaven, a young Quax son who is also gray in color, was one of the few of his progeny at the 1971 show. He was V2 but by 1972, in tough competition, had moved up to V1. An interesting feature of this event is that, up to this time, the strength of the Sieger Zibu line has been through the more sophisticated dogs such as Sieger Dido v. Werther Königsalle, Quido v. Haus Schutting and the latter's sons. Quido, incidentally, also brings in the Alf v. Nordfelsen influence. He, to date, has been the strongest carrier of the Zibu line. By 1971 this whole line, carried through the males, was down to three V males but doesn't include the interweaving influences. Again by 1972, the line carries on largely through Quido's son, Lido v. Allmonsforte, who also happens to be on that twelve top stud "a" list.

The 1963 Sieger, Ajax v. Haus Dexel still had progeny showing in the young classes in the 1971 show. A few years earlier he sired the wonderful E-litter Haus Park, a litter that as youngsters hit the German fancy particularly through the bitches. Three of them finished One, Two, Three in their class and their brother was also rated V. Eventually, I think six of them got the "a" stamp and one of the bitches went on to Select. One male, Enno, was owned by Heinz Roper of Zu den Sieben Faulen, who would never show under Dr. Funk, so the dog was never shown in the Sieger Show while Roper owned him. However, the breeders used him, and when Mr. Roper died he was bought by Dr. Redlich of the United States. His progeny excelled and, in spite of his absence from Germany, eleven of his progeny were entered in the 1971 show; three were Excellent, one was as high as V7, but by 1972 had slipped to eighth place. The E-litter breeding was out of Select Biene zu den Dreitzen Bucken, who was by Sieger Mutz v. Kuckstrasse on the mother's side to quality Busecker Schloss breeding. Drietzen Bucken held onto the sister of Biene and

Betty, and seeing the success of that combination, wisely bred to Ajax. Then he kept a son, Falk, who by 1972 was V19, which makes him one of the youngest Ajax sons, and he will probably be used on that basis. A slightly older Ajax son was Olaf v. Haus Altena Land. In 1971 he was V3, but in 1972 he wasn't there, although his progeny were. He was tenth on the show Stud List. Ex v. Haus Pari, who stayed in Germany, produces a few good dogs, but so far none near the quality of his brother Enno. Ajax is so interwoven through the pedigrees of some of the great ones, his influence is even stronger than I had realized.

Often I have written of the wonderful Eremitenklause phenomena. They found a successful combination and kept repeating the breeding. This wonderful combination, containing no R-litter or Axel blood, gave beautiful broad breeding partners, the most prominent and greatest being Klodo. He is bred into the pedigrees of the greatest, including the 1969 and 1970 Sieger Heiko and many more.

Jupp v. d. Murrenhutte seems to have made his first and apparently only appearance at the Sieger Show in 1968. One year he cut his foot prior to the show and couldn't be entered. His progeny started coming in 1969. In the early days, he was pushed by Murrenhutte Kennels and Dr. Simon of Piastendamm. Obviously, they found something special in this dog, who was born late in 1964 and rated V at that one show. Perhaps it is his bloodlines that make him so valuable. He is no doubt, if not the last, the most prepotent of the Klodo sons, his mother being inbred 3-2 on Ulbert v. Piastendamm, the grandfather of Raps; in fact, she is by Raps. Here we have a dog of exceptional quality and prepotency in the country dripping with the blood of Rolf—Rosel, Hein, Axel, Alf and Vello—and this dog goes back to none of them. He is probably compatible with any bloodline in an era when broadening of the lines is the order. The results bear out their wisdom. By the 1972 show he was the sire of the Select Two male, and Selects Two, Three and Five in adult bitches, plus eight Very Good young dogs. He is listed on top of the Stud List, above such dogs as Mutz, Quanto and the 1972 Sieger Marko, and all of his Selects were out of different bitches. His Select son, Hero v. Lauerhof, is a fine animal with excellent character who is well liked. The future will show how well he can produce.

The 1971 Sieger, Arras v. Haus Helma, by 1972 was moving up as a producer, although most of them were young stock. The offspring of his predecessor, Heiko, are showing fairly well as young dogs, but, surprisingly, his half-brother by Alf v. Convent, Panther v. Eschenzweig (who was far down the Vs in 1971), shows a more promising producer.

The Raps v. Piastendamm Select son, Dago v. Schloss Dalhausen, whose prominence as a producer probably brought out the importance of the Rap's blood, has a half-brother out of the same mother by a Hein son. This dog produced a Select dog in 1969 called Frei v. d. Gugge, but he has just missed ever since. His mother is Connie v. d. Gugge who is 5-5-5 on Rolf, 3-5 on

Ino-Rosel. With Hein on the father's side, a concentration of R-litter blood is evident. This dog is very popular, being Number Five on the Stud Dog List in 1972 and actually the top producer of "a" stamp stock in the top twelve "a" producing Stud List. In 1972 he had three "a" progeny at the show, fourteen SG and two G. One bitch was V1, and her older sister had gone Select in 1971. Another of the 1969 Selects, Zigan v. Firnskuppe, shows himself to be a producer. He is tenth on the "a" Stud List. In the 1971 show he had twenty-seven progeny entered, all in the young classes, but by 1972 they were not in evidence. There is a young half-brother of Zigan, Grimm by name, who was V in 1971 out of the same mother, Venus. He could be one that may show up again. Venus is linebred 3-2 on Donar v. Firnskuppe, again giving a concentration of R-litter breeding.

One of the strong, apparently desirable Hein lines is through his last, great son, Greif v. Elfenhain. Grief's son, Sam v. d. Schinklergrenze resulted from combining with Arno v. Haus Gersie blood. Sam, when bred to the Sieger Mutz daughter, Siegerin Blanka v. Kisskamp, produced Zanto aus Kattenstroth. In 1971 Zanto produced Select Three and Eight bitches, but by 1972 wasn't so evident. His strength in quality bitches should be very beneficial in future generations. Sam has other good lines through Fiemerick and Herforderring. The 1972 Select List shows Select Two stemming from Sam. Sam's brother, Quai, when bred to Siegerin Blanka v. Kisskamp, produced two bitches who were rated Excellent. One of these, Xanta aus Kattenstroth, was sold to the author and became one of her foundation bitches.

Gero v. Haus Eikemann is now becoming more important by being the maternal grandfather of Mutz v. d. Pelztierfarm; the father of Lasso v. Tollenstrand, who also represents a blending with Alf v. Nordfelsen blood; and through being the father of a dog that keeps cropping up, Kay v. Hexenkolk. Gero's influence in the pedigrees is likely there because he didn't upset the pattern and allowed the excellence of his breeding partners to prevail in some progeny.

Kay v. Hexenkolk is one of these. As a young dog, he won his class at the Sieger Show. Occasionally his progeny appear with marked effect. His daughter, Rommy v. Driland, was 1971 Siegerin; his son, Erko v. Dinkelland, was Select Two in 1971; and his grandson, Pascha v. d. Bayernwaldperle, was Select Six in 1972.

Another supporting line is the breeding from Sieger Arno v. Haus Gersie. It ties in somewhat through Sam Schinklergrenze, but also through Valet and Viet v. Busecker Schloss. Troll v. Schloss Ahaus by Valet, and whose mother is a daughter of Sieger Condor v. Hohenstamm, has been used very successfully in producing the Sudfeld dogs of which Iwo was Select in 1971 and 1972. In 1972 he produced the winner of a Young Bitch class.

In 1971 Marko v. Cellerland was Select Four at the Sieger Show, up from the last Select position the year before. Something in him appealed to the breeders and it was obvious they were going to use him. His father is a Herding Dog with the "a," and his grandfather was Cyrus Baltikum, who was Select Two in 1965. Cyrus is a great-grandson of Cralo v. Haunstetten, and Select Amor v. Haus Hoheide. His father's mother is a Jalk daughter out of a Raps daughter. Now Marko's father, when bred to his mother, brought in the influence of Sieger Mutz a. d. Kuckstrasse and the Sieger Alf v. Nordfelsen son, Sieger Veus Starrenberg. This beautiful example of open breeding of quality-plus dogs produced Marko. This open pedigree is similar in style to Axel v. d. Deininghauserheide. His progeny at the 1972 Show placed amazingly high in all the Youth Classes with seventeen SG out of the twenty-four progeny there. As a young dog he is just getting started and has already moved up to Sixth place on the "a" Stud List. Dr. Rummel must believe in this young dog, for, in 1972, he made Marko v. Cellerland the Sieger.

THE END

Index